IMPOSSIBLE INDIVIDUALITY

IMPOSSIBLE INDIVIDUALITY

ROMANTICISM, REVOLUTION, AND THE ORIGINS OF MODERN SELFHOOD, 1787–1802

Gerald N. Izenberg

PRINCETON UNIVERSITY PRESS

PRINCETON, NEW JERSEY

LIBRARY OF CONGRESS CATALOGING-IN-PUBLICATION DATA

IZENBERG, GERALD N., 1939–
IMPOSSIBLE INDIVIDUALITY : ROMANTICISM, REVOLUTION, AND THE
ORIGINS OF MODERN SELFHOOD, 1787–1802 / GERALD N. IZENBERG.
P.   CM.
INCLUDES BIBLIOGRAPHICAL REFERENCES AND INDEX.
ISBN 0-691-06926-3 (ACID-FREE PAPER)
1. SELF IN LITERATURE.   2. ROMANTICISM.   3. LITERATURE AND
REVOLUTIONS.   I. TITLE.

PN751.I94   1992   809'.93384—dc20   91-30848   CIP

THIS BOOK HAS BEEN COMPOSED IN LINOTRON CALEDONIA

PRINCETON UNIVERSITY PRESS BOOKS ARE PRINTED
ON ACID-FREE PAPER AND MEET THE GUIDELINES FOR
PERMANENCE AND DURABILITY OF THE COMMITTEE ON
PRODUCTION GUIDELINES FOR BOOK LONGEVITY
OF THE COUNCIL ON LIBRARY RESOURCES

PRINTED IN THE UNITED STATES OF AMERICA

1 3 5 7 9 10 8 6 4 2

For Ziva, Noam, and Oren

CONTENTS

ACKNOWLEDGMENTS

THAT a book is a long time in the making does not necessarily make it better, but it does ensure that the author accumulates considerable debts along the way to completion. It also makes it possible that he has forgotten some. I want to thank those who read and commented on the manuscript, in part or as a whole, at various stages of its evolution over the years: Ernst Behler, Rudolph Binion, Gregory Claeys, Richard Davis, Harold Ellis, Peter Gay, Martin Jay, Kenneth Johnston, Chris Kendrick, Naomi Lebowitz, Michael Luetzeler, Fritz Ringer, John Toews, and an anonymous reader for Princeton University Press. Early versions of some of the main themes of the book were presented at the University of Saskatchewan, the University of Texas at Dallas, and Washington University, and to the Study Group for Applied Psychoanalysis in St. Louis. Jonathan Arac gave me encouragement at a strategic point in the process. I also want to thank Lenita Newberg for her help in typing and editing the manuscript, Eric Oberle for his assistance in preparing it for the press, and Robert Brown of Princeton University Press for his efforts on my behalf. My editor for Princeton, Alison Johnson, was a discerning and careful reader who made many valuable suggestions. I am grateful to Washington University for a leave of absence in 1986–87 that allowed me to work on the book. My special thanks, and a half-point, to Steven Zwicker for indispensable friendship. And above all, to Ziva, Noam, and Oren for not only suffering patiently through the vicissitudes of writing but for their active support and encouragement.

IMPOSSIBLE INDIVIDUALITY

INTRODUCTION

THERE is a strange tension between the concepts of "individualism" and "individuality" in both modern thought and contemporary public sensibility. The authors of *Habits of the Heart*, a recent sociological investigation of individualism in American life, identify individuality with the "expressive individualism" of Romanticism and see it as originating historically in opposition to utilitarian individualism. Expressive individualism stresses the unique core of feeling and intuition in each person that must be developed if individuality is to be realized, utilitarianism the self-interests common to all human beings that each strives to advance and maximize.[1] Karl Weintraub, writing in a European context, points out in *The Value of the Individual* that individualism, defined as a social theory that advocates the free and independent action of the individual, does not necessarily lead to a concern with individuality as a personality ideal. If in a society dedicated to individualism everyone freely opts for the realization of a common model—for example, that of the rational person—a society of homogeneous personalities may be sought that denies or ignores the value of the unique individual.[2] Yet at the same time both works seem to see the development or self-realization of the unique individual as an extension of the ideas of self-government, economic liberty, and rights to freedom of thought and expression. Although *Habits of the Heart*, for example, notes the differences between expressive and utilitarian individualism, it conceives them as subsets of one overarching concept.[3] And Weintraub argues that the political and social freedoms of a society devoted to individualism seem to be the theoretical and institutional precondition for the very possibility of individuality.[4] Finally, a recent work on liberalism and Romanticism claims that, while the concept of the person in classical political and economic liberalism as the bearer of rights or as a creature driven by self-interest does not take individuality, spontaneity, and expressivity into account, so that the liberal view of society appears "cold, contractual, and unlovely," there is a strong enough affinity between Romanticism and liberalism to make the work of reconciling them not only conceivable and fruitful but necessary to fulfill the true spirit of each.[5]

In the light of this contemporary urge to see individuality as a legitimate derivative of, or as consistent with, individualism, it is interesting to recall that an earlier generation of social theorists, whose work contributed decisively to the currency of the idea of individuality in the twentieth century, argued that individualism and individuality were quite anti-

Individuality (Romantic) vs. Individualism

thetical to one another. When Friedrich Meinecke and Georg Simmel took up the idea of individuality at the beginning of the twentieth century, they argued that *Individualität* was a largely Romantic creation in direct opposition to the Enlightenment idea of individualism. The Enlightenment in their view defined humanity as a collection of essentially similar beings endowed with universal rights or motivated by similar hedonistic desires; this was a conception abstracted from modern commercial society in which individuals were seen as pursuing a uniform self-interest. At most, *Individualität* could be seen as having evolved historically from Enlightenment individualism, but the process had so changed the idea that it turned against its predecessor. "First," Simmel wrote, "there had been the thorough liberation of the individual from the rusty chains of guild, birthright and church. Now the individual that had thus become independent also wished to distinguish himself *from other individuals*. The important point no longer was the fact that he was a free individual as such, but that he was this specific, irreplaceable given individual. . . . The new individualism might be called qualitative, in contrast with the quantitative individualism of the eighteenth century. Or it might be labelled the individualism of uniqueness [*Einzigkeit*] as against that of singleness [*Einzelheit*]. At any rate, Romanticism perhaps was the broadest channel through which it reached the consciousness of the nineteenth century."[6]

One of the most important differences between the two concepts of the individual from the viewpoint of these twentieth-century thinkers was in the way each theorized the relationship between individuals. "Individualism" was an antisocial or at best asocial concept that imagined a society of atomized individuals separate from, or in competition with, one another, bound only by contract and the self-interest and coercion that sustained it. But the idea of individuality was seen as extending from individuals to groups and as somehow uniting both. "Out of this deepening individualism of uniqueness," wrote Meinecke, "there henceforth arose everywhere in Germany in various forms a new and more living image of the state, and also a new picture of the world. The whole world now appeared to be filled with individuality, each individuality, whether personal or supra-personal, governed by its own characteristic principle of life. . . . Individuality everywhere, the identity of mind and nature, and through this identity, an invisible but strong bond unifying the otherwise boundless diversity and abundance of individual phenomena—these were new and powerful ideas which now burst forth in Germany in so many ways."[7] The concept of an individuality of collective entities seemed to make possible the idea that personal individuality could be fostered through identification of the individual self with the unique personality of the culture or nation to which it belonged, and so create a seamless harmony between self and whole that would be damaged if the self asserted itself in independence from, much less against, the group. "[T]his individualism, which restricts freedom to a purely inward sense of the term," Simmel noted, "easily acquires an anti-liberal tendency."[8]

Simmel's point was not only a historical assessment of the sociopolitical bearing of Romanticism, it was also a contribution to a contemporary debate. In the late nineteenth and early twentieth century, many German intellectuals defending the ethos of the recently united German Empire were attempting to define a specifically German form of individualism not only different from but superior to the shallow, mechanical, and materialistic individualism of Britain and France. German concern for uniqueness and spirituality, for personal *Bildung* with all of its cultural and ethical overtones was contrasted with "Western" utilitarianism and mechanical liberalism.[9] This ideological mobilization sometimes involved scholars, even the more liberally inclined skeptics like Simmel who were worried about the conservative, statist implications of extreme organicism, in significant distortions of the history of their cherished concept of individuality. The first explicit defense of individuality as a personality ideal in late eighteenth-century Germany, for example, was linked with an attack on state intervention in personal and social life and argued for the minimal state as the essential political precondition of individuality. In Wilhelm von Humboldt's view, the state as a coercive collectivity was not the fulfillment of, but the most serious obstacle to, individuality.[10] Steven Lukes, who makes a number of important conceptual distinctions in his introductory work on individualism, ignores this very important difference when he classes Humboldt with Schlegel, Novalis, and Schleiermacher as originators of the term individuality and suggests that it entered the liberal tradition only with John Stuart Mill's integration of Humboldt in *On Liberty*.[11] Lukes, along with Simmel and Meinecke themselves, glosses over the important issue of just how the idea of personal individuality was extended and transformed into one of the personality of supraindividual entities (or regressively identified with Herder's earlier concept of unique organic cultures). For while it is true that German Romantics historically did make the move from personal to collective individuality, that fact only pushes a conceptual problem one step back. The question of the transition from singular individuality to collective individuality is an abyss to be bridged rather than a bridge to be crossed. The Romantics' own definitions of individuality, for example, emphasized the idea of differences among unique individuals, of uniqueness understood as determined *against* others, a conception that would seem to rule out any kind of nonconflictual organic synthesis between self and other or self and collective identity. Moreover, the Romantics understood their idea of individuality not only as the highest degree of individ-

view, best expressed by the work of M. H. Abrams. Abrams's interpretation of Romanticism may be termed "reconciliationist." In his own words, "Romantic philosophy is . . . primarily a metaphysics of integration, of which the key is that of the 'reconciliation,' or synthesis, of whatever is divided, opposed and conflicting."[16] Romanticism is the secularized and naturalized transformation of the Neoplatonic strand in Christianity, which posits a three-stage developmental history of Being as paradigmatic also for human reality: primal cosmic unity and goodness, subsequent differentiation into multiplicity and individual particularity, which is equivalent to a fall into evil and suffering, and then a return to unity and goodness that retains individual differentiation. The central trope of Romantic writing, Abrams claims, is the circuitous journey in which the visionary writer, as prophetic representative of all humanity, falls from primal unity into individuated and conflicted existence, separated from the whole and divided within himself, but returns at the end of his journey to a higher unity that restores his original harmony with the world while preserving his separate identity.[17]

Locked in polemical embrace, the reconciliationist, and what for shorthand purposes may be called the demystifying, views encompass only two alternatives: either the harmonious synthesis of subject and object, infinitely free self and infinite cosmos, epitomized for example in Wordsworth's famous image of the marriage of mind and nature in his "Prospectus" to *The Recluse*, or the unbridgeable metaphysical chasm between the absolutely free, self-positing individual consciousness and the world, which has whatever meaning it gets only from consciousness. (A more strictly defined deconstructionist criticism, while rejecting the idea of subjectivity in favor of the supposed determinism of language, reaches essentially the same position with regard to truth. All efforts by Romantic works to express objective eternal Truth are undermined by the very language that attempts to formulate it.) Whatever the Romantics may have hoped for, say the demystifiers, their own discoveries about the nature of imagination and mind, or their own linguistic practice, deconstruct the very possibility of a coherent notion of absolute Being, turn it into a pure fiction, and doom any efforts at a conceptual or poetic realization of oneness with a timeless world and final truth.

Without calling into question the validity of the critique of Romantic reconciliation, I want to suggest nonetheless that both it and reconciliationism anachronistically misinterpret Romanticism to suit contemporary projects. Significantly, both approaches seem to agree that what the Romantics at least overtly wanted was some sort of equal partnership between the human and the absolute, however the latter was conceived. Abrams sees the human equality inherent in the Romantic vision of the mind's cocreation of the world of human experience as directly rooted in the civic and political equality of the French Revolution, which political disillusion then displaced into the spheres of philosophy and art. In the textual examples he cites to illustrate the paradigmatic Romantic three-stage journey, the original undifferentiated oneness is often figured as the unity of mother and child, while the reunification at the end of the process of separation and individuation is represented as the joining together in marriage of adult equals. The demystifying view on the whole does not doubt the Romantic aspiration to partnership, only the possibility of imagining or saying (writing) it without contradiction, since totality and unity are either categories of the creative mind or mere verbal aspirations rather than possible attributes of the world or of truth. On this reading, the ideal of partnership with the world conceals the inescapable transcendence, hence ultimate separateness and aloneness, of the human.

Undoubtedly, both reconciliationist assertions and deconstructive underminings are present in Romantic works, but Romanticism is more paradoxical than even the modernist view suggests. For in Romantic imagery and concept, whether it be that of humankind's relationship with nature or with the state, whether it be the artist's relation to the work of art or the lover's relation to the beloved, the Romantic idea of infinite individuality is always linked with the notion of an all-inclusive totality other and greater than the self, in a relationship not of reciprocity but of dependency. The Romantic contradiction is that the individuated self's dependency on, even fusion with, this totality, invariably figured in maternal terms, is the very condition of absolute free individuality; or to reverse the terms, the absolute, ungrounded agency of the self is seen to derive from the dissolution of the self into a larger whole. But since the self's creative agency *is* held to be absolute in Romanticism, the contradiction is doubled: for human individuality is also held to be superior to, even the very source of, the overarching totality to which it submits itself. And finally, to compound these contradictions, the self, as the passage from Hölderlin quoted above clearly shows, *knows* its own originary superiority, knows that it is the source of the idea of an objective absolute, but does not allow its knowledge in any way to shake its belief in the externality of the absolute and its ability to rely on it.

One condensed example here can stand for many and will serve to introduce what is to come. In the poet-visionary Novalis's Romantic political fantasy *Belief and Love*, written in 1797 to celebrate the accession of Frederick William III and his queen to the throne of Prussia, radical individual freedom is held possible only through complete obedience to the ruler in a state headed by a loving, happily married royal couple. The king's rule is justified neither by Hobbesian or Christian assumptions about the need for absolute authority over an unruly or sinful humanity, nor by enlightened absolutist notions of the ruler as the sole nonpartisan agent of universal reason above particular interests. Rather, the king rules because he is the embodiment and model of absolute freedom. He is the transcendental ego incarnate, the absolutely free "I" that not only "posits" or produces the world by opening it up through his activity to its infinite possible meanings, as every "I" does, but knows himself as doing so, and is therefore conscious master of his own implicit freedom. The king, however, has this knowledge, and hence his freedom, only through love: because he loves, and is loved by, the queen. She is the true locus of infinite freedom. It is because of her virtues that he knows and loves her as the ideal, that is, infinite and absolute, object. Knowing that he is drawn to her precisely for her ideality, he comes to know his own infinity, and that knowledge alone makes him worthy of the throne. As Novalis says, "Only he who is already more than king can rule as king, so let him be king who loves the most noble woman."[18]

But the monarch's rule, while absolute, is so only provisionally and instrumentally. For the king's ultimate purpose, inherent in the very quality by virtue of which he reigns, is to negate himself, to cancel out his absolute authority by preparing all humanity for freedom. All men, Novalis claimed, were in principle, and ought to become in fact, worthy of the throne; all men indeed originally sprang from ancient royal lineage. The king is the educational means of returning all men to their royal status, their absolute free selves. In this sense, the ideal monarchy is simultaneously the ideal republic, the polity of self-governing equals. In fact, Novalis insisted, there is no republic without a king and no true king without a republic. In his myth of the state, political submission, the equivalent of filial submission, to the royal couple is only the indispensable condition of absolute transcendence, achieved by each subject through identification with the king (whose infinite freedom is, as we have seen, actualized only in the nexus of his loving marriage with the virtuous queen; one of the conditions of maturation to freedom in Novalis's state is the receiving of a bride at the hands of the queen). In view of the ultimate goal of absolute freedom for each individual, the king's political "transcendence" could be nothing but the projection of the transcendence of universal human selfhood, not a justification for royal absolutism. Absolute tutelage is the precondition for absolute freedom.

The same complex and contradictory pattern of interdependence between autonomy and submission can be found in many Romantic works on aesthetics, love, philosophy, and politics. Some modernist criticism has assembled elements of this pattern. In a controversial reading of Wordsworth's poem "A Slumber Did My Spirit Seal," Hillis Miller touches on themes strikingly similar to those in Novalis. On a first superficial level, he says, Wordsworth's impossible idealization of the young Lucy in the poem as one "that could not feel / The touch of earthly years" is the realization of Wordsworth's own psychobiographically rooted wish to join again in an eternal bond with his dead mother. But that wish is merely an empirical instance of a more fundamental ontological trope, "a constantly repeated occidental drama of the lost sun," the universal metaphor for ultimate enlightenment or wisdom. Lucy's name, Miller points out, means light, and "To possess her would be a means of rejoining the lost source of light, the father sun as logos, as head power and font of meaning."[19] Apart from the fact that, as Abrams complains,[20] Miller reads too much of Wordsworth into one small poem, which makes his interpretation of basic themes in Wordsworth seem far more arbitrary than it actually is, his reading misses or reverses essential Romantic positions. In Wordsworth's poetry, as in the work of other Romantics, the subject, or writer, does not wish simply to join with the ultimate "font of meaning"; he sees himself as that font of meaning itself. Romanticism propounds a version of the self that in the most crucial respect is the opposite of that recurrent occidental drama to which Miller refers. At the same time, for all its reveling in the undecidable cruxes of Wordsworth's poem that show its aspiration to be unachievable, Miller's interpretation misses the contradictions that are essential to understanding Romanticism's break with Miller's allegedly traditional plot. The first contradiction is that in Romantic works the symbol of an external source of all power and meaning is retained even while the warrant for its legitimacy is simultaneously completely nullified by the power of the self. The second contradiction lies in the strange logic of maternal possession (not union with the father, which, contra Miller, is not an end in itself but a way to the mother) as the instrumentality for the appropriation of power. The fantasied fusion with the maternal figure is consciously understood on one level as an abnegation of self, which would appear to destroy the possibility of its becoming the source of meaning, yet turns out, as we have seen, to be the precondition for its own primacy.

One source of the problems in Miller's interpretation is the dehistoricizing of the Romantic movement, which is homogenized into yet another instance of Jacques Derrida's master plot of the Western metaphysical tradition: the "logocentric" effort to establish the normative truth of supposedly eternal beliefs as the ground of all knowledge and judgment. This dehistoricizing occludes the essential difference not only between Romantic and modernist versions of the self but between Romantic and pre-Romantic versions of the purportedly constant myth of recovering and rejoining the absent ground of truth. The Romantics themselves were explicitly aware of standing on the threshold of a new moment in history precisely with regard to that myth. The era of the French Revolution seemed to promise the liberation and reign of what Hölderlin called "the God in us," an idea that suggests a decisive break with previous ideas

of an external and univocal Truth and a quest for the source of truth in
the self. At the same time, awareness that humans project divinity onto
nature did not prevent Hölderlin from asserting its objective presence
there. To the extent that Romanticism itself both consciously approached
and consciously retreated from positions about the self and the origins of
truth that resemble those of existentialism and deconstruction, it presents interpretive and explanatory problems different from those presented by "logocentric" texts. Romantic works are not just un-self-aware
"totalizing" enterprises that unconsciously struggle to repress certain
refractory truths that would undermine the objective reality of the totality they claim to discover; such works are therefore not adequately
explained when their conceptual or linguistic repressions are exposed.
The interpretive work that reveals the contradictions in Romantic texts is
in a sense the beginning, not the end, of the explanatory task, especially
when Romantic writers not only admit but insist on, and even glory in,
contradiction.[21]

III

A more recent strand of contemporary criticism, rejoining an older Marxist tradition, has in fact criticized the deconstructionist approach for its
ahistoricism but has also argued that it mirrors the Romantics' own denial
of history. Within English criticism this charge paradoxically enough is
leveled even at Abrams's apparently historical interpretation of Romantic
origins. Where Abrams sees in the preceding revolutionary hopes for a
regenerated, free, and harmonious mankind a source for the Romantic
vision of reconciling humanity and nature, historicist critics see an evasion and a problem: how do secular political ideals and programs get
translated into unhistorical visions of the eternal power of imagination
and its fusion with timeless nature?[22] From the historicists' point of view,
the Romantics' move is not a logical progression from, but rather a suppression of, the political. As Jerome McGann succinctly summarizes this
position: "The poetry of Romanticism is everywhere marked by an extreme form of displacement and poetic conceptualization whereby the
actual human issues with which the poetry is concerned are resituated in
a variety of idealized localities."[23] An analogous approach is to be found in
much of the modern criticism of German (and to a lesser extent of French)
Romanticism, which sees the Romantic preoccupation with the idea of
aesthetic revolution as the displacement of an original concern with political revolution into the cultural sphere.[24]

To get at the "actual human issues" with which Romanticism is ostensibly concerned, historicist critics have proposed a method of reading that

restores the supposedly original historical context of Romantic works, their suppressed content, without prejudice to their manifest substance. "A socio-historical method," McGann insists, "helps to expose these dramas of displacement and idealization without, at the same time, debunking or deconstructing the actual works themselves."[25] In fact, however, the force of the historicist exposé is much more sweeping than this methodological disclaimer suggests. McGann speaks of the "displaced" and "idealized" content of Romantic work as "ideology," in the explicitly Marxist sense of "false consciousness."[26] The Romantic preoccupation with consciousness, imagination, art, and their cognates is a large self-deception that conceals the Romantics' failure or refusal to deal with the "real"—that is, social and political—issues with which they were originally concerned. Commenting on the extreme level of abstraction in Wordsworth's "Intimations Ode," for example, McGann writes of its apparent triumph over a deep sense of loss, "Wordsworth's poem does not actually transcend the [social and political] evils it is haunted by, it merely occupies them at the level of consciousness. . . . What he actually discovered was no more than his desperate need for a solution. The reality of that need mirrored a cultural one that was much greater and more widespread. Wordsworth transformed both of these realities into illusions. The process began with the displacement of the problem inwardly."[27] Similarly, of the now famous passage in Book VI of *The Prelude* in which Wordsworth celebrates the autonomy of imagination, Alan Liu writes, "History is denied, and the 'I' engenders itself autogenetically as the very crown of . . . objectified subjectivity: a mind knowing itself only in the impersonal."[28] The Romantic concern with the "I," according to Liu, is altogether a snare and a delusion; where the Romantic writer says "I" he really means "history."[29]

McGann's insistence that the sociohistorical method does not debunk its objects, however, betrays his uneasiness about his procedure. In fact the same flaw he finds in Abrams's reasoning shadows the historicist argument. In what way can a "displacement inward" be said to be dealing with the external political and social realities? There is a strong flavor of reductionism in the idea that talk of the "I" is really disguised talk about history, society, and politics. In rejecting the ahistoricism of existentialist and poststructuralist criticism, the historicists have thrown the baby out with the bathwater, essentially eliminating what appears to be the central explicit concern of Romantic writing and thought.

They do so at least partly because of an a priori, essentially Marxist, assumption about what is historical—and political. In this view history concerns only group issues—social stratification, economic exploitation, legal and political inequality—and group struggles to end or correct them. There seems to be no awareness in recent historicist criticism of the possibility that the self might also be a historical issue and a political problem rather than an escape from history. But the idea of freedom during the period of the French Revolution pertained to the individual just as much as it did the group. Rebellion against monarchical authority and social privilege in the name of individual rights and universal equality did not mean only the institutionalization of collective ideals like popular sovereignty; it meant ideological rebellion against fundamental general principles of external authority in favor of a new source of autonomy in the self, which led in turn to a qualitatively new kind of autonomy for the self. As Philip Gilbertson has noted, one of the most distinctive features of Romantic writing is the challenge to the idea of fixed, insurmountable limits to human nature inherent in its recurrent language of boundary-breaking.[30] In breaking the boundaries of legitimate authority, the Revolution also unraveled the traditional limits (even those of the Enlightenment) that had previously confined the self.

There is an explanatory price to be paid for ignoring the politics of selfhood. Since the central concern of contemporary historicist criticism is to expose the fact of Romanticism's ideological suppression of history, it pays only the most cursory attention to the question of why the suppression took place. Or rather it generally seems to assume that the reasons are obvious and do not require much examination. The failures of the Revolution, its apparent degeneration from the goals of freedom and self-defense into violence and imperialist domination, presumably frightened and disgusted the naive young Romantics who, ideologically hampered by their class-based biases, could not distinguish the desperate defensive measures and momentary excesses inspired by the revolutionaries' fears from social stereotypes of mass barbarism and ideological fanaticism. But the explanation of the Romantic defection from the revolutionary cause is hardly so clear-cut as disaffection with the Revolution's anarchy, violence, and oppression. Of the figures in this study, Chateaubriand left France for America, apparently disenchanted with revolutionary violence, as early as the middle of 1791, even before the September Massacres, but only turned against radical republicanism, and that only equivocally, in the context of his experience in the United States. Schleiermacher, Schlegel, and Wordsworth, however, all supported the French Revolution through the Terror—Schlegel, for example, wrote his most explicitly political work, an essay defending democratic republicanism, in 1796. And even in the case of Wordsworth, the only one to cite an actual event, the French invasion and occupation of Belgium in 1795, as the straw that broke his allegiance to the Revolution, historical events only turned him away from any hope of realizing his political ideals in radical political action, not away from the ideals themselves. It was precisely at the point of disenchantment with praxis that he turned to radical political theory and reached the furthest extent of his own theorizing. In every case, as we will see, it was not "history" but a radical theory—and practice—of the liberated self that frightened the Romantics away from radical politics. But not away from history. The Romantics never suppressed "history" from their work. They were not only highly aware of themselves and their literary and philosophical innovations as the products of the historical process, but always saw themselves as the bearers of a historical mission.

IV

The central Romantic concern with self I have just emphasized raises the obvious question of the place of the Romantics' biographies in understanding their work and its development. Perhaps the only thing that deconstructionist and historicist criticism agree on is that biography is irrelevant to textual interpretation, that biographical explanation commits the long-condemned fallacy of reducing literature to something else, or, since these approaches in fact operate their own reductions of texts, of reducing more fundamental linguistic, ontological, or social issues to the merely individual, hence accidental, life.

In the case of the Romantics, this critical prejudice runs up against the stubborn fact that so much of their work was autobiographical, either explicitly, as in the case of *The Prelude* and the *Mémoires d'outre-tombe*, or in only thinly disguised form, as in *Lucinde* or *René*. This is not wholly to be got around with the modern critical argument that autobiography is itself in crucial respects a fictive construct. It was after all out of their personal lives that the Romantics chose to make exemplary fictions. One way of dealing with this fact is to acknowledge, as Miller does, the obvious autobiographical referentiality of the work but to make the contingent facts of the individual life either mere instances of universal myths, tropes, and ontological structures, or defensive displacements of collective historical events. The Romantics themselves, however, will not let us have it this way.

Toward the end of the "Prospectus" to what was to have been his epic poem "On Man, on Nature, and on human Life," Wordsworth ventures what seems like a gratuitous *apologia pro vita sua*, an apparently out-of-context plea for his reader's understanding if he introduces the humble details of his own life into the universal and exalted themes of the poem:

> And if [with] this
> I mingle humbler matter, with the . . . thing
> Contemplated describe the mind and man

> Contemplating and who he was and what
> The transitory being that beheld
> This vision, when and where and how he lived . . .
>
> . . . .
>
> Be not this labour useless.

(Another version of this last line in the draft reads "If such theme / Be not unworthy.[31]) Wordsworth seems to be concerned that biographical detail might be considered merely incidental to the poem, a self-indulgent excrescence, but elsewhere the "Prospectus" says exactly the opposite. The central theme that he announces for his project is

> th'individual mind that keeps its own
> Inviolate retirement, and consists
> With being limitless, the one great Life;
>
> (8–11)

With these apparently simple lines, we are at the heart of the Romantic enterprise and the Romantic claim: the finitude of the unique individual, inviolate in his or her self-contained individuality, is consistent with the individual's infinity and fusion with the cosmos in the one great life. Autobiography is not incidental; it is the demonstration and thus the proof of the great new truth that Romantic writing wishes to announce. From this point of view the details of the individual life are not merely particular, or rather, individual particularity is elevated in Romanticism to a universal principle. Individuality is not only compatible with infinity, it is the very vehicle for realizing the union with infinity.

For the Romantics, the conceptual moves from the private self individuated from family, political, and religious dependencies to the idea of the authority of the autonomous self over all previous grounds of authority and from there to the (problematic) infinity of the self were not illogical leaps. From the beginning, public events and philosophical, political, and aesthetic concepts were read through the most personal events of the Romantics' lives, and lives were reciprocally interpreted through events and concepts. It was the impact of the French Revolution on the Romantics' preexisting struggles for self-definition, freedom from heteronomous authority, and original creative achievement that produced a new idea of selfhood, and it was the convergence of that idea with crises in their personal lives and in contemporary historical events that seemed to reveal the idea in action as acutely dangerous to others and in need of revision. These processes can only be traced by attention to the dialectical interaction between life and concept, or between "textualized" life and lived idea in the texts themselves. Events in the Romantics' lives functioned as catalysts for ideas whose ramifications emerged once again in their lives;

those ramifications must be read in the texts that are (direct or displaced) versions of the life but are also arenas where the personal was made paradigmatic and tested and probed in its general implications for humanity.[32]

The necessity for this method, I repeat, is integrally related to the Romantic idea of individuality that made that notion the very vehicle of objective truth and the path to infinite freedom. This study is organized to try to demonstrate this claim and its consequences. I begin by contrasting two concepts of individuality developed by German writers in the 1790s, Wilhelm von Humboldt's "humanist" concept early in the decade and Friedrich Schleiermacher's Romantic conception towards its end, in order to bring out as sharply as possible the distinctive features of Romantic individuality. The next three chapters, on Friedrich Schlegel, William Wordsworth, and François-René de Chateaubriand respectively, all begin with conceptual and rhetorical analyses of their subjects' matured Romantic positions around 1800 and then move back to offer historical accounts of the origins of the contradictions in those positions. Although narrative in form, these accounts are intended not just as developmental chronologies but as explanations that rely on the interaction of psychological, political, aesthetic, and philosophical factors. The key to the crucial contradictions of Romantic selfhood lies precisely in the process of its development, a process that reveals not only the birth pangs of a central modern ideal of the self but some of its continuing tensions.

V

In view of the fact that the figures at the focus of this work are all male, it could plausibly be argued that the book should have been subtitled "The Origins of Modern Male Selfhood." My omission of the gender qualifier, however, does not mean that I do not see a gender issue in Romanticism, or that I believe that issue to be insignificant. Quite to the contrary; it will quickly become apparent to the reader that the problem of gender is central not only to the conflicts that the Romantics experienced in regard to the power of the self, but to the solution they devised to deal with those conflicts.

The Romantics were as contradictory on the issue of gender as they were about the self generally. On the one hand, their concept of unique individual experience as the ground of all meaning and as the sole avenue to the infinite endowed women with a dignity and power hitherto unimagined in the history of the West. Friederich Schlegel, for example, can plausibly be seen, at least in one dimension of his work, as a pioneering theorist and propagandist of women's equality. On the other hand, the problem created by the gendered way in which the Romantics conceived the aggressive reach of the infinite self and the problems it caused led to a gendered solution that simultaneously deified and denigrated women, a not unfamiliar split that haunted European culture long before Romanticism, though the Romantics gave it new meaning.

The resulting complexities create an equivocation in the Romantic concepts of self and gender that is impossible to resolve if not to explain. When Wordsworth writes of the awesome power of the human mind, when Schlegel proposes infinity as the goal of Romantic poetry and the Romantic poet, their abstractions are gender-neutral. This is not a matter of unknowable "intention," but of concept and language, or more accurately, of intention as revealed by discourse, level of analysis, and fictional creation. What the Romantics believed about the new authority of human individuality, or of mind, imagination, and desire, cuts across gender distinctions; the category of individuality is authentically universal and warrants the ungendered rubric of "modern selfhood." But the gendered language of the Romantics is equally telling. It is, furthermore, significant of something other than an unconscious equation of personhood with maleness. Although the residue of such an equation persists, the Romantics were far too aware of their own beliefs in the power of women for their sexism to be either one-sided or unsubtle. Yet given their own experience, the Romantics understood the foundational and infinite self as not only creative but aggressive, imperialistic, and potentially destructive, and given the social relations and stereotypes of the day, they could not help thinking of those characteristics as inevitably male. Indeed they hoped that was the case, for otherwise there would be no salvation to be found in the feminine. Whether the notion of human selfhood as sole and infinite foundation of meaning and value entails the negative consequences that the Romantics feared, whether a genuinely gender-free version of that notion would eliminate or modify the Romantic dilemma of the self—these are, I believe, as yet unanswered questions that are among the most important of the problematic legacies of the Romantic idea of individuality.

ONE

TWO CONCEPTS OF INDIVIDUALITY

I) Friedrich Schleiermacher: The Divided Self

IN THE SECOND EDITION of *On Religion: Speeches to Its Cultured Despisers*, which appeared in 1806, Friedrich Schleiermacher proclaimed a categorical, though compelling, definition of the human condition:

> Both the transient actions and the permanent dispositions of the human soul show that it exists as only two opposing drives [*Trieben*]. Pursuing one of them, it strives to establish itself as a unique and separate being. To accomplish this, to expand itself no less than to sustain itself, it draws its surroundings to itself, weaving them into its life and absorbing them into its own being. The opposing drive is the dread fear of standing as a single individual alone against the whole; it is the longing to surrender and be completely absorbed in it, to feel taken hold of and determined by it.[1]

The conflict within the self that Schleiermacher described here seems clear enough. On the one hand, each person desires to be an individuated being, separate from everything (and everyone) else, and unique; on the other, each desires to lose his or her individuality and be absorbed into everything else. Yet the formulation raises immediate questions even if its generality is disputed and it is regarded as merely the projection of its author. Why should the human soul contradict itself so radically? Why should the same being that wishes to maintain its unique individuality and even expand it to incorporate the universe wish simultaneously to dissolve itself into the universe and disappear? And there is yet another contradiction that Schleiermacher did not note. Individual particularity is by definition finite, because it is delimited by its difference from others. If, however, the self tries to expand by a constant absorption of the world into itself, its tendency is to become infinite and hence to obliterate its individuated identity. It follows that the two ostensibly opposite drives aim at the same thing, though by opposite means. Both aim not at individuality but at the infinity of the self, the one by absorbing everything into itself, the other by dissolving itself into everything.

To compound these puzzles, the corresponding passage in the first edition of *On Religion* from 1799 seems to have a quite different, indeed opposite, thrust. It too speaks of a conflict of drives, one of which is described in precisely the same terms as in 1806—the drive to maintain and expand individuality by incorporating the external world. But the second

drive is described as the self's longing "to expand from its inmost self
outwards into the world, and so to permeate everything with itself, to
share of itself with everything, and never to be exhausted . . . [I]t wants
to penetrate everything and fill everything with reason and freedom."[2]
The systolic and diastolic, or masculine and feminine, movements of absorption and penetration certainly represent a polarity of passive and active relationships to the world, but in the end they are both modes of
mastering the world. The self first makes the world its own by discovering
the world's objective qualities and possibilities, absorbing what it has
learned about reality and metabolizing its knowledge in its own unique
way; it then moves outward to modify the world in accordance with the
creative synthesis it has made of what it has internalized.

The difference between the two passages clearly indicates that some
change had taken place in Schleiermacher's thinking about the self between 1799 and 1806; by 1806 he was well on his way to the "feeling of
absolute dependence" that would define the quintessential religious experience fifteen years later in *The Christian Faith*. Yet the change is not
as radical as it first appears. The contradictions of 1806 between self-
assertion and self-surrender are also present in the work of 1799–1800. If
the desire to surrender was openly acknowledged as being in direct conflict with individuality only in 1806, it was no less explicitly described in
chapter two of the first edition of *On Religion*, in the image of the self
merged in a fantasy of ecstatic union with the whole. At certain moments
of love and wonderment, Schleiermacher wrote, something, whether
person or natural scene, is mysteriously but affectively transformed for
the individual into a representation of the whole universe: "As the beloved and always sought after image [*Gestalt*] forms itself, my soul flies to
meet it, and I embrace it not as a shadow but as the holy being itself. I lie
in the bosom of the infinite world; I am in this moment its soul, for I feel
all its powers and its infinite life as my own. It is in this moment my body,
for I penetrate its muscles and its limbs as my own, and its innermost
nerves move as much in accord with my meaning and intention as do my
own" (*Religion*, 254–55). Further on, what has been simply description of
ecstatic merger becomes advocacy of total surrender, characterized in the
same terms as in 1806. Addressing those who would seek personal immortality in this life, Schleiermacher appealed, "Try out of love for the
universe to surrender your life. Strive here to annihilate your individuality and to live in the one and all; try to be more than yourself, so that you
lose little when you lose yourself" (*Religion*, 289). And this self-annihilation seems to be in absolute contradiction not only to the idea of individuality defined earlier in the text, but to its much fuller exposition the
following year in the companion piece to *On Religion*, which Schleiermacher regarded as his most important contribution to the theory of personality and to ethics. "Each human being," runs the famous manifesto in

the *Soliloquies*, "should represent humanity in his own way, combining its element uniquely, so that it may reveal itself in every mode, and all that can emerge from its womb be realized in the fullness of infinity."[3]

A closer look, however, reveals that in 1799–1800 Schleiermacher saw no fundamental contradiction between the idea of individuality and the idea of union with the "one and all." The fusion of the soul with the beloved produces not self-loss but a sense of personal mastery through the soul's identification with its object and the appropriation of the object's powers: "I lie in the bosom of the infinite world; I am in this moment its soul, for *I feel all its powers and its infinite life as my own. It is in this moment my body, for I penetrate its muscles and its limbs as my own*" (italics added). The rhetorically elegant and powerful passage repeats in its structure the reciprocity of the symbiosis it evokes. The world's infinity becomes the self, the self's intentions animate the world. The "religious" experience of self-annihilation seems not only compatible with the sense of the individuated self's active mastery of the universe, it is the vehicle for it.

But Schleiermacher also derived the paradoxical relationship between individuality and infinity in a way that does not depend on a perhaps rare experience of ecstatic fusion. The infinite is potentially available to consciousness in the phenomenology of everyday life, in the common experience of enjoying a particular activity as an end in itself. "Whoever . . . can . . . resolve to do and to promote some particular thing for its own sake with all his strength cannot help but recognize other particular purposes as things which can also be undertaken for their own sakes and which have a right to exist. . . . This recognition of the alien and annihilation of what is one's own, which obtrudes on consciousness everywhere, the simultaneous love and contempt for everything finite and limited, which such recognition demands, is not possible without a dim intimation of the universe and must necessarily bring with them a clear and definite longing for the infinite" (*Religion*, 309–10). The intimation of the infinite is given precisely in our appreciation of limited particular ends. Through the recognition that our enjoyment of the particular activities we have chosen lies in the unalienated activity they allow us, we can appreciate similar passions in others for very different kinds of things. Such a recognition frees us from the limitations of our own narrow preoccupations, enabling us to enter into other, potentially infinite, activities and states of mind. In this case, the way to the universe, to the sense of infinity, is dependent on individuality itself, on our passion for self-fulfillment, for the secret of authenticity is empathy, and hence infinity.

The organic link between individuality and infinity is also part of Schleiermacher's more detailed exposition of the concept of individuality in the *Soliloquies*, though it is less immediately apparent. Here individuality has many of the apparently unproblematic features commonly assumed in the contemporary, ordinary language meaning of the term. To be a unique self means above all that one's behavior is governed by one's own ideas and impulses. Suiting method of exposition to content, Schleiermacher offered his own development as an example, negative in this instance, recounting how his late-awakened spirit had long borne the "alien yoke" of his Pietist education and had remained ever fearful "lest it be subjected again to the domination of alien opinion" (*Soliloquies*, 40–41). The lesson he derived from his early life in fact constitutes the peroration of the book: "[W]hatever you become, let it be for its own sake. A stupid self-deception to think that you ought to want what you do not want! . . . Attempt nothing unless it proceeds freely from a love and desire within your soul. And let no limits be set upon your love, whether of measure, of kind or of duration! It is, after all, yours; who can demand it of you? Its law is wholly within you; who has to command anything?" (*Soliloquies*, 101–2).

To be unique, however, means not only to be authentic to oneself but to be different from everyone else, an arduous task because the price of uniqueness is eternal vigilance: "[O]nly if he requires himself to survey the whole of humanity, opposing his own expression of it to every other possible one, can he maintain the consciousness of his unique selfhood. For contrast is indispensable to set the individuality in relief" (*Soliloquies*, 32). Such differentiation might even demand, as it had demanded for Schleiermacher himself, an initial antagonism toward new points of view represented by others, at least until the individual has worked each new idea through for her- or himself (*Soliloquies*, 41). Finally, individuality requires that each individual integrate all his or her varied experiences into a harmonious whole in order to create an internally consistent individual personality. It is of particular interest in the light of contemporary poststructuralist theories of language and text that Schleiermacher posed the issues of originality and self-integration in terms both of language and of art. Language, he implied, might indeed consist of a conventional stock of signifiers, but from them selections could be made and orchestrated to produce an original harmony expressive of a unique self: "Each of us need only make his language thoroughly his own and artistically all of a piece, so that its derivation and modulation, its logic and its sequence exactly represent the structure of his spirit, and the music of his speech has the accent of his heart and the keynote of his thought" (*Soliloquies*, 66).

Important as these features of individuality are in the *Soliloquies*, however, they are not yet its essence. Schleiermacher's concept of individuality ultimately derives from a variety of sources: Pietism, German Enlightenment and neoclassicism, the cultural particularism of Herder, the idealist philosophy of Kant and Fichte, Hemsterhuis's Platonism,

Garve's ideas of communicative sociability. In the *Soliloquies*, however, he chose to simplify his intellectual ancestry and present his idea of individuality in both its filiation from and its opposition to Kant. This choice was historical, ideological, and tactical. To the younger generation of the *gebildete Stände*, Kant was the seminal thinker of the age, the originator of the modern philosophy of human autonomy, and the uncompromising ethicist who had posed, but failed to resolve, the problem of achieving the highest good, the reconciliation of morality and happiness. He was also the thinker who had first introduced Schleiermacher to modernity and liberated him from the stifling Pietism of his earliest education. For Schleiermacher to take on Kant was not only to take on his intellectual progenitor but to take on the challenge of offering a counter-ethic to the most imposing intellectual structure of his time.[4] It was also, however, to situate himself within Kantian values and concepts, which meant that his countervision had to satisfy the two essential Kantian demands of freedom and universality.

What Schleiermacher had found liberating in Kant's philosophy was the Idealist notion that the world as experienced was as much the product of internal categories of apprehension as it was of external determinants, indeed more. "[W]hat I take to be the world is the fairest creation of spirit, a mirror in which it is reflected. . . . All those feelings that seem to be forced upon me by the material world are in reality my own free doing; nothing is a mere effect of that world upon me" (*Soliloquies*, 16–17). The most important Kantian demonstration of freedom was in the realm of morality. Kant had shown that true morality was autonomous rather than heteronomous because the concept of "duty" entailed the idea of an imperative imposed on the self by itself in the name of reason rather than a command imposed from the outside in the name of authority. This imperative was necessarily the same for all human beings; its only logically consistent form was a universal law that demanded that all persons be treated as ends in themselves. In this way rational morality reconciled the diverse goals of free individuals. "For a long time," Schleiermacher related, "I . . . was content with the discovery of reason alone" (*Soliloquies*, 30). But at some point something changed for him. Just what, and when, he did not say, but the result was that he came to find the Kantian notion of rational moral autonomy inadequate (*Soliloquies*, 31). For although the moral law was unquestionably free because it was self-imposed, its form as universal law meant that "there is but a single right way of acting in every situation, that the conduct of all men should be alike, and that people differed from one another only by reason of their different situations and places. I thought humanity revealed itself as varied only in the diversity of outward acts; the individual human being was not a uniquely fashioned being but only an exemplar of the universal [*ein*

Element] and everywhere the same" (*Soliloquies*, 30). The individual differences that constituted one's uniqueness, that is to say, were not a matter of free will. In the Kantian conception, individual impulses and desires were part of a person's biological nature and hence belonged to the
realm of determinism rather than freedom; the behavior they produced
was determined, like all natural events, by causal force. Freedom was an
idea of reason suggested only in the experience of obligation, which entailed both the concept of a general law and the notion of an ability to
choose to act according to it. The free individual was thus free only in his
or her moral capacity, as universal human being; in his or her particular
identity, the individual was not free and therefore not truly human. But
precisely this sense of freedom, Schleiermacher complained, "gave no
meaning to my personality, nor to the peculiar unity of the transient
stream of consciousness flowing within me" (*Soliloquies*, 31). Rational
freedom was not enough if it dismissed the most intimate sense of personal selfhood as meaningless.

In good Kantian terms, however, unique individuality could have
"meaning" only if it could be understood both as an expression of individual freedom and as a source of ethical value, in other words if it had a
universal, as well as a particular, dimension. This was the ultimate challenge for Schleiermacher because for a Kantian, particular desires and
the acts they motivated were in principle unfree as well as egotistical.
Schleiermacher's solution to the problem of freedom was to combine two
different ideas: the notion that a genuinely individual choice was a choice
of *shared* elements of humanity, hence *universal*, but also a genuine
choice, hence *individual*, because of the possibility of its negation: the
person could imagine doing other than he or she in fact did. "Whenever
I now act in keeping with my own spirit and disposition, my imagination
gives me the clearest proof that I do so by free, individual choice, in
suggesting to me a thousand other ways of acting in a different spirit, yet
also consistent with the universal laws of humanity" (*Soliloquies*, 33). Negation was the important new element in Schleiermacher's post-Kantian
thinking about freedom, one fraught with great consequences. It introduced the idea of the infinity of the self because in order to be free, the
self could not be identified with any of its actual choices and dispositions.
In principle it was necessary for freedom that the self always have the
potential to negate any, and hence all, of its actual choices.

Schleiermacher, however, did not think of the infinity of the self as a
mere negative potentiality, as the essential but hypothetical indetermi-
nacy that was the condition for the possibility of freedom. Even as mere
infinite potential, of course, the self had no predetermined bounds; it was
infinite because in thought at least it was never identical with, never fully
exhausted by, its concrete choices and determinations, no matter how

many. But Schleiermacher went beyond the idea of pure potentiality to posit a drive in the self to realize, to make actual, its infinite nature. "What I aspire to know and to make my own is infinite and only in an infinite series of attempts can I completely fashion my own being. The spirit that drives man forward, and the constant appeal of new goals, that can never be satisfied by past achievements, shall never depart from me. It is man's peculiar pride, to know that his goal is infinite, and yet never to halt on his way, to know that at some point on his journey he will be engulfed, and yet . . . to make no change either in himself or in his circumstances" (*Soliloquies*, 96–97).

Individuality, then, was the aspiration to the most complete freedom; but it was also the highest form of ethics. It was, according to Schleiermacher, not only compatible with the welfare and development of all humankind but a prerequisite for it. Since each individual could realize only an infinitesimal of humanity's potential, the fullest possible development of each was necessary if the goal of the full development of humanity was to be seriously pursued. Moreover, the free development of each was at least contributory to, and perhaps even the very condition of, the fullest free development of all. This belief is the heart of Schleiermacher's sketchy social-theoretical ideas in the *Soliloquies*, in particular of his notions of the three core social relationships—friendship, marriage, and citizenship. "As soon as I have genuinely appropriated anything new in respect to culture and individuality, from whatever source," he wrote of friendship, "do I not run to my friend in word and deed to let him know of it, that he may share my joy, and himself profit as he perceives understandingly my inner growth? My friend I cherish as my own self; whatever I come to recognize as my own, I place straightway at his disposal" (*Soliloquies*, 44). Even more importantly, individuality was the foundation of his idea of love, which he saw as both the ultimate precondition and the finest product of individuality:

> The highest condition of one's own perfection in a limited sphere is a sense for the general [*allgemeiner Sinn*]. And how can this exist without love? Without love, the very first attempt at self-formation would be shattering because of the frightful disproportion between giving and receiving; without love, the spirit [*Gemüt*] that would want to become an authentic being would be driven to extremes, and either be wholly broken or else would sink into vulgarity. Yes love, you gravitational force of the world! Without you no individual life and no development is possible; without you everything would dissolve into a crude homogeneous mass. Those who don't want to be more than that don't need you; for them, law and duty suffice, uniformity in conduct and in justice. . . . No development without love, and without individual development no perfection in love; each completes the other, both grow only indivisibly. (*Soliloquies*, 38–39)

Love individualized, while desire was everywhere the same; yet in its very essence directed towards an idealized other, it also universalized the self.

Individuality was thus for Schleiermacher the basis of the most perfect sociability. When each was concerned to foster the individuality of the other, recognizing how his or her own individuality benefited from such concern, a common will was produced that was something more than the homogeneity of consensus, where "each makes sacrifice of his individuality to suit the other, until they become alike, but neither like his true self" (*Soliloquies*, 57). This pluralism was the premise of Schleiermacher's attack on the minimal state posited by liberalism, whose purpose, as he saw it, was merely negative and defensive, the protection of the narrowest kind of homogeneous individualism—material self-interest. People were not wrong in thinking that they needed such a state in modern society, since accumulation was an inherently antagonistic activity. Not only did such an association fail to be truly ethical, however, it did not foster true individual freedom either. "All . . . is concentrated on this one end: increase in outward possessions or in knowledge, aid and protection against fate or misfortune, stronger alliances to keep rivals in check. This is all that men nowadays seek and find in friendship, marriage and fatherland; they do not seek what they need to supplement their own efforts toward self-development, nor enrichment of the inner life" (*Soliloquies*, 60).

> What has become of the fables of ancient sages about the state? Where is the power with which this highest level of existence should endow mankind, where the consciousness each should have of partaking in the state's reason, its imagination, its strength? Where is the devotion to this new existence that man has conceived, a will to sacrifice the old individual soul rather than lose the state. . . . The present generation . . . believe[s] that the best of states is one that gives least evidence of its existence, and that permits the need for which it exists to be least in evidence also. Whoever thus regards the greatest achievement of human art, by which man should be raised to the highest level of which he is capable as nothing but a secondary evil, as an indispensable mechanism for covering up crime and mitigating its effects, must inevitably sense nothing but a limitation in that which is designed to enhance his life in the highest degree. (*Soliloquies*, 58–59)

Despite these arguments, however, there are many indications throughout the essay of Schleiermacher's awareness that his concepts of individuality and community are not mutually entailed, indeed are perhaps not even wholly compatible with one another. "Freedom," he pointed out, "finds its limit in another freedom"; and while those limits actually defined the very idea of human community, they were nonetheless imposed on the individual from the outside on an original freedom that knew no limits in and of itself: "Outside us is necessity, a chord determined by the harmonious clash of various inner liberties that thus reveal themselves. Within me I can behold nothing but freedom" (*Soliloquies*, 18; translation slightly modified). The native internal standpoint of an individuality that was primarily concerned with its own self-development meant that often in fact and always in theory the contribution of individuality to the community was secondary, a by-product of its action rather than an original intention: "If the purpose of my actions is to shape what is human in me, giving it a particular form and definite characteristics, thus contributing to the world by my own self-development and offering to the community of free spiritual beings the unique expression of my own freedom, then I see no difference whether or not my efforts are at once combined with those of others and some objective result immediately appears to greet me as part of the world order. My efforts have not been in vain, if only I myself acquire greater individuality and independence, for through such development I *also* contribute to the world" (*Soliloquies*, 20; italics added). The first concern of individuality was itself.

Above all, however, the notion of the infinite aspirations of the self brought the concept of individuality into direct contradiction with Schleiermacher's understanding of the interdependence of community and individuality. The latter rested on the self's acceptance of its limitations or finitude; such acknowledgment made the quest for infinity or universality a cooperative, communal enterprise. To the degree that each individual was driven by a personal striving for infinity, no matter how realistically chastened by the awareness of death, that individual was brought into a very different relationship with others. Necessarily, his or her infinitely tending self-expansion encroached upon that of others, as of course did theirs upon him or her. Individuality turned from a venture of cooperation into the same kind of competitive conflict Schleiermacher had scorned in the accumulation of wealth: "[T]he sphere occupied by each sets a limit to the rest, and they respect it only because they are not able to possess the world individually" (*Soliloquies*, 59). At points, moreover, the conflict between individuality and sociability becomes even more glaringly evident, as in Schleiermacher's insinuation that the self's infinity is not only an aspiration but an achieved and achievable reality: "[I]n the future as in the past I shall take possession of the whole world by virtue of inner activity" (*Soliloquies*, 82). This puts a different light on his notion that love and patriotism were both the finest social result of individuality and its very conditions: the beloved and the fatherland not only fostered individuality but tamed it by embodying the totality that the self appropriated as its own through devotion to them. The *Soliloquies* of 1800 thus present the same contradiction in the conception of individuality as *On Religion* of 1799, with lover and country substituting for divinity: on the one hand, the image of the self striving for a personal infinity, on the other, the image of individuality dependent on a whole greater than the self.

II) Wilhelm von Humboldt: The Whole Man

The peculiarities of Schleiermacher's concept of individuality can be brought into sharper focus by comparing it with that of Wilhelm von Humboldt, Schleiermacher's generational peer and fellow Prussian. In 1791–92, nine years before the publication of the *Soliloquies*, Humboldt had written a book in which the ideal of individuality was explicitly advocated as a personal ethic for perhaps the first time. The manuscript was not published in Humboldt's lifetime, though a number of its chapters did appear in contemporary German periodicals in 1792; in any case, Schleiermacher had other means of access to Humboldt's ideas because he frequented the same Berlin salons in the late 1790s that Humboldt had attended in the 1780s. In a passage that would subsequently become famous in the English-speaking world through its citation by John Stuart Mill in *On Liberty*, Humboldt wrote, "The true end of man, that which is prescribed by the eternal and immutable dictates of reason, and not suggested by vague and transient desires, is the highest and most harmonious development of his powers to a complete and consistent whole. . . . [T]hat on which the whole greatness of mankind ultimately depends— towards which every human being must ceaselessly direct his efforts . . . [is]: individuality of energy and self-development."[5] The possibility of uniqueness and its harmonious development had two essential preconditions—freedom of action and "a variety of situations" in which to exercise it (*Limits*, 16). Humboldt's appeal to the "eternal . . . dictates of reason" points to the same Kantian pressures behind Schleiermacher's insistence that individuality be the foundation of universal ethic. Humboldt too made individuality the source of a tie that binds human beings together rather than one that isolates them within their own egos: "[I]n all stages of his life, each individual can achieve only one of those perfections which represent the possible features of human character. It is through a social union, therefore, based on the internal wants and capacities of its members, that each is enabled to participate in the rich and collective resources of all the others. . . . [It creates] a union formative of individual character" (*Limits*, 17). Schleiermacher's and Humboldt's conceptions of individuality would thus appear to be much the same. Yet precisely because of this, the differences are all the more striking and crucial. Some of these differences might seem a matter of style or emphasis, Humboldt's dryness and objectivity, his rational mode of argument and his historical concerns contrasting with the warmth and confessional subjectivity of Schleiermacher's exhortations. But the stylistic differences are also an expression of differences in substance.

Humboldt, for example, was much less concerned to celebrate the sheer uniqueness of individuality than was Schleiermacher. Not that he excluded it, of course, since uniqueness partly defines individuality. But where Schleiermacher emphasized individual differences and the somewhat combative need to resist alien influence, Humboldt stressed a more inner-directed, less comparative feeling of authenticity. There is nothing in *The Limits of State Action* corresponding to Schleiermacher's complaint that Kant's universalist ethics gave no meaning to *his* unique personality, nothing in general of the autobiographical referentiality of the *Soliloquies*. Humboldt wrote instead of the importance of freedom of action as a necessary condition of genuine selfhood because only that which comes from free choice enters into a person's very being; otherwise it remains alien to him or her and is performed with at best mechanical exactness but without genuine desire and spirit. Perhaps oddly for an ethic of individual diversity, the personal "I" does not seem very significant in Humboldt's work; there is an impersonality both in the tone of his argument and in the articulation of the concept.

The other side of this absence of subjective voice is a conceptual difference that clearly cannot be thought of as simply a matter of texture and personality. Unquestionably the goal of individuality for Humboldt was to a degree quantitative, as it certainly was for Schleiermacher. Diversity was part of his definition of the "whole man," not just in man's external situations but within the self; Humboldt's goal was for each person to develop the fullest range of his faculties. But Humboldt specifically eschewed the idea of infinity. His true individual did not aspire to it. It is precisely because no one human being could develop and perfect every faculty that individuality could be the foundation of a social ethic for Humboldt. Schleiermacher made the same conceptual move from individuality to sociability, but Humboldt was more consistent and less conflicted on the compatibility of the two goals because he did not have the same ambitions for individuality as did Schleiermacher.

In Humboldt's version of individuality, internal harmony and unity were at least as important as freedom, authenticity, and diversity, if not more so. His stress was on integrating apparently antithetical or ill-consorting human faculties and desires. In particular, Humboldt's insistence that sensuousness was natural, hence good, encapsulated *his* version of the struggle with Enlightenment, and specifically Kantian, rationalist morality. Fervently committed to a Kantian ideal of moral perfection knowable and realizable through reason alone, he nonetheless felt that to make it an exclusive goal betrayed a one-sided and arid understanding of human nature. "The impressions, inclinations, and passions which have their immediate source in the senses . . . constitute the original source of all spontaneous activity, and all living warmth in the soul. . . . Energy appears to me the first and unique virtue of mankind" (*Limits*, 71–72). If, however, Humboldt was here attacking Kant's absolute formal separation of duty and desire and his privileging of duty, it was through Kant's aesthetics that he thought to rectify Kant's ethics. "When the moral law obliges us to regard every man as an end in himself," he argued, "it becomes fused with that feeling for the beautiful which loves to animate the merest clay, so that even in it, it may rejoice in an individual existence" (*Limits*, 72). "It is only the idea of the sublime which enables us to obey absolute and unconditional laws, both humanly, through the medium of feeling, and with god-like disinterestedness, through the absence of all ulterior reference to happiness or misfortune" (*Limits*, 77). Abstract concern for human beings as ends in themselves and objects of duty did not need to be and should not be divorced from emotional concern and love for particular individuals; the disinterested recognition of beauty or sublimity in them made it possible to have feelings for them without the selfishness and desire for personal gratification that necessarily inhered in passion and desire. The main problem for Humboldt's "whole man" was to achieve a balance of reason and feeling, to be able to be concerned simultaneously both for the abstract and for the particular: "his nature should always be developing itself to higher degrees of perfection and hence . . . especially his powers of thought and sensibility should always be linked in their proper proportions" (*Limits*, 79).

Not only is there no invocation of Schleiermacher's infinity of striving in this notion, Humboldt explicitly rejected it. He made the point in the discussion of a topic most significant for a comparison of the two men, religion. The initial purpose of the discussion was to argue that striving for moral perfection did not depend on a belief in divinity. Humboldt understood and sympathized with the desire of the heart, moved by a vision of beauty, to go beyond the limitations of what thought could legitimately claim to know and to imagine an infinite creative Being. But the less speculative way of critical thought yielded more certain, if less spectacular, results, and Humboldt asserted that "man is often compensated for the loss of the drunken exaltation of hopeful anticipation, by a constant consciousness of the success of his attempts not to allow his attention to wander away into infinity" (*Limits*, 62). Humboldt conceded that the idea of perfection in beauty approached the notion of an "absolute, unlimited totality," but questioned whether it was necessary to believe that it entailed such a notion (*Limits*, 62–63). In any case, however, he emphatically believed that such a notion was antithetical to individuality itself, insofar as such a totality was held to be incarnated in the idea of a "wise order" preserved among an infinite number of diverse and even antagonistic individuals by a divine being. Those for whom individuality seemed more sacred than order, he argued, preferred a system in which "the individual essence, developing itself out of its own resources, and modified by reciprocal influences, itself creates that perfect harmony in which alone the human heart and mind can find rest" (*Limits*, 62). Although it can be argued that there was inconsistency in Humboldt's own thinking—how, for example, did he conceive the possibility of "perfect harmony" within open-ended diversity without at least some notion of a "limited totality"—he was not tempted by the idea of totality at all, and indeed feared it as the opposite of freedom, because he could not conceive it except as an order created and sustained by something external to the self. For Schleiermacher the exact opposite was true. As Martin Redeker notes, "Individuality is not merely particular existence. If it were that, it would be determined and not really free. . . . [T]he individuality of Schleiermacher's self-intuition is the organ and symbol of the infinite."[6] Although Redeker's language here is fuzzy, the important point is that the connection Schleiermacher made between infinity and individuality was integral, not simply one of feeling but, as we have seen, a deduction of the conditions of the possibility of individuality from the experience of it.

The second major difference between the two paradigms of individuality is that Humboldt's was rooted in political and social considerations apparently peripheral to Schleiermacher's essential concerns. And to the extent that Schleiermacher's concept of individuality did have political implications, they were in crucial respects almost the diametric opposite of Humboldt's political ideas.

Humboldt attributed the origins of his ideal of the "whole person" to classical antiquity. The ancients devoted their attention to the "harmonious development of the individual man, as man" (*Limits*, 12); they were concerned to develop all human faculties—intellect, moral sense, passion and imagination—and to integrate them into an unconflicted whole. Modern individuals and modern government, by contrast, were primarily concerned with material happiness, with comfort, prosperity, and productivity. But Humboldt's contrast between ancient and modern was not a simple antithesis of good and evil. For the ancients, the development of the whole person was the means to an end, the creation of the virtuous citizen. The youth of the republics of antiquity were subjected to a systematic communal education in order to subordinate them to communal life. Regulation and interference were directed at the "inner life of the soul" rather than at outward behavior only, so that the restrictions imposed on freedom in the ancient states were in important respects more oppressive and dangerous than in modern times; all the ancient nations betray a "character of uniformity" (*Limits*, 12) because they produced homogeneous rather than diverse personalities. Although, according to Humboldt, the modern individual's social circumstances were much more limiting in the range of personal qualities they promoted than classical civilization was, with the result that the idea of the whole person was sacrificed in modern times, the individual in a modern commercial society was formally less restricted than was the individual in the ancient city-states of Greece and Rome. There was less legal and institutional pressure to conform to a specific pattern of behavior; laws and regulations governed property rather than character, and it was therefore possible for an individual to struggle against the limits and constrictions of his external environment with his internal resources. The ideal of human development then, according to Humboldt, was to combine the ancient desire to cultivate the whole person with the modern values of individual liberty and privacy.

Even without any reference to specifically political issues, this analysis of individuality was more fully and self-consciously situated in contemporary cultural, legal, and sociohistorical issues than was Schleiermacher's. Humboldt clearly aligned individuality with eighteenth-century neoclassicism, with the aesthetic ideals of Greek civilization as interpreted by Winckelmann, Goethe, and Schiller, and with the ideal of personality associated with the tradition of classical republicanism.[7] But he rejected the ethicopolitical ideal of republicanism—the primacy of "political man," and the pursuit of civic virtue—in favor of the basic outlook of the jurisprudential or natural law tradition, with its concern for the defense of individual rights based in human nature and its historical unfolding, even if he rejected that tradition's focus on property rights. Humboldt had been tutored in political economy by Christian Wilhelm von Dohm, the widely read Prussian diplomat and administrative reformer who argued for the laissez-faire views of the Physiocrats;[8] Humboldt himself had read the Scottish political economist Adam Ferguson, whose picture of the evolution of society from primitive to commercial societies in *An Essay on the History of Civil Society* of 1766 he at least partly accepted (*Limits*, 50). Humboldt thus explicitly positioned his ideal of individuality within the contemporary debate over the relative merits of the civic virtue of ancient republics and the self-interested individualism of modern commercial society and put himself in the modern camp to the extent of insisting on the freedom of private life and recognizing its historical linkage with the growth of commerce. "Men have now reached a pitch of civilization," he wrote, "beyond which it seems they cannot ascend except through the development of individuals; and hence all institutions which act in any way to obstruct or thwart this development, and press men together into uniform masses, are now far more harmful than in earlier ages of the world" (*Limits*, 50–51). Schleiermacher, as we have seen, to the degree that he dealt with the issue at all, explicitly pitched individuality *against* modern individualism.

Humboldt went even further in his critique of the Greek ideal of wholeness by accusing it of a paradoxical narrowness. The Greeks regarded all occupations connected with the exercise of physical strength or the production of material goods as harmful and degrading, concessions to the necessity of survival, and so not legitimate manifestations of human freedom; that is why they approved of slavery, sacrificing one part of humanity to the cultivation of another. They were wrong, Humboldt argued, not only morally but theoretically. It was not the content of an activity that mattered so far as free human self-development was concerned, but the manner in which it was carried out. "There is no pursuit whatever that may not be ennobling and give to human nature some worthy and determinate form. The manner of its performance is the only thing to be considered. . . . [A] man's pursuits react beneficially on his culture, so long as these . . . succeed in filling and satisfying the wants of his soul; while their influence is . . . pernicious, when he . . . regards the occupation itself merely as a means" (*Limits*, 28–29). What was done for its own sake became a genuine part of the self and expanded its capacities and sensibilities; what was done as a means to ulterior advantage was merely instrumental to self-interest and did nothing to further the range of the self. Although the sweeping assertion that any pursuit could contribute to human development, depending on its motive, in theory sanctioned even commercial pursuits as potentially legitimate modes of self-cultivation, Humboldt could not relinquish the classical (and aristocratic) idea that gainful pursuit was inevitably a means only to the ends of economic subsistence and material acquisition and furnished no other—no intrinsic—satisfactions.

It is not only its rootedness in social thought that marks the distinction between Humboldt's model of individuality and Schleiermacher's. The entire framing purpose of Humboldt's exposition of individuality was radically different. Schleiermacher's discourse is confessional and homiletic; Humboldt's is explicitly political. Individuality was the basic principle from which Humboldt worked, but he did not argue it in the text. He used it rather as the premise of an argument for a particular view of the purposes and function of the state. The state should do the minimum necessary to guarantee the mutual security of its citizens in relationship to one another and against foreign enemies. It must, however, abstain from all solicitude for the positive welfare of its citizens in order to allow for the freest possible development of individuals. Humboldt examined the spheres of social life that he took up in the book specifically from the point of view of the legitimacy of state action with regard to them. His discussion of the possible connection between moral perfection and religion, for example, tested, and rejected, the proposition that because religion is necessary to form the moral character that conduces to good citizenship, the state has the right to regulate the religious life and duties of its citizens. Of the implications of individuality for the organization and duties of the state, Schleiermacher, on the other hand, had nothing concrete to say in the *Soliloquies*. What he did say negatively, however, is significant. He expressly repudiated Humboldt's notion of the negative state and implied a view of fatherland and patriotism much closer to the classical republican ideal rejected by Humboldt. The state was an embodiment of wholeness and an object of devotion not incompatible with individuality, indeed contributory to it in the way that love was, though perhaps not, at least at this point, the indispensable condition of it that love seemed to be.

Humboldt's book is political in a more topical and concretely historical way as well. The chapter on religion, for example, is not simply an abstract philosophical analysis of the desirability of religious toleration. Behind it in part is the shadow of the 1788 law of Frederick William II of Prussia declaring Lutheranism the state religion and threatening penalties for those who did not conform. The death of Frederick the Great in 1786 had been followed by a retreat from the relative liberalization of his enlightened absolutism, and Humboldt's book was a shot in the war against a return to religious obscurantism and centralized control of conscience. But the broader historical occasion of the essay was unquestionably the French Revolution. The opening pages suggest that Humboldt intended nothing less than that his book serve as the theoretical charter of a bloodless revolution in Prussia. His strategy in the book was one of indirection, indeed reversal. Under the guise of rejecting revolution, he proposed that the Prussian monarchy virtually reform itself out of existence, or at least out of its traditional historical identity. "Real political revolutions," Humboldt wrote, "always produce unfortunate consequences; whereas a sovereign—whether it be democratic, aristocratic or monarchical—can extend or restrict its sphere of action gradually and unnoticed, and in general attain its ends more surely as it avoids startling innovations" (*Limits*, 10). Humboldt's rejection of violence was utterly genuine, but the force of the passage's rhetoric was directed not at condemnation of revolution but at exhortation to change, if indeed change from above. At points his desire virtually breaks into open flattery and pleading: "If to see a people breaking their fetters . . . is a beautiful and ennobling spectacle . . . it must be still more fine and uplifting to see a prince himself loosing the bonds and granting freedom to his people"

(*Limits,* 11). Although the essay is certainly not simply a *pièce d'occasion,*[9] it was a clear response to the new sense of possibility opened up for Germans by the French Revolution. Many of the elements that went into Humboldt's program of individuality (similar to many in Schleiermacher's concept)—Enlightenment rationality, especially in the form of Kantian critical idealism, the idea of *Bildung* derived from neoclassical aesthetics, sensibility and *Sturm und Drang* feeling and passion, Pietist concern with sincere intention and the inner light of the soul, Herder's doctrine of historical cultural individuality—represented advanced German thinking on the eve of the Revolution. Humboldt's essay was a synthesis and a reinterpretation of this cultural heritage under one rubric, individuality, but it represented the politicization of a previously apolitical ideal.[10]

Once again it may seem tempting to reduce these differences about the place of social and political issues in Schleiermacher's and Humboldt's approaches to individuality to personal differences, here of social background and profession. Schleiermacher was a pastor, son of an army chaplain of lower middle class origins; Humboldt was a Pomeranian aristocrat (though not of ancient lineage)[11] whose father was chamberlain [*Kammerherr*] to the crown prince, and he himself began his own career in the higher echelons of the Prussian civil service. It seems easy enough to place sociologically Schleiermacher's homiletic orientation and Humboldt's concern with state functioning. But such an explanation is too facile. Themes prominent in one writer and apparently absent in the other are in fact latently present in the second as well. There is a dynamic of suppression and emergence in the texts that reveals that the two concepts of individuality were, so to speak, different stages of one line of development; the full implications of individuality in one direction could only emerge at the cost of its curtailment, suppression, and transformation in another. Humboldt could offer an untroubled defense of sociable individuality and the limited state because he did not pursue the Faustian implications of open-ended diversity in personal development and thus did not see it as a danger to society or the state. The cost of Schleiermacher's concept of infinite individuality was the downgrading of politics and within that reduced politics the insistence on the desirability of the positive state. This entailed what appeared to be Schleiermacher's total rejection of the French Revolution. In the passage proclaiming the state the highest level of human existence, he wrote disparagingly of the dreams of the present generation, ignorant of the true meaning of the state, to reorganize it along with all other human ideals (*Soliloquies,* 59). Political revolution in general, he claimed, was futile and irrelevant: "I, for my part, am a stranger to the life and thought of this present generation, I am a prophet citizen of a later world, drawn thither by a vital imagination and strong faith; to it belong my every word and deed. What the present world is doing and undergoing leaves me unmoved; far below me it appears insignificant, and I can at a glance survey the confused course of its great revolutions. Through every revolution whether in the field of science or of action it returns ever to the same point" (*Soliloquies*, 62). Yet other passages indicate that Schleiermacher's attitude to the revolution was rather more ambivalent. In the *Soliloquies* there is a mysterious, though obviously personal, reference to the difficulty of finding and uniting with the soul-mate who will foster one's individuality, a reference that hints angrily at the contemporary social resentment that fueled the revolutionary demand for equality. "And even if he, whose heart seeks love everywhere in vain, should learn where dwelt his friend and his beloved, yet would he be restricted by his station in life, by the rank which he holds in that meagre thing we call society" (*Soliloquies*, 54). Somewhat more directly, though still without naming it, he alluded to the French Revolution in *On Religion* as "the most sublime deed in the universe." He also connected the epoch of the Revolution causally with both the personality ideal and the new religiosity he was advocating. "It belongs," he asserted, "to the opposition of the new time to the old that no longer is one person one thing but everyone is all things."[12] These passages suggest that the Revolution and radical politics were more integral to Schleiermacher's concept of individuality than he allowed in his explicit comments. It is a suppressed presence whose role and meaning must be understood.

III) Politics and the Psyche

Schleiermacher's early enthusiasm for the French Revolution has always been known but generally dismissed as a passing phase of no consequence for his later work; Dilthey's classic biography pays it very little attention and gives it no developmental significance.[13] Between his revolutionary phase and his emergence in the first decade of the nineteenth century as an ardent Prussian patriot—during the period, in other words, when he worked out his new ideas on individuality and religion—Schleiermacher is supposed to have been completely apolitical.

From both textual evidence such as that cited above and material in Schleiermacher's *Nachlass*, however, it appears that the importance of the French Revolution in Schleiermacher's early life and work has been much underestimated. Kurt Nowak proposes to apply the model developed in the modern literary criticism of early Romantics like Schlegel and Novalis as a heuristic for analyzing the Revolution's role in Schleiermacher's thought. He offers the suggestion (long familiar in English Ro-

mantic studies from M. H. Abrams's work) that Schleiermacher's interpretation of religion, especially his idea of the revolutionary period as a
movement of potential rebirth at a time of religious collapse, represented
a recasting of the revolutionary impulse in spiritual terms.[14] The transformation of the political revolution into a holy revolution extended both
the content and the scope of the revolutionary idea. Religion entailed a
universal horizon of meaning that would be relevant to all spheres of
life, including art and morality as well as politics, a meaning extending
beyond the parochial vicissitudes of merely national politics to embrace
the whole of humanity.[15]

Nowak is undoubtedly right about the revolutionary impulse behind
Schleiermacher's religiosity, but there is an ambiguity in his conclusion.
To say that Schleiermacher's religion was a broadening of the revolutionary impulse would seem to mean, or ought to mean, that spiritual revolution subsumed revolutionary politics in a more complete synthesis. As
Nowak summarizes the modern consensus on the early Romantics' trans-
figuration of revolution, "it would be a mistake to interpret their philosophical and poetic program as escapism. . . . Their concept of praxis
reached beyond a concept of political praxis and stood in close connection
with a new understanding of the autonomy of the spiritual.[16] The evidence, however, suggests a more complicated and contradictory conclusion about the role of politics in Schleiermacher's central texts of 1799 and
1800. If politics was "sublimated" in a higher religious synthesis, its concrete concerns were demoted, and any revolutionary content was eliminated or reversed, its republican-sounding terms modulated into an anti-
individualist organicism. On both counts, however, Schleiermacher was
repudiating radical political ideas he had fervently held as recently as
three years before he wrote *On Religion*.

Schleiermacher—like the other early German Romantics—defended
the Revolution after most of the German intellectuals who initially supported it had abandoned it because of its increasingly violent cast or because of the outbreak of war between France and Prussia in 1792.[17] In a
letter to his father written after the execution of Louis XVI—his first,
Schleiermacher himself significantly pointed out, on the subject of politics—he expressed his continued ardor for the Revolution despite his sorrow at the "wretched death" of the king:

> I do not know how it has happened that I have never written to you on these
> subjects; now however, they occupy my mind too much to pass them over in
> silence. Being accustomed openly to communicate to you all my thoughts,
> I am not afraid of confessing that upon the whole I heartily sympathize with
> the French Revolution; although . . . I do not of course approve of all the
> human passions and exaggerated ideas that have been mixed up with it,

however plausibly these may be represented as a natural consequence of the previous state of things; nor am I either seized by the unhappy folly of wishing to imitate it and of desiring the whole world to be remodelled according to that *standard*. I have honestly and impartially loved the Revolution.[18]

Schleiermacher pointedly stated that he opposed the execution of Louis XVI because he believed him innocent of the crimes of which he was accused, not because he was king. The letter, and subsequent comments by Schleiermacher, leave open the question of just what new political arrangements he did favor for Prussia. He unequivocally supported the French republic, however, for a good time longer; a letter of 1799 expresses anxiety over Napoleon's coup of the eighteenth Brumaire, which he calls an "unnecessary revolution" that threatened the overthrow of the republic.[19] Within Germany, he claimed to his father, his criticism of both sides and his failure to take an unequivocal stance opened him to attack from all sides: "Such has been my fate in relation to French affairs more than a thousand times. I cannot refrain from correcting the onesidedness and partiality of people . . . and from giving them now and then a little practical advice . . . and thus I get into the black books of all. . . . [P]oor me . . . I am looked upon by the democrats as a defender of despotism . . . while . . . the royalists deem me a Jacobin, and the prudent people consider me a thoughtless fellow with a tongue too long for my mouth" (*Life*, 110).

We can accept Schleiermacher's account without taking it wholly at face value. His father certainly did not. It is difficult not to see in the letter's wording the delicate maneuver of a rebellious but anxious son, especially in the light of the troubled history of father and son over Friedrich's loss of religious faith six years earlier. As a boy of seventeen, while at the Moravian Brotherhood seminary at Barby, Friedrich had announced to his father that he no longer believed in the divinity of Jesus, and his father had responded that he was repudiating him, though in fact communication between the two was never broken off (*Life*, 46, 52). Now, Schleiermacher wanted to stake out a rebellious position and win at least his father's tolerance and perhaps even a measure of approval for it by taking cover under the masks of Olympian moralist and ineffectual talker. His father obliged him with the first but not the second, and he indicated that he saw through his son's show of impartiality: "You might also ask your democrats," the elder Schleiermacher wrote, "if they really think it is possible that a republic of such dimensions as France could ever prove permanent" (*Life*, 113). Without confronting his son directly—he too wanted no repetition of the anguished breach of 1787—he took for granted his son's republicanism and even his democratic sympathies. Not long afterwards, Friedrich rejected the Jacobin regime and greeted the fall of Robespierre as a blessing for the French people and a necessary precondition for the peace accord of 1795 between Prussia and France. But this was not inconsistent with his fundamentally republican political ideals and his basically favorable attitude to the idea of revolution itself.

In comparison with Humboldt's beliefs then, Schleiermacher's political ideas were initially more radical. Yet in their respective works on individuality, Humboldt was explicitly political and reformist and Schleiermacher largely apolitical and to the degree he was political, antiliberal. There is a paradoxical double relationship between their politics and their concept of individuality, one direct and one inverse. Schleiermacher's initially more radical political stance towards the Revolution led to his development of a more ambitious and extended concept of individuality. On the other hand, although Humboldt's more restrained concept of individuality remained allied with a liberal politics, Schleiermacher's radical concept of individuality involved the suppression of radical politics. This difference emerged strikingly in the arguments between the two men over the founding of the University of Berlin in the first decade of the nineteenth century. Although their common ideal of individuality meant a shared belief in a humanistic education aimed at developing the whole person rather than a specialized professional or technical training, Humboldt favored a curriculum centered in the liberal arts and established independently of the Prussian government, that would equip the student to serve society, while Schleiermacher favored a general education in the arts and sciences with the state supervising the school. Since he believed that the educational process should prepare the student to honor and serve the state, he argued that the state should be allowed to direct the preparation of material taught in the classroom.[20]

Schleiermacher's notebooks dating from the early part of his residence in Berlin reveal just how dramatic the suppression of radicalism in the 1790s actually was; they offer an almost visual representation of the second, inverse relationship between radical individuality and radical politics. He first began keeping notebooks for jotting down ideas when he came to Berlin in 1796 to take up his position as pastor at the Charité Hospital. Over a period of one year, until the summer of 1797, there are only ten entries, written in a fragmentary or aphoristic style. The next ten entries, however, cover a period of three weeks in September of 1797, very shortly after Schleiermacher met Friedrich Schlegel. Not only the tempo but the tenor of the aphorisms changed radically after that encounter. The notebook was originally clearly intended for political ideas: its marginal notation reads "Politics" and five of the first ten entries deal with political theory. All of them attack "unlimited" [*uneingeschränkte*] monarchy with the conceptual weapons of natural law and the general will. "An unlimited monarchy," runs the first, "cannot have arisen in a condition of natural simplicity, for then men guard their rights too jealously, nor in a condition of cultivation, for then they take more measures [against it]. Thus only a crude mass, that does not take time to reflect, and has no other interest than bread and circuses will constitute an unlimited monarchy."[21] A second entry asserts: "The defenders of unlimited monarchy inevitably fall into the following dilemma. Either there is no general will in such a state, or the people have alienated not only the exercise of sovereignty but sovereignty itself. For if I consider the monarch as a member of the state, there is then no general will, because there is one will in the state that is not subjected to it; if I consider him as something external to the state, then the exercise of sovereignty is outside the state and is thus alienated" (KG, 1:2:3, 2). In a third entry Schleiermacher attacked the theory of the philosopher J. A. Eberhard that a people has no right to change its constitution because it has made a contract of submission [*Unterwerfungsvertrag*] with its rulers; Schleiermacher insisted that Eberhard's conclusion could not be a universal generalization because such a contract is not the juridical basis of the relationship between rulers and ruled in a republic and holds at most for an unlimited monarchy, not even for all monarchies (KG, 1:2:4, 3). By far the most substantial entry, longer than all the others combined, was ostensibly concerned with the state's role in making and enforcing contracts but was in fact concerned with sexual freedom and the limits of state action. It argued that the state had the right to prescribe the form of contracts but not their content. It could, for example, establish the legal forms of exclusive sexual intercourse, by setting up the system of marriage, but it could not make marriage the only permissible form of sexual intercourse. According to rational moral principles the law could only act in cases where individuals were prevented from fulfilling their duties or asserting their rights (KG, 1:2:4-7, 4). Although Kantian in its expression, the concept of appropriate state action could be right out of Humboldt.

None of the notebook entries after the first ten, however, have anything to say about these or any other political matters. The original purpose of the notebook seems to have been abandoned entirely. Instead there appear in a three week period in September 1797 a number of aphorisms about the absolute ego and the infinite. The fifteenth entry, for example, reads, "There are only two virtues: 1.) The philosophical virtue or pure love of humanity. That is, the striving of the I to posit itself absolutely, to produce humanity and elevate it. 2.) The heroic virtue or the pure love of freedom. That is, the striving to ensure for the self's domination [*Herrschaft*] over interconnected [*verbundene*] nature everywhere" (KG, 1:2:9, 15). "The amiable person," says another entry, "is the one who finds the infinite in the finite, the great person is the one who discards the finite for the sake of the infinite. The complete person is the one who unites both" (KG, 1:2:17, 48). The Fichtean language and Schlegelian paradoxes of these fragments represented a radical change in Schleiermacher's terms of discourse and apparently also in his concerns.

The political concerns of the earlier entries, furthermore, were not just a matter of a few isolated fragments. During his first year in Berlin, in 1796–97, Schleiermacher was working on a large-scale systematic study of contract theory whose purpose was to explore the grounds in natural law that might be used to legitimize the coercion of others.[22] The impulse of his thinking was radically libertarian, though legalistic in its method and apparently narrow in its focus. He attacked what he regarded as the merely subjective theories of such writers as Hufeland, Mendelssohn, and Schmalz, who had argued that a person's right to coerce others was founded on their duty to fulfill what they had undertaken to that person, because their promises aroused certain expectations about their future actions that affected the fulfillment of the person's own goals and so affected his or her freedom. Neither a person's subjective expectations, however, nor even the fact that others had objectively bound their own wills by promises were sufficient grounds to warrant the use of force against them, Schleiermacher argued; it was illegitimate to bind the freedom of others by refusing them the right to change their minds. For Schleiermacher, the will was the essence of personality in human beings because it was the locus of freedom. If it could be shown, however, that their actions were no longer the expressions of their wills—as arguably was the case when there was an inconsistency between their declared will and their actual behavior—their actions could be taken (on Kantian grounds) as natural events rather than as the expression of a free person, and it was then legitimate to use coercion to make them fulfill their own expressed will, whether in the interests of the affected person's freedom or their own. Although Schleiermacher did not extend his discussion from the moral and legal grounds of legitimate coercion to their political implications in his notes, the fragments not only make it evident that his analysis was to be the foundation of a political argument but give some hint of what that argument would have been.

This project, and indeed political references in general, were abruptly broken off in September 1797. It seems obvious from the chronology and conjunction of events that there was a connection between this sudden rupture and the new concerns with the absolute positing of the self, the domination over nature, and the pursuit of the infinite, but the inner meaning of this connection is not clear. Closer analysis shows that the transition was more complicated, more dialectical, than it seems at first. The new Fichtean language represents in a number of respects a further extension of the idea of freedom inherent in Schleiermacher's previous thinking. But this radical extrapolation carried with it for Schleiermacher

such enormous and potentially dangerous consequences that it had to be
severed from its original legal and political foundations.

To understand this transition, it is necessary to know more about the
nature of Schleiermacher's previous political radicalism. There is an important clue to its nature in the lengthy notebook fragment from 1796–97
dealing with sexuality and the state. Most of Schleiermacher's youthful
reflections on freedom in the years before he came to Berlin were concerned with purely formal issues of self-determination couched in Kantian terms—the nature of the free will, the question of whether the will
had to be thought of as motivated or not, and similar philosophical questions. Although they seemed utterly devoid of politics, these issues had
political implications for Schleiermacher; his so-called "deterministic"
critique of Kant in "Über die Freiheit," for example, allowed biographical, psychological, and social factors a role in influencing the possibility of
moral action, a possibility that Kant's identification of the pure moral will
with freedom excluded.[23] But Schleiermacher's treatment of these factors
was so abstract that they could in turn be treated by Schleiermacher's
biographers and interpreters as purely metaphysical issues.[24] In his letters, Schleiermacher occasionally discussed political matters, expressing
support, for example, for the idea of disestablishing the church in order
to prevent state interference in the religious life of its subjects,[25] but the
notebook fragment on sexuality is Schleiermacher's most extended discussion of a substantive issue of freedom in this period.

On the basis of a broadly permissive definition of morality, the fragment called for a complete revolution in the social norms of sexuality.
Neither "concubinage"—nonmarital sexual relationships—nor even pros-
titution would be immoral by this definition; these forms of social relationships created moral difficulties only under the legal and economic
conditions of the period. Women were completely dependent on men
and if men had no legal obligation to their sexual partners and to any
children born of an extramarital relationship, such women and children
were either helpless and destitute or charges on the state. If, however,
marriage were to be legally abolished and replaced with an arrangement
in which children belonged to their mothers and inherited from them,
and the estates of males reverted on their deaths to their sisters or sisters'
children, "the satisfaction of the sexual drive without a legal contract
[would] not be a bad thing even without any state intervention" (KG,
1:2:5–6, 6). Schleiermacher argued that at least some degree of relaxation
of restrictions was possible even as things then stood; the state ought not
to insist that a child legally have only one father but should "allow all
participants [a woman's lovers and the possible fathers of her children] to
assume their relative part." Schleiermacher proposed to himself to treat
these issues in much greater detail in a work on "The social relationships

that arise out of the sexual drive from a moral and legal standpoint." Among the issues to be considered in such a work was the question of whether the present system of inheritance entailed such negative consequences as promoting the amassing of wealth and creating division between the *Stände*. But underlying the concern with sexual freedom there seemed to be above all for Schleiermacher the idea of the liberation of women. "If marriages were merely concubinages," he concluded, "the female sex could accomplish much more, and a woman would never again count for more than she was worth [that is, she would no longer simply be valued because of her sex]. She would have the opportunity to rise [*emporzuschwingen*]" (KG, 1:2:7, 7).

That Schleiermacher was not alone in these advanced ideas would be evident simply from the fact that he took the specifics of alternate arrangements to marriage from an anonymous article in a respected journal, the *Neue Teutsche Merkuhr vom Jahr 1793*, published by one of the greatest of contemporary poets, Christoph Martin Wieland. But the date of the publication of the article is of special significance for Schleiermacher's life. That was the year that he left the employ of Count Friedrich von Dohna, the powerful Prussian aristocrat to whose family he had been tutor for the previous two and a half years. While there, he had fallen in love with Dohna's seventeen-year-old daughter Friederike, and though he tried to keep his passion secret, Friederike apparently guessed its existence.[26] Schleiermacher's sister later suggested that her brother had kept silent because the daughter of one of the greatest houses in the kingdom seemed to him absolutely unattainable. His uncle even expressed the fear that his feelings would spoil any possibility of future married happiness with a bourgeois girl.[27] Somehow, years later, Schleiermacher got hold of a prayer written by Friederike in 1800 justifying her decision to oppose the wishes of her parents that she marry a man she did not love. One passage read "My Father, I know there are no more beautiful duties to be fulfilled than those of a virtuous wife. But these are also the most difficult if one has not a friend but only a husband."[28] Whether Schleiermacher kept the prayer because he still cherished the hope that Friederike had loved him—she never married—or because he cherished the aspect of her character expressed in the ideal of friendship joined with sexuality that she defended along with her rebellious independence is uncertain. Even before he obtained the prayer, however, he had written in the *Soliloquies* of the Schlobitten years, "I saw that it takes freedom to ennoble and give right expression to the delicate intimacies of human nature, whereas they remain forever obscure to the uninitiated who respects these only as the bonds of nature" (*Soliloquies*, 74)—a cryptic hint that he had discovered that his wish to approach Friederike as a friend and equal represented the difference between love and mere sexual desire, but also that the freedom to do so was balked by the social gulf between them. Under these circumstances it does not seem coincidental that it was also during his stay at Schlobitten that he first expressed his support for the French Revolution. The dawning of political consciousness was linked with his sexual and romantic awakening and with the frustration caused by an impassible social gulf between him and the object of his desire. Not one to be frightened into silence by authority, as he had proved in the matter of his religious crisis, Schleiermacher expressed his political views openly and clashed directly with the conservative and outspoken Count Dohna, who repudiated everything the Revolution stood for. Finally the two had a bitter argument ostensibly over the count's interference with the tutor's methods of instruction, and in a fit of temper the count threatened to dismiss him. The real issue, however, was the count's superior position and authority, which Schleiermacher could not tolerate. As Schleiermacher reported the argument to his father—whom he knew from past experience would disapprove of his son's defiance and stubbornness: "Of course, the word of a nobleman and soldier cannot so easily be retracted as that of a simple citizen. . . . On the other hand, it would not have been dignified in me to beg him to take it back; and had I done so, I should, inevitably, have placed myself in a very dependent and unpleasant situation, in which I should have been obliged to keep silent on a great many subjects. On the other hand, even if the Count has wished to retract, he could not but fear that, in doing so, he would be giving too much scope to my desire for independence and to my apparently arbitrary conduct" (*Life*, 114). In fact, contrary to Schleiermacher's expectations, the Count did wish to retract; in their next meeting he backed down by saying he had spoken too hastily and wished his threat of dismissal to be forgotten. It was Schleiermacher who insisted on continuing the conversation, pointing up their differences on education and finally provoking the dismissal. He later admitted that it was his resentment over the Count's intrusion in his sphere, a basic conflict over power and authority, that was the cause of the rupture. He won a symbolic victory by rejecting the Count's apology and refusing to submit to his dominance by remaining in his household.

Four years earlier he had rebelled against Pietist orthodoxy by invoking Enlightenment rationalism against Christology, defying his father and precipitating a painful, if temporary, break between them. Now he extended religious and filial rebellion to political and social rebellion, at least on the level of values and symbolic behavior. It is in this context that the new turns his thought took at this time can be understood. In May 1792, while still at Schlobitten, he had written his father: "[N]o one has the right to say to another, My way of being happy is the true one, and every other is only fancy—for, in reality, happiness depends entirely upon the feelings and the consciousness of the individual; . . . the tranquility of mind which the individual enjoys must in truth be his own; the sentiments from which it springs must be natural to him and in perfect harmony with the whole character of his mind" (*Life*, 99). Biographers, citing Schleiermacher himself, have pointed out that the seed of his concept of individuality first germinated at Schlobitten,[29] but following his own evasions, they generally ignore the implications of that fact: that its origins were specifically connected with the erotic-social-political awakening in the Dohna household and that its more fully developed expression in the *Soliloquies* was in part a radicalized version of the rebellious idea expressed in the letter to his father. At the time, however, the most important intellectual result of his discovery that his drives were as much expressions of free personality as were his moral faculties was an extremely insightful philosophical critique of Kant's moral doctrines.

The moral will, Schleiermacher argued in his earliest writings, could not be held to be completely independent of psychological motives, as Kant insisted; our reasoning was always bound up with being inclined and disinclined towards things, even if these were maxims or rules of action rather than just objects. The influence of reason on our intentions was always by means of incentives, which involved feelings; morality thus acted on us not by some abstract determination of will but through a moral feeling.[30] "In my theory," wrote Schleiermacher in an unpublished manuscript on Spinoza, to whom he was drawn because of his understanding of the force of human drives, "the will signifies the understanding occupied with desire."[31] Kant's doctrine of freedom, according to Schleiermacher, was either circular or contradictory. If "will" designated a faculty determined by nothing but pure practical reason—the categorical imperative—then the will was good by definition. But since such a will was human freedom, in that it acted only according to self-legislated maxims, the will could not be said to be free to choose between good and evil. Schleiermacher avoided this dilemma by arguing that will in itself was neither good nor evil. The incentives of moral reason had to compete with the incentives of sensuality. The problem for moral behavior was to bring knowledge of the moral law and desire together: "'Knowing and desiring should not be two in me, but one. . . . Complete invariable consonance of the two, in the fullest degree to which both are possible in me, unity of both in purpose and object, that is humanity, that is the beautiful goal established in human nature. And the first condition I make upon life is to furnish objects which not only occupy each of these powers individually, but also exhibit this consonance of both, and through which it can be promoted.[32] In the context of what Schleiermacher said he had learned at

Schlobitten, the reference to Friederike von Dohna seems obvious. But an equally important implication followed from his psychological revision of Kantian moral thinking. If motives and incentives were an essential aspect of morality, and these, as part of nature, were (unlike the pure Kantian moral will) amenable to influence from the outside, then external social and political factors could contribute to the possibility of moral behavior. If as Schleiermacher said, the first condition he made upon life was to furnish objects that exhibited and promoted the consonance of morality and desire, and life put obstacles in the way of furnishing such objects, then life had to change if moral behavior were to be promoted. Moral philosophy, sexuality, social discontent, and political rebellion all come together in Schleiermacher's early manuscripts on human freedom and the value of life.

Three years after leaving Schlobitten, Schleiermacher had the opportunity to gratify at least some elements of the desires aroused in Schlobitten, if in sublimated form. On moving to Berlin, he became part of one of the most extraordinary sociocultural phenomena of the period, the salon society maintained by a number of young Jewish women, Henriette Herz, Dorothea Veit, Rahel Levin (later Varnhagen), a society centered in the Herz and Veit households. It was a uniquely egalitarian and cosmopolitan enclave in a highly stratified and still parochial world, a place outside official society where aristocrats could meet on an equal footing with commoners, enlightened Christians with skeptics, all hosted by Jews; its very structure and composition embodied its ideals of a universal moral and aesthetic cultivation in which differences of class, religion, and gender were insignificant.[33] In a fine, but not incidental, irony, Schleiermacher was introduced into this society by Count Alexander zu Dohna, the son of the aristocratic employer whose service he had left. The young count had become the tutor's friend during the time Schleiermacher lived in his home, and the Dohna family were patients of Markus Herz, Henriette's husband, a man of philosophical culture and reputation as well as a physician, a favorite former student and friend of Kant. Writing to his sister two years after he gained entry into these circles, Schleiermacher explained their attraction in terms that reveal his own rebellious egalitarianism:

That young intellectuals [*Gelehrte*] and society types regularly visit in the great Jewish houses here is quite natural, because they are by far the wealthiest bourgeois families here, almost the only ones that hold open house, and homes where one can meet strangers from all classes because of their widespread connections in every country. Whoever therefore wants good society without any hindrances gets introduced into such houses, where it is taken for granted that every person of talent, even if it is only social talent, is

welcomed, and he is certain to enjoy himself because the Jewish women—
the men are plunged too soon into business—are very cultivated, can talk
about anything, and usually are very skilled in one or another of the fine
arts.[34]

The Berlin salons were the antidote to Schlobitten, a place where a
Schleiermacher could socialize with a Dohna on the common ground of
philosophy and art, one open to all talents regardless of rank. The salons
also provided the compensation of female company of a sort quite different from what was available at Schlobitten but equally inappropriate and
scandalous for someone of Schleiermacher's background. He became
close friends with Henriette Herz, the charismatic, beautiful, and flirtatious center of the circle. More than one man in the group fell in love with
her—Alexander Dohna among them—but Schleiermacher had a particularly strong penchant for emotional involvement with married women.
During the period of his previous clerical post at Landsberg, he had been
very attracted to the wife of his cousin and in 1799 was to fall in love with
Eleonore Grunow, the unhappily married wife of a Berlin clergyman,
whom he tried for years to win away from her husband. Henriette Herz
and Schleiermacher's professedly platonic relationship was based on a
strong common interest in the Kantian ideal of the moral life embodied
in true friendship, but there were rumors of a more emotional involvement, and the very letter in which he denied any erotic basis to their
relationship seems to affirm it as a potentiality denied primarily because
of Schleiermacher's self-consciousness over his height and physical
appearance:

> It is a very warm and intimate relationship, but it has nothing to do with man
> and woman; isn't that easy to imagine? Why there hasn't been any other kind
> of involvement and why there never will be is indeed another question, but
> that too is not hard to explain. She never affected me in such a way as to
> disturb my serenity. Whoever understands anything about how the inner
> soul expresses itself outwardly recognizes immediately in her a nature with-
> out passion, and if I were to consider only the external effect, she doesn't
> attract me at all, although her face is indisputably very beautiful, and her
> colossally queenly figure is so much the opposite of my own, that if I imagine
> that both of us were free and loved each other and we got married I would
> always find it from that [the physical] point of view rather ridiculous and
> absurd, so that for these decisive reasons I can put the thought aside.
> (*Briefen*, 1:261)

The friendship between the two invited a good deal of gossip not only
because Henriette was married (and older by four years) but also because
she was Jewish. For a clergyman to frequent the Berlin salon at all, much

less to form an intimate friendship with someone like Henriette was highly suspect to conservatives inside and outside the Reformed church. Schleiermacher's superior Sack warned him about the possible effects of the company he was keeping on his chances of advancement in the church and even went so far as to advise him to take a position in Sweden for a while until the talk died down (*Leben*, 187–88). In 1796–97, Schleiermacher's political concerns were consistent with the way he was leading his personal life; rebelliousness in his social contacts and at least the appearance of impropriety in his erotic life were matched intellectually by researches into contract theory in the effort to find the basis for an idea of government by consent and for the limiting of state interference in the private sexual life of its citizens.

Implicating Schleiermacher's involvement in the Berlin salons and Henriette Herz in his political radicalism, however, raises a serious question about the causal significance of this involvement when one compares his ideas with those of Wilhelm von Humboldt. Humboldt after all had preceded Schleiermacher not only in the salons but in Henriette's affections, and his involvement with both the salons and Henriette played a considerable role in his emotional and his intellectual development. Ten years before Schleiermacher's participation in the Berlin salons, Humboldt had, as a young man of nineteen, been introduced by his tutor into the Herz household and had soon begun an intimate correspondence with Henriette; she even taught him Hebrew script so that he could pour out the details of his emotional life to her in cipher. A few years later, he joined the *Tugendbund*, the League of Virtue that Henriette had formed with Brendel (Dorothea) Veit and others, a secret fraternity dedicated to friendship much in the spirit of the age, bound by promises to seek together moral perfection, purity of soul, and nobility of heart, as well as by effusively physical demonstrations of hugging and kissing.[35] Humboldt, too, in short, owed a good part of his theoretical interest in the freedom of the affective life to his own personal awakening. Furthermore, Humboldt's affective liberation soon went beyond the sublimated emotionality of the Berlin circle's Enlightenment ideal of friendship. Within the next two years he grew away from the *Tugendbund* as he met another group of people less conventional in their behavior and less morally high-minded in their attitudes. It included a number of young women such as Therese Forster, wife of the famous traveler and writer Georg Forster, women who had acted on their frustration with the constricting social conditions of their lives by disparaging conventional virtue as self-suppression and hypocrisy and engaging in extramarital affairs.[36] Influenced by their example, Humboldt began to express his own desire for absolute personal freedom and a variety of "new situations" and soon translated these ideals into behavior. Although he became engaged in 1789, he indicated to his fiancée that he could not be bound to sexual fidelity and continued a compulsively active sexual life with prostitutes that became notorious amongst his acquaintances.[37] Humboldt understood something of the psychological reasons for his behavior, though he generalized his own needs in the standard moral terms of the Enlightenment. He justified his promiscuity on the grounds that marital love, which should be based on mutual respect and appreciation for the individuality of each of the partners, was incompatible with the male sexual drive; this drive was, as he told his fiancée, "always too selfish to be lovingly considerate of the delicate feelings of a wife," and it was inherently connected with a will to dominate. His biographer even suggests that his idealization of mutual freedom as the basis of true marital happiness was a kind of reaction formation, an attempt to keep this element of domination out of their relationship.[38] In any case it is clear that personal issues, not least among them strong sexual needs, were a major driving force behind Humboldt's ideas about the importance of freedom in private life and therefore in his initial sympathies with revolutionary events in France. In this he and Schleiermacher seem to have been much alike.

What then accounts for the differences in their concepts of individuality, for the much greater scope of Schleiermacher's claim for individual development coupled with its less political orientation? First of all, Humboldt seems to have been initially more conflicted about the legitimacy of male sexual impulses because they seemed to him dangerous in their very essence to the welfare of women. Although he did not believe that the suppression of these impulses was possible or even desirable in life, his way of reconciling sensuality [*Sinnlichkeit*] and morality philosophically in *The Limits of State Action* seems to involve a repressive sublimation of sexuality in the Kantian ideal of disinterested beauty. The theoretical result, which apparently carried over into his actions in private life, was that sexual behavior was split off from the ideal integration of the cultivated "whole man" and left unincorporated. No less concerned to moralize sexuality, Schleiermacher felt no need to sublimate it; in the right kind of relationship, sexuality itself could be the epitome of moral behavior, an idea he pursued with consistency from his early notes on politics to his defense of Schlegel's *Lucinde*.[39] From the beginning, Humboldt was more concerned with harmonious integration than with unrestricted self-expression; "feeling" could be integrated in a way that sexuality could not be.

Secondly, and perhaps partly as a consequence of this first point, Schleiermacher's politics in his radical phase were more radical than Humboldt's were in his. Humboldt certainly greeted the Revolution with enthusiasm, and even traveled to Paris in August of 1789, though with what precise purpose is not clear. But despite his admiration for the "courageous citizens" whose taking of the Bastille he thought a noble act of freedom, he never showed enthusiasm for the idea of radical political change;[40] he was certainly never a republican even in theory, as Schleiermacher was. Glad as he was for the overthrow of despotism, Humboldt's revolutionary sympathies did not have the militant antiauthoritarian and egalitarian thrust that aimed even theoretically at the overthrow of kings and social hierarchies. When on his return from France, Humboldt heard a law professor praise the French nobility's renunciation of its feudal rights on the night of August 4, Humboldt replied: "It has happened too fast, it will not produce beneficial results, and has aroused chimerical ideas of equality."[41]

Finally, beginning with a less assertive rebelliousness than Schleiermacher's revolutionism, Humboldt did not undergo the even more radicalizing transformation of an encounter with Fichte's philosophy, as Schleiermacher did when he met Friedrich Schlegel in Berlin. It was through Fichte's conceptions of the absolute I and infinite striving that Schleiermacher extended his idea of freedom to the notion of the self's infinity and its domination over nature that suddenly appear in the notebook entries quoted above.

This radicalizing transformation, however, was fundamentally ambiguous in its consequences for the goal of revolutionary autonomy. Although it extended Schleiermacher's idea of individuality into a claim for freedom that was new and absolute in its scope, it entailed for him not only a retreat from radical politics but a regression into a form of dependency on an external totality that at the same time became the very condition of absolute freedom. This paradoxical development seems to have been connected with Schleiermacher's relationships with Henriette Herz and the Berlin salons, or, more accurately and fully, with his interpretation or understanding of his feelings and behavior in terms of the Fichtean absolute ego. The reinscription of selfhood within this conceptual framework gave his actions and impulses a philosophical significance that extended the meaning of his claims to personal freedom from the negative ideal of "liberation from" to the positive ideal of expanding the potentially infinite self. At the same time, the breaking of social, religious, and marital boundaries that this ideal entailed showed how dangerous it could be when translated into interpersonal action; it turned others into the instruments of one's own individuality. That made it necessary to retreat from the political implications of the infinite self and to establish the polity as a transcendent whole to which the self subordinated itself and from which it drew the sustenance for its self-expansion. Beyond that, it meant reinscribing the divinity as ultimate source of the self's infinity, a move that might look to Schleiermacher's less religious friends as a retreat to old-fashioned belief but was in fact understood by religious conservatives as a suspiciously heterodox version of religion. They were right; at this point, divinity for Schleiermacher could be "nothing but a single religious form of intuition" (*Religion*, 284–85) rather than a hypostatized "God," an intuition of "being one with the infinite in the midst of finitude and being eternal in a temporal moment" (*Religion*, 290). It is this contradiction that needs to be grasped if the Romantic idea of individuality is to be understood.

IV) Toward European Romanticism

The history of Schleiermacher's concept of individuality situates it at the conjunction of personal, political, and philosophical events in his life. None of the English or French writers we call Romantics used the word individuality; only the German Romantics did. But the essential features of the concept without the word can be found in English and French Romanticism. In crucial respects, and with due allowance for the differences in national cultures and histories that are important for the distinctiveness of national Romanticisms, the contradiction of Schleiermacher's concept of individuality is paradigmatic for European Romantics of the first generation. All of them put the unique individual—and more specifically, their own histories—at the center of experience, all of them believed that individuality demanded the expansion of the self towards infinity, and all of them insisted that this was not only compatible with, but dependent on, a fusion with totality conceived, or at least named, as a finite entity—nature, woman, form, Absolute, God, state. Schleiermacher's personal development was also in crucial respects paradigmatic for other European Romantics as well. All of them were primed by personal development and by Enlightenment thought and art to greet the French Revolution as the dawn of a new kind of personal as well as political freedom. Out of the needs of their own development they extrapolated the ideological foundations of revolutionary radicalism to a new and extreme claim for human autonomy beyond anything available in contemporary revolutionary political and social theory. And out of the same conjunction of personal issues and radical thought, they ultimately recoiled at the implications of their radical idea of individualism. Although they had been repulsed by the Terror, most Romantics had weathered it intact. But first in their private lives and only then in their political ideas, they came to see their new ideal in action as self-aggrandizing, isolating, aggressive, and destructive, in principle incompatible with the liberty of others. Not wanting—indeed, not able—to surrender the truths they thought they had learned about human freedom, they tried to find ways to hold on to their infinite claims for the self while making them less dangerous by reformulating individuality as a dependent relationship with an all-inclusive totality other and greater than the self.

In its beginnings, European Romanticism was a generational affair. All of the early Romantic writers—Wordsworth, Coleridge, and Southey in England; Chateaubriand and Constant in France; Schleiermacher, the Schlegel brothers, Novalis, Tieck, Wackenroder, and Hölderlin in Germany—were born within a period three years on either side of 1770, the majority of them between 1770 and 1772. (To this group could be added the painters Turner, Constable, and Friedrich, also usually thought of as Romantics, and Beethoven and Hegel, strongly marked by the Romantic climate, if in important respects resistive and even hostile to it.) They were in their late adolescence when the French Revolution broke out, in the midst of struggles for familial, sexual, vocational, and intellectual independence, and though many were initially indifferent or even mildly hostile to the Revolution, they sooner or later became without exception ardent supporters. Long ago, Richard Samuel, biographer and editor of Novalis, suggested that the fundamental reason that the younger generation of German artists and intellectuals adhered to the Revolution was psychological, that it lay in the analogy between their personal experience and the events of world history.[42] More recently, John Toews has commented that although there is nothing historically unique or startling about generational rebellion, the rebellion of the generation of 1770 had a peculiar and decisive significance in European thought because its members identified their own crises with the historical crisis of European culture and connected the possibility of a satisfactory personal solution to the hopes for a collective transformation aroused by the French Revolution.[43] The Romantics themselves were quite self-consciously aware of their identity as youth and saw youth as a factor in the Revolution itself. The most famous expression of this consciousness, at least in the English-speaking world, is Wordsworth's outburst in *The Prelude*, "Bliss was it in that dawn to be alive / But to be young was very heaven," but it was not unique, and other such utterances were more analytical. "The contemporary conflict over forms of government," Novalis claimed with typical hyperbole and metaphorical compression, "is a conflict over whether ripe age or blooming youth is superior."[44] Even more startling is his interpretation of the Revolution as a stage of adolescent development: "Most observers of the French Revolution . . . have declared it to be a life-threatening and contagious illness. They have, however, not gone beyond the symptoms and have confused them. . . . The cleverest opponents insisted on castration. They noted rightly that this alleged illness was nothing but the onset of a puberty crisis."[45] Nor was Novalis alone in this

diagnosis; Chateaubriand for another attributed the "passion for the indeterminate" that he argued had helped to cause the Revolution to the adolescent character of the age.[46] It is this passion that is incarnated in Chateaubriand's fictional *René*, who is along with Werther the archetypal
modern adolescent.

If there is a problem with all of these interpretations, modern as well
as contemporaneous, it is that they biologize or universalize a crisis that
was in important respects new. As historians of youth have pointed out,
adolescence is a historical concept; it is not adolescence but "youth" that
is a biological-social constant in all cultures as the stage between childhood and adulthood.[47] The modern idea of adolescence involves both a
specific set of social and cultural ideals and the psychological, familial,
and social conflicts that arise in the course of their troubled realization. If
Romantic literature often displays brilliantly sensitive descriptions of
what we now take to be paradigmatic stages of adolescent development—
Chateaubriand's autobiographical account in the *Mémoires d'outre-
tombe* is a classic example[48]—it must be remembered that the issues of
modern adolescence, which was emerging at this time as a new phase of
personal development at least among a vanguard of European youth,
were also the issues of individuation emerging as a new philosphical/
psychological ideal and cultural ethos. The factors that fed into this
change—political, economic, social, and intellectual—amount to a history of the seventeenth and eighteenth centuries and can hardly be can-
vassed here. They range from the self-interested individualism promoted
by commercial revolution in England and France and hotly debated in
eighteenth-century thought to the ideal of a universal humanity fostered
by "new men" of bourgeois origins, able to rise within the meritocratic
bureaucracies of the absolutist German states and evade the stratified
inequalities of corporate and caste society; from legal concepts of rights,
developed in conflicts with monarchical absolutism and imperial pretensions out of both old corporatist and new jurisprudential traditions, to
religiously-derived ideas about inner conviction as the sole legitimate
foundation of belief and to arguments for the merits of cultural individuality against the tyranny of a universalizing classicism. Research in French
and especially German Romanticism has established the continuity of Romanticism with the Enlightenment against older ideas of a sharp break,
and correspondingly, the idea of a "pre-Romanticism" has fallen into discredit.[49]

But if the revolt of the generation of 1770 was thus historically unique,
what it produced was also historically unique. It is too simple a model to
argue that personal crisis provided the fuel for political revolution, or that
politics, by furnishing a public model and set of public symbols for personal development, transposed the issues of personal freedom into the

world of political action and the problems of public authority. The specific issues of the future Romantics' private lives, which had been refracted and interpreted through Enlightenment thought and culture, in turn transformed the ideals of the Revolution into something different from, and in crucial ways more far-reaching than, what those revolutionary ideals originally encompassed. It is not possible to gain an adequate understanding of the concerns and cruxes of Romanticism without an appreciation of the convergence of the private with the public, the erotic with the political, the psychological with the philosophical and aesthetic. The case of Schleiermacher should already suggest the causal importance of these convergences; I want to demonstrate their role and impact in more detail by considering the work of three of the most important representatives of Romanticism in its national variants—Friedrich Schlegel in Germany, William Wordsworth in England, and Francois-René de Chateaubriand in France.

TWO

FRIEDRICH SCHLEGEL

What I have doubtless sought instinctively and been pleased
to find in books . . . has not been the reflection of . . . infinite
incompleteness . . . but rather the exact opposite:
definitive overviews, wholes which, thanks to their bold
structure, arbitrary yet convincing, give the illusion of being a
total picture of reality, of summing up all of life.
—*Mario Vargas Llosa*, The Perpetual Orgy

I) Irony as Possession and Demystification of Infinity

IN THE SUMMER of 1797, en route from Jena to settle in Berlin, Friedrich Schlegel made an entry in the notebooks he kept for literary and philosophical jottings that, though portentous, seems cryptic even by the standards of their typically fragmentary style: "Tendency of modern poetry to satanism."[1] Schlegel had been critical of modern literature for some years, was indeed staking his cultural role and reputation on antimodernism, but the severity of this indictment was new; he had never before taxed modern literature with being demonic. A few entries later he continued in the more usual terms he had been using to condemn modernity as inferior to antiquity, reasserting the importance of the classical ideal: "Confusion, awkwardness, inconsistency ⟨absence of character, even meanness⟩ [are the] failings of progressive man. ⟨Refined = classical.⟩ Without the classical, progressive men become regressive. ⟨Our whole age is also a progressive man. . . . ⟩ Herein lies the deduction of philology, the necessity of the study of antiquity" (KA, 18:24, 66; the angular parentheses indicate material in the margins of Schlegel's text included by the editor of the *Kritische Ausgabe*). These words, however, do not explain the new charge; however undesirable they might be, confusion, awkwardness, even meanness of character do not add up to satanism. Not until a few months later did the notebooks seem to throw more light on what Schlegel might have meant by the term. But astonishingly, this new entry completely reversed the clearly implied value judgement of the earlier one, with an exclamatory emphasis rare in the large corpus of Schlegel's unpublished fragments: "One can make the small-scale beauty of the Greeks [appear] laughable and contemptible next to the unformed colossalness of the moderns!"[2] It was, then, the "colossal" pretentions of the moderns that had seemed satanic. Now, just a short time later, these same claims made the long-praised ideal beauty of the Greeks seem merely petty.

Schlegel gave no explanation for this sudden change in his estimation of modern literature anywhere in his writings. Literary critics and historians of Romanticism have generally emphasized its epochal significance for criticism without explaining how and why it occurred; even the dating of the change has remained imprecise. This study will attempt such an explanation, but its adequacy will necessarily depend on an accurate description of what is to be explained, and there are problems with the current understanding of the new position Schlegel had reached somewhere between the two notebook entries of summer and autumn of 1797.

Although abrupt, the shift was not without preparation. Under the influence of Fichte's philosophy, which he had been studying intensively during the year before his move to Berlin, Schlegel had gradually been moving towards two contradictory conclusions. One was that his beloved classics, which he had been relying upon to provide the model for a regenerated, free, and harmonious humanity in modern times, in fact offered only a limited view of humanity and of the world because they did not deal with human aspirations to totality. The other was that limitation both in art and in life was inevitable, an ontological necessity; indeed art depended upon limitation for its very production (KA, 18:24, 63). It was precisely the grandiose claims of modern literature to encompass all of reality that made it seem colossal and satanic. But in reversing his attitude to it, Schlegel had come to accept the legitimacy of its goals. His problem now was how to reconcile them with his belief in the inescapability of limitation.

That was the central point of the concept of irony that appeared in his work in late 1797. Irony was to mediate the two opposite demands Schlegel now made on an exemplary work of art: that it be fully individuated on the one hand—unique, original, concrete, and formally delimited—but that on the other, it should embody totality, the Absolute. How that mediation happens, how irony "works"—a much discussed subject in the literature on Romanticism—depends on what Schlegel meant by the Absolute, a more vexed topic, and one generally less explicitly considered. The abstraction that bedevils Schlegel's theorizing is mirrored in the frequently all-too-vague theoretical glossing of this one of his key concepts. The shorthand of Idealist philosophy, which he condensed even further in his fragments as "absolute," "infinity," "fullness," "universe," "totality," is usually either simply repeated in critical work or translated into the existential language of "Being" and more recently the deconstructionist language of "presence." At the risk of oversimplification, it is necessary to cut through these abstractions to recover in a preliminary way the breathtakingly radical nature and the enormous excitement of the Romantic project as Schlegel conceived and felt it in the summer and fall of 1797 and over the next few years. There would be important shifts of emphasis and even real change in the period between 1797 and 1800; in particular, the language of religion, though present from the very beginning, would become more prominent and less metaphorical, increasingly traditional over those years. Nevertheless, for an initial statement of Schlegel's Romantic contradiction, the work of those four years can be treated as evolving phases of one central idea.

For Schlegel, the Absolute was nothing less than the sum total of all the ways humans and things could *be* in the cosmos, and for the first time in history it seemed that this totality was available to the human mind—and even more, to human action. The Idealist breakthroughs of Kant and Fichte seemed to contemporaries to show definitively that the human species was above all the meaning-producing creature, that all the ways that things in the world appeared and interconnected were only opened up to humanity by its own subjectivity, through the categories of human cognition and the enactment of human possibilities. It was purposive consciousness reaching out into the world, an active principle, that disclosed the world as it apparently "was." Even its "objective" qualities were in a crucial sense the product of human consciousness: not created ex nihilo by the subjective mind—though human creativity could see and fashion connections that were not yet realized and existed only potentially in the given—but there for us only through the human sensorium and human acts of delimitation of boundaries, of categorization and conceptualization.

In Idealism, particularly in its Fichtean extension, humanity was revealed as God-like in its ability to create even in apparently passive perceptual receiving and in the fact that there was no a priori limit to the potential of its creativity. This made it thinkable that humanity was infinite, in the sense that, because humans were the source of meaning, they could in principle know all there was to know, connect things through perception, thought, practice, and imagination in all the ways there were to connect and consciously enact all the ways there were to be. Kant had excluded any such possibility, and even Fichte, as we will see, had stopped short of it, but Schlegel saw the notion of an individualized "lived totality" as the idea to which Idealist philosophy inevitably led. If this language seems excessively naive, Schlegel himself occasionally allowed the same naive directness of expression to peek through his abstractions. "Only the unconditioned is useful," he asserted. "*Whoever does not want everything*, to that extent precisely approaches nothing [*geht auf Nichts zu*]" (KA, 18:289, 1122; italics added). "The antithesis of the mystic [Schlegel's term for Fichtean thinkers] is everything or nothing" (KA,

18:115, 1033). In many of the passages in which he spoke of "allness," it is true, Schlegel denied the possibility that the *individual* could be everything. "If one wants to be everything at once, one becomes precisely . . . nothing" (KA, 18:115, 1140). "The necessity of polemic is indeed to be deduced particularly from the fact that one cannot be everything. If one person is one thing, and another something else, conflict arises just from the fact that they are different, so that everything which should exist for itself will be sustained in its distinctive [*classisch*] difference and with the rigor necessary to maintain that difference, and each will be protected in its rights against the other" (KA, 18:81–82, 624). But even where he denied its possibility, Schlegel established as the self's most basic point of orientation the notion of being everything, or its desire to be everything. Schlegel's Absolute is the idea of the simultaneous being, in and for human consciousness, of all imaginable possibilities and hence the raising of the self from time to eternity, and it is nothing else. "There is nothing infinite except an I," claims one of his bluntest notebook fragments (KA, 18:301, 1282). "*God* is nothing but the individual to the highest power" (KA, 18:243, 605). But even for publication he could be almost as direct. "Every good human being is always progressively becoming God," he wrote in the *Athenaeum Fragments*. "To become God, to be human, to cultivate oneself are all expressions that mean the same thing."[3] Or to write the authentic work of literature; for it was to art even more than to philosophy that Schlegel looked for the realization of the divine. As he wrote in the *Dialogue on Poetry*, "The mind cannot bear [that one's poetry and one's view of poetry is limited]; no doubt because, without knowing it, it nevertheless does know that no man is merely man, but that at the same time he can and should be genuinely and truly all mankind."[4] Of course, where the desire is to be everything, the only apparent alternative is to be nothing, for not to have attained everything feels like having attained nothing. "[S]urely," Schlegel asserted, "the philosopher has only the choice of knowing either everything or nothing" (*Athenaeum*, 182, 164). "Nothing and everything are . . . Romantic categories" (*Notebooks*, 153, 1503). But Schlegel did not mean to present "nothing" and "everything" as either/or alternatives; the point of Schlegel's concept of irony was precisely to deny the mutual exclusiveness of those two options. In the work of art, Romantic irony transforms the disjunction "all or nothing" into a something that is simultaneously both all *and* nothing.

This is not generally the way Schlegel's irony has been understood by his critics. Most often, perhaps, it is the demystifying aspect of irony that is emphasized. Irony sees through the limitations of individuality; it attacks the pretensions of any work's claim to finality or totality by exposing its one-sidedness, blindness, imperfections, and contradictions. "Irony for

Schlegel," writes Ernst Behler, "[is] that capacity which repeatedly tears the spirit in its 'presentiment of the whole' away from the fixations of limited selfhood."[5] From this viewpoint, irony is preeminently a negative force. It is unquestionably liberating, as Behler implies, but its liberation operates through destruction. Even where critics emphasize the positive or enabling dimension of irony, which, in undermining the inflated claims of one limited perspective, reopens the vista of wholeness and so inspires new creation, the ironic moment itself emerges only as the concrete negation of an illusory embodiment of the Absolute, and the at best empty vision of mere hope for its true realization.[6]

The most consistent and uncompromising formulation of the sheer demystifying negativity of irony is that of Paul de Man, who insists that this is all irony can logically be. Criticizing Peter Szondi's rather modest version of a positive possibility in Schlegel's irony, which sees the ironist as measuring the inadequacy of all purported present realizations of the Absolute by the fiction of some idealized past or utopian future, de Man writes: "[This] is right from the point of view of the mystified self but wrong from the point of view of the ironist. . . . Schlegel is altogether clear on this. The dialectic of the self-destruction and self-invention which for him . . . characterizes the ironic mind is an endless process that leads to no synthesis."[7]

Schlegel sometimes did take the position that de Man attributes to him, but he also said quite the opposite. The contradiction makes him less consistent an ironist than de Man, but paradoxically more ironic. For Schlegel's position was both that there can be no synthesis *and that there is*. "True irony," he insisted, "requires that there be not simply striving after infinity but also possession of infinity" (*Notebooks*, 64, 500). "The novel in general [is] the union of two absolutes, absolute individuality and absolute universality" (*Notebooks*, 59, 434). "An idea is a concept perfected to the point of irony, an absolute synthesis of absolute antitheses" (*Athenaeum*, 176, 121). And, in one of his wittiest fragments, which characterizes his own contradictory spirit very well, "It is equally fatal for the mind to have a system and to have none. It will simply have to decide to combine the two" (*Athenaeum*, 167, 53). In the increasingly religious language of his notes after 1798, where the Absolute is often spoken of as God, though not yet in the traditional dogmatic religious sense, Schlegel spoke of all proper literature—indeed sometimes more broadly of any "authentic" finite entity—as an allegory of the divine (KA, 18:155, 380). Marcus Bullock, in a deconstructionist approach to language, says that for Schlegel, writing could represent the Absolute in an allegorical way because "the absolute is nothingness, rather than presence . . . [and] language is always equidistant from the absent absolute."[8] But Schlegel emphatically said otherwise, both about divinity and about the sufficiency of allegory to embody it. "We are now at the point where we must recognize God and eternal life," he insisted, "as positive and material realities" (KA, 18:164, 88). "To be enthusiastic [enthusiasm is the religious term Schlegel used to refer to genuine belief in an achieved totality] is better than to be allegorical. *Prophetic* is simultaneously enthusiastic and allegorical. So, the highest" (*Notebooks*, 138, 1314). Schlegel even anticipated and explicitly refuted those who would define irony as a purely negative moment of demystification in one of his most passionately assertive, if typically sarcastic, *Athenaeum* fragments: "There are people whose whole life consists in always saying no. It would be no small accomplishment always to be able to say no properly, but whoever can do no more, surely cannot do so properly. The taste of these nay-sayers is like an efficient pair of scissors for pruning the extremities of genius; their enlightenment is like a great candle-snuffer for the flame of enthusiasm; and their reason a mild laxative against immoderate pleasure and love" (*Athenaeum*, 172, 88).

Schlegel is to be taken with strict literalness on this point of contradiction. It is not enough, for example, to say that his notion of a synthesis of belief and demystification is one of temporal sequence, in which movements of enthusiasm that envision a totality are followed by ironic coolness and distance that relativize it. He did speak, in the *Dialogue on Poetry*, of the "perennial alternation of enthusiasm and irony." But the terms enthusiasm and irony can be found in Schlegel's notes linked in temporal simultaneity, as for example when he define harmony as "enthusiasm + irony" (KA, 18:185, 176). And he even defined irony on occasion not merely as an element in a synthesis of opposites but as itself a synthesis of partialness and totality. "In irony are united self-limitation and the participation in all life" (KA, 18:218, 291). Difficult as it may be to reconcile logically, among the many contradictory positions that Schlegel's fragments staked out between 1787 and 1800, the central one insists on the acceptance of outright contradiction on the most important issue in his work, the simultaneous impossibility and achievement of absolute totality, whether in the Romantic work of art or in the ideal philosophy. "To manysidedness there belongs not only an *all-embracing system*, but a sense for the *chaos outside it*" (KA, 18:259, 782; italics added). "Man is a chaos of the finite and infinite and *at the same time* a system. That is the nature of man, his ideal, to be a system of both" (KA, 18:287, 1091; italics added). "The transcendental separates the infinite and finite, the absolute is both simultaneously" (KA, 18:115, 1033). Such pronouncements defeat all efforts to defend Schlegel's position as "deliberately paradoxical" rather than "self-contradictory."[9] It is in acknowledgment of the contradiction he espoused that Schlegel used the word "mystical" to characterize any literature or philosophy that aspires to it. The term refers not to a supernatural or transcendent realm but to the defiance of logic inherent in the reconciliation of opposites in his "Romantic" unity: "Romantic unity is not poetic but **mystical**; the novel is a mystical work of art" (*Notebooks*, 71, 580).[10]

The sense of contradiction in Schlegel deepens when one examines the way in which he understood the combining of individuality and universality in the Romantic work of art. The individuality of the work is equivalent to its self-limitation, for it is through the author's choices and constructions that the formless chaos of unlimited raw material is delimited and defined and the work takes on unique characteristics. In the broadest aesthetic sense, "self-limitation" is thus equivalent to the principle of aesthetic form. Form-giving, Schlegel argued, is necessary "for the artist as well as the man" because "wherever one does not restrict oneself, one is restricted by the world, and that makes one a slave." By the same token, however, form-giving is the ultimate act of human freedom, not only in the negative sense that it triumphs over necessity by taking control of the conditions of limitation, but because "one can only restrict oneself at those points and places where one possesses infinite power, self-creation, and self-destruction." The act of limitation is only the negative side of the free power of creation. Yet, Schlegel went on to say, form-giving, though free, is not arbitrary. "What appears to be unlimited free will, and consequently seems and should seem to be irrational or supra-rational nonetheless must still at bottom be simply necessary and rational; otherwise the whim becomes willful, becomes intolerant, and self-restriction turns into self-destruction" (*Lyceum*, 147, 37). Form has its own internal principles that must be followed if a genuine totality is to be created out of the material at hand.

The contradiction between form as freedom and form as necessity entails another contradiction that reinforces and amplifies it: form as the very essence of self-limitation is simultaneously the very embodiment of infinity. This follows from Schlegel's idea that for the artwork, form is totality, the totalization of particulars, and thus the whole of which the individual elements of the literary work are parts. "Spirit is the determinate unity and wholeness of an indeterminate plurality of unconditioned qualities. . . . Form is a totality of absolute limits" (*Notebooks*, 59, 441). As his language became more religious, Schlegel wrote explicitly, "All matter is human, as all form is divine" (KA, 18:342, 234). The divinity of form is its infinity, which it has, or is, in virtue of its phenomenological character as totality, "everythingness." Even if the totality in any particular case is relative to the finite elements—e.g., of character, plot, figural modes—that it organizes and contains, the idea of "form" always entails the absolute sense of "allness." Moreover, as totality, form is the principle to which the writer subordinates him- or herself, the external norm by which the writer is compelled in the very work he or she is ostensibly freely creating. The author's freedom becomes a prisoner of itself, of its own aesthetic choices, servant to a structure beyond choice even though that structure emerges from its choices. The idea of wholeness conditions the parts, makes internal demands for those elements that would complete the structure, just as a geometric formula, one of Schlegel's favorite metaphors, predetermines the space it encloses once its variable parameters are chosen. (There is a nice question about which geometric form, the closed ellipse or the open-ended parabola, best symbolizes Schlegel's notion of wholeness.[11] Once again the issue is whether or not he accepted the idea of closure or finality in art and in life. Schlegel explicitly opted for the closed figure of the ellipse [KA, 18:156, 380] though his reason for choosing it rather than the circle needs yet to be explained.) Thus on the one hand, form is the very embodiment of absolute human freedom, and, on the other, it is an external totality that contains and constrains the author, making demands of its own.

How is the mystery of this contradiction to be understood? How was the writer able to produce freely the structure that unifies the work by becoming its governing force, the structure that, though a finite totality, yet refers to the infinite? In response, Schlegel offered a definition and a metaphor.

Taken in isolation, the definition seems to mystify further, rather than to clarify. In one of his unpublished fragments of 1797, Schlegel wrote that the poetic ideal—he used the word "poetry" to mean literature in general—combines absolute mimesis, absolute fantasy, and absolute sentimentality (*Notebooks*, 87, 735), that is, pure objective reality, completely autonomous imagination, and infinite love. The first two of these elements might seem to be derivable from the purely internal requirements of an aesthetic that aspires to the infinite while bowing to the inevitability of limitation. Imitating or copying reality roots literature in the concrete, the finite, and the necessary; reshaping reality through the creative imagination frees the work of art from all constraints, opening it up to infinity through the author's unconditional freedom. Mimesis thus supplies the raw matter of literature, imagination its form. But what role does this division of labor leave for love?

Love, moreover, is not just one element amongst the three in Schlegel's formula for literature; it is the crucial one. "The best explanation of the Romantic," runs his most lapidary formulation, "is perhaps chaos and Eros" (*Notebooks*, 176, 1760). Love provides both the basic material or theme of the novel (the Romantic work "presents a sentimental theme [*Stoff*] in a fantastic form" [*Dialogue*, 98]) and the organizing energy for the novel, the principle that transforms the chaos of infinite possibilities into aesthetic order, or form: "the highest beauty, indeed the highest order is . . . the kind of order that waits only for the touch of love to unfold [chaos] as a harmonious world" (*Dialogue*, 82). The Romantic literary work is not only "about" love, it is love that makes the work possible; love is its shaping spirit, the force that potentiates imagination.

What can this possibly mean? It is hardly self-evident that love is either the essential subject matter or shaping force of literature unless one thinks in terms of the early Freudian idea of imaginative literature as libidinal wish-fulfillment. But though Freud's filiation from Romanticism has long been asserted, the most instructive similarity between Schlegel and Freud is in the idea of a necessary connection between the principle of art and the problem of personality.

Schlegel, as we have already noted, made no distinction between the goal of art and the task of personality: both ideally strive to reconcile individuality and totality. In *Lyceum* fragment 37, the first detailed published notice of his new theory of literature, Schlegel wrote interchangeably of the necessary self-restriction of writer and of work. And just as he called for an art that would tear down the artificial separations between the classical poetic genres that "have now become ridiculous in their rigid purity" (*Lyceum*, 150, 60), he called for an idea of self-cultivation, or *Bildung*, according to which "A really free and cultivated person ought to be able to attune himself at will to being philosophical or philological, critical or poetical, historical or rhetorical, ancient or modern: quite arbitrarily, just as one tunes an instrument, at any time and to any degree" (*Lyceum*, 149, 55). Art is the instrument of personality (*Notebooks*, 71, 572); it is *through* art that personality cultivates itself. The ideal of the infinite work of art serves the ideal of the infinite personality: "The spiritual person is simultaneously farmer, manufacturer, salesman, soldier, civilian, doctor—but only in a symbolic sense. This universality is indisputably the ground of his privileges" (KA, 18:142–43, 243). Schlegel's aesthetics, then, are emphatically not aestheticist;[12] they are subordinated to *Bildung*, the goal of shaping the self.

There is, however, a deep ambiguity in the idea that art is the expression of personality. On the one hand, it appears, art is the necessary means of self-cultivation, which implies that human universality is achievable for Schlegel only through art. On the other hand, it is only the universal or "progressive" person who is able to produce universal art in the first place. This apparently vicious circularity is broken in the realization that for Schlegel it is love that produces the kind of personality that can, in turn, produce a literature of the infinite.

This is the burden of the novel that Schlegel wrote in 1799 at the peak of the first phase of his Romanticism. As a work that mixes epistle, poetry, fable, dialogue, and narrative, *Lucinde* is the "free form" (*Lyceum*, 145,

26) that fulfills the formal criteria for the desired new literature. As the story of a love relationship through which a young man is able to integrate the fragments of his personality and be released into creativity, it documents the event that makes Romantic writing possible in the first place. The novel is self-referential in the sense that it relates the conditions of its own production, and as such, it is part of the theory of Romanticism itself, not just an instance of it.

What is immediately striking about the love relationship as depicted in the novel is that it reproduces the contradictions in the theory of Romantic aesthetics in terms that both clarify the mystery and deepen it. It is true that the force of love for the personality is on occasion put in general, and reciprocal, terms: "Only in the answer of its 'you' can every 'I' wholly feel its boundless unity," says its male protagonist (*Lucinde*, 106). But Lucinde's love makes her lover Julius feel integrated and whole because it is her love that is infinite and he is its sole object. "You feel completely and infinitely," Julius tells her; "you know of no separations; your being is one and indivisible. . . . That is why . . . you love me so completely and don't relinquish any part of me to the state" (*Lucinde*, 101). Lucinde's infinity and her infinite positive regard for Julius are the agencies that act on him as passive recipient.

At the same time, however, the novel expresses the consciousness that Lucinde's apparently infinite being is actually Julius's own creation. The demystifying words are put in the mouth of Lucinde herself. "I am not, my Julius," she tells her fond lover, "the sanctified person you describe. . . . You are that person . . . [Y]ou see reflected in me—in me who am forever yours—the marvelous flower of your imagination" (*Lucinde*, 126). The very attribute of Lucinde in virtue of which Julius can feel whole and freely creative she ascribes to him. Julius's protest that his image of Lucinde is not simply a product of his imagination, that his yearning for her is boundless and always unsatisfied is hardly an adequate answer, because it argues the limitlessness of his desire, not of its object. But he does not register this apparently elementary logical flaw in his response. Lucinde ironizes herself, but Julius misses the point and defends his experience of her as absolute.

The contradictions in the images of Lucinde and Julius mirror and explain those that inhere for Schlegel in the relationship between author and literary work, in particular between imagination and form. Like Lucinde in relation to Julius, literary form is infinite and finite, creative and yet created, that which the author produces by his imagination yet which at the same time embraces the author totally, providing the structure that organizes his very creativity. Since it is Lucinde's love that also releases Julius's creativity in the first place, the secret of form turns out to be the secret of love, aesthetic empowerment by a contradictory relationship to a woman that involves the man's complete dependence and subordination, without any sacrifice of independence and power. But what in turn explains the contradiction of this kind of love? After all, woman only gives back to man his original divinity, which leaves the question of why he alienated it to her in the first place and why he sees and yet does not see the contradiction in his attitude toward her.

In response to the mystery of aesthetic form, I said earlier that Schlegel offered an explanation and a metaphor. The explanation by love, as we have seen, itself engenders a mystery that requires further explanation. The metaphor will turn out to be not "mere" metaphor but part of the required explanation. It too, however, soon reveals its own internal contradictions.

The metaphor that Schlegel offered to illuminate further the ideal of the new literature is politics. Romantic literature proposes to achieve totality by breaking down the rigid barriers between literary genres, by eliminating hierarchy among them, and by including all varieties of literary expression, even those regarded by classicism as eccentric and monstrous, just as the modern republic grants equal rights and equal participation to everyone in the state regardless of station. "Poetry is republican speech," runs a *Lyceum* fragment, "a speech which is its own law and end unto itself, and in which all the parts are free citizens and have the right to vote" (*Lyceum*, 150, 65).

But the political is more than just a metaphor for the literary; from other fragments, published and unpublished, it is evident that, just as literature is instrumental for *Bildung*, the formation of personality, it is also intended to realize an essentially political ideal. "[T]he essence of romantic poetry[,] mixture [*Mischung*] is a political principle," Schlegel stated flatly in the notebooks (*Notebooks*, 91, 776). The mixing of genres within one work, the "democratization" of language against the exclusionary rules of classical decorum and taste, were symbolic embodiments of contemporary political ideals made into an agenda for the first time by recent historical events. "Novels," he wrote in the *Lyceum Fragments*, "have a habit of concluding in the same way that the Lord's Prayer begins, with the kingdom of heaven on earth" (144, 18). The eschatological reference is neither to the purely religious end of the Second Coming nor to the purely personal end of living happily ever after. "The revolutionary desire to realize the Kingdom of God is the elastic point [the coordinate that determines trajectory] of progressive civilization and the beginning of modern history," he said in the *Athenaeum Fragments* (192, 22). In a fundamental sense, Schlegel's aesthetic goals and concepts derive from the political and historical spheres, a point about which he could be quite explicit: "The philosophy of man synthesizes politics and history in aesthetics" (KA, 18:272, 929). This being the case, the real meaning of art is ultimately politics: "The highest artwork of man is the state . . . and so politics is the climax of the theory of art, which is as general as history" (KA, 18:369, 580). From a practical point of view, literature is thus a propaedeutic, an education for the harmonious totality that is to be brought about in the social and political world: "Poetry and philosophy [are] only *preparation*" (KA, 18:197, 787).[13]

How do the political ideal and purpose of literature as just stated relate to the character ideal of *Bildung*? At one level, they seem to be mutually reinforcing, indeed mutual prerequisites. Schlegel had acknowledged, even insisted, that the goal of being everything was not achievable by the individual. The social coordinate of this truth about the absolute was the idea Schlegel put forward in the *Athenaeum Fragments* of *Symphiloso-phie*, defined there neatly as "a mutual search for omniscience" (215, 344). Given the limitations of individuality, totality had to be a collective enterprise in which each participant had an equal role. *Symphilosophie* was not simply a cognitive ideal but a social form because it demanded interactions based on tolerance and mutual respect among individuals all bent on developing themselves to the fullest. "A systematic *Symphiloso-phie*," Schlegel claimed ambitiously in his notebooks, "would be a com-plete philosophy for mankind. The resolution of all basic disputes, and friendship . . . agreement amongst all men; a philosophical eternal peace" (KA, 18:225, 368). The last phrase is a reference to Kant's essay *On Eternal Peace* of 1795, which laid out as the moral and political prerequi-sites of a peaceful international order among states the republican consti-tutions that would guarantee freedom and reason in each. Quite appro-priately, Schlegel could claim that "True *Symphilosophie* has perhaps no other object than contemporary history and the realm of politics" (KA, 18:328, 40). From this point of view a Romantic work is a representation of the ideal of *Symphilosophie*, which is itself a microcosm of the ideal political order.

But the fragments that concern the political ideal behind the new liter-ature point in quite another direction as well. "[The] sense for the uni-verse is historical spirit," Schlegel wrote; "Is it perhaps not impossible to have it, to get the world in one's power, as a philosopher or a poet does his little work?" (KA, 18:129, 91). "To get the world in one's power"—in other words, to have total mastery and control, as the author does over the little universe of his or her work. This notion implies quite a different political model for literature than "republican speech." One notebook fragment raises the question explicitly: "Is there a constitutive element among the elements of the Romantic mixture, or is a republican constitu-tion valid here?" (*Notebooks* 91, 776). Is there, that is to say, one literary element that dominates the others, that determines the structure of the whole and subordinates all other elements to it? The implied contrast is between a hierarchical and authoritarian structuring and a more "egalitarian" principle that would presumably be more formless, more anarchic, less disciplined, less "centered." The contrast does not remain merely implied. In outright contradiction to the apparently republican bearing of Romantic art, Schlegel wrote in one of his notebooks, "As certain as it is that there must always be people of sense and love and spirit, people raised to a higher power, so certain is it that art strives for a monarchy. But the monarch should not desire to direct, but to be the genius of the times, a representative for this form of art and humanity" (KA, 18:255, 740). On the hierarchical side of his political contradiction, Schlegel was equally clear that literature represented displaced politics. "Every state should be a hierarchy," he insisted correspondingly (KA, 18:142, 23). The same position, with the inconsistency only somewhat blurred even appears in the published fragments. "A perfect republic would have to be not just democratic, but aristocratic and monarchic at the same time; to legislate justly and freely, the educated would have to outweigh and guide the uneducated, and everything would have to be organized into an absolute whole" (*Athenaeum*, 190, 219).

The political bearing of Romantic art thus reveals itself in outright contradiction between republicanism and monarchy, egalitarianism and hierarchy. But the contradiction in Schlegel's ideas about the political foundation of Romantic literature is even more glaring. In spite of the fragments and aphorisms that make literature the instrument, or at the least the microcosm, of a new moral-political order, politics is distinguished in the published work of the period 1797–1800 by its almost complete absence. There is of course the frequently quoted *Athenaeum* fragment that celebrates the French Revolution, along with Fichte's philosophy and Goethe's *Wilhelm Meister*, as one of the three greatest tendencies of the age (190, 216); but there is little else, and that fragment typically fails to explain its sweeping assertion. Both the ending of *Lucinde* and the whole of the *Dialogue on Poetry* were meant to be representations of *Symphilosophie* in action, but the conversations in both do nothing to substantiate the statement that true *Symphilosophie* has no other object than contemporary history and politics; neither topic is discussed in either of the works. Finally, Schlegel's contradictoriness about the political bearing of Romantic aesthetics is made verbally explicit in the last collection of fragments in this period, the *Ideen* of 1800. "Don't waste your faith and love on the political world, but in the divine world of knowledge and art offer up your inmost being in a fiery stream of eternal creation" (251, 106). The links between politics and literature were here broken completely; politics and literature were represented not as instrument and end, not even as coordinate spheres governed by similar ideals, but as mutually exclusive alternatives.

So the "resolution" of the contradictions in the solution that love supposedly offered for the contradictions in Schlegel's aesthetic theory turned into its own problem. At first it appeared that the purpose of Romantic literature was both to represent and to educate for an ideal of infinite personality that could only be achieved through a specific form of political and social community, a community itself modeled in literature and in the process of literary theorizing. But the ideal sociopolitical form was thrown into question by the raising of contradictory political alternatives, and then the importance of the political was denied altogether in the elevation of literature to absolute status. Furthermore, the preeminence of art was not the last word either. "Art is only an episode," Schlegel said in another of the unpublished fragments, "love is more; only it will overcome the world" (KA, 18:191, 781). Among all the contradictory statements, this assertion of love's priority was at least in keeping with Schlegel's key notion that eros makes art possible. Distilled to its essence, it appears then that the goal of reconciling individuality and totality, though fundamentally and originally for Schlegel both a personal and a political goal, was representable only in literature, and only in and through love. But this conclusion only formulates the ultimate problem of Schlegel's Romanticism. Why are there contradictions in the political goals of Schlegel's Romanticism, and why are they fatal to the political project of Romantic art but apparently reconcilable, or at least sustainable, in the sphere of love? For the most striking feature of Schlegel's idea of love, as we have seen, is that it is simultaneously ironized and not ironized. It exists on two levels of consciousness without the mutual interference and unease that the contradiction between them ought to generate. What is impossible in politics seems possible in love, which is then suggested as the only possible politics. To understand this we must follow the progression of ideas that brought Schlegel to this conclusion.

II) The Road to Revolution

i) The Problem of Identity

Friedrich Schlegel was seventeen years old when the French Revolution broke out, a precocious, hyperintellectual adolescent tormented by highly self-conscious efforts to find some sense of purpose and inner unity. His amorphous, if intense, feelings of inner conflict and despair found their formulation in the current language of neoclassical aesthetics, and he was apparently quite indifferent to contemporary politics. Four years later he enthusiastically embraced the French Revolution as the indispensable foundation of a solution to the fragmentation and lack of freedom of modern life. Later yet, when in *Lucinde* he told the story of the resolution of his struggle for an independent and settled identity, he carefully detailed its erotic and ethical stages. He completely omitted, however, any mention of its familial and political aspects and the intimate connection among all these elements.

In gaining his personal independence, Schlegel, according to Ernst Behler, created a new independent social type in Germany, the literary intellectual, free of all vocational and social obligations, who lived only by his pen and so preserved his spiritual independence.[14] Although his early career undoubtedly marked a step beyond such forerunners as Lessing in this regard, Schlegel paradoxically achieved an independent identity both in rebellion against, and in conformity with, his family traditions. He came from a distinguished family of the *gebildete Stände*, the educated, largely middle-class elites who played so important a part in the administrative and cultural life of eighteenth-century Germany.[15] The Schlegel family had numbered among its members well-known jurists and pastors, government officials, writers, and critics. An ancestor had even been ennobled in the seventeenth century by the emperor Frederick III for his preaching, though the family made no use of the title until Friedrich and August Wilhelm petitioned for its renewal at the Congress of Vienna.

Friedrich's passionate interest in literary criticism, his ultimately rebellious attitude towards its reigning orthodoxies, and his role in founding a radical literary journal and coterie along with his older brother had startling paternal precedent. While still a student preparing for the ministry in the 1740s, his father, Johann Adolf, had joined with his own older brother, Johann Elias, who was on his way to becoming an eminent dramatist and literary theorist, in a literary group devoted to poetry, friendship, and the critique of Rococo aesthetics. A sentence in the introduction to the statutes of their group both epitomizes its polemical Enlightenment spirit and anticipates Romantic antinominianism: "Friendship needs no rules, for nature has already written them in the heart of every man."[16] These were fighting words, intended to proclaim a new freedom and equality against Baroque standards of authority and courtly conventions. In keeping with the consensual spirit of enlightened individualism, the members of the group submitted their work to collective criticism and editing, with majority vote deciding not only what was to be accepted for publication but even the details of proposed textual alterations.

Although Johann Adolph was a serious and ambitious divinity student who ultimately became an unusually busy high church official, his literary activity was not just an extracurricular avocation. He wrote a good deal of poetry that was noticed favorably, if not uncritically, by the most eminent writers and critics in Germany;[17] its central themes were the need to mediate between extremes of all kinds and achieve a balance between unbelief and religious fanaticism, moral severity and sensuous enjoyment, the classical and the modern.[18] He was equally serious about literary theory because he believed that critics equipped with the correct beliefs could instruct poets in the ways of art,[19] and his translation of and commentary on Charles Batteux's *Les beaux arts réduits à un même principe* of 1746 (in three editions, 1750, 1759, 1779) put him at the center of debate on the significant issues of the day in literary aesthetics. Although he was overtaken by later developments and criticized by *Stürmer und Dränger* like Herder for his conservatism, Johann Schlegel had been drawn to Batteux precisely because the French theorist had modified the strict classical doctrine of art as imitation, insisting that the artist does not simply copy nature but orders and beautifies it through his idealizing imagination. In fact in his lengthy notes, ultimately published as a separate volume of essays in the third edition of his translation, Schlegel attacked Batteux for not going far enough. He criticized the ahistorical, rationalist rigidity of Batteux's idea of literary taste, which needed to take into account the beliefs and preferences of an author's time and place, and he argued the legitimacy even of magic and the supernatural in literature. Attacking Batteux's traditional doctrine of genres as a priori and insufficiently empirical, he claimed the modern novel as a valid, if new, poetic form.[20] That Johann Schlegel's literary activity soon took second place—it continued, though with an increasingly religious orientation, to the end of his life—is evidence not only of the seriousness of his clerical vocation but of the practical problems that ultimately made the pursuit of aesthetic theory a luxury. Translations of important work brought in income; original theorizing was economically far riskier.[21] For whatever combination of pious and prudential reasons, he abandoned criticism and poured his considerable energies into making a highly successful career in the church, amassing by 1767 three important posts in Hanover as pastor and administrator; his literary interests were largely sublimated in the writing of volumes of church songs and sermons, though two volumes of *Miscellaneous Poems* were published in 1787 and in 1789.

The remarkable parallels in the literary interests and activities of father and son did not derive from a close relationship between them. Friedrich was the problem child of the family from birth. He was the youngest of seven children, five boys and two girls; Johann Adolph was fifty-one when Friedrich was born, his mother probably in her early forties. His three oldest brothers were sixteen, fourteen, and eleven years older than he, and the sibling closest to him in age, his brother August Wilhelm, more than four. Whatever emotional distance and loneliness these age differences produced were greatly exacerbated by the fact that Friedrich spent most of his early years out of the parental home. Ill as a young child, he was sent away, either to convalesce or to lighten the household burden,[22] first to his uncle, a childless country priest, and after the latter's death to his oldest brother, by then also a country pastor. When he first left home is not certain, but he was only four at the time of the second move, and he did not return home until he was thirteen.

The return did not end his deprivations. Johann Adolf had clear, well-developed, and firm Enlightenment ideas on education that he had worked out in considering how aesthetic taste developed; not trusting the progressiveness of contemporary schools, he had personally taken charge of the early instruction of his four oldest sons. By the time of Friedrich's return, however, he was so busy with his three posts that he did not have time for his youngest, who in any case had already been labeled as difficult to educate. Friedrich's religious instruction was left to his mother, his training in Latin to August Wilhelm, himself still a schoolboy.

Although Friedrich was not taught directly by his father, Johann Adolf's ideas were his milieu, and they were certainly mediated to him explicitly by his brother, as Friedrich's defensiveness at August Wilhelm's chastisement in their later correspondence shows. Johann Adolf believed that sense perception and feeling were more natural and immediate paths to learning than intellectual abstraction, an epistemological-pedagogical doctrine that, like his aesthetic theory, was far from ethically or socially neutral. Children were to be taught through nature as protection against the false courtly-aristocratic ideas of rules and decorum, which prescribed heroic manliness and honor, and the associated vices of arrogance, sensuality, lust for fame, indolence, and self-indulgence. A significant by-product of the stress on natural education was criticism of the exaggerated place occupied by classical antiquity in the traditional curriculum: blind respect for the past without an understanding of its inner spirit was not the way to genuine values, which must come from experience. Natural development would teach the importance of decency and respectability, as distinguished from the artificial courtesy and politeness that constricted and falsified spontaneous expression. Because they were natural, such ethical values also fostered the child's autonomy. Johann Adolf believed it both possible and necessary to enlist the child's freely willed participation in his own education and thought one ought to appeal to the child's interests and operate at the level of his or her capacities, using play, picture, and story instead of rote learning and punishment to teach religious and moral truths. This more subjective approach did not mean excluding everything unpleasant from the child's environment; to the contrary, the child could not be spared the pains of reality and hard work, lest he or she become a weakling and idler frightened of passion, tragedy, and achievement and prone to fantasies of voluptuousness and ease. But nature was to be the true teacher, so that the hard lessons the child learned were seen to derive from reality rather than from the impositions of arbitrary authority. True moral education was training in self-cultivation.[23]

Johann Adolf's pedagogical techniques and principles are an almost paradigmatic expression of the ethos of the educated middle class, which made up much of the administration of the centralizing, bureaucratized principalities of eighteenth-century Germany. The ruler's needs for educated personnel gave the middle class unprecedented opportunities for social mobility and at least relative power. Having no established place in the traditional structure of estates, they hoped to replace the hierarchical, courtly, and military values that gave exclusive prestige to the nobility with universal notions of humanity, citizenship, and social usefulness that would afford them both social worth and self-esteem.[24] At the same time they had no desire to deny the absolute authority of those rulers who had provided them their positions of administrative and intellectual leadership and no power to deny the continuing political and social preeminence of the aristocracy. The new values, reflected in Enlightenment thought and in such literary trends as the "sensibility" movement and the "bourgeois drama" of Lessing, emphasized the idea of virtue grounded in both reason and feeling, a universal morality that was the true basis of human dignity, deriving from human nature as such, rather than birth, status, or custom. Because virtue was integral to the individual's nature, the exercise of virtue also represented individual freedom. At the same time, however, full moral development was considered possible only for those who were propertied or personally gifted.[25] Lessing's dramas, for example, while attempting to ground heroic action in a virtue that was not the exclusive preserve of one class, concerned themselves with the socially high-born in an effort to promote social reconciliation through common acceptance by upper bourgeoisie and aristocracy of a new set of universalist values for the elites.[26] In the ideal of moral autonomy, as the German Enlightenment and Johann Adolf understood it, freedom and moral probity, equality of dignity and political and social subordination, cohered easily together. The distinct political culture of Hanover gave the new values particular point and relevance. The traditional estates and the old nobility were particularly well-entrenched and powerful in Hanover because the ruler, who was also the king of Great Britain, was perpetually absent.[27] This meant that the relatively newer state-service families of nonaristocratic origins had to struggle harder to maintain their position alongside the aristocracy, but also that the stakes were all the more worthwhile because the king's absence and the influence of English institutions precluded the growth of a Prussian-style absolutism and fostered the relative autonomy of the elites.

The conflicting impact of his father's legacy of freedom and authority would first be directly expressed only in Schlegel's letters to his brother.

That Friedrich was troubled, however, was evident at least from the time he returned home at thirteen. Moody, introverted, and hard to reach, he attached himself passionately to the only male in the family who seemed interested in him and was willing to give him time and attention, his brother August Wilhelm. Unlike his father, his mother was emotionally available and warmly concerned, and Friedrich's long-unsatisfied need for, and ready responsiveness to, maternal love were to play central roles in his life. His mother, however, was neither intellectual nor well educated, distinct deficiencies in a family that valued intellect and cultivation so highly; thus his brother had to bear the heavy weight of identification. The attachment to August Wilhelm, however, must even at this stage have been marked by the ambivalence Friedrich's later letters to him display. August Wilhelm was the favorite of the family, a dutiful, diligent, and talented student who was already winning notice for literary achievement and patriotic sentiment in the *Gymnasium*.[28] Friedrich admired him but showed none of his ability. Concerned for the future of this difficult child whose questionable literary interests and even more questionable talents offered dim prospects of a livelihood, Johann Adolf decided to apprentice him at age fifteen to a Leipzig banker to prepare him for the practical career of a merchant.

The attempt was a near-disaster. Apparently acquiescent at first, Friedrich was soon desperately begging his father to let him come home and prepare for a learned profession. August Wilhelm was now at the University of Göttingen, winning prizes for his precocious work in classical philology; to be shunted into a mere commercial career was a humiliation in the Schlegel family. Friedrich returned, undecided what to do and so sullen and angry, his mother wrote August Wilhelm, that one could get nothing out of him.[29] To everyone's great surprise, however, he very soon began to display both voracious enthusiasm and formidable talent for learning. Within two years he had mastered Greek and Latin well enough to read extensively in the classical authors. Friedrich wanted to join his brother at the university; lacking formal education, he made up the requirements on his own with the help of a sympathetic older teacher. It was apparent that where his passions and ambitions were aroused, he could mobilize considerable energy and ability. In 1790 he joined his brother at Göttingen with the ostensible purpose of studying law in preparation for a career in the civil service, the secular counterpart of his father's career in the church bureaucracy.

In Göttingen, Friedrich avidly, if indiscriminately, sampled the whole array of available learning from medicine to philosophy, though he apparently also devoted himself to his legal studies. So long as he was with his brother, he was able to reconcile dutiful pursuit of the professional career his father wanted for him and a still unfocused passion for humanistic and literary studies. When, however, in May of 1791 August Wilhelm left to take up a position as tutor in the home of a wealthy Amsterdam banker, Friedrich, who had transferred to the University of Leipzig, fell into a severe crisis. The separation left him to face on his own the issues of career and identity. It also occasioned the fascinating, though one-sided, correspondence—Friedrich later destroyed the letters from his brother—that has enabled later generations to follow the tortuous and painful process of self-formation by which he resolved these issues.

The correspondence was itself an essential part of that process, because August Wilhelm was not merely a sympathetic friend or a close confidant. Friedrich's long, detailed, and frequent letters put his brother into the roles of mentor and competitor, ideal and conscience, brother and father, and occasionally, in his material and emotional support, even mother. "You will have to put up with the fact that I send you books instead of letters," he wrote apologetically early on. "It has become almost a necessity for me to communicate myself to you completely. . . . For now I don't know anyone who could understand me so completely" (KA, 23:23). Friedrich worked out his independence and the beginnings of a psychological, vocational, and philosophical identity with, through, and against August Wilhelm. The details of that many-layered sibling relationship are important not only psychologically but intellectually and methodologically. They provide a remarkable piece of evidence for the interaction between personality and ideas and help explain not only Friedrich's early intellectual choices but the ongoing conflicts that drove him beyond them to a revolutionary intellectual position.

At first Friedrich tried both to follow the two tracks of duty and inclination and to avoid any sense of conflict between them. "I regard the study of jurisprudence much more seriously than you do," he wrote earnestly in July 1791. "It seems to me important to fulfill this civic vocation [*bürgerliche Bestimmung*] well, and I will always strive to do so." His attitude, however, was prompted by resignation rather than enthusiasm. "A completely perfect, or as Schiller would say, a *mature* fifer fulfills his being, after all, by fifing. But whoever is not what he is, even if he were God, makes himself into nothing, in fact less than nothing, because what he is is pure negation.—If I have to be something, that means being it completely, which includes solving all the problems that fate lays before me" (KA, 23:17). The resignation is clearly bitter, and incomplete, and the sarcasm at Friedrich Schiller is the earliest expression of what would be a long rivalry with the great writer, nine years older than Schlegel, who, when he was Schlegel's age, had become virtually overnight a major cultural figure. Schiller could afford to offer sententious advice because he had already achieved success; this also made him a convenient object for the hostile feelings Schlegel had to suppress against his brother, who had achieved more success than Friedrich and was a constant and not always silent reproach to his immaturity. Schlegel's inner conflict emerged more explicitly in his Winckelmannian characterization of the activity to which he would have liked to devote his life—literary and cultural criticism. The goal of art, he wrote in his first letter to August Wilhelm, is "to bring out the beauty of life. . . . When, however, a man is not in harmony with himself or with the world, [art] lacks the power to do that and accomplishes the exact opposite. The harmony of a single moment makes the continuing dissonances more palpable; one suffers all the more the burden of the mundane" (KA, 23:11).

Friedrich's frustration was the greater because he also defined beauty as the manifestation of "victory over fate" (KA, 23:12). Art rose above necessity by mastering time and imperfection through the idea of the eternal inherent in beauty, as well as by directly depicting in its themes the triumph of the human will over external conditions. But having bowed to "fate" in obeying his father and pursuing his legal studies, he felt disqualified from productive aesthetic activity by his submission and could only engage in what seemed to him merely passive pursuits. "We go on in our usual ways," he wrote in a frequently repeated complaint, "you write a lot and I read a lot" (KA, 23:15).

Friedrich's initial attitude to the French Revolution and politics in general was a perfect mirror of his state of mind about profession, father, and self. In a letter of October 1791, August Wilhelm suggested that he read Edmund Burke's *Reflections on the Revolution in France*; Friedrich responded that he had read Christoph Girtanner instead, a Göttingen doctor turned political publicist who published a newsletter Schlegel said was useful for "laymen" like himself because it contained selections from the most important writings and papers. He professed to find Girtanner "non-partisan," though he was in fact a staunchly conservative critic of the French Revolution; the exchange was indicative of Friedrich's casual attitude to contemporary politics: "The whole affair [the Revolution]," he confessed, " interests me primarily indirectly, as a vehicle for conversation with many people" (KA, 23:23).

This response was both true and disingenuous. Friedrich's conservatism was a reflex response, part of his unreflective compliance with his father's authority. Hanover's elites tended to follow the dominant temper of English politics; Burke was particularly widely read there, and native Hanoverians like August Wilhelm Rehberg, one of the most influential political theorists in Germany and a close personal friend of Friedrich's father, developed independent positions against the Revolution.[30] Friedrich's ritual conservatism was the local and family party line, and to that extent he was quite sincere in declaring his basic indifference to the Revolution. But his lack of interest in contemporary politics was not an indifference to politics as such. If current events did not engage him, it was precisely because the conservatism that compliance demanded ran counter to underlying attitudes that were fundamentally antithetical to the orderly hierarchical *Ständestaat*, even with the modifications the progressive conservative Rehberg had suggested to curb the excesses of aristocratic power. Friedrich had in fact recently become very interested in the politics of ancient Rome, where his thinking reflected more activist strivings. "The greatness of a nation," he wrote, "can, I believe, always be explained as the consequences of freedom or resolve, rather than fate" (KA, 23:16). When the Roman republic was overthrown, Rome's destiny was determined by great leaders such as Caesar, Cato, and Catiline, "a small number of truly *colossal* men who contested for mastery over the world," and for whom learning and art, exercise and travel—what moderns considered the noblest part of life—were not ends in themselves but preparation for action. In politics as in aesthetics, the obsessive themes of freedom over fate and the triumph of action over passivity were the measuring rod of Friedrich's judgments.

As yet, however, it was only in spheres remote from contemporary actuality, personal or political, that Friedrich could show resolve or opt for freedom of action. He clearly did not lack personal ambition and acknowledged his own plans to be an author, "not indeed so much out of the love for the work as out of a drive that possessed me from early on, the devouring drive for activity, or as I would rather put it, the longing for the infinite" (KA, 23:24). The very grandiosity of his ambition, in part a reaction to his early humiliations and his current creative impotence, may also have been one of the major factors contributing to his inability to act; an infinite goal made anything less seem like nothing and the hostile desire for superiority implicit in it demanded self-punishment. "I put myself high above the common rabble of sinners," Friedrich wrote in a classic, if self-ironic, expression of narcissistic contradiction, "but I often feel that I'm worth nothing. . . . I can hardly call myself a man. . . . What I have most to reproach myself for I cannot find words to express; part of it is that I experience constant strange mood swings from the greatest heights to the lowest depths" (KA, 23:31).[31] In the meantime, he lived vicariously through the activity of his brother. August Wilhelm, less hampered by uncreative work and inner conflict, was busy writing, though he felt himself in exile away from the German literary world and was filled with doubt about his own poetic ability, fearing that he had talent only for translation. Friedrich took an alternately proprietory and subservient attitude to his brother, constantly solicitous for his welfare, exhorting him to activity when he seemed discouraged and distracted, expressing the wish above all to be useful to him, if only by occasionally reminding him that becoming great depended only on himself (KA, 23:22–23). "Use the enthusiasm of youth and love," Friedrich wrote in an obvious projection of his own wishes, "to strengthen your soul, whose object in maturity can then be the will and thought of your own better self; that's not egotism, it's called rather being one's own God" (KA, 23:13). If Friedrich couldn't achieve independence and greatness himself, he would reach it through identification with August Wilhelm.

Early in their correspondence that identification came increasingly to focus on August Wilhelm's relationship with Caroline Böhmer, a young woman he had met in Göttingen in 1788. Caroline was then twenty-five years old, four years his senior, a widow with one young daughter living temporarily in the home of her father, J. D. Michaelis, the eminent Göttingen Orientalist. She was a forceful personality—intelligent, intellectually engaged, strong-willed, and independent. August Wilhelm had quickly fallen in love with her; though she initially denied that anything could come of their relationship,[32] she gave him some reason for hope when he moved to Amsterdam, and they began to correspond frequently. Early in 1792 she moved to Mainz, where she stayed with a childhood friend married to Georg Forster, then librarian at the University of Mainz and a strong sympathizer of the French Revolution deeply involved in local radical politics. Through Forster, Caroline's own enthusiasm for the Revolution developed into active participation in the Mainz republican movement.

Friedrich knew Caroline only through his brother and the excerpts from her letters that August Wilhelm periodically sent him. His attitude toward her was conditioned by his almost devouring need for August Wilhelm's love and by his consequent admiration and envy of her. These conflicting emotions could lead him into the most erratic and contradictory judgments as he tried to follow the twists and turns of their relationship. When he heard that August Wilhelm wanted to leave Amsterdam to join Caroline in Mainz, he applauded the step as a daring sacrifice of financial security for love and the possibility of independence and self-fulfillment as an author, though he admitted personal satisfaction in the prospect of having August Wilhelm with him in Germany (KA, 23:33). When, however, Caroline discouraged him and August Wilhelm expressed anger at her and also at Friedrich for his selfish motives in wanting him to leave Amsterdam, Friedrich quickly turned on Caroline in his anxiety to stay in his brother's good graces. "I leave it to the tenderness of a woman to selfishly seduce her friend into taking a rash step," he wrote severely, apparently blaming her for the original idea; "She can do more than that, she can with all her wiles seduce her friend into an action that would inevitably lead to the total debasing of his character" (KA, 23:37–38). He attacked her "self-conceit," her "feminine craving to rule

[*Herrschbegierde*]," and her need for praise. In sententious terms, he assured August Wilhelm that it was for the best that his relationship with her was at an end, because in Caroline he had really loved his own ideal and greatness; since the source of his own success lay not in her but in himself, he didn't need her (KA, 23:37). The devaluation of Caroline in apparent support of August Wilhelm also served the purpose of undercutting the most serious rival for August Wilhelm's love and attention.

Friedrich quickly saw, however, that Caroline was not going to be wished away. August Wilhelm, though upset, was devoted to her and criticized Friedrich's "lack of humanity" towards her; Friedrich felt it necessary to match his ambivalence, with sometimes unintentionally amusing results. "I maintain that a connection with her is dangerous for a man, because of her inclination to demand adoration. But I hold her in high esteem because this inclination is only a deviant form of the highest nobility" (KA, 23:49). His ambivalence, however, was not only on his brother's account but on his own. August Wilhelm's picture of Caroline suggested someone with the self-regard Friedrich himself both admired and feared, and the fact that his idealized brother loved her was in any case reason enough to believe her wonderful. Friedrich became increasingly obsessed with August Wilhelm's love affair and his good fortune in possessing so estimable a woman. He demanded more excerpts from Caroline's letters, scolded his brother for withholding information about her, insisted repeatedly on knowing everything about their relationship, past and present, and complained that he was being excluded. His favorite pastime, he wrote, was to guess the greatness and wholeness of her spirit out of the fragments Wilhelm sent him. "What a woman! Lucky one, do you still have the nerve to complain? What wouldn't I give to have to put up with such happiness!" (KA, 23:59). Yet Friedrich was aware on some level that he did not know the real Caroline at all, that he was involved with a "phantom,"—"a phantom whom it would perhaps be dangerous for me to really get to know" (KA, 23:58). He already sensed not only that Caroline's radical ideas might lead him astray, but that he could easily become even more emotionally involved with her precisely because she belonged to his brother.

August Wilhelm's even relative success in love exacerbated Friedrich's insecurity and already-troubled feelings about women. He expressed contempt for their supposedly low intellect yet acknowledged his own sexual need for them. "I find women in general even more shallow than men," he had written early on to Wilhelm. "I am very sensual; indeed too much so to be able to find pleasure in the company of young women" (KA, 23:18). If, however, he felt uncomfortable with his sexuality, he believed that love was indispensable to him because it was only through another's love that he thought he could find the self he lacked. "Above all, however, the one I would love must be capable of living for one thing, and of forgetting everything for one thing. . . . [I seek] the powerful love that can only come from the yearning for the infinite, for the heart supposes that it can find in the beloved the infinite good that it lacks" (KA, 23:52). Having never encountered such a "drive for the infinite" in a woman, he had not found a woman he could love (KA, 23:52); it was on masculine love, on his love for August Wilhelm, that he had pinned his hopes for identity. Now, however, August Wilhelm had found the right woman for himself. In the middle of 1792, Friedrich's two-edged jealousy of his brother drove him into an ill-fated affair.

Given the circumstances, the episode was bound, perhaps even calculated, to be an emotional disaster and to increase Friedrich's sense of failure and humiliation. His object was the daughter of a wealthy Leipzig banker (it will be remembered that Wilhelm was a tutor in the home of a banker in Amsterdam), a married but notoriously flirtatious socialite.[33] She was pretty and vivacious, but in Friedrich's perhaps suspect judgment, of neither high intellectual nor moral standards; he himself described her as "unworthy." Despite this evaluation, he drove himself into a frenzied passion over her, which, he wrote to August Wilhelm, "only makes the worthlessness of my life clear" (KA, 23:62). His attempts to woo her with the elaborately contrived schemes of a *galant* made him feel ridiculous and were in any case rewarded with mockery and rebuff. To keep up with her social circle, he spent himself heavily into debt, mostly by gambling, violating his father's cherished sense of bourgeois self-control and propriety and increasing his dependency on August Wilhelm by adding the need for financial help to the long-standing need for emotional sustenance. He found his posturing and insincerity among the most painful aspects of his behavior during this episode; they exacerbated his already intense anxiety about not having a real self. In a letter written at the height of the affair, he offered August Wilhelm an ironic but self-lacerating defense of the uses of lying: "Lying is as necessary to mankind as weakness and flight from whatever terrifies. But what is more terrible than truth? . . . [M]any who constantly deceive themselves would be killed by the pain the moment they were fully aware of the truth. . . . Every intentional error is to me a lie, and if I add that it is not necessary to be clearly conscious of one's intention, it is no exaggeration to say that I doubt whether in many lives a single moment goes by without lies. . . . *Lying* sounds to me almost as bad as *murdering*" (KA, 23:71). Friedrich's apparently abstract obsessing, with its drastic concluding moral equation, becomes more intelligible as a confession of his own conscious hypocrisy and unconscious urges. "It is good that I pretend religion to my father and respect to my family. The little art that there is in human relationships is to lie skilfully and that is something that can be learned" (KA, 23:72).

Friedrich's self-described "debauches" were not only a surrender to his sexual need and a competitive identification with his brother but also a rebellion against the father who forced him to pretend and be false to himself, a rebellion that, in light of the previous passage, amounted in his own mind to parricide.

This rebellion, however, was as much a failure as the effort to compete with August Wilhelm. "You will be loved by the best women and I will fail with the worst," he lamented. The contrast was so painful that he could not suppress an expression of hostile jealousy amidst his usual one-sided idolizing. "[Women] can esteem you as a noble man, and you seduce them just as surely as the most likeable scoundrel would; of course even the best of women want that too" (KA, 23:75). Despite the flash of hostility, however, he needed August Wilhelm more than ever, for the worse he thought of himself, the more he depended on his brother's approval. He had alienated his few other friends and acquaintances. In defensive reaction to his disastrous performance in love, he took a more than usually superior and critical tone with them, pointing out their weaknesses and errors in the name of "truth." His description of the behavior that drove away his recently acquired friend Friedrich von Hardenberg suggests both how insufferable he must have been and how helpless he felt to control himself. "I was happy to use him . . . he was interested in me and my peculiarities. . . . In order to be allowed to speak as much truth as I did (I can speak daggers) I would have had to flatter him with more lies" (KA, 23:76).

Friedrich was fully aware of the bad impression he made on people but was mostly worried lest August Wilhelm react as they did. Even before the affair, he had to report that Schiller had found him an arrogant and cold smart-mouth [*Witzling*] (KA, 23:51). Now, he acknowledged in a letter to his brother—perhaps not without perverse pride in just how bad an effect he had—"People find me interesting and avoid me. Wherever I go, the good mood disappears, and my presence is oppressive. . . . I certainly inspire many with disgust. . . . To most I'm an original, which means a fool with spirit. . . . If I were loved, I would become lovable, but I almost fear that even with you it's more interest than love" (KA, 23:70).

The effect of the Leipzig affair was to intensify Friedrich's ambivalent identification with August Wilhelm. "Let me be happy in you," he wrote to him, "since I am not happy with myself." He hit on the idea of abandoning his legal studies and finding a position as tutor in Amsterdam (KA, 23:70). Friedrich pressed August Wilhelm even more insistently to "share his joys" completely by telling him all about the relationship with Caroline, especially whether he had ever spoken about him to her. He openly expressed his desire for her approval and almost as openly admitted his desire to possess August Wilhelm, pleading that when his brother returned to Germany he would visit him before he saw her. "Allow me this jealousy—you know she did infinitely more for you than I ever could. . . . In the will [to do for you] I believe we are equal. And then you are only a friend to her—to me you are everything. I also hope in the future to be more to you" (KA, 23:75). The depth of his need made August Wilhelm's reprimands for his extremes of behavior, mood, and language hard to bear. He defended himself against his brother's reproachful assumption that the suicidal wishes he expressed were the result of his bungled erotic adventure—"the value of my life does not depend on a woman"—insisting, not very reassuringly, that he had thought of suicide daily for almost three years (KA, 23:78). In giving what he thought was the real reason for his chronic despair, however, he unwittingly uncovered the connection between it and his rivalry with Wilhelm: "My powers are much greater than my activity for I always wrestle with the thought, 'Everything is useless after all!' Too proud to believe that it is worth the effort to lower ourselves merely for 'something better,' we sink with the weakest men from the highest insight ever deeper into indolence and self-contempt." For Friedrich it was the highest or nothing. Only being like August Wilhelm would enable him to achieve the degree of success he desired, but his father's wishes blocked him from a literary career, and in any case Friedrich conflated being like August Wilhelm with being him, outdoing him by replacing him. He had as yet no independent literary stance of his own. He had sabotaged his own hostile efforts to compete with his brother romantically by choosing his object poorly and then acting badly, bringing down on himself the brotherly censure he felt he deserved yet hated. His attempts at living his brother's love life through his letters and at courting his exclusive love were no more successful, though Friedrich blamed August Wilhelm for this failure, evading both the unpleasant realities and the danger stemming from his own desires. His frustration and baffled rage at both himself and August Wilhelm ultimately produced melodramatically masochistic declarations: "Accept my warmest thanks for your reprimand and don't let it be the last . . . give me praise and blame as you see fit. I hand you the dagger myself; don't spare me and pierce through the heart if necessary. From the hand of a brother it can't hurt, and even if it does, I will gladly seal our friendship with my blood.—I believe in you—even if you used a real dagger against me, I would thank you as I died, in the certainty of your wise intention" (KA, 23:78).

The Leipzig affair ended in the spring of 1793. Deprived of his own drama, Friedrich plunged even deeper into August Wilhelm's. He drew closer in fantasy to the "phantom" Caroline he had never met. "Will you find me fickle," he asked his brother, "if I tell you that I have somewhat changed my judgment of her? You see, I believe I've done her an injustice. With all her faults she is very loveable. I couldn't stand the slightest blemish in her—but I have no right to let her feel that. I only wish I could take it back, yes I would gladly beg her for forgiveness . . . if only I had the opportunity" (KA, 23:82). His chronic dependency became even more child-like. "Don't expect anything more than renewed descriptions of a shattered heart and repeated requests for more frequent letters, advice, sympathy and support" (KA, 23:82), he wrote August Wilhelm in February. A few days later, a letter from his mother containing a sum of money to help with his debts, and no reproach for them, sent him into a paroxysm of filial gratitude. "I will always keep this letter from my mother. Only motherly love can make one so generous" (KA, 23:83).

The failure that increased his self-abasement, however, also intensified his desire to become independent and productive. Throughout his romantic involvement he had kept up his reading in philosophy, moral theory, theology, physiology, and politics—though not in jurisprudence—and felt he had accomplished much, even if it was not yet evident. "I feel now that I have powers and I hope that I may give proof of them and that I may be worthy of your approval. But I can't be bound any longer—I must and will live for myself." Independence, however, was still a tenuous idea for Friedrich, dependent on the grace of others. "My parents must give up a plan they have forced on me and that has very poor prospects, and I hope that they will do it now; if only you don't work against me with unfavorable descriptions of the life of a tutor. . . . [Y]ou would [intercede for me] if you knew what pitiful prospects I have and how my powers are being destroyed in the painful struggle with my nature and my situation" (KA, 23:91).

Typically, Friedrich expressed his evolving needs, inner states, and growing frustrations as doctrines of art. "There are only two rules for art," he announced magisterially to August Wilhelm in May 1793. "One of them is that multiplicity be combined with an inner unity. Everything must work to one point and everything else, every existence, place and meaning must follow necessarily from it" (KA, 23:97). "Only the autonomous human spirit and its deeds have intrinsic worth. . . . The greatest activity, completeness and harmony of all our powers, the inner enjoyment of our own selves can be the effect of a work of art. . . . [As for content] there is only one unconditional law—that the free spirit always triumph over nature" (KA, 23:98).

Friedrich's desperation at his impasse reached a climax in the summer of 1793. "I see the obvious impossibility of imprisoning myself in a bourgeois yoke," he declared, "of irretrievably sacrificing my spirit, the best part of my life, for a miserable wage. . . . Ought it not to be possible for me to seek out and create my own place for myself? . . . I want to follow the call; I must gamble because I must. I don't need you now to tell me what my goal is: to live, to live in freedom . . . [but] tell me, what am I destined for, what will become of me, what ought I to do?" (KA, 23:99–100). The drive to freedom was stymied in part precisely because it had as yet no content, no end other than liberation from an equally desired submission; hence the paradox of begging August Wilhelm to tell him how to live in freedom. But being himself still entailed a threatening grandiosity. "I know," he declared, "that I cannot live at all, if I do not become great, that is, satisfied with myself." He rationalized his paralysis, however, as the effect of one of its symptoms, the obsessive hyperintellectuality into which he poured all the energy of inhibited action. The problem, he thought, was that his intellect was too developed for the rest of his character. "For my intelligence is such that were everything else equal to it, and there were harmony in me, I would already have achieved greatness" (KA, 23:104). It was at this point that Friedrich became fascinated with the figure of Hamlet with whose insight, inability to act, and desperation he strongly identified; his interpretation of *Hamlet* was a self-diagnosis: "The object and the effect of this play is heroic despair, that is, endless disorder amid the very highest abilities. The ground of his inner death lies in the greatness of his intelligence. Were it less great, he would be a hero. . . . He sees an immense tangle of circumstances—hence his lack of resolve. . . . His innermost existence is a horrible nothingness, contempt for the world and for himself. . . . Unhappy is he who understands him. Under certain circumstances this play could instantly be the cause of suicide for a soul of the most delicate moral sensitivity" (KA, 23:100).

At this moment of Friedrich's deepest crisis, salvation—a word he was to use himself—appeared in the guise of Caroline Böhmer, whose fate suddenly, if briefly, fell into his hands as a result of the vicissitudes of the contemporary historical upheaval. Since October 1792, Mainz had been occupied by French troops; under their protection, the local radicals had organized themselves into a Jacobin Club with the ultimate purpose of forming a republic and requesting annexation by France. Georg Forster was directly involved in these plans, and though Caroline rejected the extremes of Jacobinism,[34] she was implicated both by her friendship with him and by her own revolutionary sympathies and activities. These had extended to a liaison with a French officer by whom she became pregnant. When the armies of the First Coalition again went on the offensive against France in the spring of 1793 and laid siege to Mainz, Caroline attempted to flee the city but was caught by the Prussians, arrested, and imprisoned. Her brother was finally able to secure her release in mid-July, and the faithful August Wilhelm hurried to her side. Since he soon had to return to his position in Amsterdam, however, he placed her under Friedrich's care in the home of an elderly unmarried doctor in

Lucka, a town just south of Leipzig. Because Caroline's travel permit allowed her to go only to Frankfurt, the arrangement was somewhat dangerous and had to be kept secret.

It was a fantasy come true for Friedrich. Suddenly he had exclusive access to his brother's beloved in clandestine circumstances. The report of his first meeting with her on August 2 was full of both excitement and a strange unease. "The impression she made on me is much too extraordinary for even me to understand and communicate clearly. . . . What she thinks of me is completely unknown and mysterious to me. Though she seems largely indifferent . . . I could be in danger of gushing over her and I believe that I have a crush on her [*schwärmen*] which would mean that I might sin against her" (KA, 23:111). Nevertheless, despite his anxieties, he wanted more. He attacked his brother for withholding information about his plans for her; August Wilhelm had not even told him she was pregnant. Friedrich somewhat maliciously reminded him that because he was the only person who would see her in this painful time, he ought to be taken into their full confidence so that he could comfort her. As he got closer to Caroline, his tone became more proprietory and provocative. "I'll spare you detailed descriptions of her suffering," he wrote on August 28 in reference to her fear of discovery (KA, 23:123). "The most I can do to lessen the necessary pain and worry (I don't spare you but I'm not after all without feeling) is to give you news quite often. . . . I can't forebear to quote you *one* thing from her last note to me (since you won't be getting anything from her today)" (KA, 23:125). He declared himself strangely "disturbed" when he discovered that she was pregnant by a French officer rather than by Forster, who he thought dominated her in everything but who was at least a known quantity. He mentioned unspecified "hopes" that he entertained but felt she didn't—"and why should she?—I have understanding, but I am so inexperienced, so limited and above all . . . I lack the sense for love. . . . I wouldn't be surprised if she found me crude . . . and in any case respect forces me to treat her as a man." Although Friedrich was ostensibly writing only about the possibilities of friendship, he found it necessary to give August Wilhelm reassurances. "We are together not because we belong together but because we meet in the same house. I believe one can not know her if one doesn't love her or isn't loved by her" (KA, 23:127–28). Clearly, Friedrich was trying simultaneously to rouse and assuage August Wilhelm's jealousy, as he finally more or less acknowledged. "I may have given you reason to think erroneously about our relationship," he wrote. "I ought to have written about it simply and seriously, not half jokingly or when I'm in a bad mood." He confessed that he had been greatly taken by her from the first and had tried for the intimacy of friendship, but he realized that under the circumstances too much closeness was inappropriate. "I place myself therefore in the simplest, most uncomplicated relationship to her, the respect of a son, the openness of a brother, the ingenuousness of a child, the undemandingness of a stranger" (KA, 23:132–33).

From Friedrich's erratic and impulsive behavior towards Caroline, it is clear enough that he was in love with her but that under the inner threat of direct rivalry with his brother he suppressed and tried to transform his feelings. In fact he succeeded in doing so in a way that enabled him to use her internally to resolve his crisis. Alternating between intense conversations with her and lonely reading and thinking in Leipzig, he began overtly to break the ties that bound him to filial obedience, though even now not without great anxiety. "I have torn the bonds or chains of nature," he said ambiguously in the letter of August 28, "and I feel more and more that the bonds of my own creativity [*Erfindung*] are weak and without power, that I stand alone . . . outside the world, that I am very superfluous and that I don't know what I need" (KA, 23:127). What he did not yet quite know was that he needed external release from the old chains as well as external permission to try something new. In the meantime, under the stimulus of his feelings for Caroline, he was defining his ideas more explicitly and more ambitiously than ever before: "When you consider all human thought as a whole, it is obvious that truth, complete unity, is the necessary if never-reachable goal of all thought. . . . [T]he spirit of system, which is something quite other than a system, is the only thing that leads to manysidedness. . . . The source of the ideal is the burning thirst for eternity, the longing for God. . . . What else is the source of our worth, but the power and the resolve to be like God, to keep infinity always before our eyes" (KA, 23:129–30). On September 29, in the midst of all this ferment, he got the news that his father had died. "I should have been expecting it for a long time," was all he reported to August Wilhelm, in the middle of a letter that began with concern about Caroline's health and went on to discuss many other things, "but never was I less prepared for it" (KA, 23:135). This lack of preparation was not wholly surprising, since Johann Adolf, though in his seventies, had been in good health and his death had come unexpectedly two weeks after the onset of an initially mild flu. But Friedrich's tone of detached objectivity and the doubled denial that he had ever anticipated his father's death suggest suppressed feelings, and the chillingly casual remarks at the end of the letter that he was anxious to know more about his father's death and that it would mean a serious change in his situation since he could no longer accept any financial support from home (because of the straitened family circumstances) hardly indicate grief. Johann Adolf's death was a release for his son, something that Friedrich had both wanted and feared as the prerequisite for his own independence.

In the event, Johann Adolf's death precipitated the final rebellion. Just a few weeks later, Friedrich announced to August Wilhelm that he had come round to Caroline's thinking about the French Revolution. She had given him the letters she had written to her sister Martha from Mainz. "When I add to them what she both now and earlier confessed to me in conversation I find what she underwent incredible. In another way, though, very understandable, given the inhumanity of rulers and their minions." He could now almost forgive her for trying to drag August Wilhelm actively into the revolutionary mess. "This enthusiasm for a great public cause intoxicates us and makes our own selves and our petty concerns seem unimportant, and must do so if it is genuine." He had begun to read contemporary political theory, though he found only Rousseau worth reading exhaustively. "History and political science are not unimportant prospects in the project of my future life. . . . In the past few months it has become my preferred form of convalescence to follow the mighty, confusing trend of current events; and then I begin to think in ways that it would be foolish not to keep hidden. I reflect on the direction and the essence of the matter, and my sympathy and approval inexorably follow. It is all connected in my head with ideas for more intensive research than I can develop in a letter" (KA, 23:144–45).

On November 4, Friedrich announced to his brother the birth of Caroline's child, Wilhelm Julius Cranz, for whom he stood godfather, with a self-revealing account of his own reaction. He had to leave the house because he could not stand to watch her pain, and even then her screams penetrated him "to the very marrow. . . . If she were mine, I would have been out of my mind. I am fine, but in my anxiety I only thought of you. . . . [Y]ou should come back to Germany" (KA, 23:150). Schlegel had expressed the forbidden wish, which perhaps increased his anxiety over Caroline and at any rate made him want August Wilhelm there to protect him from it and himself. Later he would name the autobiographical protagonist of *Lucinde* after Caroline's son, Julius. If he could not be the father of her child, he would be the child itself and pay literary tribute to her fostering of his identity as writer. In the same letter Schlegel discussed for the first time the momentous decision he had made to move to Dresden, where he could get a fresh start and make his living as a freelance writer and translator; it was a spiritual rebirth. Only August Wilhelm was to know, since both the break and the risk would be too great for the rest of his family; so far as they were concerned, he was taking a position as a tutor.

He intended to spend all his time working on a number of articles and books on Greek literature that were to advance an interpretation of classical culture that only his new political ideas had allowed him to crystallize.

At last Friedrich had a voice of his own. His father's death had made it possible; Caroline's ideas had supplied a crucial part of its language, and her role in his psychic life had given it sanction. If Friedrich was not aware of the first, he at least knew something about the second and third: "Caroline's opinions have been of great value for me in this recent period," he wrote. "This above all has strengthened and cheered me. I have no claims to her gratitude but she has my friendship forever. *I have got better through her, and she probably doesn't know it*" (KA, 23:164; italics added).

Two years later, on the anniversary of their meeting, Friedrich acknowledged some of this in a direct tribute to Caroline. "Think about it, I stood before you and thanked you silently for all you did for me and to me. What I am and will be I owe to myself; that I am it, in part to you."[35] This was a generous tribute, but Caroline had done even more for him than he realized. An important part of what he could now become derived from her. Her political ideas enabled him to translate his personal struggle for freedom not only into a public and universal cause, but into an understanding of the cultural creativity of his beloved Greeks as the product of their political freedom. He was able to make the translation, however, only because he was able to identify with her and thus overcome the conflicts that had blocked his passage to independence. By surrendering any romantic or erotic claims to Caroline, he had submitted to August Wilhelm in the internal rivalry between them. But in that very submission he established and internalized Caroline as a maternal figure who—because of her age and her relationship to August Wilhelm—could authorize his rebellion against his father through her revolutionary ideas. Simultaneously, he could win an independent identity against August Wilhelm, who did not sympathize with Caroline's politics or with her influence in political matters on Friedrich (KA, 23:163). If he did not possess Caroline physically or romantically, he possessed her in a way that August Wilhelm had to accept to the extent he accepted Caroline herself. And in this way he was at last able to identify also with his brother, becoming a writer and a critic without dissolving his identity into August Wilhelm's or destroying him by displacing him. Finally, he also both identified with and bested his father. He took up the vocation his father had respected but set aside as risky; he took up his father's ideas about freedom and morality and developed them not only much more boldly than Johann Adolf but in the context of a revolution and in the form of an obsession for the Greeks—"Graecomania" Schiller was to call it contemptuously—that his father had decried. It was not only for the present that Schlegel achieved an identity through Caroline, however. This complex process of identification established a model that was to be of great theoretical importance in the future.

ii) Classical Individualism and the Primacy of Politics

Apart from the deviation from his father that it represented, there
seemed little that was revolutionary in the classical program of Friedrich
Schlegel's early writings. Idealization of Greek art was the received literary wisdom of late eighteenth-century German culture;[36] Schlegel's uncompromising assertion of the absolute superiority of classical over modern art and his attack on modern individualism could even make his
version of it appear somewhat conservative by contemporary standards,
in comparison with Schiller, for example.[37] In fact, the case was just the
opposite.

J. J. Winckelmann had largely set the terms of the neoclassicism that
became widespread in Germany after 1760 with his dictum that the only
way for moderns to become great was by imitating the Greeks,[38] because
Greek art aimed neither at the merely realistic imitation of particular
objects in nature nor at the projection of the artist's particular individual
taste, but at an objective and absolute ideal of beauty—the celebrated
"noble simplicity and tranquil grandeur."[39] Greek art preserved the freedom of naturalness while making nature more perfect and beautiful, in
particular by depicting heroic impassiveness and serenity in the face of
suffering and passion. Winckelmann had been Friedrich's indispensable
guide to classical culture when he was teaching it to himself in the years
before Göttingen, and when he finally began to write himself, he wanted
to extend Winckelmann's vision of the ideal unity in Greek visual art to
Greek literature, as Lessing had begun to do in *Laocoon*. Apparently
unhistorical in its conclusions about the universal validity of Greek ideals
(though relativist in its assumptions about the uniqueness of the Greek
environment), Winckelmann's aesthetic enterprise was in fact aimed at
his own culture. In part it intended to provide Germany with the paradigm of a nation united culturally rather than politically in order to
challenge the primacy of the Roman imperial idea that underlay the predominant French cultural model.[40] Ideologically, the fusion of "noble
simplicity" and "tranquil grandeur" implied a synthesis of the moralized
nature of the Enlightenment with an aristocratic notion of heroic superiority stripped of false showiness and arrogance—a synthesis in keeping
with the Enlightenment ethos of the *gebildete Stände* described earlier.
From a psychological point of view, in placing the highest aesthetic value
on the integration of sensuousness and self-restraint, Winckelmann's aesthetic norms were an effort to heal the self-division inherent in the
conflicting paradigms of courtly sensuousness and bourgeois morality,
though the tortured effort to accommodate nature while denying a corrupted, exploitive sensuality perpetuated self-division in the asceticism
of his aesthetic ideal, which allowed passion and sensuality only under

the form of restraint.[41] On this issue Schlegel broke with Winckelmann and sided with Lessing in insisting that the Greek ideal of beauty in literature allowed for, indeed demanded, the inclusion of strong emotion.[42] He accepted but extended Winckelmann's position on another crucial issue as well: the place of politics in the development of the Greek ideal. Winckelmann had argued that only liberty had provided the conditions that elevated Athenian art to the level of perfection; Schlegel interpreted Athenian republican freedom in the light of the radical egalitarian republicanism of the French Revolution.

Classical literature, Schlegel wrote in his central essay *On the Study of Greek Poetry*, was concerned with the beautiful alone, defined as that which was "objective" in nature, especially human nature—that is, "the universally valid, constant and necessary.[43] By contrast, modern literature dealt only with "the particular and the mutable," with *original and interesting individuality*" (KA, 1:245; italics in original). "Individual," "interesting," and "characteristic" (i.e., idiosyncratic) were negative characterizations for a literature that Schlegel saw as preoccupied with novelty and effect, with the faithful rendering of events and people whose sole claim to interest was their capacity to stimulate or arouse. His conceptual language here is partly Kantian. He reinforced Winckelmann's Greek ideal of objective beauty with an abstract definition of the beautiful from *The Critique of Judgment*. "The *beautiful* . . . is the universally valid object of a disinterested pleasure, which is equally independent from the coercion of necessity and law, free and yet necessary, without purpose and yet absolutely purposeful" (KA, 1:253). For Kant the beautiful was that which was experienced as an end in itself, serving no subordinate purpose, whether sensuous pleasure, moral instruction, or utilitarian ends. It was precisely this quality of "disinterested pleasure" that distinguished the idea of beauty from merely subjective taste, preference, or sensibility.

But Schlegel's Kantian terminology conceals a quite un-Kantian, in fact, anti-Kantian concern with the psychological rather than the formal conditions of beauty. His attack on mere particular individuality was not at all what it seems. Above all it was not an attack on the idea of individual freedom, sensuality, or even the value of personal uniqueness. His target was the self he had been, and hated, and was trying to outgrow, the self he saw reflected in the characters of modern literature.[44] Modern writing deformed selfhood because it was dominated by the intellect, the rational understanding whose function was primarily analytic. "The isolating understanding begins by dividing up nature's wholeness into individual parts. Under its direction, therefore, the role of art is completely exhausted by the faithful imitation of the individual" (KA, 1:245). Schlegel here confusedly and confusingly mixed description of what he thought was wrong in the depiction of character in modern literature with a diagnosis of why it went wrong. What was really problematic for him about modern individuality was its exclusive connection with the intellect. Even the analytic approach of modern literature, Schlegel conceded, could represent the universal in the particular, and such representation could yield a genuine work of art, but it would be "didactic" or philosophical rather than purely "aesthetic." The highest achievement of such philosophical art was Shakespeare's *Hamlet*. Unquestionably *Hamlet* had to be considered authentic art by Schlegel's standards because it was a unified whole; all the individual parts of the drama developed necessarily from a central point, the character of the hero. But all the strength of Hamlet's character was concentrated in his intellect; his ability to act had been totally destroyed. "His soul was divided, torn in opposite directions as if on a torture rack; it disintegrated and went under in an excess of rumination that oppressed him even more than it did those close to him. There is perhaps no more complete a portrayal of relentless disharmony, which is the authentic object of philosophical tragedy, of such an enormously false relationship between the intellectual and the active forces, as in Hamlet's character. The total impression of this tragedy is a maximum of desperation" (KA, 1:247–48). Hence, while Shakespeare's tragedies were formally unified and complete, they were not "beautiful." Beauty required harmony of content as well as structural unity, but Shakespeare's plays incorporated the ugly in such a way that content undermined formal completeness and the effect of his dramas was often "relentless disorder, and the result of the whole infinite conflict" (KA, 1:251).

The example of Hamlet gave substance to Schlegel's abstractions. He thought the modern ugly because it dealt with the ugly disharmonies of strong individuals at odds with themselve because their intellectual faculty was developed at the expense of all their other faculties. Unable to act, they were cerebral monsters who obsessionally analyzed everything and turned it into abstractions. By contrast, the heroes of Greek literature were men who had developed all of their capacities and got them into a comfortable balance with one another. Although Schlegel ranked the dramas of Sophocles as the epitome of Greek beauty in this regard, the only Greek hero he discussed in any detail in the essay as a classical contrast to Hamlet was a figure from the earlier epic period of ancient greatness. In the light of the internal struggles disclosed in his correspondence, the passage stands as a wishful self-portrait:

In the ethics of [Homer's] heroes, force and grace are in balance. They are strong but not coarse, gentle without being weak, and clever without being cold. Achilles, though in anger as fearsome as a fighting lion, knows tears of tender pain at the faithful bosom of a loving mother; he chases away loneliness through the soft pleasure of a sweet song. With a sigh of mourning he looks back at his own error, at the enormous harm caused by the obstinate presumption of a proud king and the hasty anger of a young hero. With ravaging sadness he dedicates a lock of hair at the grave of his beloved friend. On the arm of an honorable old man, his hated enemy's father, whom he has made unhappy, he can dissolve into emotional tears. . . . Even in battle, in the very moment when anger so carries him away that [unmoved by the youth's pleas] he stabs the defeated enemy through the breast, he remains human, even likeable, and reconciles us by an enchantingly moving reflection. (KA, 1:279–80)

The greatness of Greek art was that it gave scope to every side of personality—impulse, feeling, ego, morality, and reason—without allowing any to usurp or obliterate the others. Greek heroes, in Schlegel's conceit, could be sensuous and passionate, even violent and murderous, yet tender, ethical, and spiritual; they could give free rein to their most aggressive instincts and selfish desires without destroying their own finer sensibility and cultivation or their feeling for others. In Schlegel's list of the excesses that they avoided—coarseness, coldness—one hears the language in which Schiller and others had criticized him, language that he had just recently used to criticize himself. In the image of Achilles comforting the grieving Priam, whom he himself has injured by killing his son, there is present the shadow of Friedrich's recent struggle with his father, whom he too had hurt, or wanted to, by killing off the "good," obedient son—his former self—and also the struggle with his brother, with whom he had been engaged in deadly inner combat. And in the images of "weakness" and "tenderness"—Achilles crying on his mother's breast, comforting his own loneliness with song, mourning the death of his friend, or weeping on the arm of the man whose son he had killed—can be read the infantile and "feminine" traits that Schlegel feared in himself, the submissive dependency that was both an integral part of his character, as his letters abundantly show, and a reaction against his murderous impulses and grandiose ambitions. Contained within a hero who combined both action and reflection, however, these traits were not only acceptable but noble, necessary for roundedness of character.

The boldest, most provocative programmatic statement he gave of the Greek ideal was in his description, that is, his mythic idealization, of the essential characteristics of Greek comedy; it is another projection that reveals the extent of his rebellion and desire, as well as the conflict it aroused and the consequent need for a "classical" synthesis:

Above all freedom is presented through the removal of all restrictions. A person who therefore determines himself solely by his own will and who makes it evident that he is subject to neither external nor internal limitations displays complete internal and external personal freedom. In that he acts only from purely arbitrary choice and caprice, in happy enjoyment of himself, intentionally without reasons and against reason, internal freedom is made evident; external freedom is displayed in the wantonness with which he violates external limits while the law magnanimously waives its claims. This is how the Romans displayed freedom in the Saturnalia; a similar idea was probably the basis of the carnival. That the violation of limitations should only be apparent, that it contain nothing really evil or ugly, and that freedom still be unconditional: that is the real task of any such portrayal, and so also that of ancient Greek comedy. (KA, 1:23)

Under these ideal conditions, beauty and individuality are *not* enemies but mutually necessary. "In general," Schlegel claimed, "complete universal validity and the highest individuality in art do not contradict one another. . . . [T]he material, the language of art cannot be too individual. . . . The ground of the comic muses' depiction must be the highest individuality" (KA, 1:26).

How did Greek art reach such a happy state? For one thing, according to Schlegel, it had developed under the guidance of spontaneous, natural human impulse, rather than of analytic reason and its rules. Allowing human nature—which for Schlegel included ethical and aesthetic as well as "biological"—i.e., selfish, impulses—free rein, Greek culture could tame man's animal nature without subduing it and create an art free both from the coercion of instinctual need and the domination of the abstract intellect. In the civilization of ancient Greece, law became spontaneous inclination (KA, 1:274). But Greek naturalness, Schlegel insisted, did not exist in a vacuum; it was only made possible by certain cultural and social conditions, and its perfection was possible only with the perfection of those conditions. He was vague about the specific nature of these conditions in the early stages of Greek culture in Homeric times. What he did insist upon was that the achievement of epic Greek art was not just a matter of individual genius. "One ought to guard against the idea that what was worthy of imitation in Greek poetry was the privilege of a few chosen geniuses, as every more excellent originality is in modern writing. . . . Greek beauty was a common possession of public taste, *the spirit of the masses*" (KA, 1:282). The portrayal of wholeness in Homeric heroes not only expressed but was made possible by an ethos that linked people in shared communal and heroic values.

As Greek civilization advanced from its early epic stage, however, spontaneous inclination developed into forms of self-conscious education and cultivation; the perfection of Athenian art epitomized in the drama was achieved through human freedom, not blind nature, through cultural institutions established by human wit and ingenuity that transformed free natural impulse into rational practice (KA, 1:285). "Where was cultivation so genuine, and genuine cultivation so general? Indeed there is hardly a more sublime spectacle in all of human history as that offered by the great moment when there appeared simultaneously . . . republicanism in the Greek constitutions, enthusiasm and wisdom in the sphere of ethics, logical and sytematizing procedures in the sciences instead of the mythic connections of fantasy, and the ideal [of beauty] in the Greek arts" (KA, 1:286). Republicanism was the political correlate of the highest Greek aesthetic achievement, the logical political outcome of making self-conscious and institutionalizing those natural human drives for free self-expression and spiritual greatness that animated the Homeric heroes.

Indeed, Greek republicanism was not just one of the manifestations of those drives but the privileged one, the one upon which all the others depended. "Political judgment is the highest of all standpoints; the subordinate viewpoints of moral, aesthetic and intellectual judgment are equal to one another. . . . The point of the political is to order the individual forces of the whole spirit and the individuals of the whole species into a unity." On the other hand, since politics in its ideal form is the practical institutionalization of freedom and wholeness, it must always be thought of as instrumental rather than an end in itself, a precondition, if the most necessary one, for freedom of the individual. "Political practice may put limits on individual freedom . . . but only under the condition that it does not inhibit progressive development, and does not render impossible a future of complete freedom. Politics must at the same time strive to make itself superfluous" (KA, 1:325).

With this blunt assertion of both the necessity and instrumental nature of political freedom and participation—an important reversal of emphasis both from classical republicanism's stress on the primacy of civic virtue and republican ideas of "patriotism" in eighteenth-century Germany[45]— Schlegel's classicism reveals itself as the opposite of an anti-individualistic aestheticism. The real meaning of the objective ideal of beauty emerges as the ideal of a radically free, yet psychologically and socially integrated, personality and the republican polity that is both its political expression and its precondition. If Greek individualism was more wholesome than modern individuality, it is because it did not deform the personality one-sidedly in the direction of sensuousness or intellect or allow one personality to develop at the expense of others, and this in turn was possible because Greek individualism was the product of social arrangements that provided for the development of the whole man, and of all men (though not yet women—for Schlegel one of its major defects). By contrast, modern society, that is, his native Germany, was a totally unfavorable environment for the ideal: "The process of modern cultivation, the spirit of our time and the German national character in particular do not appear very favorable for [ideal] poetry. How tasteless are . . . all the tendencies and institutions, how unpoetic all the usages, the whole way of life of modern man! Everywhere there predominates ponderous formality without life or spirit, violent disorder and ugly conflict. I seek in vain free wholeness, unity" (KA, 1:256). Although hardly a specific, much less a political, analysis, this is an accurate transcription both of Schlegel's internal state and of his quite untheoretical feelings about the external conditions he knew at first hand—the rigidities not only of the Baroque classicism his father had attacked but also of the hierarchical, bureaucratic estate society that his father was part of, the petty-minded soullessness of the commercial life his father had initially tried to force on him despite Johann Adolph's own educational ideals and personal values of cultivation. Above all, Schlegel's words express the storm of internal rage and envy resulting from suppressed individuality and competitiveness, which he knew firsthand from his own psyche.

The logical conclusion of Schlegel's argument was a call to revolution, and this is precisely what he offered. It was not overtly a call for political revolution, and in this respect might be thought to sound like the parallel call issued by Schiller in his *Letters on the Aesthetic Education of Man*. "The moment seems indeed ripe," Schlegel wrote, "for an aesthetic revolution, through which the objective could become dominant in the aesthetic education of modern man" (KA, 1:269). In light of his views about the causal primacy of politics, this might seem like an anticlimax or a retreat, but such a conclusion would be a misunderstanding of Schlegel's personal relationship to the practice of radical politics. Political revolution was for him the counterpart in institutional life of the personal rebellion in which he overthrew paternal authority and became capable of action in the world. Fate and personal environment, however—or as Schlegel would have it, the distorting forces of modern life—had made him an intellectual rather than an activist. If the one-sided over-development of intellect at the expense of action had been his curse before his enlightenment (when action had to be suppressed because it would have been equivalent to attacking or destroying his father and brother), he could use his intellectualism after enlightenment to promote the cause of cultural revolution, thus realizing his personal ambition for greatness within the framework of a universal ideal of freedom.[46]

Fate had also made him a German, a serious disadvantage if liberation were simply equivalent to revolutionary action, because Germans were debarred from effective radical politics. However, through a philosophy of culture and of history derived in part from Herder and Kant but modified to suit his own purposes, Schlegel was able to turn his identity as a German as well as an intellectual to his advantage. He did not renege on the position that politics is the ultimate foundation of personality and hence of culture. If modern writing was deformed and impoverished, it was not because modern humunity was organically inferior to the ancients, but because it was politically inferior. "The rarity of genius [in the modern era] is not the fault of human nature but rather the fault of inadequate human art, of political bungling [*Pfuscherei*]" (KA, 1:360). However, there was no doubt in Schlegel's mind that the French Revolution was in the process of creating the modern equivalent of those Greek republican institutions that were the conditions of Greece's enormous cultural achievements—and hence of creating the prerequisites for a modern aesthetic revolution. It is true that Schlegel did not fully equate the spirit of modern republicanism with the concrete events of the French Revolution; as he wrote: "In the communication of knowledge, ethics and taste the French have been far superior to us for a long time. As a result of this they can reach a higher stage of perfection in civic poetry than other cultivated nations of Europe. One may wish to explain this unexpected phenomenon as the result of [France's] new political structure, which however can be nothing more than the fortunate outer stimulus that drives the force long present in quiet readiness to mature bloom" (KA, 1:361–62). But this statement was not a denigration of the importance of modern republicanism, only a comment on its contamination by less salutary French political ideals. If France was ahead in civic poetry, she was behind in the drama and other literary forms that demand absolute universality of cultivation and complete freedom from national limitations. This was because France's new political form simultaneously intensified the one-sidedness of her national character, exacerbated her nationalism, and isolated her from other nations. Here Germany had the advantage. "In Germany, and only in Germany, has aesthetics and the study of the Greeks reached a height that must have as its necessary result the complete renovation of poetry and taste" (KA, 1:364). Germany's political backwardness in the matter of national identity and unity gave her the advantage of cultural cosmopolitanism.

Why did the discipline of aesthetics matter so much for the total revolution Schlegel advocated? Precisely because it was an *intellectual* enterprise, and thus gave Schlegel a leadership role. The glories of Greek culture, Schlegel had insisted, even its more rational and self-conscious Athenian phase, were the fruit of natural cultivation. "This cultivation [*Bildung*] was none other than the first development of the most fortunate endowment [*Anlage*] whose universal and necessary kernel is grounded in human nature itself" (KA, 1:306). But natural development was the weakness as well as the strength of Greek culture. It was just as natural that Greek poetry declined in its later years from the most elevated peak to the deepest decadence because, as Schlegel put it, "Instinct

. . . which guided Greek cultivation is a mighty moving force but a blind leader. If a number of blind moving forces are released together, without their being unified by an overarching law, they will destroy themselves in the end. So also in free [i.e., natural] cultivation; even when it is law-directed there is something alien in it, because instinct is a composite of human nature and animal nature [*Thierheit*]. Since the latter comes into existence first and even causes the development of the former, it predominates in the earlier stages of cultivation. The animal nature prevailed in Greece in the case of the large mass of completely undeveloped male and female citizens of educated peoples . . . and while a group did mature and become independent, it was only a smaller ruling mass amidst a larger, governed one" (KA, 1: 316). Supplemented by slaves and barbarians, the coarser masses pulled Greek culture down because it was not self-consciously guided by rationally articulated principles. Only one thing could have saved it: "Only the guiding act of an intellect matured through varied experience could have given the development of cultivation a happier direction" (KA, 1:317).

But this intellect was precisely what was available to the modern, that is, to the intellectual, that is, to Schlegel himself. The modern had the virtue of his or her defects or, as Schlegel put it, "Our deficiencies are themselves the sources of our hopes."[47] The historical process that had freed the intellect to the detriment of the drives and passions had also given humanity the only tool capable of restoring the original balance. Greek culture had blossomed never to flower again, but reason made possible new aesthetic perfection that could reach even greater heights. For although it was true that the ideal of beauty—defined as harmony among the elements of multiplicity, unity, and universality—was timeless in its form, so that the most that modernity could do was repeat the formal accomplishments of Greek aesthetics, the constituents of experience that required harmonizing were capable of change and increase and hence beauty was capable of infinite progress and perfection. The analytic understanding of the rules of beauty made it possible for the creation of beauty to become for the first time a self-conscious program in a changing world. Thus what was needed for the aesthetic revolution Schlegel called for—which was equivalent to nothing less than a revolution in the modal personality of the culture—was aesthetic law-giving, and the only force that could furnish the necessary laws for the aesthetic education of modern man was theory, theory that by basing itself on the Greeks understood the law of beauty in its full universality untainted by the particularism of modern nationalism. The German aesthetic philosopher thus turns out to be the most radical and most genuine revolutionary, the veritable leader of the revolution that would create the new free individual. Schlegel's synthesis of Enlightenment ideas, neoclassical aesthetics, contemporary politics, and personal needs had produced a vision of individuality and universality that created a special role for him without impinging on the freedom of others, a role that indeed made his contribution a necessary condition for the individuality of others.

iii) The Politics of Cultural Revolution

Because Schlegel's essay was, in its practical intent, concerned with promoting an aesthetic revolution and contains no concrete political discussion, commentators have differed over whether his intended revolution entailed radical political change. Recent criticism recognizes and even emphasizes the general political context of Schlegel's literary classicism. But while the decisive impact of the French Revolution on Schlegel's early aesthetic writings is universally acknowledged, some critics insist that the result was a purely cultural program, not a political one, and argue that the ideals of the Revolution were sublimated into Schlegel's ideal of *Bildung*—aesthetic and spiritual liberation and cultivation.[48] Whatever the case after Schlegel's turn to Romanticism—and we have already seen how complicated its so-called apoliticism is—the assertion is not true for the years 1795–96.

Even in the *Studium*-essay, Schlegel explicitly insisted on the primacy of politics: "It is the destiny [*Bestimmung*] of political capacity [*Vermögen*] to unify the individual powers of the whole human spirit and the individuals of the whole species" (KA, 1:325). Schlegel's researches into the political history of classical antiquity proceeded simultaneously with his study of Greek literature, and though they were not published—a manuscript of 1795 titled *A Treatise on Ancient and Modern Republicanism* was lost—they seemed to be of greater interest to him than his literary studies. The structure of his argument dictated that an explanatory political analysis should follow his historically conceived classification of Greek literary genres, so that the plan for the larger project envisioned a volume on the history of Greek poetry to be followed by another on "the political revolutions of the Greeks and Romans" (KA, 23:304). But, as he wrote his brother in January 1796, complaining about the slowness of his work, "If I were finally working on the political material, how easily and pleasantly it would all go, and much more productively" (KA, 23:275). The letter also clearly indicates that Schlegel's interest in the history of ancient revolution was not purely scholarly but was explicitly linked to contemporary political commentary. In response to his brother's concern about the dangers of censorship he wrote: "There is, thank God, no danger in Greek politics. The rigor of scientific investigation alone makes it possible for me to hold back from even the remotest hint about current events. The obscurity of abstract metaphysics will protect me, and when one writes only for philosophers, one can be unbelievably bold and say much before the police take notice of it or even understand the boldness" (KA, 23:275). By May of 1796, his impatience and his desire for as much activism as his vocation as writer and his situation as German would allow reached their peak; he was willing to dare the censorship and go public: "I am heartily sick of [literary] criticism and I will work with unbelievable enthusiasm on the [history of] revolutions. At the same time I will write something popular on republicanism. I will be happy when I can wallow in politics. . . . I won't deny to you that republicanism lies a little closer to my heart than divine criticism and even than poetry, which is the most divine" (KA, 23:277–78). The fruit of this resolve, *Versuch über den Begriff des Republikanismus*,[49] published in 1796 and written in the philosophical idiom of Kant and Fichte, was hardly popular in any ordinary sense, but it was political theory, not history, and so was an undisguised staking out of position in the contemporary ideological wars. The essay took the form of a critique of Kant's *On Eternal Peace* and essentially taxed Kant with not being radical enough in the vision he put forward there of a world federation of free republics.

In Schlegel's view, Kant's republicanism was minimal, abstract, and contradictory. A republican constitution required that the members of a state be free and equal citizens, but Kant defined freedom as the right not to obey any law except that to which the individual *could* have consented, and he defined equality as equal subordination to the law. There were in Kant's theory no actual mechanisms of consent. Although Kant identified republicanism with representation in terms of constitutional principle, he thought of representation as an idea of reason that bound the ruling authority in its conception of its task, rather than an institutional practice of voting or legislative bodies. More central to Kant's definition of republicanism was the principle of the separation of the legislative from the executive functions of government, the ultimate protection against tyranny, but the important consequence he drew from the need for separation was the incompatibility of republicanism with democracy. Democracy necessarily resulted in despotism because it established an executive power based on the general will, that is, on universal consent, which in practice meant that the majority would act against individuals who did not consent. The general will would thus contradict itself and infringe on universal freedom. These contortions in Kant's political thought derived from his fundamental belief in the necessary split between the moral will and the natural or sensuous will, a split that inevitably produced the individual's asocial selfishness and thus in Kant's view necessitated the retention of an authoritarian, monarchical form of government.[50] A king might at least plausibly claim to be the servant of the general will; in a democracy it was impossible for the people as a whole to claim this because the desire of all to rule would pervert the expression of the general will.

Schlegel accused Kant of stopping short of the logical implications of his own principles. A more consistent concept of political freedom entailed the right of the people to obey no law that the whole of the people ideally could not have willed and that the majority of the people through their representatives had not *in fact* willed (KA, 7:13). Since the absolutely general will was a pure concept, an unreachable idea, a "fiction" was necessary to approximate it as closely as possible in reality. "The will of the majority shall count as a surrogate for the general will," Schlegel asserted. *"Republicanism is therefore necessarily democratic"* (KA, 7:17).[51] An even more far-reaching idea of freedom would be the position that Kant had rejected as a tautology: the right to do whatever one wishes as long as one does not commit injustice. The idea of such a right, difficult though it was to realize in practice, was not logically circular and therefore represented an ideal to be striven for: the right to be circumscribed by no external laws whatsoever, but only by the inner moral law. In short, Schlegel's regulative principle of republican freedom was political anarchy.

Just as radical was Schlegel's maximum program for equality. "The maximum would be absolute equality of citizens' rights and responsibilities which would put an end to all domination and dependence" (7:13). Kant's assumption that disagreement between the individual and the general will was inevitable was the sole root of his belief in the need for political domination, i.e., monarchy. That assumption, however, was in fact an empirical generalization from modern society, not a logical necessity, and it could not therefore be used to determine the pure theoretical form of the state. Schlegel's confidence on this point was based on history, on the advanced degree of freedom and equality once actually attained by the Athenian polis, in comparison to which modern political society was in its infancy (KA, 7:18). It was therefore not true in principle that the state had to be founded on relationships of superior to inferior. To find a social principle that could form the basis of a political association embodying the radical personal autonomy that Kant reserved to the moral sphere but denied in the political because of man's "unsocial sociability," Schlegel turned to Fichte's concept of ethical sociability. Following Fichte, Schlegel attributed to human beings a "capacity for communication [*Vermögen der Mitteilung*]," a capacity for social interdependency so fundamental to human development that it underlay the growth of all other human faculties. From this capacity he derived a political categorical imperative as the foundation of all legitimate political associations: "There shall be a community of humanity, or the 'I' shall be communicated" (KA, 7:17). Although this idea remained unspecified and vague in its concrete political implications for a future state (except as a justification of democratic equality), its concrete exemplar was once again Schlegel's beloved Athenian state, which, though lacking the advanced formal structures of modern republicanism, was far superior to modern states in the spontaneous affective communalism of its ethical life. As an ethical association the Greek polis was noncoercive, based not on law but on the internal acceptance by each of universal ethical principles, its spirit manifested in communal festivals and public art.

To appreciate Schlegel's political thought adequately is to understand both how *politically* radical it was and the extent to which it was rooted in a goal that was not for him essentially political. The goal was the ideal self conceived in dialectical relation to its pathological form, the modern personality generally and his own in particular. Subservient, torn by conflicting impulses and varied interests, consumed by concern for its own ego, the modern self wanted absolute freedom from external coercion, an inner harmony without the surrender of multiplicity, variety, and development, and an affective cooperative fellowship with others. Schlegel's maximum political ideals of freedom, equality, and ethical community were the projected realizations of those ideals of personality as well as the means to them.

Neither the radical nature of his political goals, their extrapolitical source, nor their rootedness in an idealized antiquity made Schlegel an unrealistic utopian or a pseudo-political thinker. He was well aware that regulative ideas of reason offered only approximations of unreachable goals, not practical possibilities. Under the influence of the actual historical events of the French Revolution and of his own needs, he maintained in 1796 a more optimistic view of what was historically possible that did Kant. That his ideal was set in the classical past did not mean that it was forever unattainable but precisely the opposite, that it was a real empirical possibility for the future; because it had already existed, it corresponded to real human capacities. That is why Schlegel made distinctions between maximal ideals and concretely realizable constitutional forms and criticized Kant for the remoteness and abstractness of his political thinking. Kant did not conceive of politics as a practical science whose purpose was to realize the political imperative; he was only concerned with the theoretical possibility of the perfect constitution. Schlegel, on the other hand, was concerned with the realizability of this constitution and this demanded a study of political history, both ancient and contemporary. "One can reach a satisfactory *conclusion about the relationship between political reason* [i.e., ideals] *and political experience* [i.e., what is real or realizable] only from the historical principles of political education [*Bildung*], from the theory of political history" (KA, 7:24). History, in other words, furnished the material from which a theory could be derived to guide legitimate practical aspirations. In a provocative ending to the essay, Schlegel raised the question of whether a republican constitution could allow a right of revolution and concluded that "A revolution whose motive is the destruction of the constitution [i.e., an existing despotism or usurpation] whose regime is purely provisional, and whose purpose is the organization of a republic, is . . . lawful" (KA, 7:25).[52]

In the middle of 1796, when this essay appeared, Schlegel was a radical political intellectual. That is not to say that he was a political activist in an organizational or insurrectionary sense. He had already defined the nature of his own activity in the *Studium*-essay in keeping with his interests and abilities. He was an idea man. His job was to furnish the cultural and political theory for the political praxis of others. But there is no question that for him, aesthetics and politics were one and that he was interested in promoting practical political results. "Kant," he wrote in his notebooks, "mistakenly confused the *ethical maximum* (the holy will and the Kingdom of God in his sense) with the *practical*, out of a lack of political and aesthetic sense. The formal object of ethical action is not the ethical but the practical maximum" (KA, 18:20, 24).

The admiring, and under the political circumstances provocative, appreciation of Georg Forster that Schlegel wrote during this period was in fact a description of how he conceived his own character and role as a political intellectual.[53] Forster, the friend of Caroline Böhmer, famous throughout Germany before the Revolution as a naturalist, world-traveler, and writer, notorious after it for his revolutionary partisanship and republican activism in Mainz, had died in Paris in 1794, impoverished, alone, and reviled by Germany's most powerful literary figures, including Goethe and Schiller. Schlegel's *Charakteristik*, a new genre form, tried to develop a category that would capture the unifying theme and purpose of the whole body of Forster's work as well as the organic connection between his work and his life. In keeping with his own current cultural ideals, he praised Forster as a "classical" writer, one who pursued an ethical life yet not at the cost of the simultaneous pursuit of individual greatness, which Forster had valued despite his awareness of its inevitable excesses. His work itself, moreover, aimed at the twin classical virtues of inclusiveness and inner unity: "To finally reunite into an indivisible whole all the fields of knowledge, which, though essentially interconnected are at present separate and fragmented, seemed to him the most sublime goal of the researcher" (KA, 2:99). Conceding that there were contradictions in Forster's work, Schlegel argued their virtues: the contradictions were the very evidence of Forster's love of truth and his many-sidedness. In any case, that many-sidedness did not preclude Forster's holding unchanging principles: a belief in the unshakeable necessity of the laws of nature and in the indestructible capacity for human perfectibility. These beliefs were not by chance the very poles of contemporary "higher political criticism": there was thus a fundamental harmony between Forster's literary and his political work.

If Forster's writing was classical in form, its public significance lay in its social intent. Schlegel described Forster as a "universal educator," a consciously cosmopolitan and "social" writer who worked to realize the egalitarian ideals his own work represented by popularizing for a wide audience contemporary specialized knowledge. As the mediator of higher cultivation to broad social circles, he wrote not only to develop himself but to "stimulate, to cultivate, and to reunite all the essential powers of mankind." This was from Schlegel's point of view the highest form of political activity. He did not omit Forster's concrete political views and indeed obliquely defended them. He wrote for example that Forster never excused the violence of the Revolution though he believed that too much blame for what had gone wrong had been assigned to the revolutionaries rather than to their circumstances—a view one may assume Schlegel shared. But he clearly viewed Forster's historical activities as means to his broader spiritual ends.

No doubt, in downplaying Forster's concrete political activity, Schlegel was to an extent recreating him in his own image. Schlegel had chosen a different form of political activity for himself. But there should be no mistake about its explicit political content and aim. The point needs to be stressed because the mystery of Schlegel's sudden abandonment of revolutionary partisanship a short while later has led some of the most sophisticated Schlegel interpreters, in an effort to explain it, to downplay the political specificity of Schlegel's original program. "The revolution itself," writes Claus Behrens, "was understood by Schlegel and his contemporaries not so much as political event as rather above all an arbitrary act of historical discontinuity or as the outbreak of a 'new time' whose content and goal is not yet determined."[54] And while he acknowledges that it is virtually impossible to separate aesthetic and political culture in Schlegel's neo-classicism, the emphasis is on the word "culture": "What links the French Revolution and the cult of antiquity together is the humanistic aspect of a renewal of human culture, both as regards the cultivation of the individual in community with others and the relationships of states to one another and the possibility of "eternal peace."[55] But this approach is essentially a short cut around a difficult problem. It is not possible to soften Schlegel's transition to the more apparently symbolic politics of early Romanticism by downplaying the hard reality of his politics in the preceding phase.[56] The puzzle must be solved in another way.

iv) Radical Autonomy

Schlegel's first step away from his classical aesthetic and republican positions—though at the time he did not and could not see it as such—was taken with the intensive study of Fichte that he began when he moved to

Jena in the summer of 1796. The excitement of Fichte's early major philosophical work, *The Foundation of the Entire Theory of Knowledge*,[57] was
that it promised a more radical version of human freedom than Kant's
philosophy. For Kant, unconditional human freedom lay in the moral law
alone, because only the moral will could legislate imperatives for the self
undetermined by any external conditions. For the rest of its activity,
however, the self was subject to the physical, natural world, including the
world of its own natural impulses. Although the mind supplied necessary
forms and categories for the organization of sensory experience, knowing
and desiring or knowledge and interest were nonetheless causally determined by the external forces of nature. Moreover, since what was given
in actual experience was only what had already been organized by the
categories of the understanding, the mind had no direct access to the
causal external world, the notorious thing-in-itself or noumenal world. It
was thus doubly at the mercy of the external world. The thing-in-itself,
unknowable by the mind yet in its ineluctable thereness the absolute
limitation or constraint on human knowing and doing, was the unsurpass-
able limit of human freedom.

Fichte's great breakthrough, as not only he himself but the whole first
generation of Romantics saw it, was to expand the scope of human freedom by getting rid of the pure externality, and hence sheer coercive
force, of the thing-in-itself. For, as Fichte argued, the "thing-in-itself"
was itself a concept, that is, a human construct. It was the mind that
conceptualized the objective world as objective, as world without subjective admixture. In this sense, strictly speaking, there was no such thing
for the mind as a world without mind; thinking the world was already
classifying or conceptualizing it. That was not to say that the world was
not real in the usual common-sense understanding of the word. But since
the world was always given to consciousness only in terms of meaning, it
literally made no sense to talk about something that was not conceptual-
izable; any such talk involved conceptualization. All address to the world
was a "positing," a picking out, or a defining, of something as something.

In ordinary experience the self was not aware of doing any such thing.
It was aware of its objects but it did not catch itself in the act of positing
them. Nevertheless, Fichte argued, philosophical deduction showed the
necessity of just such a conclusion. If there was a consciousness of something, it must be the case that the self had picked it out and addressed
itself to it as that thing. And if that were the case, then there was something even prior to positing the world. In positing the world (i.e., in
saying "A is A", or "I address myself to that as A"), the self was positing
itself; the self was aware of itself as that which picks out a certain portion
of reality or addresses it in terms of certain of its qualities ("I am I"). "The
self posits itself (*Theory of Knowledge*, 97)" was Fichte's first principle. It

was, he acknowledged, not provable, that is, not demonstrable through observation, because it was not a datum of consciousness. In the Kantian sense, however, it was a deduction, the logically necessary condition of consciousness as we experience it, and hence a philosophically tenable position. Moreover, it was from the standpoint of freedom an extraordinarily powerful one. For nothing caused or forced the self to posit itself. It was a free act of the self that recognized/defined the self in terms of its free activity in positing the world. Self-positing was an unconditionally or absolutely free act. "That whose being or essence consists simply in the fact that it posits itself as existing, is the self as *absolute* subject" (*Theory of Knowledge*, 93).

Schlegel was fascinated by, and ambivalent about, the brutal way Fichte cut through to his fundamental principle without proof. In his earliest notes on Fichte's philosophy, he called it a mysticism, and wrote, half-deprecatingly, half-admiringly, "If one has permission to arbitrarily posit something unconditional, there is nothing easier than explaining everything . . . the mystic is really *Pope* in his domain, and has the infallible power, to open and close heaven and hell with his key" (KA, 18:3, 2). Nevertheless, precisely because of that power, Schlegel acknowledged, "It is really the mystics from whom we must now learn philosophy" (KA, 18:5, 11). "If one postulates knowledge [*Wissenschaft*] and looks only to the condition of its possibility, one winds up in mysticism, and the most consistent, from this standpoint the only possible solution of the task is—the *positing of an absolute I*" (KA, 18:7, 32).

It was not simply by lifting the constraints of the thing-in-itself that Fichte's philosophy expanded the idea of freedom for Schlegel. In positing itself, Fichte pointed out, the self made a fundamental distinction between self and not-self; it posited not-self along with the self. That it chose to address reality in terms of this disjunction did not mean that the self "created" the external world. It meant that it was important to the self that such a distinction between self and not-self could exist to be made. "[T]he not-self," he wrote, "has reality for the self only to the extent that the self is affected" (*Theory of Knowledge*, 136). To conceptualize the world as not-self, in other words, meant that *that* aspect of reality, its alien or oppositional character to the self, *mattered* to us. The self experienced it affectively, in frustration or challenge, as a limitation on its ability to master the world, make it its own. The self's relationship to the world, then, was not primarily one of passive knowing but of active appropriation, what Fichte called activity or striving. The goal of that striving was total self-determination. Positing the world as not-self meant defining it as a field for the striving of the self.[58] Fichte argued that reason was at base practical, that is to say, aimed at activity, making the world subject to human ends and intentions; it only became theoretical in the application of its laws to a not-self that restricted it (*Theory of Knowledge*, 123).

Fichte's denial of the thing-in-itself clearly did not mean a denial of the limitations of the self. On the contrary, limitation was definitional of the self. If the self were completely unlimited, totally self-determined, it would not posit—that is, delimit and define—anything. It was active precisely because it was limited by an external reality that it reached out to transform into meaning. Furthermore, every action was also a limitation because by its very nature an action excluded the possibility of another action; positing as action both encountered checks and set boundaries.

Limitation then was both the condition and the consequence of striving. It was also the condition of philosophical reflection, or self-awareness, an act that opened up a new level of freedom. It was the awareness of a check on its striving that opened up the possibility for the self to take cognizance of striving. To be sure, self-awareness initially involved an awareness of limitation, a particular, bounded approach to the world. "[I]ts outward, striving activity was, as it were, thrown back (or reflected) into itself, from which the self-limitation . . . would then very naturally follow" (*Theory of Knowledge*, 191). But by the same token, the awareness of the limited nature of the outwardly reaching activity, the experience of check or boundary, pointed precisely to the fact that the striving was for absolute, unbounded freedom. Why else would the self experience, be conscious of, check, boundary or limitation? "This is possible only if the activity . . . in and by itself . . . reaches out into the unbounded, the indeterminate and the indeterminable, that is, into the infinite" (*Theory of Knowledge*, 191). "The activity of the self consists in unbounded self-assertion; to this there occurs a resistance . . . then it must posit itself to that extent as not positing itself . . . if it has to do that, it must be infinite" (*Theory of Knowledge*, 192).

Reflection on the preconditions of ordinary experience yielded to Fichte a concept of self that experienced itself as finite and limited not simply because it was so but because it had infinite aspirations and infinite capacity. Although it had to define the world in concrete and delimited ways, the self chose, as it were, where to draw its lines and boundaries and could choose to draw them in different places, including more or less, stopping there rather than here. "The self is finite," Fichte wrote, "because it is to be subjected to limits; but it is infinite within this finitude because the boundary can be posited ever farther out, to infinity. Thus it is not confined by this absolute positing of an object, save insofar as it absolutely and ungroundedly confines itself" (*Theory of Knowledge*, 228). It was this combination of concrete finite activity and infinite potentiality and aspiration that made up the being of the self. Its infinity was not something that it could realize in an activity but was the ground of its activity, the point of its striving. It could extend itself continuously toward infinity, but given its nature (as revealed in its experience), could never reach it, for then it would no longer be a human consciousness, but something like eternal, self-creating presence: "The self is infinite, but merely in respect to its striving; it strives to be infinite. But the very concept of striving already involves finitude, for that to which there is no counterstriving [i.e., the resistance of the not-self] is not a striving at all. If the self did more than strive, if it had an infinite causality, it would not be a self. . . . But if it did not endlessly strive in this fashion . . . it could oppose nothing to itself; again it would be no self" (*Theory of Knowledge*, 238). This was the ultimate paradox of the self, that it strove to reach a goal that its very nature as finitude, the characteristic that made it want to strive, made unreachable. "We are obliged," Fichte wrote, "to resolve this contradiction; though we cannot even think it possible of solution, and foresee in no moment of an existence prolonged to all eternity will we ever be able to consider it possible. But this is just the mark in us that we are destined to eternity" (*Theory of Knowledge*, 238). And though Fichte had pronounced the task that the self sets itself as unsolvable, he sketched out a poignant, if abstract, description of the kinds of efforts the self makes to solve it that amounted to a definition of the self, a description whose tone was not as pessimistic as the previous passages would have made appropriate: "The interplay of the self in and with itself, whereby it posits itself at once as finite and infinite—an interplay that consists, as it were, in self-conflict, and is self-reproducing, in that the self endeavors to unite the irreconcilable, now attempting to receive the infinite in the form of the finite, now, baffled, positing it again outside the latter, and in that very moment seeking once more to entertain it under the form of finitude—that is the power of the *imagination*" (*Theory of Knowledge*, 193).

Both what Schlegel took from Fichte at this point and what he criticized reveal much about his development. Generally Schlegel scholars have treated the fragments of the *Philosophical Notebooks* from 1796–98 as a more or less homogeneous mass and have not sufficiently discriminated between the stages of Schlegel's assimilation and transformation of Fichte's thought. When Schlegel moved to Berlin in the summer of 1797, however, not only his thinking on aesthetics but his thinking about philosophy changed, and the change can be documented by a careful distinction between those fragments written in Jena and those written after his arrival in Berlin.

Schlegel's brief summary of the essence of Fichte's philosophy in his review of Niethammer's philosophical journal of 1797 shows at least what he found significant in it: "The sole beginning and the whole basis of the *Wissenschaftslehre* is an *action* [*Handlung*]: the totalizing of reflective abstraction, a construction of the self founded on observation, the free inner immediate perception [*Anschauung*] of selfhood [*Ichheit*], of the positing of the self, of the identity of subject and object. The whole philosophy is nothing but an analysis of the one action understood as a movement and portrayed dynamically [*in ihrer Tätigkeit*]. Whoever is not able to deal with this free action is excluded from the sphere of the *Wissenschaftslehre*" (KA, 18:28). The somewhat defensive belligerence of the last sentence was a sign of Schlegel's own problems with Fichte's work. Fichte's philosophy legitimized his quest for an understanding and construction of his own self and both systematized and deepened his understanding of what went into such tasks. Self-reflection and self-construction were grounded in the very being of selfhood; for humankind, to be was to be self-conscious. Self-consciousness revealed, and was an enactment of, the unfettered freedom of the self to determine itself. For while there were givens in the world, the self was not equivalent to any one of its particular engagements with reality. In its awareness of the limits of any concrete positing of world and self, the self could separate itself from the act and realize its own infinite potential. Here was a major step beyond what Kant's philosophy made feasible, though it was very much in keeping with the spirit of Schlegel's own drive for complete freedom and greatness and gave him for the first time a language to articulate its general principles. Kant's freedom was negative and regulative: freedom from the coercion of nature in the ability to will the selfless universal law, though not to enact and live the law consistently because in its desires and passions the self was otherwise unfree. Fichte's freedom meant a vision of the infinity of the self both as the ground of all human action and as the summation of all human striving. And finally, reflection yielded a picture of the positing self as the unifying center of all the apparently discrete and separate forms of human action and all the objects of apparently distinct fields of knowledge.

Given Schlegel's earlier ideas and ideals, however, Fichte's philosophy was not usable in its original form without correctives. Fichte was content to deduce first principles in a purely abstract way; Schlegel wanted at least an image of the actual realization of the goals implicit in those principles—freedom, fullness, and unity. He made the same criticisms of Fichte on this score that he had made of Kant. Fichte was not interested in the concrete and the historical (KA, 18:8, 48, 50, 52) and in focusing exclusively on the subjective conditions of experience, he paid no attention to the real objects or content of experience. "As between *representation* and *object*, one must be the center and the other the horizon, or both mutually and reciprocally make one another possible, necessary and real.—This would be beyond Fichte" (KA, 18:66, 460). A more complete philosophy, a genuinely "critical" philosophy that would supplement

Fichte the way Fichte supplemented Kant would raise the question of the progressive realization of the infinite self over time and in the concrete results of human activities.

What Schlegel was suggesting, however, was not simply a supplementation of Fichte but a subtle though radical subversion of him. Fichte had written of the infinity of the self as something that subsisted only implicitly in its striving and was an unrealizable paradox. In calling for the translation of the striving into a conscious goal of action in history, Schlegel expressly suggested the possibility of a concrete totality of knowing and hence of being. "If there is a ⟨genuine⟩ critical philosophy, there must also be a genuine method and a genuine system, which are inseparable from one another. System is a thoroughly articulated totality of scientific material in thoroughgoing reciprocal interaction and organic connection.—Totality is a unified multiplicity which is complete in itself" (KA, 18:12, 84). Schlegel's goal was now nothing less than a unified field theory of human knowledge, in which every sphere of human endeavor would be connected with every other by necessary principles that would still allow for the independence of each. This was another expression of the classical ideal of harmony celebrated in the *Studium*-essay but applied to modernity with the added ideal of achieving totality, not only in the sense of an integration of conflicting elements but of an infinity of elements. "In every false philosophy *limitation* and *fixation* arise only out of inability, stubbornness, exhaustion, the gratification of one's wishes, powerlessness etc. to raise oneself to the unconditioned" (KA, 18:521, 24). "The essence of philosophy," he insisted, "is to be sought in the totality of knowing [*Allheit des Wissens*]. In that goal there is implied already a rejection of all arbitrary positing (which is opposed to knowing) and all contradictions (which oppose the idea of unity and therefore also of totality)" (KA, 18:13, 101). This last point is especially noteworthy in light of the high value Schlegel was very soon to put on contradiction. For Schlegel, the demand for infinity did not mean a surrender of the desire for complete reconciliation of conflicting goals and desires. Given the personal roots of that need, it is not surprising that Schlegel not only persisted in, but re-emphasized the demand for, inner consistency. Fichte's philosophy had very much raised the ante for the self. Reconciling the opposites of instinct and morality, tenderness and aggressiveness was one thing, and difficult enough; admitting an ideal of infinite expansion of human selfhood raised new possibilities of chaos and excess. "In the highest sense, the [Biblical verse] God created man in his image is the true beginning of history and philosophy, [whose purpose is] to copy this image" (KA, 18:518, 10). And Schlegel left no doubt in his notes that he had in mind not only an ideal of knowledge but a personality ideal when he talked about an all-encompassing system. "When an original thinker

[*Original*] can only *make* systems, without himself *being* one; that is only *talent*" (KA, 18:67, 465).

Schlegel fought shy, however, of this most extreme implication of the idea of totality—the individual as God. On the contrary, a number of the notes of this period criticize the apparently radically individualistic implications of Fichte's thought or the possibility of reading radical individuation into it.[59] The level of abstraction at which the *Wissenschaftslehre* operated made it unclear to contemporaries just what the status of the Fichtean absolute "I" actually was—whether, for example, it was one of an indefinite number of human or finite egos, metaphorically preparing a range of self-consciousness that is "for it" or whether it was a solipsistic ego producing a world that is "for it" but incommunicable to any other.[60] Whatever Fichte himself intended, Schlegel warned that "The *Wissenschaftslehre* must be everywhere very rigorously purified of empirical egotism" (KA, 18:508, 34), and he cited approvingly a remark of Schelling's that it was pure empirical egotism to say of the absolute self "*my* self." Although in one sense Schlegel was correct about the non-empirical nature of Fichte's "absolute I," he was distorting the thrust of Fichte's thought in trying to sever the connection between it and the empirical individual ego. His own concern, however, was with the dangers and the absurdity inherent in the grandiosity of the claim he was making if it was about individuals. "Humanity [*der Mensch*] is omnipotent and omniscient and all-benevolent; but the person in the singular is only so piece-meal, *not wholly*. The individual can never be wholly so" (KA, 18:506, 2). Our knowledge of the world, Schlegel insisted, was not just the result of our own personal experience but of knowledge transmitted to us by other human beings as reliable witnesses. "The positing of a totality of 'I's happens a priori (and belongs in the *Wissenschaftslehere*)," Schlegel claimed (KA, 18:508, 31). In keeping with this assertion, his own ur-definition of philosophy had to be somewhat modified. "To philosophize means to seek totality of knowledge [*Allwissenheit*] *communally*" (KA, 18:515, 97). The dangers of the unbridled egotism that he believed inherent in the Fichtean system also caused Schlegel to reaffirm his classicism all the more strongly. "Classical antiquity is one of the branches of knowledge which fascinates the mystic. For *harmony* is the essence of classical antiquity. *Winckelmann-Hemsterhuis. Love, marriage* suchlike through absolute unity, annihilation of the personality. Similarly art and its theory, whose essence is also harmony" (KA, 18:47, 8).

Communality, however, did not mean for Schlegel eradication of individual ambition or the elimination of competition. There was in fact a continuing tension between the ideal of god-like self-expansion and the notion that totality could only mean the totalizing of the knowledge and power of humanity at large.

From the [concept of] the totality of knowing, for which the philosopher strives, it follows of itself that no more than one system is possible.—One cannot even imagine the case, therefore, that the philosopher could refute all genuine opponents, or all the attacks which were at least possible within his system, and that nonetheless there could still be another system, which did not impinge on his and which perhaps had rights equal to his or was an even better system. If the philosopher had really refuted all real and possible attacks, his system is the true one. Every different opinion in philosophy is an opposed one. (Brotherhood or death!) The *refutation of all others and complete internal connectedness* are the authentic criteria of the system. (KA, 18:520, 21)

This passage describes an intellectual ideal that at the same time says much about the nature of Schlegel's ambitions, his internal conflicts, and his relationships with the great contemporary figures of German criticism and philosophy. His insistence that the quest for a total system could only be a communal venture was not only an acknowledgment of the finite nature of the individual but a reaction against his desire to be the sole author of that system through the systematic reduction of all possible competitors. For that is precisely how he saw his intellectual co-workers—as engaged not in a cooperative but in a competitive enterprise. In a number of entries he characterized the goal of philosophical striving as "polemical totality"—a totality arrived at through combat. In one of those entries he tried to deduce totality out of what he called "the assumption of communicability" (KA, 18:515, 98), but this was at best a partial truth and at worst an evasion, since communicability did not necessarily entail war to the death. Just a few lines later, Schlegel implicitly acknowledged this in the same words he was to repeat later in the same notebook, in the longer note cited previously, a repetition indicating the compulsive pressure of the thought: "Every *different* opinion in philosophy is an *opposed* one. Therefore *polemical totality* [is] a necessary condition of [philosophical method] and a criterion of the system" (KA, 18:515, 101).

Schlegel's drive for personal preeminence and his competitiveness were of course not new. His new conceptual formulations, however, not only served to legitimate these drives but, reacting on them in turn, raised them to a higher level of claim. The ideal of "polemical totality" gave him an ideological platform from which to challenge the other claimants to predominance in German thought and letters, Kant, Fichte, and Schiller; only Goethe was, at this point, largely beyond challenge. The choice and the exclusion of objects repeated a pattern of the past, though on the new level much more was at stake for Schlegel both publicly and privately. In relation to Goethe and Kant, the generation of the "fathers," Fichte and Schiller represented a generation of older brothers. Kant had already been more or less successfully challenged by Fichte, who was widely regarded as his legitimate philosophical heir; there was no real danger in attacking him. Goethe was—as yet—untouchable. But in the cases of Schiller and Fichte, Schlegel could see older contemporaries, men who had made seminal contributions in the fields Schlegel wanted to claim as his own, men whose work had either significantly formed or inspired his own, or was threateningly similar in its inspiration. His attitude to them was an ambivalent mix of admiration, love, identification, envy, and devaluation. Because his thought had been so influenced by theirs, he had, in order to assert his supremacy, either to underestimate their work or to surpass it, both hostile acts. He variously tried both.

Schlegel's initial reaction on meeting Fichte in person when he came to Jena oscillated between inhibiting reverence and contemptuous dismissal. He was so intimidated the first time he was invited to Fichte's that he could hardly approach him and spoke only about "indifferent matters" when he did.[61] Yet when he heard Fichte lecture publicly, he described him as "remarkably trivial" and as weak and out of his element [fremd] in every discipline that had a concrete subject matter.[62] As he grew to like Fichte personally and found himself well received, a friendship developed between the two, but in reaction Schlegel claimed to be distancing himself from Fichte's philosophy. By the end of January 1797, he wrote that he had decisively separated himself from Fichte as author of the *Wissenschaftslehre*, now spoke with him only about peripheral work, and would not show him his own writings.[63] Some months later, while claiming his ever-growing affection for Fichte, he expressed regret that he couldn't show him "all the rubbish of my notebooks. Oh, that one has to be so worldly wise!—He wouldn't understand it anyway."[64] Despite his earlier assertion, Schlegel was far from through with Fichte's philosophy—in another letter to Novalis he equated philosophizing with "Fichteanizing"[65]—but he was obviously uncomfortable acknowledging to Fichte either his indebtedness or his criticism. His words give him away: "Oh, if only I could be quite openly against him! But at least I am never dishonest with him, and I never could be."[66] Fichte was the angel Schlegel felt he had to wrestle, and to get his philosophical blessing, he had to defeat him and replace him, at least internally.

The conflict with Schiller was older, more intense, and more out in the open. It is no accident that it reached a climax precisely during this period and became so fierce that it forced Schlegel to leave Jena for Berlin. The two men had first met when Schlegel was a student in Leipzig, in an inauspicious encounter that left its scars. But the reasons for Schlegel's ambivalence went much deeper than personal injury. Not content with being one of Germany's foremost dramatists and poets, Schiller had preceded Schlegel into the field of literary theory, with the specific task that

Schlegel had taken on as his own—the development of a new aesthetics, based on Kant and the classics, adequate to the problems of modernity. The *Studium*-essay in fact presented a program that implicitly challenged Schiller's *Letters On the Aesthetic Education of Man*, published while Schlegel was still writing the essay. Schiller's aim was to circumvent revolution by spiritualizing and internalizing it; Schlegel's program, as we have seen, depended on political revolution.[67] In turn, Schiller's *On Naive and Sentimental Poetry*, which Schlegel had read only after completing his own essay, challenged its conclusion by making a powerful defense of modern literature against classical.[68] Commenting on Schlegel's love-hate for Schiller, Ernst Behler notes: "The more Schlegel was fascinated by Schiller's brilliant arguments, the more passionately he fought for his spiritual independence, the more sharply he emphasized what despite everything separated him from Schiller."[69] During this first Jena period, however, the battle went beyond independence; Schlegel believed he had at least the beginnings of ideas that would enable him to surpass Schiller.

The last phase of the conflict was triggered by Schlegel's review of Schiller's contributions to his own periodical, the *Müsenalmanach für 1796*, which was written even before Schlegel came to Jena. What followed was not wholly Schlegel's doing. His criticisms were not without justification, and Schiller was sensitive. But Schlegel's points of attack and choice of language were not simply fair critical comment, and only willed naiveté about his own intentions could have blinded him to the likely effects of his remarks. Willed naiveté and identification—because Schlegel saw himself, or at least his own ideals, in Schiller, something that made it all the more necessary to cut him down and all the more difficult to recognize what he was doing. "Schiller's lack of completeness," he wrote, "springs in part from the infinitude of his goal. It is impossible for him to limit himself and approach a finite goal undistractedly. His restlessly fighting spirit pushes ever onward with what I would almost want to call sublime immoderation. He can't complete anything, but even in his aberrations he is great" (KA, 2:7). In remarks before and after this assessment, he suggested that one of Schiller's poems would benefit if it were translated into prose and read backwards by paragraphs, that Schiller's imaginative power suffered from incurable poor health, and that he was inferior to Goethe as a poet—comparisons were important to Schlegel. Small wonder that Schiller did not respond to Schlegel's letters or to a manuscript he submitted for publication in Schiller's periodical and that he came out with a series of biting epigrams against Schlegel. Schlegel reviewed the volume containing the epigrams with grace and restraint, but when Schiller finally rejected his manuscript with an unconvincing excuse, he retaliated, though indirectly. In a review of another of Schiller's periodicals, he attacked the historian K. L. von Woltmann, once a friend of Schlegel's but now a protégé of Schiller's, accusing him of plagiarizing Gibbon. Woltmann owed his academic position in Jena to Schiller and Goethe; the damning review forced him to give it up and leave the university and the town. Schlegel had his vicarious revenge, but at high cost; Goethe persuaded him that it would be better for him also to leave Jena in order to restore peace to the intellectual community. In late July of 1797, after a stopover in Weissenfels to visit with Novalis, Schlegel moved to Berlin. His doctrine of "polemical totality" had had unexpected, if not inappropriate, results. In a new set of circumstances, it was to have yet greater ones.

III) The Birth of Romanticism

The move to Berlin was decisive for Schlegel's development. Within a month of his arrival his ideas underwent an abrupt change. Even during the journey, in the notebook he kept as he traveled, Schlegel had reiterated his old position, defending classicism and attacking modern literature. But in the *Lyceum Fragments*, begun in the late summer of 1797 and published that fall, Schlegel suddenly turned against the fetishizing of classicism in general and against a number of its sacrosanct doctrines. "My essay on the study of Greek poetry is a mannered prose hymn to the objective quality of poetry," he wrote of the piece that had been intended as a revolutionary manifesto on behalf of a new classicism in an age of modern republicanism. "The worst thing about it, it seems to me, is the complete lack of necessary irony; and the best, the confident assumption that poetry is infinitely valuable—as if that were a settled thing" (*Lyceum*, 143, 7). The "necessary irony" was now supplied in the very terms of Schlegel's re-evaluation of the essay: its style, he acknowledged, contradicted its message. Subjective and passionate, the writing was the antithesis of the harmonious calm and detachment of the classical ideal of beauty that the essay advocated. This ironic assessment, however, was intended as a criticism not of the essay's style but of its uncompromising classicism. "All the classical poetry genres have now become ridiculous in their rigid purity," he proclaimed (*Lyceum*, 150, 60). And the repudiation of dogmatic classicism was just the negative side of Schlegel's reversal. The positive side was his favorable valuation of modern literature. Schiller had anticipated this attitude in his *On Naive and Sentimental Poetry*, published in 1794, and it is not surprising that Schlegel would express his new position in a competitive reckoning with Schiller. In one of the earliest unpublished fragments documenting the change, Schlegel wrote, "Only through absolute progressivity (striving for the infinite) does the sentimental become sentimentally and aesthetically interesting. Otherwise it is just psychologically, that is physically interesting or morally interesting as part of a worthy individuality" (*Notebooks*, 9, 2). The implication of this hit at Schiller's definition of the modern is that Schlegel's own was grounded in a more radical concept involving a deeper appreciation of the modern spirit. For Schiller, modern literature had to strive self-consciously to synthesize those aspects of humanity, particularly the sensuous and the moral, that classical literature had integrated "naively" or intuitively, because moderns, in developing their individuality, had become aware of the possibility of difference, separation, and conflict. Mere psychological or moral integration, however, was no longer an ambitious enough goal for Schlegel because it did not draw the full consequences from the modern idea of freedom. "Where one tries to form the constituent parts not just uniformly but with variety one is striving for wholeness, not just unity" (*Notebooks*, 46, 24). "As long as one seeks after *absolute* poetry or *absolute* philosophy or absolute criticism, one is never satisfied by any one work" (*Notebooks*, 35, 181). Schlegel did not hesitate to personalize his criticism of Schiller's ideal, in keeping with his own critical principle that the work was an expression of the man. "Schiller is a rhetorical sentimentalist full of polemical vehemence, but without independence, who for a long time stormed and raged but then clipped and cultivated himself, became a slave, and regressed" (*Notebooks*, 152, 33). The rebellious Schiller of the *Sturm und Drang* had retreated from the demands of liberation into a tamed neoclassicism; the judgment was an indirect affirmation of the extent of Schlegel's claims for the revolutionary and liberating force of his own new Romantic doctrine.

With such claims, however, Schlegel was not only finally surpassing Schiller but himself, finally accepting the most radical implications of his own reading of Fichte. He did not surrender his ideal of a collaborative or communal approach to totality—it was in fact only at this point that Schlegel publicly put forward the ideal he called *Symphilosophie*, or collective philosophizing. But in embracing modern literature as the correct aesthetic standard because of its progressivity and universality, he was also asserting the idea of infinite individuality. "[Romantic poetry] alone is infinite, just as it alone is free," run the celebrated words of *Athenaeum* fragment 116, "and it recognizes as its first commandment that the will of the poet can tolerate no law above itself" (*Athenaeum*, 175). The passage conflates the work's freedom with that of the poet. The sentence shifts from the lawlessness of aesthetic form to the lawlessness of the poet's will. Taken along with Schlegel's claims that there is no literary form so fit as Romantic poetry (specifically the novel) for expressing the entire spirit of an author and that the essence of Romantic poetry is that it is forever becoming, never perfected, tending therefore to infinity, it is clear that the poetic will was to Schlegel the symbolic expression of a general human will to infinity. Furthermore, in the very act of proclaiming the principle, Schlegel was exemplifying and enacting it by assuming the position of aesthetic legislator. Others would be needed to fulfill the program of totality—this was the point of *Symphilosophie*; he was the one who was establishing the agenda. The tension between "egotism" and solidarity in the Jena period persisted in Berlin, but the balance had been tipped in the direction of egotism. "The highest virtue," he wrote in a notebook entry in 1798, "[is] to promote one's own individuality as the final end. Divine egotism.—People would have a legitimate right to be egotists if only they know their own ego, which one can do only if one has one" (KA, 18:147, 134). The difference between "true" individuality and the merely "worthy" individuality for which he castigated Schiller was precisely the divinity of the egotism to which true individuality aspired, an egotism that was not mere narcissism because it transcended the particular self even while constituting it. Fichte's "absolute I" was the inescapable human structuring of the world of experience, a general principle. Nevertheless, Schlegel believed the transcendental ego was also and just as inescapably the foundation of the unique and concrete self. Whether or not Ficthe understood the absolute I as a psychological concept, something inhering in each individual, Schlegel came explicitly to understand it this way. In doing so, he—along with Novalis and Schleiermacher—created a new concept of individuality whose most striking, most paradoxical feature was precisely the linking together of finite and infinite self. The two were not conflated into one; rather, infinite free creativity, the constituting of a totalized world, was inherent in all particular human action in the world, though not necessarily self-consciously so; only an act of philosophical reflection revealed it. Art, because it was self-consciously concerned with form, the principle of totality, represented the ego fully conscious of its own driving principle. Suiting his own creative action to his principle, Schlegel did not content himself with merely proclaiming it. The most telling indication of the synthesis of the personal and the infinite was Schlegel's new readiness to challenge the reigning figure of German letters, Goethe himself, for ultimate supremacy in the world of critical theorizing.

What accounts for this extreme and sudden change in Schlegel's basic position? Both its timing and its content point to only one conclusion. Put simply, though only in preliminary terms, it was his falling in love with Dorothea Veit and simultaneously, if secondarily, his friendship with Friedrich Schleiermacher that precipitated Schlegel's intellectual revolution. He had met them both in the salons of Henrietta Herz and Rahel Levin at the end of August 1797. The mutual attraction between Friedrich Schlegel and Dorothea, though not without digressions on Schlegel's part, was both instantaneous and profound, producing a transformation simultaneously emotional and intellectual. And in Schleiermacher he found a soul-mate who not only could understand his ideas but validate, supplement, and stimulate them actively in a creative dialogue made possible by his own parallel yet independent development, an ideal partner for *Symphilosophie*. The inner coherence of all these elements in Schlegel's new intellectual turn is graphically evident in a letter that he wrote Novalis on September 26, 1797, containing the first reference to Dorothea, whom he had met almost exactly a month before. The letter was a response to one from Novalis that Schlegel felt had reopened their conversation on philosophy and poetry after a hiatus and made it possible for him to reveal himself intimately and passionately.

In [Fichte's] philosophy I always discover more. Now it has become at times a serious question for me whether he is too little an idealist or too little a realist? The less his philosophy satisfies me, the more I learn from it.—I have written much and I believe I have taken some big steps forward.

How remarkable I found your newly awakened love for poetry. I had just been in full flood for two days, as I was last winter in philosophy. Worlds upon worlds opened to me, and within three days I felt as if I had understood absolutely nothing about poetry before. You can imagine, since you know me, that I have thought up a whole host of projects, almost as many as in philosophy. . . . All of them are such that no contemporary, not even Goethe, could do them and yet I can prove, on the basis of ur-texts and philosophy, that they *must* come, whoever does them, whenever they are done. The ideas, however, will strike you specifically at first glance as sudden and they will quite please you.

My letters on [Wilhelm] Meister are turning into a book. . . .

. . . Can you not send me everything you have written on *Meister*, and do you give me enough credit for understanding and discretion to serve me in that way as a critical editor? . . . I have just sent a *critical Chamfortiade* a few pages long into the world [the *Lyceum Fragments*, whose fragment form was suggested, or legitimized, by the epigrammatic style of a recently published work of N.-S. Roch de Chamfort]. . . .

There is also *one* philosopher in Berlin; he is called Schleyermacher. He is a Reformed clergyman, and contributes much to my satisfaction here. He has sense and depth, and above all, a critical spirit; along with it almost enough feeling for mysticism. . . .

. . . Things are going very well for me. I feel much powerful life within me. It has also, thank God, come to the point of some explosions, in which I can release volcanic material. Do not be surprised at the (somewhat) dithyrambic tone of this letter. I am anticipating a pleasant tryst [*Notturno*] this coming night. (KA, 24:20–22)

Even if the last paragraph did not tie all the themes of the letter together and in some sense explain them, the significance of the juxtaposition of events in the letter is unmistakable. The critique of Fichte's inadequate ambitions, the breakthrough to a new view of poetry, the belief that his insight has made him superior to Goethe at least in regard to his vision of the necessary future of literature, the relationship with Schleiermacher, and the anticipated first night of sexual love with Dorothea are all facets of one event, one "volcanic" explosion. It was the love relationship with Dorothea that somehow created the context in which Schlegel could finally lay claim to the most extreme consequences of his developing philosophical position without falling into the extreme egoistic dangers it represented. Their mutual love furnished Schlegel with a new source and a new kind of unity. It replaced the static, timeless objectivity of classical rules and liberated an open-ended creativity within the shelter of the beloved, whose being was the guarantor of both wholeness and goodness. But how was that possible?

The shaping force of loving and being loved for the personality was not a new idea or experience for Schlegel. He had already felt its transformative and empowering capacities in his relationship with Caroline Böhmer. Their attachment, which, though stronger on his side was nonetheless genuine on hers, had enabled him to internalize her revolutionary politics as a legitimation of his desire for an independent identity and to generate his own cultural-political program, an amalgamation of the classical ideal of beauty with revolutionary republicanism. Through Caroline he had come to appreciate the full humanity and capacity of women, and because of her role in his political conversion, his interpretation of republicanism not only demanded women's absolute equality with men in the present but argued that ancient Greek civilization had flourished and decayed in direct proportion to the degree of equality it accorded women.[70] Although he continued to accept the traditional notion of characterological differences between the sexes, he now thought these less important than their common humanity; both masculinity and femininity ought to be subordinated to the higher ideal of a perfected humanity.[71] But the classical female figure Schlegel was most drawn to represented something more than an equal partner. Diotima, the friend and intellectual companion of Socrates in the *Symposium* had also been the one who by his own admission had taught him about love. Schlegel referred to Caroline as his own "independent Diotima" and wrote an essay attempting to prove that the historical Diotima was not, as conventionally accepted, a courtesan, but an independent intellectual, equal to the greatest men of her day.[72]

Caroline's relationship to his brother put rather strict limits on the kind of love Schlegel could exchange with, or even allow himself to feel for,

Caroline, limits most easily discerned in their displaced form in his work in literary history. In the essay on Diotima he emphasized that the love she taught Socrates was not physical but spiritual, love for the ideal of the perfected human being, the pure goodness of a completed soul. In this connection he cited a Platonic dialogue of the Dutch philosopher Hemsterhuis, *Simon*, which he praised for renewing the Socratic lesson of love in modern times. Hemsterhuis's Diotima teaches his Socrates that the highest virtue is based upon and manifested in an equilibrium of all the faculties, the same ideal of personal and aesthetic harmony that Schlegel advocated in the *Studium*-essay.

But Hemsterhuis's Platonism also involved some rather different ideas about love that Schlegel was not yet in a position to appropriate. In his *Letter on Desire* (1770), Hemsterhuis had asserted that the highest goal of human desire was the most intimate, perfect fusion of the soul with the object of its desire. The more homogeneous an object was with the soul's essence, the greater the desire for it and the greater the possibility of fusion. Since the soul was like God, simple in substance, and had a capacity for infinity insofar as it could conceive of it and long for it, God was the highest possible object of desire. Yet despite the apparent valuation of soul over body inherent in this argument, Hemsterhuis ranked the attractions of friendship lower than sexuality in the hierarchy of desire, because he believed sexual desire to be the most intense manifestation of the soul's striving to be physically united with its desired object. His claim of a mutual interaction between our sexual organs and our ideas made physicality part of physical-intellectual being and infused physical eroticism with conceptual content.[73] For Schlegel, torn as he had been by urgent sexual needs and the fear of their incompatibility with ethical behavior, Hemsterhuis's erotic Platonism could support the ideal of harmonizing sensuousness and morality. But both the conditions of his relationship with Caroline and his classicist concept of *Bildung* meant that his main concern about sexuality during his classical phase was not with the aspiration of the erotic towards the infinite but with its compatibility with ethical existence, which meant the effective subordination of sexuality to a spiritual idea of friendship between the sexes.[74]

It was only through the encounter with Fichte's ideas that Schlegel could begin to assimilate Hemsterhuis's deeper understanding of desire. Not coincidentally, that assimilation also enabled him to acknowledge more completely the full force of his own sexuality because he now had a compelling philosophical framework that gave it both meaning and legitimacy. As his ideal of self-cultivation moved beyond the idea of harmony to totality, he understood his desire for sexual union with a woman as a desire not only for the synchrony of body and spirit, sex and friendship, but precisely as a quest for totality. This awareness entailed both a different appreciation of the differences between men and women than he had had before and a shift in the weight he gave to sexuality. "Only in marriage," he wrote in his notebook on the way to Berlin, "can there be complete friendship. Only there can the connection to some extent constantly approach the absolute through sensuality, children, since woman is the absolute antithesis of man.—[I]nseparable being together, a kind of community of goods—cannot take place among men. . . . Though marriage can learn much from friendship. . . . Whoever has no sense for friendship is not capable of true marriage" (KA, 18:28, 111).[75] By marriage Schlegel did not mean a legal or sacramental status but the physical union it sanctified. To strive for totality rather than merely for harmony demanded something other than the subordination of sexual difference to common *Menschlichkeit* in order to make friendship possible between men and women; it demanded precisely that the differences be highlighted, that men and women indeed be conceived as complete opposites, so that their union would amount to totality. But difference did not at this point preclude equality. In keeping with his efforts in the Jena period to hold individual egotism in check, Schlegel insisted that men and women were equal in that each was only a half of the whole. Marriage was the symbol of a form of relationship that put sexual difference within common humanity in the foreground in order to realize totality.

The most telling document of the Jena period concerning Schlegel's views of love and male-female relationships is his impassioned, at times almost savage, review of Friedrich Jacobi's novel *Woldemar*.[76] It brought together themes from his classicist and Fichtean phases whose inconsistency with one another was masked only by their common antipathy to Jacobi's views of women and sensuality. The merit of Jacobi's novel, Schlegel acknowledged, was that it was animated by the most delicate official sensibility and by an inward striving for the infinite (KA, 2:57). But it ended with an unresolved dissonance, which made it impossible for the hero to raise himself to the dignity of a truly free man (KA, 2:61). Jacobi did not overcome the "real original sin" of modern *Bildung*, the complete splitting and isolation of human powers that can only remain healthy when freely united (KA, 2:58). His hero, Woldemar, lives with two women—Allwine, his lover, and Henriette, a friend with whom his connection is supposedly on the highest spiritual level. Their friendship is ostensibly more complete as a relationship of opposite genders than a male friendship could be and allows for more complete self-development because in it, aggressive male intellectuality is complemented by woman's more altruistic ethical nature. But this functional division of labor, which ostensibly enables Woldemar to have everything, sexual and spiritual fulfillment as well as absolute freedom, rests on his exploitation and stunting of both women, and so undermines the possibility of his own wholeness. Woldemar claims to possess Allwine completely without her possessing him in return, because neither her sensuality nor his desire for her encompasses his whole spirit. As for Henriette, Jacobi deprives her of her sexuality, since pure friendship is a selfless communion of equals who do not use one another for personal gratification. But aside from his hypocrisy in allowing Woldemar to fulfill the sexual dimension of his personality with someone else, he has made Henriette too stereotypically feminine even for his own ideal of friendship. She is "too much woman and girl," too immersed in passive loving. A genuine friendship between a man and a woman is possible, Schlegel insisted, but the man must be less sensual and vain, more master of himself than Woldemar is, and the woman more able to love ideas actively, less desirous of living so completely in her beloved and her children than is the domestically inclined Henriette. Jacobi's feminine representation of Henriette looks much more like prudery than spirituality, since, as Schlegel acidly pointed out, Jacobi's allegedly rare idea of friendship as depicted in her relationship to Woldemar is all too often realized in ordinary marriages: the most intimate sexual unity at the cost of the woman's independence (KA, 2:65). Jacobi had made Henriette characterologically fit only for a traditional marriage and then deprived her of the sexuality that might make a traditional man want to marry her. The resulting portrait of Woldemar is of a "repulsive egotist," for whom everyone else in the world would seem to be there only for his sake (KA, 2:66), an egotist who precisely because of his need for dominance, fails in his desire for wholeness.

This aspect of the critique focused on the internal contradictions of the novel with regard to the ideal of wholeness of character, the impossibility of coherently depicting the harmonious integration of personality when sexuality is still seen as something negative to be segregated, and woman's intellectual independence as a threat that must be suppressed through nonrecognition. But Schlegel also talked about Jacobi's approach to the infinite by linking his views of gender, sexuality, and friendship to his literary style, his philosophy, and the personality they revealed. The real unity of the novel, Schlegel argued, was neither aesthetic nor philosophical, but personal; its supposed depiction of "humanity" was actually nothing but Jacobi's self-portrait. Jacobi's starting point was what Schlegel called subjective need rather than an intellectual grasp of the objective requirements of human fulfillment. His prose style was "genial" to the extent that it derived from a dialogue with many different thinkers— "For what else is genius but the legally free inward community of several talents"—but the real guiding force of the novel was the inner light of Pietist subjectivity, the authority of pure inward feeling: "obviously his inner constitution is not genuinely republican; that is why he is only genial but not a genius. The theological talent rules with unbounded despotism over the philosophical and poetic" (KA, 2:73). Equating such arbitrary subjectivity with political despotism, Schlegel argued that a spirit like Jacobi's, which relies only on a personal drive for pure love, produces bad art because it is dangerously indifferent to form and law. The desire for the absolute as a purely personal urge is despotic because it does not recognize formally, that is, as a matter of law and obligation, the equality of others demanded by the republican ideal. That is why Jacobi's supposed ideal of friendship turned into a relationship of submission and domination. The hope for unity based on feelings rather than law and constitution first led to idealization of femininity, because of the supposedly purer ethical nature of feminine impulses and woman's tendency to boundless submission, and then led to exploitation of that tendency.

At this point, without being explicit, Schlegel had introduced a new element made possible by the convergence of his Fichteanism and the Christian Platonism derived from Hemsterhuis. Idealizing a woman involves not simply valuing her moral character but seeing her as ideal—perfect, complete, or absolute. The absolute, Hemsterhuis had taught, is experienced not primarily as an idea, an "it," but as a person, the object of desire, an insight Schlegel translated dialogically : "In religion one considers the absolute as you [*Du*]" (KA, 18:37, 199). Unlike Novalis, Schlegel did not work out conceptually the way in which the experience of the absolute is logically present or given within the experience of idealizing love; *Lucinde* would novelize the implication without the philosophical analysis. But his position was essentially the same as Novalis's. In the feeling of loving another, the limited and finite "I" experiences its determinateness in relationship to a "you" experienced as unconditioned and unlimited. This sense of absoluteness can be recovered for the self because it is already part of it; it is only against its own desire to be absolute that the self can experience itself as limited and the other as unlimited. But the very situation that is so full of promise for the self is also full of danger. Undoubtedly, Schlegel wrote in relation to Jacobi, the striving for the infinite is the driving force in a healthy, active soul, and if there is an equally powerful striving for harmony, and the capacity for it, the good and the beautiful will combine with the great and the sublime into a complete whole. Assume, however, a striving for the infinite in a soul without such a capacity for harmony, a soul of live and delicate sensuality but infinitely vulnerable, and it will fail to combine opposites. It will constantly oscillate between the most closed-off loneliness and the most unconditional surrender, between arrogance and humility, between delight and despair, unbridled anarchy and slavery (KA, 2:76).

This amazing characterization has clearly detached itself from Jacobi's novel; although it takes off from Woldemar's self-contradictions, it turns the tables on itself and becomes, via a *Charakteristik* of Jacobi, another one of Schlegel's self-descriptions, or self-extrapolations. It makes plain what temptations and pitfalls Schlegel felt lurking in his own Fichteanism, when applied to the sphere of love. The drive to totality was absolutist, although, in relation to the "other," it was so in a very complicated way; woman was simultaneously divinized and subordinated, so that man could experience his own subordination without having to acknowledge it. Recognizing this, Schlegel insisted that the purely emotional impulse for the divine had to be checked and limited by the republican insistence on formal recognition of the genuine otherness, specifically in this case the rights and powers, of women. Without such a "republican constitution" in human relationships, be they political or erotic, the questing individual (male) would swing wildly between domination and submission. Once again the classical ideal of objectivity, reason, and law was upheld and maintained even more fiercely, perhaps, in this Fichtean period than in its earliest phase, as a necessary defense against the despotic anarchy of individuality. Schlegel tellingly extended one of the central doctrines of classical republican political theory into the domain of love. The greatest danger to the public good in classical republicanism was the growth of personal luxury and corruption; concern for the common interest was undermined by the opportunity and consequent drive for self-interest. Inequality of wealth made some within the republic dependent on others, destroying the freedom that equality makes possible. The same, Schlegel argued, held with regard to the most intimate personal relationships. "All luxury ends in slavery; even if it is luxury in the enjoyment of the purest love for the holiest of beings" (KA, 2:74). Ultimately, Schlegel's critique of *Woldemar* was that it was too modern a novel, not classical enough.

The description of the dangers of the quest for the infinite in love at the end of the *Woldemar* review was an almost uncanny anticipation of what was to happen to Schlegel when he and Dorothea Veit met and fell in love in the summer of 1797. Suddenly, everything he had hoped for, everything that he had been balked of since he had fallen in love with Caroline, seemed available to him. In crucial respects, Dorothea was a duplicate of Caroline. The well-educated daughter of the great Enlightenment philosopher Moses Mendelssohn and an important figure in the Berlin salons, she had a considerable intellectual pedigree and was independent and intellectually-minded in her own right. Married to the banker Simon Veit, she too belonged to someone else, and like Caroline, even had two children. Again like Caroline, she was older than Schlegel—in this case, by eight years. This time around, however, he succeeded in winning the object of his love sexually; moreover, he succeeded in taking her away

from the other man. And this time the victory had a different meaning for
his sense of being than it would have had previously, interpreted as it was
through a different philosophical framework. The fulfillment of erotic
passion and the competitive triumph was simultaneously a symbolic
breakthrough to the infinite individuality he had both been arguing for
and trying to contain in his assimilation of Fichte's philosophy.
Dorothea's intellectual, marital, and maternal status fitted her to be not
only Caroline's replacement but the emblem of that totality which had
now become his conscious ideal. As an independently-minded intellectual she could think for herself and thus was self-contained, but her moth-
erhood meant that she was so complete in herself that she could give to
others. At the same time, since she also "belonged" to another, Schlegel's
will in relation to her was limited by the not-self of her husband's possession. Winning her from her husband conferred on him the totality she
represented through his act of overcoming limitations. Yet though in a
sense he "appropriated" Dorothea, his love escaped the "repulsive egotism" with which he had charged Jacobi. Dorothea possessed the attributes Jacobi had denied Allwine and Henriette; she was both intellectual
and sexual, and Schlegel did not have to feel that he was condescending
to her by denying her what he valued for himself. As he would later generalize in the *Athenaeum Fragments* "Women are treated as unjustly in
poetry as in life. If they're feminine, they're not ideal, and if ideal, not
feminine" (*Athenaeum*, 167, 49). In these respects, then, she was his
equal; as an older woman, wife, and mother, she was his superior. Their
love thus contained the objective checks and balances to egotism that
Jacobi's merely inner urge to wholeness did not. Schlegel no longer
needed the lawlike controls and the external forms of classicism with its
rigid genre conventions and ideals of proportion and controlled serenity
as a counterbalance to the infinite individuality of his new Romanticism.
He could go beyond the classical ideal of harmony to embrace unequivocally the modern ideal of totality because eros, love, furnished a replacement organizing principle that offered the control of form without limiting the freely inventive capacities of the creative imagination. Love
supplanted law as the form of restraint while making possible a much
greater, an infinite freedom. Nevertheless, as *Lucinde* shows, the experience of Romantic love did not escape the contradictions Schlegel had
already discerned in Jacobi.

How is the connection between Schlegel's novel and Schlegel's life to
be understood? On the one hand, the autobiographical elements are so
obvious that to dismiss the relevance of the life for the novel seems like
a simple denial of reality; on the other hand, modern critical theory has
made hopelessly naive the idea that writing the life, even in un-
ambiguously intended autobiography, much less in fictional form, is

merely a transcription of the life. We have already seen that as a novel about the formation of an artist's identity through love, *Lucinde* is part of Schlegel's aesthetic theory because it documents the event central to the theory of artistic production and form, the event that indeed makes the theory itself possible. As the male protagonist Julius says to his lover Lucinde early in the novel, excusing himself for writing about lovers in general rather than of themselves, "I'm only concerned with the objectivity of my love. For this objectivity and everything connected with it really confirms and creates the magic of writing" (*Lucinde*, 63). But while that makes writing the end and love the means, the distinction is not so simple. For the purpose of writing is to describe and celebrate the event that makes writing possible, since writing is at least partly the realization of the totality that eros also achieves (as well, of course, as the expression of the necessary irony about that love). Beyond the intertwining of life and writing through the bond of eros, however, Schlegel provided yet another model for thinking about how biography and the novel interconnect. In his *Dialogue on Poetry* (written very shortly after *Lucinde*), he went beyond the idea that Romantic literature should be mimetic to insist that the novel must be based "entirely on a historical foundation" and that a good Romantic novel will almost always have "a true story at its source, even if variously reshaped" (*Dialogue*, 100). This is entirely consistent with his expressive notion of art, according to which novels are "compendia, encyclopedias of the whole spiritual life of a brilliant individual" (*Notebooks*, 78, 152). That Boccacio, Cervantes, and Sterne are held up as examples shows that Schlegel was not espousing realism as understood later in the nineteenth century; for the novel's purpose in both charting and embodying character formation or *Bildung*, it was necessary that it be referential in the broad sense that it encompass the reality sense itself, that is, a human subject's sense of the facticity of life: engagement in time and place, history, the body. But the autobiographical referentiality of his own novel also indicates that the mimetic requirement originated in the desire, and the idea, that the novel both document the shaping of its author's life and contribute to that shaping. *Lucinde* not only describes retroactively how love enables Julius to write but enacts his production as a writer. And the course of the novel modifies the very story it tells about the connection between love and creative identity.

The *apparent* way that love produces writing is by creating the unified and whole personality that alone is capable in turn of creating—indeed even just conceiving the idea of—the Romantic work of art. The central and longest section of *Lucinde*, "Apprenticeship for Manhood," describes Julius's exemplary biographical itinerary from fragmentation to wholeness, a journey consummated only when he finds his ideal love. Julius is

a turbulent, directionless youth, alternating between passionate but in-
discriminate enthusiasms and empty, detached indifference: "Everything
could fascinate, nothing satisfy him . . . his whole existence was a mass of
unrelated fragments" (*Lucinde*, 78). A series of encounters with women
gradually enables him, through their inner unity, to integrate his own
being by reconciling what had seemed to him till then irreconcilable opposites: sensuality and moral integrity, passion and independence, variety of interests and inner coherence. His first genuine love is for a woman
who is not available to him; she is in love with his "friend" and therefore
can only be a friend. But even this unexpressed and unrequited passion
initiates a major transformation. The unnamed beloved is a symphony of
dissonances. She can be mischievous but refined and feminine; playful
and mocking yet serious and sublime; a flirt but also inspired, solicitous,
and maternal; responsive but assertive; tender and lyrical but strong and
courageous. "Every single characteristic was freely and strongly developed and expressed as if it existed for him alone; and yet this rich, daring
mixture of such disparate elements formed a whole that was not chaotic
because it was animated by a single spirit, a living breath of harmony and
love" (*Lucinde*, 92). The "worship" of this "sublime friend" becomes the
center of Julius's world, the impetus to inner change, sense of purpose,
and action. "He broke with all former ties, and with one stroke made
himself completely independent. He dedicated his strength and his
youth to sublime artistic inspiration and achievement. He forgot his own
times and modeled himself on the heroes of those former ages whose
ruins he loved to adoration. And for himself the present didn't exist
either, since he lived only in the future and in the hope of someday completing an immortal work as a monument to his virtue and honor" (*Lucinde*, 93–94).

Unreciprocated devotion, however, is not sufficient to complete Julius's development. He remains too serious, too rigid, too intense, and
his work suffers correspondingly. Finally he meets Lucinde, an artist who
replicates the qualities of his first love, but with the added virtue that she
loves him in return. She lives through her imagination; her paintings,
though technically crude, harmonize in a unified emotional whole so obvious as to seem inevitable (*Lucinde*, 97). She is a nonconformist who has
in some unspecified way "renounced all ties and social rules daringly and
decisively and lived a completely free and independent life" (*Lucinde*,
98), yet having been a mother (her child died soon after birth), she is
"inspired by an ardor and a profundity which only a mother can possess"
(*Lucinde*, 100). Julius is enraptured and Lucinde responds to his sexual
importuning. The consummation is more than physical. "They were completely devoted and joined to each other and yet each was wholly himself
more than he had ever been before, and every expression was full of the

deepest feeling and the most unique individuality" (*Lucinde*, 99). This seemingly paradoxical fulfillment, in which individuality is contingent on union, relaxes Julius's will to creativity into spontaneity and flexibility. His paintings come alive with light and color, and though they disregard conventional rules of artistic beauty, they appeal because of their ability to capture disparate aspects of life in a unified whole. His own life also becomes a work of art for him, because he can see its structure and feel himself to be at its center. He is the author of his own actions and their unity, yet "It seemed to him that everything in his life had been predestined and created since the beginning of time" (*Lucinde*, 102). The reason for this contradiction is that the inner unity and necessity of his history are produced by external intervention; they emerge only in relationship to Lucinde: "by telling her about it he saw his life for the first time as a connected whole" (*Lucinde*, 98). She is the necessary audience for his narrative because she is the ending that makes a *story* possible at all. Her listening to his story is her acceptance of him, the reception that gives his life point and structure, a sense of closure. Julius's narrating and Lucinde's listening are the enactment of the lesson of identity that Julius learns: "Only in the answer of its 'you' can every 'I' wholly feel its boundless unity" (*Lucinde*, 106). (In the notebook fragments connected with *Lucinde*, Schlegel added to the same sentence, "before that is chaos" [*Notebooks*, 152, 1481].) In the light of this consummation of love and personal identity it becomes clear why Schlegel chose the ellipse as the geometrical symbol, or perhaps more accurately as the allegory, for the novel. It takes two centers or foci to produce an ellipse. A circle only has one, and the other geometrical figures are not complete, closed universes. "The ellipse, the circle, the parabola and the hyperbola are only explosions, developments of the point, which must be thought of in highly mystical terms. In the primitive point there is duality. The ellipse is the first symbol of that duality; the circle and parabola are only deviations, extremes of the progression, all nuances of the ellipse, otherwise nothing more" (KA, 18:156, 398). "That the novel seeks two centers points to the fact that each novel wants to be an *absolute* book, points to its mystical character. This gives it a mythological character; in this way it becomes a person" (*Notebooks*, 173, 1728).

The implied reciprocity of this lesson in identity-creation is, however, misleading, although there are moments in the novel when Schlegel clearly wants to assert complete reciprocity between the lovers. In "Metamorphosis," the section that immediately follows "Apprenticeship for Manhood," he writes: "There exists a pure love, an indivisible and simple feeling without the slightest taint of restless striving. Each person gives exactly what he takes, each like the other; everything is equal and whole and complete in itself, like the eternal kiss of divine children" (*Lucinde*,

106). Reciprocal moments such as these, however, are wishful evocations in a much more complex, unbalanced, and conflicted relationship between Lucinde and Julius. The relationship between eros and writing is more tortuous that it first seemed.

At the first level of the novel's consciousness, the power is Lucinde's. She is the infinite who in loving Julius is able to make him whole and infinite because he is then "the object of an infinite love" (*Lucinde*, 101). Women already are what men have to become—finished, whole, and self-contained—and their love of man can therefore be empowering. In the erotically charged "Dithyrambic Fantasy" near the beginning of the novel, as the two prepare to make love, Julius says to Lucinde, "You feel completely and infinitely; you know of no separations; your being is one and indivisible. That is why you are so serious and so joyful. That is why you take everything so solemnly and so negligently, and also why you love me completely, and don't relinquish any part of me to the state, to posterity, or to my friends" (*Lucinde*, 47). Being total in herself, Lucinde can claim Julius totally: nothing of him escapes the security of her embrace, therefore of her validation of him. This is the child's wish-fantasy of the omnipotent mother who lives for nothing else but to love him and to attend to everything he does. It seems wholly appropriate that when Julius's art blossoms in the light of Lucinde's love, his favorite subjects include "a young man looking with furtive pleasure at his own image in the water, or a fond, smiling mother with her darling child in her arms" (*Lucinde*, 101).

But Lucinde's power is inversely a source of instability and insecurity. Being absolute, it is beyond Julius's will to contain or control, a gift gratuitously bestowed or withheld. Significantly, the novel begins not with the assurance of possession but with the anxiety of absence. In a letter to Lucinde, Julius describes a daydream of lovemaking inspired by his longing for her. He pictures them embracing "with as much wantonness as religion." He begs her that "for once" she might give herself over to frenzy and be insatiable. He, however, listens with "cool composure" for even the faintest sign of her passion "so that not a single trace might escape me and leave a gap in our harmony. I didn't simply enjoy but felt and enjoyed the enjoyment itself" (*Lucinde*, 44). The enjoyment, however, was an illusion, he tells her, merely a daydream. "[E]verything was an illusion except that a moment ago I stood by the window and did nothing, and that now I am sitting here and doing something, a something which is perhaps only a little more, or even a little less than doing nothing" (*Lucinde*, 45).

What Julius is doing, of course, is writing the letter we are reading. That the act of writing is "more" than the "nothing" of mere fantasizing seems obvious, but why then is it also less? Because fantasy seems to produce the immediacy and reality of fulfillment that writing cannot; the very act of writing is a distancing, a description *of* the experience, a reflection *on* it that separates consciousness from it. Yet the description of the embrace shows that consciousness is separate from the experience even in the imagined embrace itself. Julius, after all, imagines himself detachedly watching himself, not involved in the embrace as Lucinde is. Writing thus turns out to be not only more "real" than fantasy but more "real" than love itself; though writing is only mediated communion, it is more substantial (the letter will reach Lucinde, as it reaches the reader) than the love embrace it describes, which is actually an experience of separateness. And there is another ironic way in which writing is more than love. It may be impossible to live love or even fantasize it without the threat of separateness disrupting the communion of the lovers. But language may *assert*, however self-deceptively, the communion of love. Love, in this analysis, appears to make writing possible in quite the opposite way from what the theory might first imply; writing is about love's impossibility. Is this, however, the whole story?

In the letter, Julius explains his detachment from the embrace in two ways. Observing it, he says, makes it more complete for him. By enjoying his enjoyment, he joins his participation in the act with his consciousness of the act in a synthesis of all the possible modes of existence; he possesses his own experience. The act of observing also makes the union of the two lovers more complete, for nothing of Lucinde's passion, her being for him, escapes his attention. Yet Julius's explanation is disingenuous. The gap between his involvement and his detachment, between her desired frenzy and his coolness, destroys the possibility of union between them; they are the very definition of disharmony. The distance between the lovers is not only disclosed, it is widened in what is supposed to be the effort to bridge it. The gap, moreover, is not just the necessary, the ontological abyss that forever divides the self between being and self-consciousness or separates self and other. It is above all the gap between Lucinde as an idealized being, as absolute, and Julius as finite and contingent. His need to watch her, to reassure himself that there is nothing to her other than her desire for him, exposes both his belief in her infinite freedom and significance and his fear of his own negligibility. He watches her with anxiety because she has the power not to look at him.

As we have seen, however, at another level of the novel's consciousness, Lucinde's power turns out to be not original and self-subsisting, but borrowed. Lucinde demystifies herself to a resistant Julius by pointing out to him that her divinity is but the reflection of his imagination. Julius's protest that his yearning for her is boundless argues the limitlessness of his desire, not of its object. Julius appears to have conceded this when he says at the beginning of the section, "Only in yearning do we find peace . . . only when it can find nothing higher than its own yearning" (*Lucinde*, 126), but he does not draw the conclusion that his fulfillment in loving Lucinde is unreal and insubstantial. That she is the product of his boundless desire ironically puts him in control of the object he nonetheless continues to desire. Lucinde is Julius's mirror, and the light by which he sees himself in her is the light of the night, the moon—she is "the priestess of the night"—which is nothing but his own originating light reflected in her.[77] The very fact that women are by nature what men have to make of themselves makes them less than men, for their being is not their own achievement. Humanity, Julius says, is really divided into two separate classes, the creative and the created, the male and the female (*Lucinde*, 108). Ultimately, woman is nothing and man is everything.

The contradiction in the image of woman and of her relationship to man is now complete. She is on the one hand the absolute, making the individuated and whole man possible by loving him, thus allowing him to identify with her and with her perfected image of him. At the same time she is nothing but his mirror, a passive object reflecting his infinity—even if it is but the infinity of his desire. Two factors make this contradiction sustainable, that is, maintainable even in the face of its ironic undercutting both here and at the beginning of the novel. One is that the contradictory structure of love hearkens back to forms of relationship in which, because of the imbalance of power between infant and mother, it is plausible—indeed inevitable—that the mother will be seen as the real source of power. It is precisely the maternal configuration of the erotic relationship that not only obliterates the separation between self and other but obviates the possibility of making such a distinction. But, in the second place, what makes this configuration sustainable in the face of adult (authorial) self-consciousness is the will to regress, the need to abnegate power and find it instead in an external source. Regression to a maternal structuring of eros accomplishes this without fully surrendering the power that is feared. It is the arrogation of divine power to the self that produces the need for the kind of love that *Lucinde* depicts.

The contradiction in that love, as I suggested earlier, both contains and explains the contradiction in Schlegel's aesthetics, in particular the contradictory notion of form. Like the feminine "*Du*" in relation to the male, form is infinite and finite, creative yet created, that which the author produces by his imagination out of his life, and which at the same time embraces the author totally and autonomously provides the structure that organizes his very creativity. The secret of form, we have seen, is the secret of love, the secret of a contradictory relationship to woman that involves complete dependence without the sacrifice of complete independence. But the secret of that relationship is the compartmentalized consciousness that contains separately the self that depends on the mother as mirror and the self that holds the mirror up.

It is now perhaps possible to understand why Schlegel's breakthrough to the modern and his abandonment of pure classicism not only made the republicanism with which the latter was allied highly problematic but threw into question the whole political foundation of his Romanticism. As a system of formal guarantees for the freedom and equality of each, republicanism was no longer necessary for the protection of others against the self if such guarantees were inherent in the spontaneous relationship of love. Furthermore, the idea of constitutionalism suffered from the same defects of externality as did the rules of classicism. But there was a more serious source of incompatibility between republicanism and the new doctrine of Romanticism. Romanticism entailed the idea of the infinite, rather than the merely free, whole, and equal individual, whether that individual was the ideal Romantic poet—who in any case did not yet exist, Schlegel had asserted—or the theoretician who had conceived the ideal and was at the present historical moment its only avatar. The political implications of such an idea were decidedly antiegalitarian. Schlegel gave them remarkably open expression in a letter to August Wilhelm on October 31, 1797, one month after the letter to Novalis in which he had alluded to the great changes his thinking had undergone. In the letter to his brother, he proposed to launch a project that the two had vaguely discussed before, the publication of their own periodical. The plan, however, not only became concrete but took on a quite different significance now that Friedrich felt himself the originator of a new view of literature. In the past, controlling his own journal would have meant not being at the mercy of others in getting his own work published; now it meant having a platform to launch a new movement headed by himself. "I must however confess to you that I proposed the plan . . . in terms somewhat different from those you have considered till now, for all I know; either far broader or far narrower, however you take it.—Specifically, a journal not only edited by us, but *wholly* written by us *alone*, without any other regular collaborators. . . . Imagine the infinite advantage *in being able to do and allow whatever we see fit.* . . . Another big advantage of this undertaking would certainly be that we would gain for ourselves great authority in literary criticism, enough for us to be in five or ten years time the critical dictators of Germany" (KA, 24:31–32). Of course the proposal was for a joint dictatorship, but the idea and the initiative were Friedrich's, and later in the letter he referred to the journal as "my project"

(KA, 24:35). Above all, Friedrich saw it as the vehicle for collections of fragments such as he had recently published in Reichardt's *Lyceum der Schönen Künste* (KA, 24:34), and though he expressed the desire to write such fragments in collaboration with others and repeatedly tried to encourage August Wilhelm, Novalis, Schleiermacher, and even Caroline to contribute fragments, he was in no doubt that the fragment was his peculiar form of self-expression. "I can give no other sample of myself, of my whole 'I'," he wrote his brother a few weeks later, "than a system of fragments, because that is what I am" (KA, 24:67).

Two further suggestions for the periodical reveal much about its political meaning for Schlegel. He proposed to his brother that each of them as editor have the right of absolute veto both over any outside contributions that either might propose as well as over one another's contributions. This not only institutionalized a patently ambivalent drive for absolute power in the most contradictory way, it reproduced the editorial procedure used by his own father and his collaborators many years before in their collectively published journal. He also proposed, in the event unsuccessfully, that the periodical be named *Hercules*, the name by which Schiller had referred to Shakespeare, whom Schlegel had termed superior to Goethe among modern writers in the *Studium*-essay. The psychological convolutions of the suggestion were Machiavellian. The periodical would use Schiller's own classical reference to a half-human, half-divine figure to declare its editors' supremacy over Schiller's great friend Goethe, whom Schlegel had also declared to be Germany's preeminent writer over Schiller. The proposed title of Schlegel's new periodical was both the final revenge against Schiller and a declaration of revolution that proposed to overthrow Goethe, the reigning deity of German culture.

Schlegel issued his most direct challenge to Goethe in his review of *Wilhelm Meister*.[78] The review appears to be a highly positive appreciation of the novel, with some subtle qualifications. Ernst Behler points out that Schlegel was far more critical of Goethe in his private notes than in his publications. Yet the devaluation of Goethe takes place within the review itself, and in the most ironic way. Schlegel's very analysis of what Goethe does, or attempts, in the novel is a criticism because Schlegel presented himself as seeing what the author himself did not see and what, in not seeing, he could only grope toward rather than realize. Indeed, Schlegel announced his triumph over Goethe in the programmatic prescription he offered for reading any author correctly:

> It is pleasant and necessary to submit wholly to the effect of a poem and to let the artist do with us what he wants. That is the first and most essential step. But it is not less necessary to be able to abstract from every particular,

to grasp the implied universal, to survey a mass of detail and to hold on to the whole, to penetrate even the most hidden and pin down the most remote. *We must rise above our love, above what we worship, and be able to destroy it in our thoughts; otherwise we lose . . . the sense for the universe.* . . . So we may gladly tear ourselves away from the magic of the author, after we have so willingly allowed ourselves to be bound by him, most gladly spy out what he wants to remove from our sight or not at first show, and what makes him most an artist: the secret intentions he pursues in silence and which we cannot assume the genius has too many of. (KA, 2:131; italics added)

The italicized words are usually quoted out of context, robbing them of their specificity. They are not simply another expression of the procedures of Romantic irony; they were aimed at Goethe in particular. Schlegel conceived the critic's agon with the writer as a (homo)sexual conflict in which the reader initially submits only to dominate subsequently. He granted the work of art its necessary temporal primacy because it exists before the work of criticism; the critic is wholly dependent on it, has nothing of his own. But the critic transcends his slavish devotion by destroying the work and remaking it in the light of his own vision of the hidden whole that the work constitutes or intends. Schlegel explicitly said in the passage that the meaning the critic finds is the secret intention of the author, and his language here has something of the flavor of uncovering the primal scene. But there is simultaneously also something disingenuous about his concession that the critic merely discovers the author's secret. Even in the passage itself there is a hint that the critic alone can generalize from the author's details, that he alone sees the figure in the tapestry. This hint is borne out by much more direct assertions in the notebooks. "Goethe had no idea of Romantic wholeness" (*Notebooks*, 49, 341), Schlegel asserted flatly in a note from the late summer of 1797. "*Meister* is incomplete because it is not wholly mystical" (*Notebooks*, 49, 351). "A more complete novel would have to be a much more romantic work of art than *Wilhelm Meister* is" (*Notebooks*, 48, 289). But similar evaluations are implicit in the negative comments Schlegel made in the review about the character of the novel's hero, whom in one of the notebook entries he called a "weakling" (*Notebooks*, 135, 115): "After a few light attacks of anxiety, defiance and remorse his independence disappears. . . . He formally resigns his own will, and now his apprentice years are complete, and Natalie becomes the supplement of the novel" (KA, 2, 144). What was great in *Wilhelm Meister*, according to Schlegel, was not its accomplishment but its tendency (cf. *Athenaeum*, 216), and it took Schlegel to discern that tendency. The Romantic work of art that the times awaited had not yet been written, and the strong implication was that it could not be written until Schlegel had discerned it as the agenda for modern literature.

But what of the ideal of *Symphilosophie*? How does Schlegel's notion that the quest for omniscience is a mutual or collective quest fit in with his challenge to Goethe and with his ambition for a "critical dictatorship"? The brief answer is that it does not. The lack of fit is betrayed in two ways: in the incoherence of *Symphilosophie* with Schlegel's erotic ideas as revealed in *Lucinde* and in the internal inconsistencies within the image of *Symphilosophie* itself as portrayed both in *Lucinde* and in the *Dialogue on Poetry*.

Almost immediately after Julius declares that the I-thou relationship with Lucinde is all-encompassing, a series of intrusions disrupts the self-contained closure of the couple and opens their relationship up in a way that seems to suggest retroactively that others were necessary for totality after all.[79] First there is the announcement that Lucinde is pregnant, to which Julius reacts with the acknowledgment that the two of them are after all part of a larger community and that especially with a child coming, they need to find or create the right kind of society, one that will be both a marriage of the "two classes"—male and female, that is, the creative and the created—and a "universal brotherhood of all individuals" (*Lucinde*, 109). Shortly afterwards, Julius attacks a statement in a French novel about two lovers who "were the universe to each other" because it is an erroneous, constricting form of passion that, unlike their own, is exclusive rather than inclusive. "They discover the universe in each other because they've lost their sense for everything else," Julius says sarcastically. His relationship with Lucinde, by contrast, has given them both "a feeling for the whole world," for "the infinity of the human spirit."

But Julius/Schlegel's repudiation of "French passion" is also a self-repudiation; it contradicts the all-inclusive image of love not only depicted but asserted in the middle section, when Julius says to Lucinde, "I see . . . all humanity in me and in you" (*Lucinde*, 46). A fragment from one of the notebooks is even more explicit: "It is a necessary aspect of love that each reciprocally finds the universe in the other" (*Notebooks*, 152, 499). However unstable the dyad of Julius and Lucinde, which oscillates between the poles of his own grandiosity and his idealization of her, it claims a self-sufficiency that conflicts with the later acknowledgment that a consistent universality embraces the whole human community. The conflict is even more glaring in light of the fact that the main purpose of the dyad is to achieve the integration and infinite extension of its masculine half: "We two are one, and man only becomes man and completely himself when he thinks and imagines himself as the center of all things and the spirit of the world" (*Lucinde*, 118). The strain is finally evident in a letter from Julius to his former friend Antonio in which he blames the breakdown of their friendship on Antonio's critical attitude toward another of Julius's friends, whose character differs from Antonio's. Antonio's tendency to rank character in a hierarchy shows that he does not understand the true nature of friendship, which is a harmony of multiple differences. But in both attitude and tone Julius behaves as arbiter and judge, laying down the law without giving Antonio a hearing and displaying the very intolerance and lack of understanding of which he accuses Antonio (*Lucinde*, 122–23).

The contradiction between the ideal of collective enterprise and the claims of personal authority are more striking, if also more subtle, in the *Dialogue on Poetry*. The dialogue would seem to be the form ideally suited to *Symphilosophie*, implying as it does a colloquy of equals. Seduced by the image of the Romantic circle in Jena from the fall of 1799 on—though in fact Schlegel began the *Dialogue* while still in Berlin—critics have tended to treat it as a *roman à clef*, even looking for exact correlations between its fictional characters and active members of the group.[80] But as Ernst Behler has succinctly observed, "The dialogue form is the surface and not the essence. . . . Ultimately nothing but the opinions of Friedrich Schlegel himself are revealed. That is to say, he speaks through the mouth of his puppets" (*Dialogue*, 10). In the light of the present analysis, the word puppets may signify even more than Behler intends. There are no genuine interlocutors in this dialogue, because it is, and can only be, a monologue.

That a monologue is inevitable derives from Schlegel's core idea that individuality strives for the sublime, for totality in its own right (*Dialogue*, 87). He anticipated the problems for the individual work of art in the *Lyceum Fragments* when he pointed out the inevitable tension between the ideal of all-inclusiveness and the need for closure in art. A "motley heap of ideas," he said there, "animated by the ghost of a spirit and aiming at a single purpose" may have more unity than an apparently more coherent work. That the flattering comparison is in favor of his own kind of form, the collection of fragments, does not lessen the critical force of his analysis. "What really holds [the motley heap] together," he claimed, "is that free and equal fellowship in which, so the wise men assure us, the citizens of the perfect state will live at some future date; it's [the] unqualifiedly social spirit." The problem with the more rounded work, he claimed, is that the "instinct for unity" is so powerful in man "that the author himself will often bring something to a kind of completion which simply can't be made a whole or a unit; often quite imaginatively and yet completely unnaturally" (*Lyceum*, 155, 103). What Schlegel failed to realize is that he did not escape this problem by the relative formlessness of the fragment form. It is the author's arbitrary will that composes, selects, and arranges; there is no democracy in the single-author work, and the analogy with the modern egalitarian republic breaks down. Furthermore, Schlegel was effectively debarred by his own premises and desires from what appears to be the obvious alternative: the collective work. The *Athenaeum Fragments* made an effort in that direction, including as it did fragments by Novalis, Schleiermacher, and August Wilhelm. But it was Schlegel who initiated the idea and solicited the contributions; in any case, the preponderant number of fragments were his and no one doubted that he was the animating spirit of the collection. In the *Dialogue*, despite himself, Schlegel reaffirmed the inevitable recourse to the single voice, the single authority. The writer, said Schlegel, cannot bear that either his own work or his view of literature should be limited; therefore he must strive continually to expand both by integrating his work with the entire body of literature. He can only do this "when he has found the center point through communications with those who have found theirs from a different side, in a different way. Love needs a responding love. . . . [T]he true poet . . . is a social being" (*Dialogue*, 55). But in the immediately preceding paragraph the conclusion is exactly the opposite. The writer cannot bear limitation because he knows obscurely that "he can and should be genuinely and truly all mankind. Therefore, man, in reaching out time and again beyond himself to seek and find the complement of his innermost being in the depths of another, *is certain to return ever to himself*" (*Dialogue*, 54; italics added). Where the legitimacy of the only source of authority that we have, the positing act of the individual self, depends on its being "transcendental," that is, not merely psychologically, but ontologically, necessary, individuality and universality are fused. The unique experience of the individual is the model for the validity of all experience, even shared experience, which can only get its authority from the choice or assent of the individual ego. There is no authority higher than the unique individuality; the personal authenticity of its choices is what validates them and guarantees their universality.

Politically, the analogue to Schlegel's erotic and critical breakthrough was a revolution that overthrew a monarch but replaced him with one-man rule behind a facade of collective leadership. It is not by coincidence that the letter in which Schlegel proclaimed his ambition to be critical dictator of Germany contained an attack on the politics of Johann Friedrich Reichardt, editor of the *Lyceum der Schönen Künste* and supporter of the French Revolution; the attack heralded a complete break with him just a few weeks later: "The man has much that is good, but since he is not open-minded [*liberal*] it would be stupid . . . to continue collaborating with him in literary matters. . . . His self-styled political and literary *re-publicanism* is old-hat Berlin Enlightenment, a spirit of opposition to obscurantists and pro-French bias" (KA, 24:30). This is the first explicit sign of Schlegel's distancing himself from his former political ideals, a distancing quite in keeping with the tendencies of his new critical thinking and its implications for the politics of culture. But replacing republicanism in politics was a more difficult issue than finding a subordinate position for classicism within the new hierarchy created by the preeminence of the Romantic principle. There was no obvious political parallel to Romanticism in politics, no clear alternative to republicanism. Critical dictator he might wish to be, but the principle that was the warrant for his authority, the poetic doctrine of an infinitely free, progressive universal poetry did not translate into the regressive models of Old Regime absolutist politics. In both aesthetics and erotics, moreover, the Other was still an equilibriating force preventing the collapse of all authority into the self, even if this collapse was no longer prevented by the model of natural law and republican equality; indeed, the Other was in a crucial sense the very condition of the Romantic self's infinite freedom. Unlike Novalis, who in *Belief and Love* projected a "monarchical republic," an idealized Prussian royal couple able to educate all subjects to be monarchs through the special virtue of the queen's maternal love, Schlegel could find no political analogue in his early Romantic phase for his conception of the relationship between love and individuality. Furthermore, Schlegel conceived of the Romantic principle as a revolution on the scale and in the image of the French Revolution. "All your fragments," Novalis wrote to Schlegel in terms he knew Schlegel would take as the highest praise, "are thoroughly *new*—genuine revolutionary handbills [*Affichen*]" (KA, 24:69).

The result was that at least at the beginning of the Romantic breakthrough in the late summer of 1797, and in diminished degree until 1802, Schlegel retained a republican rhetoric and applied republican metaphors to art. The reality, however, was that he withdrew from radical politics without yet committing himself to an authoritarian politics. The price he paid for the principle of infinite individuality was a retreat from any effort to realize it in the sphere of political practice, and one of the most important reasons for the retreat was that the implications of the concept translated into action were competitive, dictatorial, and destructive. A few of Schlegel's less inhibited notes on politics reveal that he did not escape these implications by sublimating his ideal into art. They show a radical change from his classicist phase, when he argued that the highest achievement of art was founded on republican politics. "*Monarchy* also in the history of art; there could be only one *Sophocles*. . . . As certain as it is that there must always be people of sense and love and spirit, people raised to a higher power, so certain it is that art strives for a monarchy.

But the monarch should not desire to direct, but to be the genius of the times, a representative for this form of art and humanity" (KA, 18:255, 740). "Only a monarch can found mythology [the new mythology Schlegel called for in the *Dialogue on Poetry*]; he will be the last, and then the republic will begin" (KA, 18:256, 754). Schlegel even tentatively extrapolated this conclusion directly to politics. "There must also be monarchs for the practical sphere. Here too the essential thing is to find the monarchs" (KA, 18:256, 754). "The true reform of states must begin with the *formation* of masters and servants" (KA, 18:258, 771).

Not that Schlegel's monarchism was ever unequivocal in the period between 1797 and 1802. Republican and egalitarian fragments are continuously and confusedly mixed in with the more authoritarian epigrams. "The age strives for a revolution in the family as much as it does for a republic. Only in the family ought there to be a free monarchy, every state must be a *republic*" (KA, 18:398, 1379). "Liberty, equality, and community are the principles of all universality" he insisted in one place (KA, 18:333, 123), even though he would also assert virtually simultaneously that there was never greater liberty, equality, and fraternity than in the various peasant, regional, and communal leagues and federations of the Middle Ages (KA, 18:299, 1255)—a foreshadowing of the turn his political theorizing would take after 1808. As we have seen, *Athenaeum* fragment 214 brings together the conflicting desiderata in as clear a synthesis as Schlegel could achieve: "A perfect republic would have to be not just democratic, but aristocratic and monarchic at the same time; to legislate justly and freely, the uneducated would have to outweigh and guide the educated, and everything would have to be organized into an absolute whole" (*Athenaeum* 190). The apparent confusion of political forms was not necessarily as contradictory to contemporaries as it seems to us; in German political thought of the time, as we have noted in the case of Kant, the idea of a republic was not in principle incompatible with that of a monarchy, since republicanism could refer either to a mixed constitution or to one with a clear separation between executive, legislative, and judicial functions. But as both his earlier work and even his fragments from this period clearly show, Schlegel used the word *republic* in its egalitarian and antimonarchical sense. The political formula in the fragment above required a unity of genuine opposites to create the "absolute whole" that was his ideal of the polity as well as of the literary work and of the individual personality.

The monarch in these fragments was the constitutive force whose adequate individuality and authority alone could unify the state. Adequate individuality was the divine egotism (KA, 18:134, 147) that strove for the infinity and integrity of the self and could thus pose such an ideal for society as a whole. Without it, society would be a chaos of individuals, not an organized totality. But without the democratic consent of all, there would be no genuine totality either, but an arbitrary, forced obedience akin to the regimentation of an artistic work with a forced, artificial closure. Precisely what constitutional functions each element was to have in the state Schlegel did not say, except for an opaque fragment in which he wrote that "The administration should be monarchic, the management [*Direction*] democratic and the representation aristocratic" (KA, 18:129, 83). His lack of clarity did not stem from the fact that he was not thinking in essentially political terms but from the fact that his political principles at this point were in conflict with one another. The monarch could not constitute the state in Schlegel's sense without impinging on the freedom of its members, who in turn could not be whole and unified unless subordinate to a unitary principle that could only come from the will of one person. Yet Schlegel was aware of the danger to universal freedom inherent in absolutizing a particular will; it was precisely what had led the French Revolution astray. "The French Revolution began with the self-deification of the nation and ended with it," he wrote during this period (KA, 18:243, 595). In the light of the theoretical impasse his political thinking had reached, it is perhaps not surprising that his enthusiasm about the future of literary criticism was tempered by severe doubt about its ability to accomplish what it was supposed to in the historical realm: "Might it not also be the case, however, that human history will come to a miserable end, half tragic, half comic, *so that nothing will come of it*, and those who seek the kingdom of heaven only in the afterworld are right?" (KA, 18:192, 789; italics added).

Both the authoritarian tendencies and their incompatibility with Schlegel's republicanism that were revealed in these political notes could be at least partly concealed within the theory of aesthetics by the regression it required. The dictatorial will of the writer could be allowed to prevail because it was checked by its subordination to form, even though the writer had created this form. But the theory and practice of literary criticism allowed no such equivocation; here Schlegel's desire for "critical dictatorship" had burst through and revealed the full implications of the Romantic project of individualized totality. "The essence of the modern," he wrote, "consists in *creation ex nihilo*—Such a principle lay in Christianity—a similar one in the revolution, in Fichte's philosophy—and similarly in the new poetry" (KA, 18:315, 1473). In Schlegel's Romantic vision, humankind had taken over the heritage of the divine and was on the verge of becoming God. But this ideal made the individual who even imagined it, much less tried to live it, dangerous to others in his or her desire for personal totality. It was only in the sphere of love as defined in *Lucinde* that the regressive consciousness could maintain both its absolute priority on the one hand and its total dependence on the other. The

THREE

WILLIAM WORDSWORTH

I) Criminals and Prophets

ON March 6, 1798, Wordsworth wrote his friend James Tobin to thank him for sending his copy of Henry Brooke's drama *Gustavus Vasa*. The correspondence does not indicate why he wanted to read the play just at that time. In the 1805 *Prelude*, Wordsworth mentioned the story of the heroic sixteenth-century Swedish general, who had freed his country from the tyranny of foreign rule, in a list of possible topics he says he considered for a great epic poem.[1] But in early 1798 Brooke's play might have been interesting to him for quite other reasons. *Gustavus Vasa* had been forbidden performance when it was written in 1739 and had not yet appeared on the London stage. One of its central characters was a malevolent royal minister who had helped seduce his king into tyranny by insisting on the necessity of basing governance on fear; the Lord Chamberlain, in charge of censorship, had taken the character as an attack on Walpole.[2] The scheming adviser of *Gustavus Vasa* had some striking resemblances to the character Rivers in Wordsworth's recently completed play, *The Borderers*, which had itself been rejected the previous December for production at Covent Garden. In any case, Wordsworth took the occasion of the letter of thanks to discuss his own recent theatrical disappointment. Although he made light of it, the rejection clearly rankled. He made some snidely dismissive remarks about the current London success of a melodramatic Gothic play by Matthew Gregory Lewis, but acknowledged that Lewis's triumph would have thrown him "into despair" if he had had no other method of employing himself. And he insisted that he didn't need to be urged not to publish his play, since he dreaded the prospect "as much as death itself"—an expression he immediately tried to take back as "hyperbolic."

It was only after venting his feelings about this obviously still-painful failure that Wordsworth made his well-known announcement of the large work in progress that was clearly intended to elevate him to the ranks of the great poets. "I have written 1300 lines of a poem in which I contrive to convey most of the knowledge of which I am possessed. My object is to give pictures of Nature, Man and Society. Indeed, I know not any thing which will not come within the scope of my plan." The next sentence confirms how much the announcement of the new poem was part of his reaction to the fate of *The Borderers*. "If ever I attempt another drama, it shall be written either purposely for the closet, or purposely for the stage.

There is no middle way." He went on to say, however, that he had no
intention of going back to playwriting because he had his work "carved
out" for him for a long time to come, and he intended to put all his eloquence into his poem.[3]

The context and the rhetoric of the announcement make the new project seem almost like compensation for the rejection of *The Borderers*,
and the vast claims for its scope seem a measure of the ego whose pride
had been wounded. But if vanity was involved, it was not purely personal. *The Borderers* was itself an ambitiously philosophical play that attacked what Wordsworth took to be the essential spirit of modernity. In
its own way it made the same claim to totality as the projected new work,
and the fact that Wordsworth had chosen the dramatic form and that he
wanted the play produced despite its acknowledged static quality indicates that he wanted to convey his message as forcefully and directly as
possible. That *The Recluse* could replace *The Borderers* as the object of
Wordsworth's energy and ambition shows how closely linked they were
for him in theme and purpose despite all differences of genre and subject.
The Recluse was the positive to *The Borderers'* negative; the latter
showed the bankruptcy of one ideology, the former offered a substitute.

But the personal aspect of the slight that Wordsworth felt cannot be
ignored or dismissed as merely psychological; it has poetic significance.
The authority of the poet's particular experience and voice was important
to him because, as the fragments of *The Recluse* that had been written by
then make plain, his individuality was the instrument of the grand synthesis that the new poem was to achieve and the warrant for its validity.
Wordsworth's personal touchiness was an inextricable part of his concern
for the validity of his poetry, because the poetry proposed the paradoxical
idea that the unique particularity of the poet and the poet's experience
was the principle of absolute universal authority and the agency by which
the poetry attained the infinite totality it strove to evoke.

The implication of this view, however, is that there is an even closer
connection between the play and the poem than already suggested, one
perhaps less comfortable to Wordsworth's intention in linking them.
They represent negative and positive not simply in the sense that one is
destructive and the other constructive. The villain of *The Borderers*, Rivers, who incarnates the bankrupt ethic, is the negative of the exemplary
figure of the Pedlar in *The Recluse*, who articulates the new ethic, as the
photographic negative is to the positive: they are in crucial ways the same
person, with the valence reversed.

Rivers creates a new ethic by refusing to feel remorse at his unwitting
crime of abandoning an innocent man to his death and then making a
virtue of his refusal. Remorse, he reasons, would be an even greater
crime than his original error because it would destructively turn the awesome power of the human mind against itself. That power has been built

up, as he has learned in his solitary wanderings, from "mighty objects" that "impress their forms" upon it.[4] To recognize this immense power within the mind is to become a special being who can transcend all the traditional constraints on human action, the "tyranny of moralists and saints and lawgivers" (*Borderers*, 3.5.24–35), and create his own world:

> When with these forms I turned to contemplate
> The opinions and the uses of the world,
> I seemed a being who had passed alone
> Beyond the visible barriers of the world
> And travelled into things to come.
>
> (4.2.141–45)

The Pedlar's development has not been initiated by trauma, as Rivers's has been, but his self-fashioning is described in almost the exact same language Rivers uses to describe the origins of the mind's powers:

> He had perceived the presence and the power
> Of greatness, and deep feelings had impressed
> Great objects on his mind.
>
> ("Pedlar" 29–31)[5]

These objects and feelings made his being "sublime and comprehensive" (129); he became, though untaught and undisciplined in the "dead lore of schools," "a chosen son" (326) who could pass beyond the barriers of the merely visible to give "To every natural form, rock, fruit, and flower, / . . . / . . . a moral life" (332–34). As with Rivers, this ability made him a creator whose originary power transcended the understanding of ordinary men:

> He had a world about him—'twas his own,
> He made it—for it only lived to him,
> And to the God who looked into his mind.
> Such sympathies would often bear him far
> In outward gesture, and in visible look,
> Beyond the common seeming of mankind.
> Some called it madness; such it might have been,
> But that he had an eye . . .
>
> .   .   .   .
>
> Which from a stone, a tree, a withered leaf,
> Could find no surface where its power might sleep.
>
> (339–53)

The fundamental difference between Rivers and the Pedlar is neither in the nature of their power nor even in its source, because both attribute it initially to the effect of "great objects" on the mind. The difference is that while for Rivers the effect of external objects is apparently to stimulate or waken the mind to its own powers, so that once awakened it is no longer beholden to the outside, the Pedlar retains, or tries to retain, his links with his source. In the Pedlar's case that source is seen not as merely initiatory but as foundational, hence indispensable, so that, having "felt the power / Of Nature" ("Pedlar," 86–87) and having "received so much" from her "and her overflowing soul" (203–4), his heart, despite its sublimity, remains "Lowly, for he was meek in gratitude / Oft as he called to mind those exstasies / And whence they flowed" (132–34). Dependent on the bounty of his source, "he perceived, / Though yet he knew not how, a wasting power / In all things which from her sweet influence / Might tend to wean him" (159–61). It is this maternally-figured relationship, counterbalanced with the radical absolutism of the Pedlar's autonomous creation of world, that produces the enormous tension between the active creation and passive reception that modern criticism has established as the essence of Wordsworth's idea of the imagination and what Thomas Weiskel called, with regard to the Snowdon vision, Wordsworth's "astonishing . . . indifference to priority" about what the mind confers and what it perceives.[6] The juxtaposition of *The Borderers* and "The Pedlar" shows that the tension is present from the very beginning of his "great" period, at the heart of the poem that was to be his contribution to social poetry. If Wordsworth was continually blocked in his efforts to complete that poem, it was in important part because *The Recluse* was itself anchored in a consuming dialectic of absolute autonomy and absolute dependence, neither pole of which was compatible with a reconciled vision of social man, a dialectic that could not, however, be dissolved because of the dangers represented by its repressed origins in the frightening character of the revolutionary Rivers.[7]

In recent decades, two lines of Wordsworth interpretation have emerged (in one case, perhaps, reemerged), both equally subtle and methodologically sophisticated in their address to texts and contexts, but to their proponents—despite occasional disclaimers—mutually incompatible. The first, reversing the terms of nineteenth-century criticism, sees Wordsworth not as nature poet but as the poet of visionary imagination or modern self-consciousness.[8] A more recent trend describes a much more concrete and historical Wordsworth, whose poetry not only reflected the political and social issues of the day but was a partisan contribution to them, even when—in some views, especially when—it was least overtly or self-awaredly political.[9] The one major effort to connect Wordsworth's poetics of the imagination with his politics has met with serious objections from both camps. In his *Natural Supernaturalism*, M. H. Abrams links the visionary with the political Wordsworth by suggesting that the poet's vision of the regeneration of humanity through the union of autonomous mind with nature was a displacement of, and a compensation for, the failed hopes of the French Revolution.[10] Against this interpretation, critics who have made the transcendence of imagination central to Wordsworth's enterprise make essentially two arguments. First, it is claimed, Wordsworth's poetics of consciousness deals with ontological —and therefore ultimate—structures of man's relationship to self and world that transcend, or subtend, historical events; the historical is at best mere occasion for their emergence. "What Wordsworth suffered so acutely," Geoffrey Hartman writes in an especially clear expression of this view, "may lie in the destiny of all men: a betrayal into autonomy, into self-dependence. This is the story wherever the tragic sense of life is strong: in *Oedipus Rex*, in *King Lear*, in Albee's *Who's Afraid of Virginia Woolf*, and in Wordsworth's own drama, *The Borderers*, (1796–1797). The wound inflicted is self-consciousness: 'And they knew that they were naked'."[11] It also follows from this view that Wordsworth's poetry did not in any case achieve—could not have achieved—the reconciliation between mind and nature that Abrams claims for it, for consciousness is forever separated from the world.[12] On the other hand, the historicist camp has argued that Abrams concerns himself only with large generalities about the Revolution and that in any case he either oversimplifies the politics or gets them wrong by missing the hidden ideological agenda and the decisively antirevolutionary, Burkean cast in the poetry of Wordsworth's "great decade."[13]

The atmosphere of the "visionary" criticism may indeed seem at times too rarified, too abstract to capture Wordsworth's often all-too-concrete concerns—and evasions. Yet despite the often fine textual and historical detective work of the historicists, it would be a serious mistake to surrender the visionary Wordsworth. To do so is to flatten his work to one-dimensionality as much as visionary criticism does and to deny Wordsworth concerns that were not only passionately his but which made him part of a pivotal moment both in English poetry and in the history of Western mind. In order to appreciate the historicity of Wordsworth's poetry, it is not necessary either to ignore the visionary mode or to reduce it to ideology in the sense of a "resumption" of detailed sociopolitical themes "at the level of image and of metaphysics" and to concrete social and political issues disguised as abstract philosophy "because they were deadlocked at the practical level."[14] The problem with the line of visionary criticism is not its focus on the emerging "apocalyptic" consciousness of self in Wordsworth's poetry but its refusal or inability to see both the timing and the very form of that consciousness as historically specific. Wordsworth's principle of autonomy, if also shared with other Romantics of his own generation, is radically different from anything that had come before.

Those critics who redefine Wordsworth as the poet of imagination or self-consciousness have also pointed out the profound incoherence of his consciously professed central doctrine on the subject. Geoffrey Hartman characterizes the Mount Snowdon episode, Wordsworth's most detailed proclamation of mind and nature as parallel creative forces, as "a transference," "one of the most complexly deceptive episodes in literature."[15] On the summit of Snowdon, Wordsworth's perception unites the moon looking down from above him, the active mist-sea of clouds reaching outwards at his feet, and the voice of waters mounting up from below into an Agency whose creation of forms ("headlands, tongues and promontory shapes") usurps the dominion of empirical nature. Here, says Hartman, "Wordsworth sees Imagination by its own light and calls that light Nature's."[16] Tracing a similar poetic move in "Tintern Abbey," Harold Bloom speaks of Wordsworth's "repression" of the imagination. In describing the "mighty world of eye and ear" as a blending of what they "half create / And what perceive," Wordsworth denies the full creative power of his own imagination, for the qualification "*half* create" weights the balance in favor of passive perception. This, Bloom argues, is a rather more modest claim than Wordsworth had made a few months before in the early draft of the "Prospectus" to *The Excursion*, where he had praised the mind as a creative force more exalted than heaven and more terrifying than hell.[17]

Hartman and Bloom have forever alerted readers to the conflict in Wordsworth's conception of the nature and functioning of mind. Their own explanations of that conflict, however—Wordsworth's fear of an "apocalypse of the imagination" that would blot out the natural world in the assertion of its own supremacy or his anxiety over Milton's priority in poetic divination, which required a suppression both of Milton's power and his own—are, by themselves, either too broad or too narrow. They omit the historical and the personal contexts in which and out of which the contradictions in Wordsworth's ontology of consciousness developed, contexts that conditioned the very idea of autonomous imagination in Wordsworth, the forms of its contradictions, and his attempts to resolve them. As a result of these omissions, despite the critics' generally superbly sensitive readings, their explanations ignore important details of the poetic context itself.

It is not necessary to look to the "Prospectus," whose dating is in any case so highly problematic, to detect the repression of power in "Tintern Abbey" that Bloom notes; the process goes on in full view within "Tintern Abbey" itself. The opening section of twenty-two lines is a tour de force of imaginative construction in which both the materials and the labor of the "poetry work" (by analogy with Freud's "dream work," which produces the manifest from the latent dream) are visible in figure and diction. The poet's visual choices and metaphors transform a landscape of difference, of human habitation and untouched nature, into one of natural unity and totality. The "steep and lofty cliffs" of the "wild secluded scene" are seen to "connect / The landscape with the quiet of the sky" to produce the frame, the harmonious blending of motion and stasis.[18] Within it, the (humanly cultivated) orchards with their unripe fruits are as green as untamed nature and so "lose themselves / 'Mid groves and copses" (13–14); the (artificial) hedgerows—"hardly hedgerows," Wordsworth asserts, stripping them of their human shaping with an adjective— are but "little lines / Of sportive wood run wild" (15–16); and the pastoral farms, "Green to the very door," blend indistinguishably in with the woods. Against the refractory particulars of reality, separated into the natural and the worked, the poem has created its own world by main force, a homogeneous universe whose "power / Of harmony" can, when recalled, lighten the burden "Of all this unintelligible world" (47–48, 40).

But each step after this first section is a retreat from what has happened within it. The retreat takes place in two ways: Wordsworth attributes the harmony that the imagination has just visibly produced to the unitary life inhering in things themselves (49) and then casts doubt on the objective reality of the harmonious "life of things" as soon as he has proclaimed it ("If this / Be but a vain belief" [49–50]). The two moves are repeated sequentially in spiraling cycles of rising and falling action; each expression of doubt is followed by a poetically heightened reaffirmation of real presence. In the major climax at lines 106–11 Wordsworth finally acknowledges that the eye and ear half create the mighty world they perceive but then backtracks even further to language in which nature becomes sole anchor, "the nurse / The guide, the guardian of my heart." The repression that Bloom notes in "Tintern Abbey" is actually a regression; the relationship between mind and nature at this point is one of almost explicitly maternal tutelage, protection, and nurturance. Nurse and guardian, nature "feeds" the mind "with lofty thoughts" (127–28) in order to protect its "cheerful faith." Nor does the regression reach its end point with a metaphorical and abstract evocation of the feminine. The apparently climactic affirmation of nature's tutelary power—or of Wordsworth's ability to learn nature's lesson—is called into question in one final turn of the spiral of doubt. And within the very sentence that gives it voice, consolation appears again, this time in the person of Dorothy, whose presence is suddenly announced as the addressee of the poem all along.

Nor perchance
If I were not thus taught, should I the more

Suffer my genial spirits to decay:
For thou art with me here upon the banks
Of this fair river; thou my dearest Friend,
My dear dear Friend; and in thy voice I catch
The language of my former heart, and read
My former pleasures in the shooting lights
Of thy wild eyes.

(112–19)

Dorothy seems to be the ultimate repository and guardian of Wordsworth's vision of harmony, the guarantor of its permanence, hence of its very possibility. In the hope that he may behold in Dorothy "what I was once" (120) and that Dorothy's memory will be the "dwelling-place / For all sweet sounds and harmonies," the original act of creation is completely abjured and handed over to her.

It is the consensus of modern criticism that Wordsworth's indirect admission that the "one life" is a vain belief results from his half-acknowledged, half-suppressed awareness that he himself has projected it on to nature. What Wordsworth has denied by this projection, however, is not the abstract constitutive power of the imagination; it is the specific poetic act that has constructed the unified world of the opening lines of the poem through a process of blending and exclusion. And it is not only human artifacts that poetic vision has eliminated; it has also removed the human inhabitants of the space it has reconstructed. The evidence of wreaths of smoke rising from the trees shifts its testimony from the existence of settled farms to an "uncertain notice" of vagrants in the woods, to, finally, the lonely hermit in his cave. Just as all objects have been blended into nonhuman nature, all humans have been blended into the hermit, who is at home alone with nature; the poet has obliterated other individualities in the interests of his own harmony. This is not only the benign creativity of the Pedlar—"He had a world about him —'twas his own, / He made it"—but the malign creativity of Rivers, who has built the sense of his own autonomous world-making upon the (originally unintended) sacrifice of others.

Marjorie Levinson has also argued that the first part of the poem represents an ideological act of denial because it omits all of the contextual associations to the problems of poverty and vagrancy that a contemporary would have made to Tintern Abbey and its locale. But leaving aside the theoretical question of whether and how what is not present in the poem can legitimately be said to be suppressed, Levinson has matters almost exactly the wrong way around when she claims that in constructing the "idyllic landscape, lines 1–22, Wordsworth establishes a literary immortality for the endangered farms and woods" only by denying all the commercial forces that were threatening them at the time.[19] The opening lines do not celebrate those farms at all but function in fact to obliterate them completely—along with their owners and inhabitants. Nothing is to be allowed to undermine the eternity of objective nature, not the power of human cultivation, which testifies to the human capacity to transform nature and hence to nature's malleability and temporality,[20] but not the power of the poetic imagination either. In "Tintern Abbey" the power of the poet only referred to in "The Pedlar" is actually exercised, and its exercise shows more ominously its substantive links with the ideas of Rivers. Those links certainly suggest the political context of Wordsworth's venture into the poetics of nature and imagination in 1798 that Abrams and Levinson also argue for. But that venture was neither the linear sublimation of collective politics into imagination that Abrams sees, nor the escapist displacement of collective politics into transcendence that the historicists claim. The exercise of individual power in the poem is real, and in some ways goes far beyond the claims for individual authority envisaged in any revolutionary ideology of the period. At the same time, the submission to nature that the act of autonomy produces poetically is more profound than any curbing of individual freedom demanded by the ideals of political equality or social solidarity. And finally, the investment of the vision of the one life in Dorothy sustains the contradiction by enabling Wordsworth to affirm both sides. Only if she is the repository of his (created) vision can he be secure in the belief that its power is benign. In her the "wild ecstasies" of that vision will mature "Into a sober pleasure." Yet in the end, the power remains his, for should she ever suffer solitude or fear, pain or grief, she will be healed by remembering his vision and his exhortations. In the fusion between them, she is the precondition of his power. If he forgets his vision, the shooting lights of her wild eyes will remind him of it, but as in Lucinde's relation to Julius in Schlegel's novel, what Dorothy's eyes will reflect back to Wordsworth is himself. To understand this contradiction, we must trace the rise and the crisis of Wordsworth's idea of freedom.

II) The Road to Revolution

Wordsworth's conversion to the cause of revolution has always been something of a puzzle. He was sufficiently troubled by it himself to devote a whole book of *The Prelude* to an attempt at explaining it. The effort is clearly vexed; he offers a number of explanations, and, like the excuses in the archetypal story of the man who borrowed a pot and returned it broken, they are mutually inconsistent. Inevitably they also contain serious, but revealing, factual errors and misleading statements.

The difficulty is, on the surface, straightforward enough. Wordsworth made two trips to France in the early years of the Revolution, the first in July 1790, when he was twenty years old, the second a year later in November 1791. Despite the portentous words with which he later described the plausible attractions of a visit to the Continent in 1790—" 'twas a time when Europe was rejoiced, / France standing on the top of golden hours, / And human nature seeming born again" (*Prelude* VI.352–54)—he showed little initial interest in the epochal prospect of human regeneration. He observed, he even joined on occasion with the celebrating French, but only as a pleasant episode in what was intended as a walking tour of the French and Swiss Alps. The fact is that he was fundamentally indifferent to revolutionary politics in 1790. He recalled, on seeing the revolutionary army marching off to battle, that he "look'd upon these things / As from a distance . . . / Was touched but with no intimate concern" (VI.694–96). A year and a half later, after a stay of barely two months in the French provinces, away from the main scene of revolutionary politics, he became a passionately committed "Patriot," fully involved both in the cause at large and in the minutiae of politics: "my heart was all / Given to the people, and my love was theirs" (IX.125–26). What had caused him to change between the two visits?

At the end of Book VI, Wordsworth attributes his early political indifference to his being "A Stripling, scarcely of the household then / Of social life" (VI.683–84). The words suggest a retrospective judgment of youthful immaturity leavened, however, by retrospective approval of the intimacy with nature that made him as yet socially unaware. "I needed not that joy, I did not need / Such help: the ever-living universe / And independent spirit of pure youth / Were with me at that season" (VI.700–703). This is close enough to the truth to count as a distortion rather than a falsehood. If his few letters to Dorothy from France did in fact contain animated social observation in familiar eighteenth-century terms—he particularly appreciated the French for their politeness, sociability, and benevolence—his deepest emotions were undoubtedly reserved for the natural sublime. "Among the more awful scenes of the Alps," he wrote her, "I had not a thought of men, of a single being; my whole soul was turned to him who produced the terrible majesty before me" (*Letters*, 105). Yet contrary to what he implied here, nature did not exclude man for Wordsworth even at that time. Describing in Book VIII the early "Love of Nature" that supposedly only later led him to "Love of Mankind," he remarks his youthful obsession with human suffering in the midst of sublime nature:

> images of danger and distress,
> And suffering, *these took deepest hold of me*,
> Man suffering among awful powers and forms:

Of this I heard, and saw enough to make
The imagination restless; *nor was free*
Myself from frequent perils.

(211–16; italics added)

These lines are much more in keeping with the tenor of the poetry Wordsworth was writing in the years before the Revolution than were his assertions of socially oblivious communion with nature.[21] In particular, they accurately reflect the spirit of his only published prerevolutionary poem, "An Evening Walk," with its central episode of the female beggar, the first important figure of her type in the long line of Wordsworth's female outcasts and solitaries.

Wordsworth did not suddenly discover suffering humanity in 1791; it is not even accurate to say that humanity moved at that time from the periphery to the center of his concerns. What happened rather is that he discovered humanity *in a different way* than before, as the object of social oppression and the subject of political rights. Wordsworth's revolutionary experience represented both change and continuity in a preoccupation with the socially marginal with whom, as the lines quoted above suggest, he had always identified, if in oblique and complex ways. It transformed his understanding of, and his approach to, a preexisting social concern just as that concern helped prime him for revolution.

The true nature of that preexisting concern, however, is further buried in the second set of explanations Wordsworth offers in Book IX for his delay in taking up the revolutionary cause. There he attributes it not to an indifference to things political but to a personal history that enabled him to take politics for granted. He already possessed, he claimed, the freedom that the French were just now fighting for, which was for them "A gift that rather was come late than soon" (IX.254). As an Englishman, one furthermore from a locality where claims of wealth or blood brought no particular "attention or respect"; as a student at Cambridge, the republic of letters where all were equally "Scholars and Gentlemen," and "wealth and titles were in less esteem / Than talents and successful industry" (IX.218–37), Wordsworth already believed in "equal rights / And individual worth" and enjoyed their benefits. Even if all this were true, of course, there would still be the question of why these ideals should have sparked in 1791 a political ardor they had failed to arouse the previous year. Wordsworth avoids the obvious inference that something had changed for him. Aside from this, however, his description of himself radically misrepresented what was a far more complicated national, regional, and personal situation in 1790–91 than he cared to acknowledge in 1804.

It is true that the English constitutional structure had been a model of liberty for some notable Frenchmen in the eighteenth century, though Wordsworth exaggerated and even mythified when he wrote of the welcome he received in 1790, "we bore a name / Honoured in France, the name of Englishmen" (VI.409–10). It is true too that the balance of large and small landowners in his native counties of Cumberland and Westmoreland differed from the one prevailing in many other areas in England in that these two counties contained a larger number of small freeholders than was the case elsewhere.[22] But the northern counties also had one of the most traditionally hierarchical political structures in unreformed eighteenth-century England. Powerful landed families exerted tight and extensive control over the electoral system. William Wordsworth knew the structure of political authority at first hand: his family was an integral part of it. His father John Wordsworth had been law-agent for Sir James Lowther (after 1784, Lord Lonsdale), a grandee who at the height of his political power personally controlled nine seats in the House of Commons, more than any other landholder in England.[23] The senior Wordsworth was essentially Lowther's political manager, buying up houses and land when Lowther moved into a new area, riding the circuit of the counties to keep the voters in line at election time with liberal expenditures for drink and other persuaders. It was not a popular position; Lowther was, according to one historian who studied his political career closely, "A megalomaniac . . . tyrannical, ruthless, without tact,"[24] and local dislike for him spilled over onto his agent. William Wordsworth knew this face of Cumberland "democracy" quite directly as well. In 1790–91, his family was still embroiled in a long-standing lawsuit against Sir James for recovery of a large sum of money he owed John Wordsworth when the latter died in 1783. As was customary for election agents, Wordsworth had apparently been spending his own money in Lowther's service, anticipating reimbursement upon the settling of accounts after the elections.[25] Lowther, however, had successfully abused his agent's trust, neither paying him during his lifetime nor reimbursing his estate after his death. As for Cambridge, Wordsworth's claims about its equality and integrity are contradicted not only by his own observations elsewhere in *The Prelude* (e.g., III.644–68) but by historical evidence that, despite the beginnings of efforts at reforming the university, it still seethed with intrigue, favoritism, and injustice and worldly success for its graduates depended on influence and connection rather than merit.[26]

There was perhaps good reason for not recounting the Lowther episode in 1804, when the France books of *The Prelude* were written. Lowther's heir had paid the debt voluntarily in that year, and Wordsworth was on good terms with the man who would later become his patron. But this understandable tact does not explain the other inconsistencies. Furthermore, Wordsworth concealed more than the conflict with Lowther in his account of the events of his revolutionary conversion. There is something odd in general about the tone of that account. The explanation is autobiographical in form, a subnarrative within the larger narrative of the growth of the poet's mind that is the poem itself; but this section is more vague in description, more abrupt in transition, more distanced and impersonal than others. Its omissions and distortions are not sufficiently accounted for by the accepted critical notion that the poem was not meant as personal autobiography, that its major biographical alterations and dislocations were imposed in order that the spiritual design inherent in the life, which had become apparent to the mature poet only in retrospect, could stand revealed as the principle that was operative from the beginning.[27]

In this connection, Nicholas Roe points out a crucial difference between the radicalism of Coleridge and Wordsworth: Wordsworth's idea of revolution did not, as did Coleridge's, reflect the philosophic and religious concerns of radical Dissenters, and he did not share their belief in divine revelation.[28] Wordsworth in fact did not fit any of the usual patterns of English radicalism in the 1790s; he was Anglican and connected through his father's service with the landed interest, while most radicals were either Dissenters who had arrived at the demand for political change through their desire for religious freedom and equality or members of the middling classes who for economic reasons wanted parliamentary reform to end the royal patronage and aristocratic manipulation that made government costly and intrusive.[29] The inevitable conclusion that Wordsworth's political enthusiasm was "initially the product of personal experience and involvement," however, makes all the more mysterious the poet's attribution of so profound an effect to so inadequate a cause. By personal experience, Roe himself means simply the personal impact on Wordsworth of Michael Beaupuy and Abbé Grégoire, the aristocratic officer and the charismatic republican orator (later president of the Convention) who were present and politically active in Blois during Wordsworth's stay there in 1791–92. The unanswered question, however, is what made Wordsworth susceptible to their influence when he had withstood the pull of a more exuberant, less conflicted, revolutionary France the year before.

Wordsworth's second trip to France coincided with the ripening and convergence of a number of crises in his life. Although it is hardly evident from the account in *The Prelude*, the trip itself was a response to one crisis, and it soon generated another. The problem of Wordsworth's finances and his liaison with Annette Vallon have been discussed frequently in the Wordsworth literature, and they will need to be considered again here. What gave them point and force, however, was their connection to a more basic and less frequently mentioned issue, the crisis of Wordsworth's poetic identity and poetic project. Wordsworth does allude to this problem, though in this case the scantiness of treatment is less a matter of suppression than of his own less than fully conscious appreciation of its motivating force. The developing crisis, however, which threatened his poetry with blockage and impasse, can be followed in the small body of work he had written up to the time of the trips.

"The Vale of Esthwaite," Wordsworth's longest boyhood poem, was written largely on the eve of his departure from Hawkshead Grammar School for Cambridge University at age seventeen. In form a descriptive poem with a strong admixture of "Gothic" or supernatural elements, it seems to be a variation on the conventional theme of leaving youth behind, with its acceptance, albeit reluctant, of the premise common to the poetic humanism of the eighteenth century that maturation involves a rejection of youthful fancy for mature reason and the moral truths it discloses through nature.[30] The conventional theme, however, reveals a strongly personal agenda. The poem is one of exile and loss, of rage and hope, of despair at the ephemerality and fragility of the containing structures of nature, and of wishful confidence that the poet has the power to sustain and fortify these structures through the right kind of imagination.

Derivative, melodramatic, and disjointed—only partly because the extant version of the poem is put together from fragments—"The Vale of Esthwaite" nevertheless has both real power and the unity of a deeply felt conflict. The cause of the young poet's pain is his imminent departure from the Vale, the only real home he has known since his mother's death in 1778, when he was eight years old. The identification of the Vale with the lost mother and the reawakened yearning for her at the prospect of yet another wrenching separation are explicit. Even if he is far away when he dies, Wordsworth says to the Vale, his soul will cast "the wistful view / the longing look alone on you"[31] because he has no other parent:

> For I must never share
> A tender parent's guardian care;
> Sure, from the world's unkind alarm,
> Returning to a mother's arm;
> Mist-eyed awhile upraise the head
> Else sinking to Death's joyless bed,
> And when by pain, by Death, depress'd
> Ah! sure it gentler sinks to rest.
>
> (514–21)

These lines would seem to be the earliest and most direct poetic evidence for Richard Onorato's psychological thesis that Wordsworth's lifelong quest for a vital relationship with nature was the unconscious rejection of the traumatic loss of his mother and the effort to restore her in substitute form.[32] Yet even in this youthful work, the longing for nature is riven by ambivalences not only about nature's goodness but about the desirability of its maternal role. The first part of the poem alternates between efforts to enumerate nature's sustaining pleasures and the irruption of fearful images that threaten to overwhelm and destroy these pleasures. Initially the images are drawn from the Gothic conventions of contemporary literature: druid spirits demand the author's sacrifice, ominous female forms haunt him in the dungeons of mysterious castles. Eventually, however, it is nature, the Vale herself, that appears as the threatening force: the Vale is "dark and dreary," the river flowing through it heaves along in "sleepy horror" (382), and on the rocks above stand terrifying forms of murder, suicide, and madness. Wordsworth abruptly apologizes to the stream for seeing it in such uncharacteristically harsh terms; his apology implies his disappointment and anger that it can no longer soothe his pain, as it has always done before (403). In the past, the Vale had consoled him for the death of his father, even, he adds in an apparent and jarring non sequitur, for his guilt at not having mourned him sufficiently (the present tense in the line "I mourn because I mourned no more" [433] suggests the guilt is not even now assuaged), and for the separation from his sister Dorothy. But now he is leaving the Vale itself, the one loss for which it obviously cannot console him. In the face of his terrors and his sense of betrayal—a sense none the less intense for its irrationality, because he is the one that is leaving—he struggles to hold on to the Vale with the thought that he can nonetheless still possess it in the future, through memory.

Wordsworth's apology is crucial but ambiguous. He might be apologizing to assuage nature for his anger because he cannot afford a retaliatory response, lest he lose what solace memory of the Vale might offer after he has left it, "Sick, trembling at the world unknown / And doubting what to call [his] own" (502–3). Such a purpose would make the apology tactical and insincere. There is, however, another possibility. Toward the end of the poem Wordsworth indicates that he knows he has projected his own gloomy and murderous feelings onto the Vale. In a sudden shift of address from nature to the imagination, he bids farewell to the "forms of Fear that float / Wild on the shipwreck of the thought," images produced by "fancy in a Demon's form" that "Rides through the clouds and swells the storm" (546–49). These words suggest that he has apologized for having blamed nature for what are really his own angry and fearful impulses.

Neither alternative, however, is acceptable to Wordsworth. The first implies the possibility that the Vale is not really beneficent, the second that it is only a screen for his imagination and therefore, if not threatening, yet without real power to comfort either. Wordsworth rejects the first alternative and fatefully modifies the second. He blurs the implications of his apology by resolving his focus exclusively onto the Vale's nurturing aspects, which he then associates with Dorothy and his friend Fleming, whose love will also sustain him in the future. As for the imagination that has projected the "forms of fear" onto the Vale, he gives it up. He is able to bid it farewell, however, without jeopardizing the power of the Vale's image to sustain him in the future because what he is abandoning is "mere" fancy, the form of imagination associated with the palpably unreal, the superstitious, and hence the obviously subjective. He is even able to say goodbye to the more cheery and hopeful face of fancy that he also feels he must leave behind in growing up. He denies *its* reality by associating it with childhood and the infantile wish to be taken care of, which must be surrendered when one enters the adult world to support oneself "in Mammon's joyless mine" (559), whose true sounds are "toil's loud din or sorrow's groan" (560). But these concessions to maturation do not mean the complete surrender of imagination. The last verse of the poem (whose fragmentary nature admittedly makes it difficult to read with certainty) seems to suggest that there is a mature form of the imagination that need not be left behind as merely projective or illusorily wishful when the child grows to adulthood. The imagination that knows true beauty can combine with external beauty in nature to produce a "softer grace" that can overcome the "dreary gloom" of the world of work. In this sense Hartman is right in saying that "The Vale of Esthwaite" anticipates Wordsworth's later hope that the imagination can be married to the world. But his further assertion that the poem acknowledges the autonomy of the imagination is oversimplified and misleading. The poem is concerned with the possibility of hope for the poetic evocation—not the constitution—of a hospitable containing structure in nature, a structure whose comfort *cannot* be seen as the mere product of subjective wishfulness and whose occasional horror *can* be dismissed as the creation of juvenile "Gothic" fantasy. What is most striking and important about the end of "The Vale of Esthwaite" is the way Wordsworth splits the imagination in two. He identifies its "authentic" and potentially generative aspect with the aesthetic of the beautiful and sees that aspect of imagination as the organ for apprehending the objectively beautiful in nature—the pleasant, harmonious, and manageably-proportioned landscape that gives pleasure and is associated with love. "Fancy," however, is linked to the emotions and perceptions associated with the sublime—the lawless, the unbounded, the violent, and the terrifying—and seen as merely subjective and childish, to be suppressed and outgrown. It is fancy that Wordsworth sees as "autonomous" in Hartman's sense, but fancy is purely arbitrary and negative, a destructive power. Wordsworth deals with the images of his rage by splitting them off from "mature" imagination, but the maneuver creates a potential problem for his intended poetry of consolation because those images are the real sources of the imaginative power of the poem. That terrible power, however, has overwhelmed the beneficence of nature in the poem; hence it is greater than the (merely) beautiful nature whose evocation in future poetry is supposed to shelter him and contain it. In fusing his personal situation with concepts of the imagination, Wordsworth had exiled the sublime from his art and in the process cut himself off from the possibility of producing an image adequate to his needs.

These considerations also suggest that it is *conceptually*, hence methodologically, mistaken to distinguish between the mind of Wordsworth as poet and as individual psyche.[33] The poem reveals the intrinsic connection between the biographical and the poetic. I do not mean by this simply to underline the evident psychological elements in the content, structure, or language of the poem. Its broken narrative and wishful conclusion are obviously driven by the loneliness of a youth who has lost mother and father, is separated from his sister, and is about to leave the one substitute for them he has had. In the confessed disturbance of language and image, one can hear the "preternatural animal sensibility"[34] that caused his mother to worry about William more than any of her other children because of what she so early sensed as his greater capacities for good or evil,[35] the "stiff, moody and violent temperament" William himself acknowledged in the angry defiance, outbursts of violence, and suicidal impulses with which he reacted to the coldness and hostility of his guardian relatives.[36] A passage that sounds to the contemporary ear like psychoanalytic satire, interpolated in the poem after his first year at Cambridge, apostrophizes Dorothy with the reason that William is so attached to her—her resemblance to their dead mother:

> Sister, for whom I feel a love
> What warms a Brother far above,
> On you, as sad she marks the scene,
> Why does my heart so fondly lean?
> Why but because in you is given
> All, all, my soul would wish from Heaven?
> Why but because I fondly view,
> All, all that Heav'n has claimed, in you?
>
> (528–35)

But these biographical details do not add up to the "meaning" of the poem. Inherent not only in the poetic enterprise as Wordsworth views it in general but in the explicit consciousness that informs "The Vale of Esthwaite" is the idea that it requires the mind of a poet, dealing in specifically poetic means, to provide an answer to aloneness, fear, and rage. That the youthful Wordsworth generalized his personal alienation is inherent in his aestheticizing its solution. It is the "pencil" placed by the muses "in the hands of taste" that can alone fix "Each Beauty Art and nature knows" (564–67) in a permanence beyond time's effacement that will once again house the self and soften the harshness of the necessary but joyless toil that bare survival necessitates. But casting the personal issue in general aesthetic (and moral) terms does not make it less personal. If the poem only anticipates the desired end without achieving it, it also explains in terms of personal impulses the bifurcation of imagination that makes the realization of an adequate nature impossible—and sets the future problem of Wordsworth's poetry.

"An Evening Walk," which dates from Wordsworth's first years at Cambridge, is usually characterized as a typical eighteenth-century topographical or "loco-descriptive" poem in genre, a view the poet himself tried to reinforce in his old age when he linked its genesis with the memory of an experience at age fourteen that first made him aware of the "infinite variety of natural appearances" and with the resolution he then made to supply the omissions of previous poets by describing these appearances.[37] Written just a little more than a year after "The Vale of Esthwaite," however, this poem affirmed both Wordsworth's poetic identity and the particular poetic project announced in that earlier poem without succeeding in consolidating either. The poem is announced self-consciously as "The history of a *poet*'s evening" (52; italics added), though the specific vantage point and task of the poet are disclosed only implicitly in the process of the poem. The walk takes place in the vicinity of Hawkshead during a summer vacation from Cambridge. The poet contrasts his melancholy mood as a visitor to the landscape of his childhood with his former happiness as its inhabitant. His purpose in the poem is to prove to Dorothy through his description of nature that despite his sadness, "some joys to me remain" (150),[38] though the present "ebb of cheerfulness" means that at best only "Sad tides of joy" may be wrested "from Melancholy's hand" (21–22). Yet, as we have seen, "The Vale of Esthwaite" gave only mixed evidence of past cheerfulness and enjoyment of the pleasures of the Vale. The new poem really represents a continuation of the sense of loss in the old, and its problem is a more advanced and sophisticated version of what it was earlier: the adequacy of nature, or the adequacy of the poet's ability to see nature—Wordsworth does not and cannot distinguish between the two—as a structured whole that can contain and order conflict and above all include the outcast, the living emblem of disorder.

Looking back on his Cambridge years in 1804, Wordsworth remembered

> melancholy thoughts
> From personal and family regards,
> Wishing to hope without a hope; some fears
> About my future worldly maintenance,
> And, more than all, a strangeness in my mind,
> A feeling that I was not for that hour
> Nor for that place.
>
> (*Prelude*, III.75–81)

The mysterious sense of alienation, which went beyond the vexation of family and financial problems, was certainly not the result of social isolation. Wordsworth was later to criticize the superficiality of Cambridge life severely, but by his own account he entered into it with zest and a measure of success. His "heart / Was social, and loved idleness and joy," he admitted (III.234); he had a wide range of connections of all degrees of intimacy, "Companionships, friendships, acquaintances," and he "sauntered, played . . . rioted . . . talked / Unprofitable talk" (III.249–52)—a typical undergraduate. But beneath this surface sociability was a deep anxiety and unsettledness that it could not answer. Whether or not Wordsworth felt himself to be at that time, as he later said, a "chosen Son" endowed with "holy powers / And faculties" (III.81–83)—the phrase dates from 1798 and the end of a period of radical transformation—he seems to have believed at the earlier time that his salvation lay in poetry, as the only way to resolve the dilemma that "An Evening Walk" reveals.

The evening walk takes place in the late afternoon when the heat of the day no longer stuns life into uncomfortable immobility and the glaring light no longer conceals discrete objects in an undifferentiated haze. Noon is a time of forced, and therefore false, stasis and unity. Only later is it possible to discern—indeed it is impossible to avoid—the variety and ferment of which the world is actually constituted. The challenge for the poet is to compose the disharmonies and dangers he sees into a landscape in which opposites balance and dangers are offset by the sense of their necessary place in a structure that would be complete and harmonious. Hence the particular choices of detail, language, and figure. A group of potters goads a laden train of horses slowly up a steep road while a peasant shoots his sledge headlong down a path along the "fearful edge" of the cliff (109–12). The "Sweetly ferocious" cock stalks around his native walks with "firm tread but nervous feet" (129–31). One group of quarrymen toil deep in the bowels of the earth while others cross bridges high up on the cliffs or hang airily from baskets (145–50). These scenes and tropes, whether invented or borrowed from other poets, are selected as oppositions of height and depth, slowness and speed, work and effortless energy, passivity and power, safe servitude and dangerous freedom: the eye of the poet unites them through description into the necessary constituents of a balanced totality. Everything has its proper place in a harmonized landscape both natural and human.

With one exception. Towards the middle of the poem, the poet comes upon a family of swans, which he describes at greater length than he has devoted to all the previous images. The male is appropriately arrogant and self-displaying (201–4), while the female, forgetting her "beauty's pride," is tenderly consumed with a "mother's care" of her cygnets (213–15). Their safe and comfortable home along the river's edge is an organic part of the natural world, nurtured by all the elements. Abruptly, the peaceful setting is broken *not* by a visual image (as virtually all readings of the poem seem to assume) but by an imagined one, an association: the image of a wretched and incomplete human family, a mother and children without a husband and father, who is away fighting in the American Revolution. They are impoverished, homeless, without resources or help, and the anguished mother is forced to watch her children freeze to death in her arms. The picture of their death is drawn out with searing, horrified vividness. It is as immediate as anything the poet has actually seen on his walk, made even more so by the minuteness of detail and the insistent cadence of a perceptual vocabulary:

> I *see* her now, deny'd to lay her head,
> On cold blue nights, in hut or straw-built shed . . .
>
> . . . .
>
> I *hear*, while in the forest depth he sees,
> The Moon's fix'd gaze between the opening trees,
> In broken sounds her elder grief demand.
>
> (257–63; italics added)

Despite the perceptual terms, however, the contrast between the swan and the beggar woman is not one of perceptions but of perceived landscape and imagination. With the image of the beggar woman, the inner world of the poet's terrors has broken in on, and at least momentarily effaced, the sensory world. The previous play of contrasts has got out of control because one visual image has called up counterassociations so powerful that they have overwhelmed the defensive containments of the poetic operation and driven the poet back to the sadness, loss, and alienation he set out to disprove, or overcome.

It is not the bare fact of consciousness, its separateness from nature in an absolute or ontological sense, onto which the poet is here thrown back by his imagination. Vertiginous freedom and the sense of finitude may well lurk at the bottom of every experience of exclusion, loss, or threat of death, as Kierkegaard thought, but stripping such experience down to the abstraction of "self-consciousness" misses not only its phenomenological texture but the nature of the relationship between the ontological, the psychological, and the physical. Consciousness of ultimate separateness and the contingency of being, while not reducible to the pain of social aloneness or the threat of physical annihilation, are, so to speak, parasitical on them, since the vulnerability of the body or the possibility of non-recognition by others are the very meaning of finitude and so can disclose it.[39] The beggar woman's helpless, anguished isolation is not merely a figure for the autonomous imagination, nor is the repeated hammering of the language of coldness in the lines describing the children's state the displacement of an existential chill:

> —No more her breath can thaw their fingers cold,
> Their frozen arms her neck no more can fold;
> Scarce heard, their chattering lips her shoulders chill,
> And her cold back their colder bosoms thrill;
> All blind she wilders o'er the lightless heath,
> Led by Fear's cold wet hand, and dogg'd by Death.
>
> (281–86)

On the other hand, though undoubtedly "social" in that they are images of other people, these are not images of social protest or even social awareness in any political sense of the term. That the beggar's husband is imagined to be fighting in the American Revolution hints at the role of historical forces, human violence, the arbitrary power of governments, and human neglect in the woman's fate, but these are not Wordsworth's concern here either. He is neither attacking nor even attending to the social causation of poverty and misery. The irruption of the scene as imagination rather than perception and the near-obsessive fascination with the most painful details of suffering suggest identification rather than social observation or criticism.[40] The numbers of widowed and orphaned poor and of unemployed soldiers roaming the English countryside increased after the American Revolution, but the beggar woman is essentially a figure of Wordsworth's inner landscape, the adequation of a set of internal fears. Although it is impossible to say what are the exact elements of Wordsworth's identifications with the mother and her children, they center suggestively on the figures of a wife deprived of her husband, a destitute mother unable to take care of her children, and unprotected children exposed to starvation and death by freezing. The central experience is abandonment and deprivation, aloneness, homelessness, and the fear of annihilation, utter exclusion from the fullness of being. If the fascination with the plight of the husbandless woman also matches some fantasy of punishing an abandoning mother and/or displacing a father, it is also suitably punished by the helplessness of the children and their destruction. In any case, what is new in "An Evening Walk" by contrast with "The Vale of Esthwaite" is that Wordsworth has found social correlates to personal problems that situate them in a peculiar space, one not wholly self and not wholly other, but a space that permits a movement back and forth between the two.

The description of the miserable family, however, is broken off with a jarring abruptness so poetically awkward that the reader can almost feel Wordsworth's need to tear himself away from the pain of the scene and the compulsive inclination to dwell on it. The line that describes the children's fate, "Thy breast their death-bed, coffin'd in thine arms," is followed with "Sweet are the sounds that mingle from afar" as the poet returns from frightening imagination to cheering sensory presence, attentive now to the sounds of evening. But oncoming night brings with it another incipient crisis. "Unheeded night has overcome the vales, / On the dark earth the baffled vision fails" (363–64). The failure of vision is dangerous because "Naught else of man or life remains behind / To call from other worlds the wilder'd mind" (375–76). Even daylight has not been enough to prevent the mind from looking into those "other worlds"; darkness threatens to plunge the mind irretrievably back into its terrors because there will be no possibility of visual diversion for escape. Just at this point the rising moon, explicitly equated in the poem with the dawn of hope, produces a new vision, one again of the inner eye, a fantasy of the future. The metaphor is exquisitely ironic, since the "Moon's own morn" is as weak by comparison with the dawn as hope is in comparison with reality, or future fantasy with current fear. The vision is of a cottage— "Sole bourn, sole wish, sole object of my way" (410)—to be shared with Dorothy, a cottage where they will dwell together in "golden days" until their deaths.

Only after imagining the Edenic repose of that sanctuary, where pain will be nothing more than the sadness of everyday life—and not, by implication, the unnatural fear of freezing that haunts the pleasures of a summer's evening walk—can the poem reconstitute the full and harmonious natural scene. Now, however, it is a night scene that the poet describes, full of sounds, not sights. The poet has reconstituted a structure made up of simulacra of his own voice. It is an expression of the specifically poetic power, of speaking the comforting presence and unity of nature. But it is only after he has been able to imagine being housed with his sister once more that he is able to hear the harmony and use that voice to express the harmony he hears.

"An Evening Walk" thus gives some idea of the "melancholy thoughts" that haunted Wordsworth at Cambridge, as well as of the way he tried to deal with them. The feelings at war in the poem are precariousness and power. They are epitomized by two sounds the poem records in its last two lines:

The distant forge's swinging thump profound;
Or yell in the deep woods of lonely hound.

(445–46)

Wordsworth senses the poetic power that will enable him to forge an image of nature great enough to contain even his sense of isolation and rage; forging it is the very act that gives him the place he otherwise does not have within it. But the poem questions whether he, and nature, are up to the task, whether his voice is nothing but a lonely desperate howl rather than a ringing productive hammer. Perhaps the natural material he has to work with is inadequate, threatening to disappear along with the light of day, threatening, above all, to disappear under the enormous pressure of his own inner life. What kind of succor could a nature so vulnerable to the onslaught of his own fantasy give him?

Here was the poetic crisis Wordsworth was facing on the eve of his trips to France. A passage from the 1797 version of "The Pedlar"—Wordsworth's "earliest sustained piece of autobiographical . . . writing," as Jonathan Wordsworth aptly calls it[41]—seems to corroborate more directly the troubled impasse of "An Evening Walk." The age reference indicates the period immediately following the composition of that poem.

> But now, before his twentieth year was passed,
> Accumulated feelings pressed his heart
> With an encreasing weight; he was o'erpowered
> By Nature, and his spirit was on fire
> With restless thoughts. His eye became disturbed,
> And many a time he wished the winds might rage
> When they were silent. Far more fondly now
> Than in his earlier season did he love
> Tempestuous nights, the uproar and the sounds
> That live in darkness. From his intellect,
> And from the stillness of abstracted thought,
> He sought repose in vain. I have heard him say
> That at this time he scanned the laws of light
> Amid the roar of torrents, where they send
> From hollow clefts up to the clearer air
> A cloud of mist, which in the shining sun
> Varies its rainbow hues. But vainly thus,
> And vainly by all other means he strove
> To mitigate the fever of his heart.

("Pedlar," 185–203)

Poetry provided the only promise Wordsworth had. If he doubted the power of his own perception or voice, there was little he could do but still the doubts and keep writing; but if he doubted the power of the land-scape, there was another recourse—to look to a more adequate land-scape, one with power great enough to overwhelm and subdue the refractory imagination whose images of alienation and destruction seemed to burst through all containments.

Some such motive lay behind his desire to travel to the Continent to see the Alps. That mighty landscape, which had become part of the convention of the eighteenth-century sublime, might shore up a sense of nature whose frailty was under constant inner attack. As he hinted later in *The Prelude*, his poetic vocation seemed to depend upon it:

> But Nature then was sovereign in my heart,
> And mighty forms seizing a youthful fancy
> Had given a charter to irregular hopes.

> (VI.346–48)

Whether the 1790 walking tour even provisionally achieved his purpose must remain uncertain, because the first poetry resulting from it was finished only after he became a political partisan, when his conception of nature and the poet's relation to it had changed. Both the passage in his 1790 letter to Dorothy that refers to the "terrible majesty" of the Alps and their depiction in "Descriptive Sketches" suggest that he had encountered there images on the scale of his feelings and needs. But that poem is properly part of the revolutionary phase of Wordsworth's career. And that only developed when another crisis, this one connected with the material conditions of a poetic vocation, forced him to the Continent a second time. The new crisis posed the question of power in a new arena.

Lord Lonsdale's refusal to pay his debt to John Wordsworth's estate meant that William was financially, as well as physically and emotionally, dependent on his unsympathetic guardians, who had to pay for his education as well as his support. Despite their coldness—in good part no doubt because of it—William felt a strong sense of obligation to prepare for a career so that he could support himself and no longer be a financial burden upon them. For someone of his social background with a university education, this meant a career in law, medicine, the university, or the church, and as a well-connected Hawkshead boy at Cambridge, he had many opportunities for fellowships and preferments open to him.[42] At least for a short time, he half-fooled either himself, his relatives, or, given the psychosomatic indications, both, into believing he was serious about the law. "He wishes very much to be a lawyer," Dorothy wrote, "if his health will permit, but he is troubled with violent headaches and a pain in his side" (*Letters*, 7). The wish, if it ever really existed, did not last very long. Wordsworth not only did very little to prepare himself for anything practical, he refused to take a systematic or ambitious approach to his own studies. A passage in *The Prelude* nicely captures the intricacies as well as the force of his rebelliousness—his conflict over it, the immobility it led to, and his exploitation of the impasse to sanction further rebellion:

> I was detached
> Internally from academic cares,
> From every hope of prowess and reward,
> And wished to be a lodger in that house
> Of letters, and no more—and should have been
> Even such, but for some personal concerns
> That hung about me in my own despite
> Perpetually, no heavy weight, but still
> A baffling and a hindrance, a controul
> Which made the thought of planning for myself
> A course of independent study seem
> An act of disobedience towards them
> Who loved me, proud rebellion and unkind.
> This bastard virtue—rather let it have
> A name it more deserves, this cowardise—
> Gave treacherous sanction to that over-love
> Of freedom planted in me from the very first,
> And indolence, by force of which I turned
> From regulations even of my own
> As from restraints and bonds.
>
> (VI.29–48)

Wordsworth alludes here to his refusal, despite high achievements in his first half-year at Cambridge, to take the courses or sit for the exams required to win honors and the fellowships that would have eased his guardians' financial burden. It was his guilt over this, he claimed, that prevented him even from embarking on an independent course of study, though he admits that the inhibition rationalized what he later judged as such "overlove of freedom" that he was glad not to be bound even by self-imposed tasks. In fact, it was not self-discipline he rejected, but any interference with his poetic ambitions.

> The Poet's soul was with me at that time,
>
> . . . .
> A thousand hopes
> were mine . . .
>
> . . . . . .
> Those were the days
> Which also first encouraged me to trust

With firmness, hitherto but lightly touched
With such a daring thought, that I might leave
Some monument behind me which pure hearts
Should reverence.

(VI.55–69)

If Wordsworth was not interested even in reading independently, it was because in the heat of his own ambition and self-belief

The instinctive humbleness,
Upheld even by the very name and thought
Of printed books and authorship, began
To melt away; and further, the dread awe
Of mighty names was softened down, and seemed
Approachable. . . .

(VI.69–74)

Why should he read when he could write, and join the company of the mighty?

At the end of his third year, instead of spending the vacation period preparing for final examinations, in which he might have earned an honors degree respectable enough for a fellowship and a good position and recouped his moral standing with his relatives, he decided to go on the walking tour. "An open slight / Of college cares and study was the scheme," he admitted, though insisting that it was not "entertained without concern for those / To whom my worldly interests were dear" (VI.342–45). The only outward sign of that concern—mostly for Dorothy—was his not telling her or anyone about his intentions in advance. Supportive of William as she was, Dorothy was more attuned to the practicalities. "I am very anxious about him just now," she wrote in the spring of 1790, "as he will shortly have to provide for himself. Next year he takes his degree; when he will go into orders I do not know, nor how he will employ himself; he must when he is three and twenty finally either go into orders or take pupils; he will be twenty by April" (*Letters*, 29). This is the first information about a change of career plan, but it is apparent that she took it more seriously than he did. When he returned to Cambridge after his first tour, he took the examinations for a degree without honors, spent the four months between January and May in London living on a small sum provided by his paternal uncle Richard Wordsworth and the next four in Wales at the home of a friend.

Dorothy reported that her brother was happy during this period; his own letters betray more ambivalence, but given his circumstances, a surprising absence of real concern. To his Cambridge friend William Mathews, he wrote on June 17 that he had passed his time in London in a strange manner," alternating between strenuous activity and indolence, though not without "many very pleasant hours." Now, he said, "he was spending the time in a "very agreeable manner" and looking forward to a walking tour of Wales (*Letters*, 49–59). On August 3, in another letter to Mathews, he admitted with some apparent embarrassment that since coming to Wales he had not done anything, adding with guilty, yet defiant, self-mockery "I rather think my gaiety increases with my arrogance, as a spend-thrift grows more extravagant, the nearer he approximates to a final dissipation of his property" (*Letters*, 56). There was, in fact, some cause for William's insouciance. In early March of that year, an injunction that Lord Lonsdale had obtained in 1788 staying proceedings against him by the administrators of John Wordsworth's estate was dissolved. In a letter of May 23, Dorothy wrote that the outcome of the Lonsdale suit looked hopeful, and in late August, a verdict was given in the case in favor of the estate and the matter referred to an arbitrator for settlement of the exact amount to be paid by Lonsdale. It looked as if the Wordsworth children would obtain a real, if modest, economic independence, and William would be free to pursue a poet's vocation unhampered by the need for some other occupation.

By September, however, the insouciance was gone. A letter to Mathews on September 23 chided him for proposing that they both give up seeking a regular livelihood and take to the road. William's financial situation had suddenly changed. The arbitration had been delayed and was clearly not proceeding to a conclusion; it appeared that no money would be available very soon, if at all. And in early September, Wordsworth had received the offer of a curacy in Harwich from his cousin. Although he could not yet take up the living because he was not of age for Anglican orders, it now seemed he would ultimately have to do so. "[W]ere I so situated, as to be without relations to whom I were accountable for my actions, I should perhaps prefer your idea . . . to vegetating on a paltry curacy," he wrote Mathews. "Yet . . . I should not be able to reconcile to my ideas of right the thought of wandering about a country, without a certainty of being able to maintain myself" (*Letters*, 59). Wordsworth's hopes for financial and thus occupational independence had been apparently all but ended by Lonsdale, whom now even Dorothy, a lover of the monarchy and established society, called "the greatest of tyrants" (*Letters*, 65). A bleak and oppressive reality was closing in on him instead. The already galling dependency on his guardians was forcing him into a vocation he despised, a vocation which in any case could provide no support for almost two more years. The powder was being heaped up for an explosion. In a desperate effort to find a means of at least temporary support and a perhaps more palatable longer-term alternative—Dorothy had referred to the possibility in her letter of the previous year—he abruptly decided to go to France again in order to learn enough of the language to become a companion and tutor to young gentlemen. It was there that the fuse was lit.

In *The Prelude*, Wordsworth made a suggestive parenthetical comment about the "feast, and dance and public revelry, / And sports and games" in which he had participated at Cambridge and especially during the summer vacation. They were, he remarked, "less pleasing in themselves, / Than as they were a badge glossy and fresh / Of manliness and freedom" (IV.274–77). Oblique as the comment is, it is one of the few he permitted himself about the sexual side of adolescence, the testing of virility and independence in competition and flirtation, but it suggests that "manliness and freedom" were an issue in this sphere of his life, as they were in terms of poetic identity and financial independence. There is no evidence, however, other than a passing reference Dorothy made to William's enjoying the company of the some young ladies on one of his summer vacation trips, of any romantic, let alone erotic, interest until his second trip to France. Suddenly, only a short time after his arrival in Orléans, where he had chosen to reside, in circumstances of heightened dependence, diminished prospects, and frustrated hope and ambition, he fell passionately in love.

So much has been written and so much made of Wordsworth's affair with Annette Vallon that it is easy in reaction to underestimate, if not entirely discount, its importance to his politics and his poetry. Seen in the light of the crises attending his trip to France, however, it takes on intensified and even new significance. Perhaps little can or should be made of the fact that she was four years his senior. But her correspondence reveals her as a warm, direct, giving, and adoring woman, as her later activities on behalf of hunted royalists show her idealistic, courageous, and capable of initiative. Although of a social status inferior to Wordsworth's, her personality and age doubtless made her appear to him strong as well as tender, a woman whose love and devotion were to be prized. In his baffled circumstances, his passion for her, and hers for him, were consolation, fulfillment, and defiance, a proof of strength and confirmation of worth. There is a striking coincidence in timing that supports the idea of a connection between Wordsworth's financial predicament and the love affair. Annette's and William's child was born on December 15, 1792. If she was a full-term baby, she was conceived in about the middle of March, six weeks or so after Wordsworth moved to Blois, Annette's home. As late as December 7, 1971, Dorothy was again entertaining hopes for a successful, even speedy conclusion to the Lonsdale suit (*Letters*, 65). But toward the end of February 1792, Lord Lonsdale alleged that the cause of the suit had been abated by the fact that one of the Wordsworth children had come of age. The suit came to rest indefinitely at this point; [43] Lonsdale had finally succeeded in completely blocking the settlement, and by the end of February all prospects for financial independence from that source seemed gone forever. These facts suggest a more concrete referent than has ever been suggested to the lines in the story of Vaudracour and Julia that allude to Julia's becoming pregnant:

> whether through effect
> Of some delirious hour, or that the youth,
> *Seeing so many bars betwixt himself*
> *And the dear haven where he wished to be*
> *In honourable wedlock with his love*
> *Without a certain knowledge of his own*
> *Was inwardly prepared to turn aside*
> *From law and custom* and entrust himself
> To Nature for a happy end of all.
> (IX.596-604; italics added)

The language points to a partly conscious intention on Vaudracour's part not only to get Julia pregnant—her own desires regarding conception are not even considered—but to do so as a protest against the barriers to marriage and an act of defiance of law and custom. The impregnation was, even within the story's own narrative frame, a political act, a protest against paternal, social, religious, and traditional authority.

It can never of course be definitively proved that the story of Vaudracour and Julia is autobiographical, but much of its content, its place in *The Prelude*, the circumstance of its excision and independent publication, and certain details of its style make any other interpretation far more implausible. A love affair between social unequals, the opposition of family (Annette's Catholicism would have made it impossible for William to take Anglican orders, and his relatives did oppose her), the birth of an illegitimate child, the unhappy outcome, the decking of the story in the images of fiction and romance, the odd editorial comments of the poet-narrator, who, for example, reports the fact of Julia's pregnancy with "reluctance," although the story is supposedly about people unknown to him told at second hand, all make the personal significance inescapable. The spirit, however, as well as the letter, of the major details is also important. Like Vaudracour, Wordsworth had claimed the sexual prerogatives of manhood in defiance of both his own impotence in the world and an authority he knew would disapprove his behavior. The rash desire to force the issue and trust "nature" for a happy ending had only compounded his situation. Cheated out of the means of self-support by the high-handedness of an aristocrat who had manipulated the legal system, Wordsworth had with his act of assertive power only increased his helplessness and dependency, creating additional responsibilities he could not manage. The issues of power and autonomy were seamless across the range of Wordsworth's self. Annette was the "dear haven where he wish'd to be," an expression cognate to his characterization of his wish for a "bourn" with Dorothy in "An Evening Walk." In taking her—the word is appropriate to his own sense of at least one of the motives of his desire for her—he had attempted to realize his long-held poetic vision of housing himself in nature, now however not through passive perception but by active appropriation, through the exercise of his own productive power. The love affair was itself symbolically a poetic consummation. In an almost incredible irony, the ultimate effect of his impregnating Annette would be to recreate in fact a version of the abandoned wife and mother of "An Evening Walk"; for the moment, however, a far different outcome seemed possible.

The story of Vaudracour and Julia, which ends with Julia forced into a convent and Vaudracour responsible for the death of his child by "some mistake or indiscretion," is set just before the outbreak of the French Revolution. Stunned by tragedy into an almost catatonic withdrawal from the world, Vaudracour could not be roused by "The voice of Freedom" that soon afterwards resounded throughout France, either by public hope or by "personal memory of his own deep wrongs" (IX.931–35). These lines explicitly link personal wrongs with a political struggle for freedom, suggesting the equation that Wordsworth himself made between his own cause and the Revolution. They imply a contrast between Vaudracour's fate and his own; unlike the tragic but pathetic figure who could not defy his father, Wordsworth was moved to political rebellion by his own ability to connect personal wrongs with their sociopolitical causes and to act on his knowledge.

As with the beginning of the love affair with Annette, the timing of events is too precise to be merely coincidental. Wordsworth's political engagement dates from the period after February 1792 in Blois, where he met Michael Beaupuy, his political mentor, and where later in the year he heard the speeches of Abbé Grégoire, whose visionary republicanism helped inspire his own early millenarian politics.[44] Wordsworth, as we have seen, had not responded to the substantial Dissenting presence at Cambridge that so influenced Coleridge.[45] Although he claimed to have read Burke, Paine, and other writers of "master pamphlets of the day" (IX.97), perhaps while resident in London in the spring of 1791, he had passed through Paris on the way to Orléans in November 1791 without lingering, pocketing a relict of the Bastille in a perfunctory gesture, "Affecting more emotion than I felt" (IX.71). Once arrived in Orléans, he had been able to converse quite comfortably with royalist officers because he was "indifferent" to the concerns of contemporary political debates (IX.201–7) and was neither offended by, nor took offense at, strongly held and divisive ideas. The abrupt transformation of Wordsworth's political consciousness between December 1791 and February 1792, above all the impact on him of Beaupuy, can only be explained by the whole complex of issues that came to a climax in Lonsdale's final triumph and Annette's pregnancy.

Wordsworth noted a number of Beaupuy's qualities that reflected his own self-image and aspirations at the time—his coupling of meekness with enthusiasm "to the height / Of highest expectation" (IX.298–301), the passion that had once made him a successful *galant* but which now served the cause of freedom as well as it had the pursuit of love (IX.324). In particular, however, three of his characterizations of Beaupuy bring out the essentials of his own crises. "[T]hrough the events / Of that great change," Wordsworth wrote, Beaupuy "wandered in perfect faith, / As through a book, an old romance or tale / Of Fairy" (IX.305–9). He had the unquestioning belief and sense of mission of a Spenserian hero, and so could evoke Wordsworth's own identity as poetic fashioner of faith. But he was fitted to do so in the circumstances because he was *not* a poet but "one whom circumstance / Hath called upon to embody his deep sense / In action, give it outwardly a shape, / And that of benediction to the world" (IX.407–10). As a man of action, a soldier of the Revolution, Beaupuy was the ideal object of identification for the young man whose own inability to act had brought him to the point of rebellion. And the purpose of Beaupuy's action, his definition of the ideals of revolution, mirrored exactly the central concern of Wordsworth's poetic aspirations. The "hunger-bitten Girl" they met one day, creeping along with a cow tied to her arm and knitting "in a heartless mood / Of solitude" (IX.512–18) was in a direct line of succession from the female beggar of "An Evening Walk," and Beaupuy's agitated response to her—"'Tis against that / Which we are fighting" (IX.519–20)— alone made him Wordsworth's more confident and purposive alter ego. It validated Wordsworth's own connection of personal emotions to the public struggle for freedom and equality. The rescue of the impoverished girl, and everything she represented *for* Wordsworth and *as* Wordsworth, was to be effected now by politics *and* poetry, working together:

> I with him believed
> Devoutly that a spirit was abroad
> Which could not be withstood, that poverty,
> At least like this, would in a little time
> Be found no more, that we should see the earth
> Unthwarted in her wish to recompense
> The industrious, and the lowly child of toil,
> All institutes for ever blotted out

That legalized exclusion, empty pomp
Abolished, sensual state and cruel power,
Whether by edict of the one or few—
And finally, as sum and crown of all,
Should see the people having a strong hand
In making their own laws, whence better days
To all mankind.

(IX.520–34)

III) The Radical Wordsworth

i) The Phases of Radicalism

Wordsworth's revolutionary phase lasted from early 1792 until the middle of 1795. It is difficult to follow or document, its end even more elusive than its beginning, though the transformation that resulted from its crisis was more profound than the initial change and created the "historical" Wordsworth. He did not reflect on the process of his changing ideas and feelings in contemporaneous writings; his letters are few and relatively uninformative, and the retroactive account in *The Prelude*, while indispensable, must as usual be used with the greatest caution. Yet this is the crucial period for the formulation of the problem that was to be the focus of his greatest work.

Two quite different kinds of writing mark the brief period of Wordsworth's relatively unalloyed enthusiasm for the French Revolution. They are usually treated separately, but neither can be fully understood except in relation to the other. Shortly after his return to England in December 1792, he made his only foray into revolutionary political theory and polemic, the *Letter to the Bishop of Llandaff*. At about the same time, in early 1793, he published "Descriptive Sketches," which had been written during 1792, along with "An Evening Walk," which dated from before his revolutionary period. In the autumn of 1793, Wordsworth wrote the first version of the "Salisbury Plain" poems, "A Night on Salisbury Plain," and in 1794 revised "An Evening Walk" in keeping with his radical political views; with "Descriptive Sketches" these poems thus comprise the body of Wordsworth's "revolutionary" poetry. The revision of "Salisbury Plain" in the fall of 1795 represents the transition away from the Revolution and the writing of *The Borderers* in late 1796 and early 1797 the first reckoning with what had become its final meaning for him.

The choice of occasion for Wordsworth's only revolutionary political manifesto is theoretically and psychologically telling. Richard Watson, Bishop of Llandaff, had just published as an appendix to a previously printed sermon a speech he had given against the Revolution. Watson been one of the few important figures within the established church to take a liberal attitude to Dissent and political reform; he had supported both the American revolutionaries and the French Revolution in its early years. He was also a professor at Cambridge and, despite the location of his see, a countryman of Wordsworth's, living as an absentee bishop on Lake Windermere in Westmoreland. Radicalism on the part of a leading English cleric who also had ties to his native counties was of great moral and emotional significance for Wordsworth. His new-found revolutionary zeal had not at first seemed to him incompatible with English patriotism; in the spring of 1792 he still could describe England to Mathews as a "free country, where every road is open, where talent and industry are more liberally rewarded than amongst any other nation of the universe" (*Letters*, 77). But this sentiment is hard to reconcile both with his reasons for becoming a revolutionary and with his political ideas at the very time he expressed it. His continuing faith in England suggests the intensity of his need to deny any split in his loyalties, as does the "moral shock" that he experienced when England went to war with France on February 1, 1793, an event that should not have surprised him if, as he claimed, he had not doubted that the day would come when England's rulers would turn against France (X.242–45). The support of figures like Watson for the Revolution helped make the compartmentalization of fact and the denial of emotion at least somewhat plausible. By the same token, Watson's apostasy made even more complete Wordsworth's sense of being groundless and adrift when war broke out, cut off by divided loyalties from the domestic landscape that he saw as his nurturant source and no longer "a green leaf on the blessed tree / Of my beloved country" (X.254–55).

The cause of Watson's about-face was of as much concern to Wordsworth as the fact of it. Watson turned against the Revolution as a direct consequence of the execution of Louis XVI in January 1793. From that point on to be a revolutionary was to approve and defend regicide, and Watson's recantation had for Wordsworth the force of a personal accusation. Watson, who had previously been a moral and psychological buffer between Wordsworth and the hostile rulers of England, now in effect abandoned him to their anger and rejection, thus reproducing the consequences of his father's death, which had left him to cold and disapproving relatives. Watson had in effect condemned Wordsworth's rebellion for freedom and power as complicity in murder. Wordsworth's pamphlet was at once a defiant defense of regicide against Watson's recently published expression of horror at the brutal establishment of the French republic and a bitterly sharp offensive on behalf of a republicanism well on the radical side of the spectrum of contemporary ideologies. The central political ideas expressed in the letter were unquestionably derivative, a mix of Rousseau and contemporary French republicanism with Paine and British democratic radicalism. But Wordsworth's political synthesis is not only unique in its emphases; it contains some political ideas that are original and reflect his personal revolutionary agenda.[46]

No doubt, he conceded, a time of revolution was not a season of true liberty. Under the circumstances, political virtues had to be developed at the expense of moral ones. There were times when despotism was so stubborn and perverse that liberty had to borrow its methods "and in order to reign in peace must establish herself by violence."[47] Morally problematic as it might be, the use of violence was to be preferred to the continued existence of the present order, for the form of government that would replace it would be much freer. Government was at best but a necessary evil, Wordsworth argued in accord with the natural law tradition (*Prose Works*, 42); a republican form of government, as the freest, would be the least of evils. On this point he attacked Watson's claim that republicanism was the most odious of all tyrannies because it represented the tyranny of equals by introducing an argument about the psychology of liberty: it would in fact be much easier to defend against an abuse of power by those who were recognized as equals than by those whom people were taught to revere as superiors (36). Wordsworth's political starting point was a strong concept of universal individual liberty that entailed absolute equality and licensed violence to achieve it.

Wordsworth's enormous sensitivity to any form of social and political oppression led him to a unique version of the blend of republicanism and natural law concepts that constituted the most radical British political theorizing during the revolutionary period. He agreed with those critics of classical republicanism (and of Rousseau) who claimed that the size of modern states made direct democracy impossible and necessitated a system of political representation. But though he used the language of "interest" in discussing representation, implicitly taking the position of the advocates of commercial society against anticommercial republicanism, he flatly rejected wealth and property as a condition of political participation. As far as holding office was concerned, "A people will not hold out wealth as a criterion of integrity. . . . Virtues, talents, and acquirements are all that it will look for" (38). As for voting, peasants and mechanics were as qualified as anyone else: "[W]hat vast education is requisite to enable [one] to judge . . . which is most qualified by his industry and integrity to be intrusted with the care of the interests of himself and of his fellow citizens?" (38–39). Wordsworth reinforced his egalitarianism with language about the common good drawn from republicanism: so long as a single man in Great Britain had no suffrage in the election of a representative, the general will of the society of which he was a member was not

being expressed and he was merely a helot; Parliament as presently constituted was not the general will (46–47). Furthermore, to safeguard
against the misuse of power by elected representatives, Wordsworth not
only proposed to shorten the term of office and prohibit anyone from
holding office twice in succession, he fell back on republican direct democracy to insist that the legislature would only propose and deliberate
the laws, while the people alone would have the power to vote them (37).

Political radicalism thus appears to be for Wordsworth the result of a
wider sense of exclusion, oppression, powerlessness, and humiliation.
The predominant tone in the pamphlet is a sense of outrage over inequality and its malignant effects in every sphere of life, psychological and
moral as well as economic and political. Wordsworth was particularly offended by the utter unjustifiability of the aristocracy's absolute monopoly
of political and social power and the disparity between its claims to superiority and its moral and intellectual stature. "What services," he demanded, "can a man render to the state adequate to such a compensation
that the making of laws, upon which the happiness of millions is to
depend, shall be lodged in him and his posterity, however depraved
may be their principles, however contemptible their understandings.
. . . [W]hat services can a man render society to compensate for the outrage done to the dignity of our nature when we bind ourselves to address
him and his posterity with humiliating circumlocution, calling him most
noble, most honorable, most august, serene, excellent, eminent and so
forth" (44). The note of narcissistic injury and rage in the conventional
antiaristocratic rhetoric is unmistakable.

But the form of inequality in the existing order most disturbing to
Wordsworth was the unnatural inequality of wealth, for which the political privileges of the aristocracy were responsible. The coupling of a radically individualist economic and political position with a concern to ame-
liorate poverty was Paineite in form[48] but personal to Wordsworth in its
inspiration. Some distinction of wealth would always attend superior talents and industry, he acknowledged, but it was through their control of
the legislative system that the aristocracy had passed laws such as primogeniture, enclosure acts, and the setting of arbitrarily low wages for work-
ers that created "the present *forced* disproportion of . . . possession" (43;
italics added). Wordsworth's rural poor once again make their appearance, now as the victims not of nature or fate but of political manipulation
and oppression. The special emphasis on the extremes of poverty that
push people to the margins of society and beyond reflects above all the
concern of his poetry with those whose lives were emblems of the precariousness of existence. He condemned aristocratic manipulation for blocking any hope of putting an end to mendicancy, which he described as a

constant shock to the feelings of humanity. Specifically, this manipulation was responsible for the miseries entailed upon the marriage of those who were not rich, miseries that "tempt the bulk of mankind to fly to that promiscuous intercourse to which they are impelled by the instincts of nature, and the dreadful satisfaction of escaping the prospect of infants, sad fruit of such intercourse, whom they are unable to support" (43). We can read here not only the story of his daughter's birth and the fate he feared for her but the shock to his own moral sensibility, the shame of a manhood potent (and heedless) enough to procreate, but not powerful enough to support its offspring, and, in the oxymoron "dreadful satisfaction," a hint of guilt at the temptation to escape such responsibilities.

If obliquely acknowledged guilt and shame intensified Wordsworth's anger, however, the pamphlet expresses no doubt about where ultimate responsibility for this situation lay. Wordsworth was most venomous in his anger at Watson's defense of the British judicial system, the root cause of his most urgent personal problems. "I congratulate your lordship upon your enthusiastic fondness for the judicial proceedings of this country. I am happy to find you have passed through life without having your fleece torn from your back, in the thorny labyrinth of litigation. . . . To be qualified for the office of legislation you should have felt like the bulk of mankind; their sorrows should be familiar to you, of which if you are ignorant how can you redress them. . . . [Y]our lordship cannot, I presume, be ignorant of our never-ending process, the verbosity of unintelligible statutes and the perpetual continuity in our judicial decisions" (47).

The political-psychological theme of the *Letter* is wounded personal power—the "outrage done to the dignity of our nature" by humiliating deference and by the material obstacles to freedom and self-respect in the poverty caused by the unequal distribution of political authority and the resulting aristocratic manipulation of society. The remedy is the appropriation of power, through the equality that would be created by the elimination of social hierarchy and the institution of democratic republicanism. But perhaps the most striking aspect of this appropriation is Wordsworth's readiness to defend the use of violence to overthrow the old order. It represents an integration of the destructive anger he had long felt but had tried to suppress in his poetry. Wordsworth could assimilate violence when it was transformed from private rage against an abandoning nature or frustrating and humiliating authorities into the shared legitimate anger of victims of a universal injustice.

In the thematics of his poetry, Wordsworth's ability to integrate political power and violence meant the possibility of desegregating and reappropriating the sublime, which had been split off and excluded in his earlier work because it was associated with hostility, rage, and the power of destruction. This appropriation is the central aesthetic event of "Descriptive Sketches." Structurally, "Descriptive Sketches" is a more complicated version of "An Evening Walk." Like the latter, its avowed purpose is to seek a balm for sadness, though here the sadness goes beyond emptiness or loss to include some unnamed source of self-chastisement or guilt. The poet is led on his walk "lur'd by hope her sorrows to remove / A heart, that could not much itself approve."[49] And as in "An Evening Walk," the vision of nature's consoling unification of opposites is disrupted by scenes of loneliness, suffering, and death, though in "Descriptive Sketches," rupture and repair, repeated a number of times with different human figures, become a structuring pattern for the whole poem.

Thematically, however, there are two major changes from the previous poem. The human suffering that the poet encounters here is frequently—though not always—linked causally with political oppression, or "slavery," and he now looks to a political remedy for it, a revolution of liberty that will restore an original natural state of freedom and integration. And the strength for such an uprising will come from humanity's—the poet's—direct appropriation of the terrible power of sublime nature.

There are, at the same time, severe, and in the end unresolved, tensions in the solution the poem calls for. For one, the poet is never wholly secure in his will to believe that the cause of human suffering results from human actions. Although recent commentators like Eric Birdsall are obviously right in insisting on the political meaning of the poem,[50] it oscillates between visionary scenes of Alpine freedom and peace and pessimistic outbursts couched in the language of an eternal human condition. It is, for example, after the evocation of "the traces of primeval man" still left in the Alps, the hardy descendants of that ur-Man, "Nature's Child," who once inhabited the mountains, "free, alone and wild," that the poem raises the lament:

> Soon flies the little joy to man allow'd,
> And tears before him travel like a cloud.
> For come Diseases on, and Penury's rage,
> Labour, and Pain, and Grief, and joyless Age,
> And Conscience dogging close his bleeding way
> Cries out, and leads her Spectres to their prey,
> 'Till Hope-deserted, long in vain his breath
> Implores the dreadful untried sleep of Death.
>
> ("Descriptive Sketches," 636–43)

And again, after the rousing call at the end of the poem for the French Revolution to end conquest, famine, oppression, and persecution, the poet urges his traveling companion in the last lines of the poem to forget for the night "the dead load of mortal ills" and renew "when the rosy summits glow / At morn, our various journey sad and slow" (812–13). The cankers of mortality and guilt lie like an unassimilable, potentially fatal source of infection, at the center of political hope.

But there is also another source of tension in the poem, potentially just as disruptive—that between the individual and the social sources of salvation. This tension also haunts the poem from the beginning. The poet's encounter with the Grison gypsy, "sole human tenant of the piny waste," who is hurled with her child to her death by a sudden mountain storm, first triggers a reflection on the benefits of social solidarity:

> —The mind condemn'd, without reprieve, to go
> O'er life's long deserts with its charge of woe,
> With sad congratulations joins the train,
> Where beasts and man together o'er the plain
> Move on,—a mighty caravan of pain;
> Hope, strength, and courage, social suffering brings,
> Freshening the waste of sand with shades and springs.
>
> (192–97)

But despite the comforts of socially-shared suffering on the plain and the contrast of the gypsy's lonely fate in the mountains, the poet prefers the isolated, dangerous life on the desolate and stormy heights of the mountains, in the face of the very elements that killed her:

> Mid stormy vapours ever driven by,
> Where ospreys, cormorants, and herons cry,
> Where hardly giv'n the hopeless waste to chear,
> Deny'd the bread of life the foodful ear,
> Dwindles the pear on autumn's latest spray,
> And apple sickens pale in summer's ray,
> *Ev'n here Content has fix'd her smiling reign*
> *With Independence child of high Disdain.*
>
> (317–24; italics added)

Although the mountain offers neither fellowship nor material sustenance, it offers something better, independence, which the language expressly characterizes as a reaction of disdain for its hardships and dangers and perhaps also for those not courageous enough to brave them.

The strength for that freedom is obtained not from social solidarity but from the very source of danger and terror itself. As the storm clears, the sun emerges from the clouds and deluges the immense mountain vista with fire. Wordsworth underscored the significance of this moment in a long footnote that signals his breakthrough to the aesthetics—and power—of the sublime. He was going, he says, to give the title of "Picturesque" to the sketches in the poem, but this would have given his reader only "a very imperfect idea of those emotions which [the Alps] have the irresistible power to give the most impassioned imaginations."[51] This power, "which distinguishes the Alps from all other scenery"—an underscoring of the inadequacy of the domestic landscape of "An Evening Walk"—derives from images that "disdain the pencil." The phrase echoes the "pencil of taste" in the "Vale of Esthwaite" and is a rejection of its aesthetics of moderation; "taste" yields to the "impassioned imagination" that alone grasps infinite power and unity. The Alps cannot be represented pictorially, for painting demands contrasts of shading, whereas the sublimity of this scene depended on the impression of unity given it by "that deluge of light, or rather fire, in which nature had wrapped the immense forms around me." But what pictorial representation cannot achieve, poetry apparently can. And that is precisely the point of the whole passage. The poet is able to appropriate the awful majesty of the fiery mountains for himself, through the representation of "the fire-clad eagle's wheeling form," which blazes "Triumphant on the bosom of the storm" (338–39). With the eagle, the poet has slipped the bonds of earth and soars in triumphant freedom sustained by the very power that destroyed the gypsy.

The sublime, however, cannot be wholly mediated by the figure of the eagle; Wordsworth is too aware of his difference, his humanity, to rest there. Immediately the scene shifts from the sky to a lake below, where:

> Behind his sail the peasant strives to shun
> The west that burns like one dilated sun,
> Where in a mighty crucible expire
> The mountains, glowing hot, like coals of fire.
>
> (344–47)

The power of the sun, which consumes the mountains, seems too strong for humanity to withstand, at least when figured as peasant, poor, threatened, and isolated. But in another abrupt shift the "overaw'd" peasant suspends his oars before the suddenly-introduced shrine of William Tell, the heroic fighter for Swiss freedom against the Austrians. The identification with mighty heroes of old raises the weak and fearful individual above his own terror to a state of near divine power:

> And who but feels a power of strong controul,
> Felt only there, oppress his labouring soul,
> Who walks, where honour'd men of ancient days
> Have wrought with god-like arm the deeds of praise?
>
> (352–55)

Having imaginatively effected this connection with past political power, the poet can once again appropriate the power of nature, rather than fear it, not only through a natural symbol but as man. He can withstand the sun by identifying with "god-like" men who have sublimated destructive energy in the service of human liberation. The political, however, appears not in the form of social solidarity but in the form of heroic, that is, individual, political action; it is the ancient hero who is expressly linked to divine power.

Yet even this moment is precarious. As the poet stands alone, "Sublime upon this far-surveying cone" (366–67), he immediately catches sight of the chamois hunter, a man who though of "fearless step," is soon nonetheless endangered and destroyed, like the gypsy, by the power of nature. The poetic appropriation of nature's power proves evanescent. It is not enough to walk where dead heroes fought, revering them as figures of the past without living connection to the present. Continuing power resides only in a self-conscious identification with their lives, which demands reenactment. Hence, when the theme of power returns, it is in the vision of the ancient Swiss mountain dweller, the ancestor of those contemporary inhabitants who still preserve some of their forefathers' virtues and the model for the contemporary struggle for freedom in Europe:

> Once Man entirely free, alone and wild
> Was bless'd as he was free—for he was Nature's child.
> He, all superior but his god disdain'd,
> Walk'd none restraining, and by none restrain'd.
> Confess'd no law, but what his reason taught,
> Did all he wish'd and wish'd but what he ought.
>
> (520–25)

Here is the desired union of man and nature, man absolutely free and unconflictedly ethical. And his descendants retain in their self-aware filiation with their ancestor at least some of the lineaments of sublimity, the connection to infinity.

> Uncertain thro' his fierce uncultur'd soul
> Like lighted tempests troubled transports roll;
> To viewless realms his Spirit towers amain,
> Beyond the senses and their little reign.
>   And oft, when pass'd that solemn vision by,
> He holds with God himself communion high.
>
> (546–51)

Even this image will give way in the unceasing oscillations of the poem. But what is again noteworthy about it is that, though derived in part from the memory of a collective struggle against tyranny, it is a vision of solitary power. The figure of man is not generic, he is the lone individual, the "fire-clad eagle" in human form, communing by himself with God, not part of "the train / Where beasts and man together o'er the plain / Move on." There is an insistent blurring in the poem between collective and

personal power that is not simply equivalent to a shuttling between political and aesthetic power. The appropriated power of the poet is not just
imaginative: the poet is identified both with the artist of the sublime and
with a series of hero-warriors, some of whom, like Sidney, were also poets
(356–64). The full self-representation of the poet is of the poet-warrior
who conquers with sword as well as with pen.

This sense of personal power and conquest is in conflict not only with
the collective aspect of political struggle but with the positive ideals of
the battle for freedom. The invocation to the Revolution near the conclusion of the poem consists of two tonally distinct wishes. The first expresses the hope for the birth of a peaceful and virtuous new order from
the flames of the struggle, an order in which

> Nature, as in her prime, her virgin reign
> Begins, and Love and Truth compose her train;
> With pulseless hand and fix'd unwearied gaze
> Unbreathing Justice her still beam surveys.
>
> (784–87)

But this pacific vision is followed by a warrior's plea to God to allow freedom to triumph over all her enemies, who are listed in a litany of anger:
Conquest, Avarice, Pride, Death, Famine, Oppression, Machination,
Persecution, Discord. The litany reaches its crescendo in a fervent prayer
for the utter destruction of arrogant kings who pretend to omnipotence:

> And grant that every sceptred child of clay,
> Who cries, presumptuous, "Here their tides shall stay,"
> Swept in their anger from th' affrighted shore,
> With all his creatures sink—to rise no more.
>
> (808–9)

The emotions and purposes of personal power inextricably but discerni-
bly interwoven with those of communal purpose seem for this brief moment to dominate the mixture, before they are suppressed in the closing
image of tomorrow's "sad and slow" journey.

Wordsworth's next poem, while picking up directly on the rageful desire
to destroy the oppressor, tilts the balance between individual anger and
social aims back toward the latter; perhaps more accurately, it strives for
a more organic relationship between them. "A Night on Salisbury Plain"
takes up the female beggar who breaks into "An Evening Walk" with the
unwelcome but inevitable force of the return of the repressed and makes
her a sustained focus of attention, sympathy, protest, and conscious identification. She is not the sole center of the poem but one of its two foci,
together with the lonely traveler on the plain who encounters her.

Wordsworth makes a point of their affinity and similarity—"her soul forever widowed of delight, / He too had withered young in sorrow's blight"[52]—and it is the field of tension between them—attraction, congruence, and difference—that determines the shape and thrust of the poem.

Commentators have noted the extraordinary bleakness of the poem's setting and mood, the preternatural emptiness of the plain that seems to bespeak an aloneness beyond even that of a hungry and weary traveler in an isolated place.[53] The writing of the poem and the event which inspired it took place at a low point of desperation for Wordsworth. He was still unemployed—the hoped-for post of tutor had not materialized—and now even further separated from Annette and their child by the war between their countries. His relatives were furious at the news of his liaison with Annette and his desire to marry her; he was no longer welcome to visit Dorothy at their uncle's home, and the offer of a curacy was either withdrawn or made conditional on his giving Annette up.[54] Meanwhile as the prospects for reunion and marriage were diminishing, she was writing pitiful letters expressing her love and longing for him and her continuing trust in him. When his friend William Calvert offered to pay for a joint tour of England and Wales in July and August of 1793, Wordsworth had every reason to embrace the opportunity for temporary financial support and diversion. The breakdown of their carriage and Wordsworth's forced walk alone along the plain must have seemed like the climax and symbol of his troubles.

"A Night on Salisbury Plain" transforms the chance event into a signifier of his current ideas on the ultimate meaning and possible resolution of those troubles. The poem's first four verses establish as the context for both its characters and its reflections the threat of suffering and loss familiar from "The Vale of Esthwaite," "An Evening Walk," and "Descriptive Sketches"; the melodramatic Gothic imagery that pervades the first and recurs in Wordsworth's early poetry at the points of greatest inner turmoil returns here as the poem's setting. The nature and meaning of contemporary suffering are defined in a contrast with the imagined predicament of the savages who inhabited Salisbury Plain in prehistoric times. Fearful and precarious as their lot was, they had nothing better to compare it with, and they at least enjoyed the consolation of a shared predicament. The suffering of the contemporary poor of the plain may be less than that of its ancestral inhabitants in physical terms, but psychologically it is far greater:

> The thoughts which bow the kindly spirits down
> And break the springs of joy, their deadly weight
> Derive from memory of pleasures flown

Which haunts us in some sad reverse of fate,
Or from reflection on the state
Of those who on the couch Affluence rest
By laughing Fortune's sparkling cup elate,
While we of comfort reft, by pain depressed,
No other pillow know than Penury's iron breast.

("Salisbury Plain," 19–27)

The two alternatives offered in the verse to explain modern suffering correspond to the conflict between the permanent and the sociohistorical causes of human suffering that alternate in "Descriptive Sketches." The "sad reverse of fate" could in the circumstances well derive from an autobiographical reflection, but a later verse suggests that Wordsworth intends an ontological rather than a merely accidental origin for human pain with the reference to the memory of previous pleasures:

Unhappy man! Thy sole delightful hour
Flies first; it is thy miserable dower
Only to taste of joy that thou may'st pine
A loss, which rolling suns shall ne'er restore.
New suns roll on and scatter as they shine
No second spring, but pain, till death release thee, thine.

(220–25)

Wordsworth's present loss has thus become a reminder or emblem of an early loss that is figured as inevitable and irrecoverable. There seems to be an inconsistency here that vitiates the contrast between modern and primitive man. The previous happiness with which memory compares the present is obviously childhood, and surely primitives have the same basis of comparison. But the inconsistency, while weakening the rhetorical force of the contrast between primitive and modern man, does not alter the central ambiguity: Wordsworth is still uncertain whether the unhappiness he is describing stems from the human condition or changeable conditions. Significantly Wordsworth for the first time here explicitly links the ontological with the psychological, timeless joy and absolute presence with early childhood.

Both the female vagrant and the traveler are avatars of modern unhappiness. The traveler in this early version of the poem is a virtually disembodied consciousness; only in the revision of 1795 will he acquire a history. The woman, however, is a much more substantial character than the beggar of "An Evening Walk," and only partly because the range of referents for her includes the earlier character. Given the time of composition, it is hard to read her poignant fate without reading Annette into her, a temptation reinforced by the erotic details of her description in stanza 24.

But there are also striking similarities between the female vagrant's biography and Wordsworth's own. Like him, she had lost her mother, then her father. Her father had been cheated out of his possessions, so that his death left her both orphaned and destitute. She too had fallen in love, and lost her beloved to war, in her case permanently. The facelessness of the traveler, qualified only by the reinforcing hint of his own early sorrow, makes him a mirror for the woman, but his otherness makes him a sympathizer, an observer, and someone in a position to console or at least make the attempt.

> Along the fiery east the Sun, a show
> More gorgeous still! pursued his proud career.
> But human sufferings and that tale of woe
> Had dimmed the traveller's eye with Pity's tear,
> And in the youthful mourner's doom severe
> He half forgot the terrors of the night,
> Striving with counsel sweet her soul to chear,
> Her soul for ever widowed of delight.
> He too had withered young in sorrow's deadly blight.
>
> (397–405)

The sequence, diction, and syntax of this stanza condense an entire narrative that recapitulates and modifies the events of "An Evening Walk." The traveler's native preference and inclination is for a solitary relationship with the glories of the sun, but the emotion aroused by human suffering occludes them. At the same time, sympathy for another helps him suppress his own terrors, which, like those in "An Evening Walk," threaten the poet/traveler most intensely at night, when the sun is eclipsed. Externalizing suffering in the woman—not by projecting or even displacing it but by focusing on the genuinely suffering other while retaining some consciousness of his own similarity—enables him to become active, no longer simply a passive sufferer but a comforter. Setting off the last line of the stanza as a separate sentence, Wordsworth makes its point of view an ambiguous consciousness; while the narrator is aware that the traveler identifies with the vagrant, it is at least questionable whether the traveler himself knows this. The sentence also brings the stanza full circle, suggesting that the traveler's original fascination with the sun is itself compensatory.

There is a continual interfusing of dialogues in the poem, an internal dialogue, only partly conscious, within the traveler, a dialogue between traveler and vagrant, and finally, one between the narrator and both characters. Toward the end of the poem the narrator emerges as the observer, commentator, and consoler. He bids farewell to the pair, generalizes their condition, and calls for a remedy. Although there is an undertone of metaphysical despair throughout, the narrator's analysis implicates domestic oppression, debasing work, and the imperial ambitions of nations as the causes of human misery; the poem is clearly in the political vein of "Descriptive Sketches." But in this poem a new note is sounded. Although the last stanza seems to breathe the same militant spirit—"Heroes of Truth pursue your march, uptear / Th' oppressors dungeon from the deepest base" (541–42)—the appeal is not to violence but to the "herculean mace of Reason," whose light alone, in the mixed metaphors of the stanza, will cause "foul Error's monster race" to die. Salvation is not to be found in armed might. Attacking the nations for resorting to war, the poet asks:

> Or whence but from the labours of the sage
> Can poor benighted mortals gain the meed
> Of happiness and virtue, how assuage
> But by his gentle words their self-consuming rage?
>
> (510–13)

This is the first evidence that Wordsworth, just a year after he had defended it, was turning against violence as a solution to the problems of oppression and misery. The next lines are a direct allusion to the Terror in France and the harm it was doing to the aims of the Revolution with its methods.

> Insensate they who think, at Wisdom's porch
> That Exile, Terror, Bonds and Force may stand:
> That Truth with human blood can feed her torch,
> And Justice balance with her gory hand
> Scales whose dire weights of human heads demand
> A Nero's arm.
>
> (514–19)

The two stanzas together suggest nonetheless a lingering tendency to excuse or at least understand the Revolution's turn to murderous violence. Its rage is indeed self-destructive, but it is an expression of the justified anger of the helpless victims, among whom Wordsworth clearly reckoned himself. The latter stanza ends with a hint of the conflict and guilt, already foreshadowed in "Descriptive Sketches," that will become so prominent a theme in 1795–97 in the revision of "Salisbury Plain" and in *The Borderers.* Guilt is unavoidable as long as the poet continues to hold law and authority largely responsible for the violence he has begun to abhor, since to blame authority is in some measure still to condone that violence.

> Must Law with iron scourge
> Still torture crimes that grew a monstrous band

Formed by his care, and still his victim urge,
With voice that breathes despair, to death's tremendous verge?

(519–22)

The "sage" of line 510 whose wisdom will replace violence seems to be William Godwin. "Salisbury Plain" shows that by the early winter of 1794 when the poem was completed, Wordsworth was acquainted with Godwin's An Enquiry into Political Justice, which offered the certainty of progress and perfectibility while repudiating any recourse to action, specifically revolutionary violence, in achieving that end.[55] Wordsworth's turn to Godwin was not unusual among English radicals at this time. There was a tendency to move away from Paine and revolutionary radicalism towards Godwin's necessitarian and pacifist rationalism as Terror in France and repression at home made loyalty to the Revolution increasingly problematic both morally and politically. For a brief moment, Godwin was the hero of the radical movement in England, the man whose theories offered a continuing purchase on the radical hopes that historical reality threatened to ruin. But in the case of this phase of Wordsworth's life, as in the preceding one, it is important not only to know what his political mentor said, but, above all, what Wordsworth made of it for his own purposes; the two are far from the same.

Book X of The Prelude documents in well-known passages Wordsworth's individual struggle with a revolution going bad, indeed mad, as "Tyrants, strong before / In devilish pleas" multiplied their crimes, murdering indiscriminately "Friends, enemies, of all parties, ages, ranks, / Head after head, and never heads enough / For those who bade them fall" (X.307–36). He describes his own nightly visions of despair, tyranny, and implements of death, his nightmares in which he pleaded "before unjust tribunals" with a sense of treachery and desertion in his own soul—a description that seems to match the conflicted sense of both personal guilt and unjust law touched on in "A Night on Salisbury Plain." But evidence from that earlier time suggests that The Prelude rather overdraws the inner struggle of the period from late 1793 to perhaps mid-1795. Even the odd structure of Book X tells a more complicated story. The narrative of events is so obscured and fractured that it is difficult to realize at first reading that at the point where Wordsworth tells of his exultation at Robespierre's fall, the narrative backtracks to the beginning of the Revolution. The most exuberantly hopeful and untroubled expression of optimism—"Bliss was in that dawn to be alive"—follows his account of bitter inner torment and guilt during the Terror. The hearkening back to the first flush of revolutionary enthusiasm at this point in the poem could be a formally appropriate rendering of Wordsworth's conflict at the time it describes, evidence of his difficulty in accepting the guilt and disappointment of 1793–94; in fact, however, the state of mind it registers accords with what the letters and poetry of 1794 indicate about Wordsworth's mood and ideas at that time. Paradoxically, Wordsworth reached the peak of his hope, and his most extreme radical position, during the period he eschewed violent revolution, a position that took him beyond anything dreamed of in the political ideology of the Revolution.

The letters to his friend Mathews certainly confirm the Godwinian rejection of the Revolution. "I recoil," he wrote in June 1794, "from the bare idea of revolution. . . . [N]eed I add that I am a determined enemy to every species of violence?" (*Letters*, 124). But the context of this often-quoted remark was a forceful and unequivocal condemnation of "monarchical and aristocratic governments," of which he disapproved, "however modified," so strongly that he could still say that if there were no gradual and constant reform of abuses, even a revolution might be desirable. This was the same year that he discussed with Mathews a plan for collaborating on a literary and political periodical and made clear his radical commitments so that there be no misunderstanding between the partners: "You know perhaps already that I am of that odious class of men called democrats, and of that class I shall forever continue" (*Letters*, 119). But by far the most illuminating material from that year is the extensive and significant revision of "An Evening Walk" that Wordsworth undertook with the help of Dorothy between April and September of 1794 at Windy Brow.

The revisions made the poem twice as long as the original. Some additions simply extend the descriptions of nature, but the longest and most important passages express strong belief in a new faith that can unite social concern with a sense of personal uniqueness and infinite power. In a reworking of a Horation ode that he inserted into the poem, Wordsworth asserts that proper homage to nature (represented in the stream beside which the poet walks) does not demand, as in the original ode, the ancient sacrifice of a kid just reaching the age of desire and battle—a symbol for Wordsworth's own sexuality and desire for power—but rather certain qualities of the mind:

> Harmonious thoughts, a soul by Truth refined,
> Entire affection for all human kind;
> A heart that vibrates evermore, awake
> To feelings for all forms that Life can take,
> That wider still its sympathy extends,
> And sees not any line where being ends;
> Sees sense, through Nature's rudest form betrayed,
> Tremble obscure in fountain, rock, and shade;
> And while a secret power those forms endears
> Their social accents never vainly hears.

> (123–32)

These lines are notable not only for their Godwinian themes of universal benevolence through truth but as an embryonic version of the doctrine of the "One Life," an idea for which Wordsworth did not have to await Coleridge.[56] Above all, however, the last lines advert to Wordsworth's two current concerns, the desire for personal power and for social connectedness; to his implied fears that they conflict with one another; and to the wish that they would not. He hopes that the mind that is favored enough to see into the secret power of nature's forms and so into eternal being does not thereby miss their social meaning. A later passage amplifies both the secret power and the dilemma it creates. Those favoured souls, taught either by the poet's "Fancy" or by the Godwinian philosopher's "Thought" to see into the unity of all things, are "proud beyond all limits to aspire" and mount "through the fields of thought on wings of fire" (209–10). But such minds are even happier

> If, like the sun, their [] love surrounds
> The [] world to life's remotest bounds,
> Yet not extinguishes the warmer fire
> Round which the close domestic train retire;
> If but to them these farms an emblem yield,
> Home, their gay garden, and the world, their field;
> While that, more near, demands minuter cares,
> Yet this its proper tendance duly shares.
>
> (213–20)

The central metaphors—the fire-clad eagle and the sun—are continued from the poststorm epiphany in "Descriptive Sketches." Through them Wordsworth denominates the aspiration of the "Godwinian" poet, armed with Truth, to grasp infinity without sacrificing the domestic and the human. Here for the first time Wordsworth states the ambition that will both power and stymie his central poetic project a few years later. Never again, however, will he make as explicit his consciousness that his ambition has two components in uneasy relationship with one another and that one of them is a sense of personal power so great as to threaten to compromise the individuality of anything other than itself. For one who would be like the sun and contain infinity—the metaphor becomes uneasy here as Wordsworth, in the image of the sun surrounding the world, forces together illumination and possession—there is a danger of extinguishing the little fires of personal concern that warm other people. At one point Wordsworth gives away his deepest and truest intention by placing himself, or rather, the individual mind armed with the Truth, above the sun itself:

> Roll on, till, hurled from thy bright throne sublime,
> Thyself confess the mighty arm of Time;

Thy star must perish, but triumphant Truth
Shall tend a brightening lamp in endless youth.

(337–40)

Appropriately, it was just at this point in his development that Wordsworth first introduced the name of Milton directly into his poetry. He had
of course been there all along, but only with his current sense of power
could Wordsworth dream of identifying with him directly. The Milton he
evoked was at once the political Milton, the republican poet, but also the
blind Milton who despite the outer darkness supplied an inner light
greater than any mere external light could ever be.

So Virtue, fallen on times to gloom consigned
Makes round her path the light she cannot find,
And by her own internal lamp fulfills,
And asks no other star what Virtue wills,
Acknowledging, though round her Danger lurk,
And Fear, no night in which she cannot work;
In dangerous night so Milton worked alone,
Cheered by a secret lustre all his own,
That with the deepening darkness clearer shone.

(680–88)

These lines have particular resonance in Wordsworth's development;
they represent an amazing reversal of the poem's first version, with its
climactic expression of his own fear of the night that eclipses the sensory
perception he thought necessary in order for him to be able to constitute
nature as home. Now he, like Milton, needs neither the sun nor visual
perception. He too has the "secret lustre," which, though it enables him
to penetrate nature's secret, is not derived from it and does not depend
on it; to the contrary, it is all the brighter when not distracted by external
light.

This is not, however, a comfortable place for Wordsworth to rest. In
the poem's revised conclusion, the poet-walker descends from his heights
to commune with the common people:

—Who now, resigning for the night the feast
Of Fancy, Leisure, Liberty, and Taste,
Can pass without a pause the silent door,
Where sweet Oblivion clasps the cottage poor?

(771–74)

Night does not overcome him, as it did in the first version of "An Evening
Walk"; he voluntarily suspends his power to join with the humble. The
precincts of the poor, however, yield a "moral interest" to "subtle
thought," which, if it does not resurrect the grander claims for the poet's

mind, at least undermines the most important rival claimants to preeminence. The huts of the poor are in the neighborhood of a ruined abbey, beside a stream, but neither of the two, religious edifice or natural entity, has the power to comfort the cottagers.

> Here sleep sheds a more refreshing dew
> Than yon dark abbey's tenants ever drew
> From the soft streamlet idly murmuring near
> At will—but now constrained with toil to rear
> The deep night-hammer that incessant falls
> And shakes the [] ruin's neighbouring walls.
>
> (797–802)

Religion is defunct, and nature—which even in its pristine form could not sufficiently refresh—has now been subdued and enslaved by commercial enterprise. The same human enterprise, turned to virtuous ends, the poem implies, could refresh the poor more thoroughly than even sleep could by altering their condition rather than by merely supplementing it with the balm of temporary oblivion.

ii) The Crisis

That Wordsworth underwent some sort of crisis of belief between about the middle of 1795 and late 1796 is evident not only from what he said later in *The Prelude* but from the radical new direction his work took as a result at the time. The problem has always been to determine not only exactly when this crisis took place but more important, just what it consisted of. Part of the difficulty is that again there is little contemporary evidence for a subjective *feeling* of crisis on Wordsworth's part. His letters, as well as those of Dorothy, from the Racedown period, the supposed peak of the crisis, report them both generally cheerful, if somewhat isolated, though Wordsworth certainly had a lengthy fallow spell in the winter and spring of 1796, as he wrote Mathews on March 21, 1796. "As to writing it is out of the question" (*Letters*, 169). More than a year earlier, on January 7, 1795, he had written Mathews an apology for the interruption and late despatch of a letter, telling him cryptically, "I have lately undergone much uneasiness of mind" (*Letters*, 138). The uneasiness might have been connected with his comments on John Horne Tooke in the first part of the letter; one of the leading radicals of the day, Tooke had just been acquitted of charges of high treason. "He seems to me," Wordsworth wrote, "to be a man much swayed by personal considerations, one who has courted persecution, and that rather from a wish to vex powerful individuals than to be an instrument of public good" (*Letters*, 137). In light of Wordsworth's later autocritique, the charge against Horne Tooke

might seem to conceal anxieties about the point of his own political involvement, but if so, they were slight and without any obvious immediate
consequence. The rest of the letter reaffirms the need for peaceful reform, and the series of personal meetings with his "sage," William Godwin, in the first half of 1795 lay yet ahead of him. The letter to Mathews
seems too early to be relevant to the crisis.

Roe suggests that the meetings with Godwin represented the high
point of Wordsworth's allegiance to the author of *Political Justice*, but
also the beginning of a gradual erosion of confidence in him, a process
that took place not in a single moment of breakdown but over a year.[57] If
any aspect of the personal encounter, or of Godwin's personality, produced such an effect on Wordsworth, there is no evidence of it, unless
silence itself is evidence. Wordsworth could be much swayed by personalities, as the effect of Beaupuy testified, but only when he was ready to
be. At any rate there are no hints of a sudden disappointing experience in
1795–96, let alone a shock of dismay such as the one Wordsworth reported when England went to war against France in 1793. To expect or
look for one, however, may be the wrong approach. The dynamic of crisis
was adequately driven by the play of tensions within Wordsworth's ideas
and the development they underwent. Given the conflict between the
already-suspect personal anger and aggrandizement inherent in his appropriation of the natural sublime—no matter how closely the "inner
light" was identified with Miltonic republican virtue—and his wish to
make power work for all of mankind, the potential for an internal rupture
in his sensibility and work was there from the beginning of his revolutionary involvement. At the same time, there was already available within the
components of his political position an element that with some modifications could be developed into a full-blown alternative to radicalism. This
may well have cushioned the shock of self-awareness and allowed the
rapid and apparently relatively easy transition from theoretical radicalism
to the astounding quietism—astounding certainly by contrast with his
previous treatment of similar themes—of "The Ruined Cottage" and "The
Pedlar" in 1797.

Four works give the material for whatever notion we can have of the deep
structure of the crisis. The first chronologically is the revision of "A Night
on Salisbury Plain" that Wordsworth made in the fall of 1795 at Racedown, where he had moved after his spring residence in London. The
change is extreme, and remarkable. The lonely, faceless traveler of the
first version of the poem becomes a much more central character. He is
now an impoverished sailor who had been impressed into war and then
cheated by the "slaves of office" out of his just claims to reward for his
service. Returning to his family starving and empty-handed, he robs and

kills a man within sight of his home; fearful of punishment, he then flees, abandoning his wife and children.

The sailor's story radically deforms the symmetry of the earlier version. The traveler can no longer unconflictedly identify with the female vagrant. She is an oppressed innocent, while he, however much the victim of unjust powers, is nonetheless a criminal. The morning light that cheers her, a light to which in the first version the traveler called her attention in an effort to console her, now only frightens him. When they meet a man on the road beating his little son, the sailor tries to intervene in the name of "manhood" (632) but is reduced to cold sweat when the father calls him a vagabond and a knave. And when the sailor suddenly notices that the child's wound is in exactly the same place where he fatally struck his own victim, his thoughts shift jarringly from the boy to himself, from sympathy to a self-condemnation whose hyperbole turns into almost mawkish self-pity: "Yet happy thou, poor boy! compared with me; / Suffering, not doing ill, fate far more mild" (651–52). Improbably, but significantly, it is the sailor's guilty suffering that makes the father reproach himself and stop the beating. Contrition succeeds where intervention fails or is halted by the would-be savior's implication in the evil he would stop.

The sailor's cup of bitterness overflows when the vagrant comes upon a dying woman and summons him to help. She turns out to be his wife; his act of murder has created the circumstances that have led to her death. He confesses his crime, though only after he is recognized, and he is executed. The ending is ambiguous, but not quite in the way suggested by Roe and others. He interprets Wordsworth as implicitly arguing the Godwinian position that the sailor's criminal behavior is the inevitable product of his circumstances, while also inconsistently calling for the Paineite virtue of compassion, in an unsuccessful effort to reconcile contradictory philosophies.[58] Although partly true, this seems less to the point than the fact that Wordsworth is now openly grappling with a profound sense of guilt for behavior he feels as murderous, while, at the same time, rejecting the integrity and legitimacy of the political and legal system that would pass judgment and execute punishment:

> Blest be for once the stroke which ends, tho' late,
> The pangs which from thy halls of terror came,
> Thou who of Justice bear'st the violated name!

(817–19)

Understanding Wordsworth's crisis hinges on correctly interpreting this sense of guilt, a complex matter because it demands sensitivity not only to the difference between literature and biography but also to the literary ambiguities of the texts themselves. The "Fragment of a Gothic

Tale," *The Borderers*, and the last four books of the 1805 *Prelude*, taken together, however, suggest both that the guilt was decidedly personal and that Wordsworth's historical and philosophical conceptualization of his inner conflicts transfigured the personal issues to universal and epochal significance.

"This was the time," Wordsworth later wrote of his "Godwinian" phase,

> when, all things tending fast
> To depravation, the [P]hilosophy
> That promised to abstract the hope of man
> Out of his feelings, to be fixed thenceforth
> For ever in a purer element,
> Found ready welcome.
>
> (X.805–10)

James Chandler has argued that the "philosophy" referred to in the passage is not Godwin's but the ideas of the French Ideologues, whose version of Enlightenment radicalism got a serious hearing during the early years of the Directorate (1795–97) and reached England in 1796–97.[59] The timing of English access to Ideologue thought, however, is not quite right for the onset of Wordsworth's crisis, and the evidence for Wordsworth's direct knowledge of the ideas of Destutt de Tracy is admittedly thin.[60] At that time the word "Philosophy" capitalized generally referred to the work of Godwin,[61] and above all, the importance for Wordsworth of Godwin's stress on the primacy of private judgment speaks for his greater influence on that aspect of Wordsworth's rationalism. But though establishing the intellectual context is a necessary aid in interpreting Wordsworth's language, it is more important to see how Wordsworth transmuted contemporary radical theory into something uniquely his own.

One of the things that Wordsworth emphasized in the retrospect of 1805 was the rationalist fetishizing of reason for defensive purposes, as a disguise for the irrational, a place "Where passions had the privilege to work, / And never hear the sound of their own names" (X.811–13). The hidden passions to which he referred were first broached in the "Fragment of a 'Gothic' Tale" and more fully explored in *The Borderers*, both of which date from 1796. A young man plans to murder a blind old man, who believes that he is being led to safety during a violent storm. Just as the youth is about to strike, a terrible sound "of uncouth horror," like a "painful outcry strange, to living ear unknown," shocks him into immobility and wakens the old man—now called the sailor, a link to "Salisbury Plain."[62] The closing lines anticipate, if crudely, the language that will later, in the 1799 *Prelude*, describe the effects of the "spots of time" in vitalizing the imagination:

And, when returning thought began to wake,
In bare remembrance of that sound there dwelt
Such power as made his joints with terror quake;
And all which he, that night, had seen or felt
Showed like the shapes delusion loves to deem
Sights that obey the dead or phantoms of a dream.

(215–20)

Kenneth Johnston writes that it would be as difficult to deny Wordsworth's emotional involvement in the "grotesque situations" of the story
as to prove it, but that "it is impossible to deny his powerful imaginative
empathy for situations in which poor, old suffering humanity is in mortal
danger from the very persons best placed to aid it."[63] Where Johnston is
looking ahead to the pattern that will lead to *The Recluse*, this poem is the
first in which that situation occurs, and it represents a notable innovation.
Up to this point, the important suffering victims of Wordsworth's poetry
had been women. The focus of the sailor's guilt in the 1795 "Adventures
on Salisbury Plain," for example, is the wife of the man he has killed,
rather than the victim himself. Now, however, a new kind of victim is
introduced into Wordsworth's work. He is as shadowy as the reasons for
the youth's murderous intentions toward him. Those are quite unmoti-
vated, irrational compulsions deriving from a strangely deformed personality seemingly opaque to both character and author. On the way across
a precarious bridge into the castle that is to be their refuge from the
storm, the youth is seized by an impulse to hurl the helpless old man to
his death, and the urge to murder is perversely only intensified by the
man's offer to make the youth his heir in gratitude for saving him:

His hopes the youth to fatal dreams had lent
And from that hour had laboured with the curse
Of evil thoughts, nor had the least event
Not owned a meaning monstrous and perverse;
And now these latter words were words of blood
And all the man had said but served to nurse
Purpose most foul with most unnatural food.

(134–40)

The figure of the youth represents a deepening exploration of guilt, and
his features connect this guilt more closely to Wordsworth than do those
of the sailor in "Adventures on Salisbury Plain." The emphasis on youth
itself is significant: the guilt here stems not from an impulsive act in response to intolerable and unjust external circumstances, but from the
character of youth itself, from unspecified "hopes" that somehow turn
into evil dreams that cause death. The stanza gives its own license to the

interpretation of the minutest detail since, in its own words, the "least event" had a sinister meaning for the youth himself. Why the old man's offer should inflame his perversity can only be conjectured, given the poverty of detail, but the conflict between youth and age on which the poem partly hinges suggests that the man's generosity seems to the youth like its opposite. The old man's offer to take the youth into his home and make him his heir can only remind him of his youthfulness and dependency, all the more galling given the old man's feebleness. The poem remained a fragment because the thinness of the characters and situations gave it no way to develop. It is the sketchy, abortive introduction of a new and disturbing theme—guilt over destructive urges against venerable figures of authority. Wordsworth tended to make the Gothic element prominent when his material was most disturbing and not yet poetically worked through; since "The Vale of Esthwaite," the supernatural was the easiest entrance for him to the preconscious sense of the terrible dimension of sublime power.

What was hint and mystery in the "Fragment" became a fully developed drama-tract just a few months later in *The Borderers*. The hybrid term reflects the criticism that prevented the staging of *The Borderers* in 1797, criticism that Wordsworth himself acknowledged to be just. The formal failure, if that is what it is, cannot simply be ascribed to Wordsworth's lack of dramatic gifts or the fact that the play was a first effort in the genre. Wordsworth was attempting too many things with it. The desire to become a dramatist was an appeal for a public voice and role and an audience more immediate than poetry could bring, at a point where Wordsworth believed he had an important message to deliver. As a manifesto, it was in its way the counterpart to the *Letter to the Bishop of Llandaff*; its form, however, represented both a renunciation of direct politics and a claim to a place with the greatest in English literature.

The parallels with *Othello* and *King Lear* are staples of critical analysis of the play. *Hamlet* has been less noticed as a source for its structure and for the character of Mortimer, but it is no less relevant. In *The Borderers*, the young man's motive for wanting to kill an old man is his belief that the old man has committed a heinous crime. As it turns out, he has been deluded by his supposed friend, who has lied about an innocent man in order to seduce his companion into murder. But the young man has not simply been innocently seduced; his vulnerability testifies to a malign spirit that he ultimately recognizes as an independent source of guilt, a spirit that makes it impossible for him to put all the blame on his friend and exculpate himself.

It would be almost perverse to deny Wordsworth's partial identification with Mortimer, the "hero" of the play, and with Rivers, its villain. As if content and context were not sufficient, Wordsworth virtually avowed the former by pseudonymously signing the name "Mortimer" to a poem printed the day before he left London after the rejection of *The Borderers* at Covent Garden (*Prose Works*, 1:344), and the repetition of Rivers's creed of independence in *The Prelude* as, at one time, Wordsworth's own, cements the identification with him. But of course the identifications are not complete or exact, nor do they exhaust the meaning of the characters, and not only for the obvious formal and aesthetic reasons. Robert Osborn writes that Rivers's "obscurity" is the "result of a complex evolution from the various sources on which Wordsworth drew and of the need to create a character who would fulfill a complex function in relationship to Mortimer."[64] But his illuminating demonstration of the connections between Rivers and Milton's Satan, Godwin's Caleb Williams, and others[65] does not preclude a source for the pair of chief characters and their interaction in Wordsworth's own psychological, political, and philosophical concerns and does not in any case address Wordsworth's transformation of his sources for his own purposes. The characters, however, are not simple transcriptions of the "real" Wordsworth"; they are extrapolations from, and developments of possibilities inherent in, his emotions and beliefs before and during his crisis, constructs that go beyond biographical fact to explore and experiment with the psychological causes, social consequences, and moral and spiritual implications of those beliefs.

Rivers's and Mortimer's commission of identical crimes marks them to that extent as the same person. But they commit their "murders" for different reasons and with different degrees of self-consciousness. Each represents an element of Wordsworth's self-perceived motives and character; the conflict between them is the representation of an inner conflict over how to interpret behavior that Wordsworth perceived and judged in retrospect to have been wrong. It is not, however, the motives of the two men that prove mutually exclusive; though logically and emotionally incompatible, they can coexist psychologically, and if one self-representation was more flattering, or at least more exculpatory than the other, both coexisted within Wordsworth. But Rivers's moral-philosophical solution, the one Wordsworth saw himself as following in his "Godwinian" period, is humanly, morally unacceptable to Mortimer, and the latter's utter repudiation of this solution is not only Wordsworth's repudiation of his ideological radicalism but his ultimate demystification of it. Moreover, the demystification works both ways, for through Rivers, Wordsworth exposes the underside of Mortimer's "finer" emotions as well. The "repetition compulsion" effect of the play, often noted, is not exact, for it accomplishes what repetition intends but usually does not achieve: a different ending. Within the frame of his conflict, Mortimer faces the deed—if not quite the need that drove him to it—and the remorse that Rivers rejects.

He does not become Wordsworth, but, by exorcising his guilt, he prepares the way for Wordsworth.

Rivers is tricked into his crime because of wounded "honor"—or narcissistic pride. "In my youth / I was the pleasure of all hearts—the darling of every tongue," he tells Mortimer, and so was ripe for the incitements of the crew of the ship on which he was sailing against the captain they hated. Convinced by them that the captain was hatching some "foul conspiracy" against him, he "brooded o'er [his] injuries deserted / By man and nature" (*Borderers*, 4.2.17–18)—rather large words for such personal circumstances, perhaps, but reminiscent of the story of Vaudracour's sense of desertion both by his father and by the nature he trusted vainly for a happy end to all. There is even a rough familial parallel in both stories: the captain is the father of the woman to whom Rivers is engaged, and further complicating the relationship between future son-and father-in-law, she has specifically charged Rivers to stand by her father and never abandon him. When he reproaches the captain for his "treachery," the captain, a man of "imperious" temper, strikes Rivers, sending him into a fury that only the intervention of the crew modulates; instead of killing the captain, Rivers is persuaded to abandon him to his death on a barren island.

The figure of the captain condenses many possible external biographical and internal poetic referents. The captain's "conspiracy" brings to mind Lord Lonsdale and the manipulation of justice, as well as the relatives who had frustrated Wordsworth's independence and opposed his marriage. The captain as father is the dramatic parallel to Baron Herbert, father of Mortimer's beloved Mathilda, the man Mortimer later abandons, and so points, as David Erdman has argued, to Annette Vallon and her "royal father"—the French king whose execution Wordsworth had approved.[66] Osborn has also pointed out the fascinating connection between the fictional mutiny in *The Borderers* and the mutiny on the *Bounty*, with which Wordsworth had a coincidental personal involvement. Fletcher Christian, the mutineer, had been a schoolmate of Wordsworth's at Hawkshead and his brother Edward, who defended Fletcher at the mutiny trial, was also the lawyer for the Wordsworths in the suit against Lonsdale. When in 1796, there appeared in the press a purported extract from Fletcher Christian's journal exonerating Captain Bligh, Wordsworth, who knew it to be a forgery, wrote one of his rare letters to the press denouncing it. Osborn suggests that Wordsworth wrote the letter because he feared, consciously or unconsciously, that Fletcher had been mistaken in believing that Bligh was hostile to him, the implication being that Wordsworth denounced the forgery in order to still his own doubts about Bligh's guilt.[67] But this could only have mattered to Wordsworth in the larger context of his fears that his own "mutiny" against British authority, or authority in general, had been unjustified and had had purely personal sources. By the time of *The Borderers* there is no longer any ambiguity, at least in the fiction: authority is innocent. Rivers insists, repeatedly and almost gleefully, in the face of Mortimer's growing horror, "The man was famished and he was innocent," "Had never wronged me," "I had been deceived," "I had been betrayed" (4.2.63, 65, 68, 70). Any point for point correspondence between this fictional exculpation of authority and Wordsworth's biography is undercut by the fact that in the unpublished Juvenal satires he composed at this time, Wordsworth was unremittingly sarcastic and hostile to the British and French monarchies and the aristocracy; nevertheless, the fictions show the direction Wordsworth was going.

In Rivers's case, however, the play's emphasis is less on his motive for abandoning the captain than on its consequence. Rivers's pride makes it impossible for him to accept the humiliation of deception, misdeed, and above all, remorse. Driven by the need to avoid shame at all cost, he uses his intellect to fashion a novel rationalization; his mind becomes a philosopher's stone transmuting the dross of humiliation into the gold of justification and power. "I saw that every possible shape of action / Might lead to good—I saw it and burst forth / Thirsting for some exploit of power and terror" (4.2.108–10). To a degree, Rivers's language is rationalist: even his sleep, he says of the new energy that powered even his dreams, "was linked to purposes of reason" (4.2.123–25). But Rivers is not a Godwinian rationalist nor, above all, is he simply adopting an available creed. In contrast to Godwin—though like Robespierre and the Ideologues—he uses the belief in reason to excuse murder; Rivers is in this sense the living refutation of Godwin's "passionless" reason. More than that, he sees himself as doing something absolutely novel in the history of thought and ethics. He abolishes remorse by rejecting the objective standards on which the feeling of remorse depends, and so becomes the sole warrant for his actions, an existentialist before his time.

> In these my lonely wonderings I perceived
> What mighty objects do impress their forms
> To build this our intellectual being,
> And felt if aught on earth deserved a curse,
> 'Twas that worst principle of all that dooms
> A thing so great to perish self-consumed.
> —So much for my remorse.
>
> (4.2.133–39)

Previous interpretations, whether they identify Rivers's ideology with Godwin, the French Ideologues, or Robespierre, have failed to take into account the significance of Rivers's belief that he is unique, that he is broaching a new idea no one else has even seen, an idea whose time is yet to come.

> When from these forms I turned to contemplate
> The opinions and the uses of the world,
> I seemed a being who had passed *alone*
> Beyond the visible barriers of the world
> And travelled into things to come.
>
> (4.2.141–45; italics added)

Whatever Rivers/Wordsworth has taken from contemporary thought, he has transformed into something else. In one sense it would not matter if he were actually correct about this: it would only matter that he believed it to be so for his sense of isolation, uniqueness, and grandeur. But in fact Rivers does represent an ideology importantly different from either revolutionary or Godwinian rationalism. This point is obscured because Wordsworth's language on the subject is confusing; it does draw on contemporary sources to say something new, and Wordsworth is confused about exactly what he is saying. In Rivers's most famous statement of his philosophy, however, the one repeated in *The Prelude*, and the one supposedly most Godwinian in content, the radical innovation is clearly present. Significantly, it comes *before* Rivers's confession to Mortimer, as a statement not about himself but about Mortimer, when he believes Mortimer has transcended his own halfway deed by actually and purposely killing Herbert.

> You have taught mankind to seek the measure of justice
> By diving for it into their own bosoms.
> Today you have thrown off a tyranny
> That lives but by the torpid acquiescence
> Of our emasculated souls, *the tyranny*
> *Of moralists and saints and lawgivers*.
> You have obeyed the only law that wisdom
> Can ever recognize: the immediate law
> Flashed from the light of circumstances
> Upon an independent intellect.
> Thenceforth new prospects ought to open on you,
> Your faculties should grow with the occasion.
>
> (3.5.24–35; italics added)

This is more Nietzschean or Sartrian than Godwinian—or would be if Wordsworth did not try to conflate the idea of radical autonomy with some lingering concept of objective "wisdom." But the assertion that the creed that informs Mortimer's action is a rebellion against the tyranny of

"moralists, saints, and lawgivers" means that it is something different
from the ethical, theological, and legal foundations of the whole previous
history of moral and political theory. Unlike all previous political theorizing, its wisdom is not that of objective laws of whatever origin or sanction.
Rivers's "independent intellect" is a purely subjective warrant for its own
actions, not one whose autonomy is justified by its possession of universal
principles. It is this that ultimately separates it from Godwin's assertion
of the supremacy of private judgment, which for Godwin was still rooted
in Dissenting theology and justified only by conscience's sure knowledge
of absolute truths of reason. Rivers's position is that of situational ethics
without the absolute ethical standards; he must innovate not only in ap-
plying standards but in inventing them.

The position Wordsworth ascribes to Rivers explains far better than
any form of eighteenth-century rationalism Wordsworth's own moral crisis as he later described it in *The Prelude*. "What delight!" he recalls, with
somewhat heavy-handed irony, of his most radical phase,

> How glorious!—in self-knowledge and self-rule
> To look through all the frailties of the world,
> And, with a resolute mastery shaking off
> *The accidents of nature, time, and place,*
> *That make up the weak being of the past,*
> Build social freedom on its only basis:
> The freedom of the individual mind,
> Which, *to the blind restraints of general laws*
> *Superior*, magisterially adopts
> One guide—the light of circumstances, flashed
> Upon an independent intellect.
>
> (X.818–24; italics added)

This passage makes explicit the contrast between Wordsworth's understanding of the "independent intellect" and the other rival candidates for
supreme principle of authority—"the weak being of the past," a reference
to history and tradition (which in 1805 was a tribute to Wordsworth's
growing Burkeanism),[68] and the restraints of "general laws," the natural-
law common denominator of all eighteenth-century rationalism and of
much more weight for the Wordsworth of 1792–95 than the reverence for
tradition he had already shed with his adoption of Paineite political
theory. The steady beat of self-referential and grandiose terms—"self-
knowledge," "self-rule," "resolute mastery," "superior," "magisterial"—
reinforces Wordsworth's confession that he has been holding himself absolutely free and authoritative, above all principle other than his own
individuality, and underlines the contradiction between the goal of asserting his individuality and that of building "social freedom." Words-

worth is not operating within any kind of recognizable rationalist or natural law tradition at this point.

This foundationless self-belief lay at the bottom of the crisis of relativism reported in *The Prelude*. It was not a conventional rationalism that made it impossible for "all passions, motions, shapes of faith" to establish their titles and honors before the bar of reason. Even Godwin, the opponent of the passions, at least in the first edition of *Political Justice*, did not hold rationalism and benevolence to be in conflict; to the contrary, benevolence and humanitarianism were for him necessary truths of reason.[69] In the well-known preface to *The Borderers* where Wordsworth sketched the self-referential "Rivers" type, he wrote, "Let us suppose a young man of great intellectual powers, *yet without any solid principles of genuine benevolence*. His master passions are pride and the love of distinction.—He has deeply imbibed a spirit of enterprise in a tumultuous age. He goes into the world and is betrayed into a great crime" (*Prose Works*, 1:76; italics added). Wordsworth's was not a Godwinian crisis, unless it was that of his own un-Godwinian version of Godwin's "private judgement." It was a crisis of the deification of pure individuality, bouyed by the sense of personal power. It is important also to distinguish this notion from the idea of "egotism" as it has been applied to Wordsworth since Keats's famous characterization of the "egotistical sublime."[70] Individuality is a paradoxical concept that validates the self in general as absolutely self-authorizing, not merely out of some personal grandiosity but precisely as a matter of principle, as a new norm of legitimate authority, but its effect is therefore to elevate the unique self of its declarer to a position of supremacy. It was not Wordsworth's personal failing but the inner logic of the principle that left him, as he tried to find in the idea of individuality a warrant for his desires and beliefs

> endlessly perplexed
> With impulse, motive, right and wrong, the ground
> Of moral obligation—what the rule,
> And what the sanction—till, demanding proof,
> And seeking it in everything, I lost
> All feeling of conviction, and, in fine,
> Sick, wearied out with contrarieties,
> Yielded up moral questions in despair.
>
> (*Prelude*, X.893–900)

This nihilistic result was logically inevitable; having precisely rejected the idea of rule and sanction, there could be no "ground" of moral obligation that could be appealed to for proof.

But if Wordsworth came to this conclusion, he does not have Rivers do so. As he presents the radical position through Rivers's development, that position makes possible Rivers's feeling of recovery from the narcis-sistic wound that comes from concern about the opinion of others, through a sense not merely of superiority, but of historical uniqueness and prescience (though the need to seduce Mortimer suggests that Riv-ers's new-found self-containment is precarious, if not illusory):

> Is not shame, I said,
> A mean acknowledgement of a tribunal
> Blind in its essence, a most base surrender
> Of our own knowledge to the world's ignorance?
> I had been nourished by the sickly food
> Of popular applause. I now perceived
> That we are praised by men because they see in us
> The image of themselves; that a *great mind*
> *Outlives its age* and is pursued with obloquy
> Because its movements are not understood.
>
> (4.2.148–155; italics added)

This is Wordsworth's judgment both of what his ideology of 1794–95 psy-chologically entailed in principle and of what his own motives were then, or how at least they could and might have to be seen had he persisted in that ideology. Rivers is the furthest extrapolation of one of Wordsworth's self-interpretations. An almost throw-away line, uttered about Rivers by a minor character in the play, makes a striking connection between Riv-ers's beliefs and the transformative experience Wordsworth described in "Descriptive Sketches" after watching the storm in the mountains. Dis-cussing Rivers's superstitious nature with other members of their band, Lennox reports that Rivers has said about his beliefs, "I hold of spirits, and the sun in heaven" (3.4.32). Since 1792, eagle and sun had been re-current images for Wordsworth's sense of his appropriation of the sub-lime in nature.

There is another aspect of the new principle of individuality repre-sented by Rivers that must be made precise. Both Hartman and Osborn, while linking Rivers's principles to the self-awareness and separateness born of the commission of a crime, diminish the significance of the crime into a symbol for the ontological separateness of man from nature. Thus, Osborn takes at face value Rivers's discourse on the peripeties of action—"Action is transitory, a step, a blow— / . . . / 'Tis done—and in the after vacancy / We wonder at ourselves like men betrayed" (3.5.60–64). He interprets this to mean that "Any action is in some sense a curse against nature, awakening us to guilty self-consciousness."[71] This is not far from Hartman's idea that the "crime against nature" is a universal stage in the growth of the mind[72] and therefore need not even be an act committed by the protagonist but may be a betrayal from the outside, by the gods, for example, so long as it leaves man in a state of isolation.

This misses what is absolutely central to Wordsworth's new sense of individuality—that it is a general *principle* and yet is inseparable from the *personal* sense of grandiosity and power, which is destructive and murderous because it *wishes* to eliminate rivals and usurp infinity. This is the same realization that created such tension for Schlegel between the goal of personal totality that leads to polemic and combat with others (manifested in his desire to be the "critical dictator" of Germany) and his goal of *Symphilosophie*. As Lennox says of Rivers, "Passion is life to him, / And breath and being; where he cannot govern / He will destroy—you know he hates us all" (3.4.11–13). Whether or not these features are inherent in any concept of individuality is beside the point; they were intrinsic to Wordsworth's, born as they were out of the psychological and historical experience that produced his idea. They invest the imagery of surgical violation, rape, and profanation in which Wordsworth describes his effort to destroy the claims of anything other than the self to be a foundation, including not least the previously ultimate ground, nature herself:

> I took the knife in hand,
> And, stopping not at parts less sensitive,
> Endeavoured with my best of skill to probe
> The living body of society
> Even to the heart. I pushed without remorse
> My speculations forward, yea, set foot
> On Nature's holiest places.
>
> (*Prelude*, X.872–78)

Denaturing or neutralizing the element of personal violence in Wordsworth's conception eliminates one of the essential features that made Wordsworth need to abandon it. The "accidentally" psychological and historical dimension of the "apocalyptic" were for Wordsworth the essence of his experience of the "ontological" truth of the autonomy of consciousness.

This is even clearer in Mortimer's story. If Rivers is the extrapolation of Wordsworth after Louis XVI's execution, the Terror, and his adaptation of Godwin, Mortimer is the more idealistic, more naive Wordsworth before the crimes and their rationalization. But neither Mortimer's idealism nor his naiveté save him from an inner conflict whose underside is at times more terrible than Rivers's blatancy. In some ways he is closer to Wordsworth than Rivers is, and his situation tells more, however indirectly, about Wordsworth's sense of his *initial* revolutionary motivations.

The play furnishes two perspectives on Mortimer, as it does on Rivers—that offered by his own actions and words and that offered by the perceptions of others, primarily Rivers. Given his clarified consciousness, however, Rivers is a far more insightful and consciously ironic observer of Mortimer than Mortimer can be of him; his words often serve for both and help bridge the two characters. In the outline of the main plot, Mortimer is the self-appointed young leader of a band of fighters who are trying to keep the peace and administer rough justice along the Scottish-English border during the interregnum created by the barons' uprising against Henry III in the thirteenth century. He is in love with Mathilda, daughter of the elderly Baron Herbert, a nobleman who has fought heroically in the Crusades only to be dispossessed of his estates during his absence. Blinded while saving his young daughter from a fire during the battle of Antioch, Herbert was forced to give up her care when they returned to England and has only recently been reunited with her as the play opens. Mathilda wishes to marry Mortimer, but the match has been undermined by the plotting of Rivers, Mortimer's older adviser and second-in-command. Rivers has convinced Herbert that Mortimer is nothing but an outlaw bent on booty, and so incited him to an unalterable opposition to the match that his loyal and grateful daughter will not defy. At the same time he has turned Mortimer violently against Herbert by manufacturing evidence that he is not Mathilda's father but a virtual white slaver who has purchased her from a poor beggar and intends to turn her over for profit to the degenerate Lord Clifford.

The first full portrait of Mortimer is a flattering description addressed by Rivers to Mortimer himself; its complex, savage irony, working on many levels simultaneously, reveals the essentials of the historical, psychological, and aesthetic-philosophical situation in which Mortimer operates. Encouraging Mortimer's resolution to punish Herbert by death, Rivers alludes first to the historical setting that makes such justice not only socially necessary but ethically noble, even glorious:

> Happy are we
> Who live in these disputed tracts that own
> No law but what each man makes for himself.
> Here justice has indeed a field of triumph!

> (2.1.51–54)

The breakdown of traditional authority—the parallel with the French Revolution is unmistakable—has created new possibilities of freedom and morality. His next words, however, are aimed directly at the vanity interwoven with Mortimer's moral sense and in their ambiguity both pique and mock it.

> Self-stationed here,
> Upon these savage confines we have seen you
> Stand like an isthmus 'twixt two stormy seas
> That checked their fury at your bidding—
>
> .   .   .   .
>
> Your single virtue has transformed a band
> Of fierce barbarians into ministers
> Of beauty and of order. . . .
>
> .   .   .   .
>
> Benevolence that has not the heart to use
> The wholesome ministry of pain and evil
> Is powerless and contemptible: as yet
> Your virtues, the spontaneous growth of instinct,
> From rigorous souls can claim but little praise.
> To-day you will assume a character
> More awful and sublime.
>
> (2.1.60–79)

Rivers's reference to Mortimer's "single virtue" that all by itself has transformed barbarians into "ministers of beauty and order" is reminiscent of Hölderlin's Hyperion sarcastically raging at himself for believing he could liberate and regenerate Greece—another symbol for the French Revolution—with a band of robbers.[73] It points up the grandiosity behind Mortimer's self-appointed mission while urging it on; by executing Herbert he will receive the acclaim he deserves but has been denied and will above all become "awful and sublime." The irony here is double at least. Rivers is urging an ethic far different from what Mortimer realizes, an ethic that in the traditional sense, as we have seen, is the abrogation of all ethics, but still holds an appeal to which Rivers believes Mortimer is vulnerable. In Rivers's argument there is a strong echo of the position Wordsworth himself took in the *Letter to the Bishop of Llandaff* that benevolent ends sometimes require, in the wonderful oxymoron, "the wholesome ministry of pain and evil." This is the Wordsworth of 1796–97 mercilessly exposing the Wordsworth of 1792–93 through the Wordsworth of 1794–95. It is interesting that Mortimer gives his age as twenty-three (5.3.238), which was Wordsworth's age in 1793.

The key to Mortimer's character in the play is his Hamlet-like hesitation to kill Herbert and the excessive guilt he feels for a death that he only accidentally brings about, a death which in any case he has had reason to believe is well-deserved. The point, of course, is that he never fully believes in Herbert's guilt and the accident is not simply an accident. David Erdman attributes "the erosion of [Mortimer's] whole system of values" to his "failure to recognize a Father,"[74] but Mortimer's failure is not wholly passive; he *wishes* to believe Rivers' story. Michael Friedman goes to the opposite extreme when he says that "*The Borderers* is a play about a man who murders a father in order to obtain a wife."[75] This explicitly oedipal formulation is not so much wrong as overly reductive and careless about the nuances of Mortimer's ambivalence. Erdman is after all partly right. A good part of Mortimer's rage at Herbert is the result of Rivers's successful plot, buttressed by apparently hard evidence—the testimony of Mathilda's putative mother—to convince Mortimer that Herbert is not her real father. The problem for Mortimer's resolve is that his intuition and emotions constantly get in the way of his reason. It is not only that he repeatedly senses Herbert's innocence (2.3.69–71) and notes the similarities of father and daughter (2.3.212, 288–89), his own yearning for a father enables him to recognize the father in Herbert (2.3.417; 3.3.12, 63–68; 4.2.178–80). At one point the peasant who has met Herbert on the heath, seeing Mortimer's distress, solicitously asks, "but you are troubled; / Perhaps you are his son?" (5.2.39–40). Yet despite all the premonitions that stay his hand from murder, Mortimer never lets them break through to confront Herbert directly with his suspicions. And in the end, his "forgetting" to return the belt that contains Herbert's food dooms Herbert to death when he abandons him on the heath.

Mortimer brings about Herbert's death in part then, as Friedman says, because he is a paternal obstacle to his possession of Mathilda. Toward the end of the play Mortimer as much as admits it when he tries to shift responsibility for what he has done to Mathilda, his words resonant with Adam's ur-attempt to blame woman for his own desire and transgression: "The fault's not mine— / If she had never lived I had not done it" (5.3.38–39). But Adam's words were intended as a defense against the ultimate and original sin—the rebellion against the absolute, against divine authority. From the beginning of the play Mortimer's hesitation seems related to fears of an even greater evil and corruption in himself than the urge to remove a frustrating father.

From the moment he confronts the prospect of judging and punishing Herbert, Mortimer senses an excitement in himself that quite goes against the desire for justice:

> Rivers! I have loved
> To be the friend and father of the helpless,
> A comforter of sorrow—there is something
> Which looks like a *transition* in my soul,
> And yet is not.
>
> (2.1.89–93)

His excitement makes him aware for the first time of something in him that he realizes has always been there. He is confronted with it again when he is unable to kill Herbert in the castle:

> Is not the depth
> Of this man's crimes beyond the reach of thought?
> And yet in plumbing the abyss of vengeance
> Something I strike upon which turns my thoughts
> Back to myself—I think again—my breast
> Concenters all the terrors of the universe,
> I look at him and tremble like a child.
>
> (2.3.59–65)

Ambiguous as the passage is, Mortimer's recoil from killing Herbert is clearly enough connected with a sense of evil in himself even greater than the "crimes beyond the reach of thought" of which Herbert is guilty, an evil whose enormity "Concenters all the terrors of the universe." This conviction of an internal evil of infinite magnitude seriously undermines any sense of the righteousness or efficacy of his self-appointed role as protector of the helpless on the border. "We look," he says to his follower Lacy early in the play

> But at the surface of things, we hear
> Of towns in flames, fields ravaged, young and old
> Driven out in flocks to want and nakedness,
> Then grasp our swords and rush upon a cure
> That flatters us, because it asks not thought.
> The deeper malady is better hid—
> The world is poisoned at the heart.
>
> (2.3.337–44)

He does not say at this point what the deeper malady is, but a short while later, when Rivers presents him with another piece of false evidence against Herbert, Mortimer's furious reaction seems grotesquely inappropriate:

> Now for the corner stone of my philosophy:
> I would not give a denier for the man
> Who would not chuck his babe beneath the chin
> And send it with a fillip to its grave.
>
> (3.2.92–95)

Rivers's response, "Nay, you leave me behind," refers not only to his failure to understand; the enormity of Mortimer's nihilism and satanism exceeds even his own and does not seem rationally linked with the provocation.

All this suggests another meaning for the passage above in which Mortimer describes how his desire for vengeance turns his thoughts back upon himself in terror. If the thought of striking Herbert makes him "tremble like a child" and concentrates all the terrors of the universe in his breast, it is because it would be not just a parricidal blow but one at the principle of divinity and authority itself. Rivers's assumption of absolute authority came as a rationalization after the fact of accidental transgression; Mortimer is planning future action and is obscurely conscious that his intended act means arrogating to himself the authority and holiness he attributes to Herbert as well as the unholy power to destroy innocence and helplessness without a qualm. He becomes God and Satan simultaneously.

It is this deeper sense of the desire behind his vengeance that makes executing Herbert impossible for Mortimer. From this point of view, the interpretations of Erdman and Friedman are only partial constituents of a more complete explanation. With all necessary allowance once again for the problems of reductionism and evidence, their separate but not mutually exclusive conclusions are persuasive, even, in a way, unavoidable. Erdman, without actually saying that Mathilda is Annette and Herbert the king of France draws a point-for-point correspondence between Wordsworth's political involvements and conflicts and the characters and situations of the play. "[T]he debate," he writes, "over the justice and necessity of the dethronement, trial and execution of Louis XVI is recapitulated in the central moral conflict in *The Borderers*."[76] More generally, he argues that the play expresses Wordsworth's growing Burkeanism, an interpretation much extended by Chandler. "In *The Borderers* . . . the error . . . is a contempt for the grey locks of tradition. In this sense grey-headed father Herbert is Custom, Law, Ancient Faith, the Constitution (in Burke's sense): and only in this wide sense is the king significant to Wordsworth."[77] Friedman, stressing the triangular nature of the father-daughter-lover conflict, makes blunt assertions about Wordsworth's own "Oedipus complex." If the theorizing goes beyond the evidence, the suggestion is a plausible personal referent for the mainspring of Mortimer's actions and conflicts. For that matter other biographical figures are equally likely candidates for the overdetermined personal sources of Herbert. Mortimer believes Herbert guilty of what Wordsworth had accused Lonsdale of: the responsibility, in Lonsdale's case indirect, for frustrating his dream of love through selfish inclinations and even worse, perhaps dooming his beloved to poverty and sexual exploitation. The identification links Herbert with Rivers's captain and through him and Captain Bligh again to the British establishment against whom Wordsworth was rebelling.

But all of these associations, psychological and political, took on their lethal power only when they were interpreted in the light of the radical ideology of Wordsworth's second revolutionary phase, between 1794 and 1795. It was when the psychological and political motives were filtered through his radicalized idea of individuality that both they and it could be seen for what they were. Neither the political nor the psychological interpretations exhaust the meaning of the characters of the play. In all of them, but perhaps especially in Herbert, there remains a node of mystery that escapes the boundaries of any or even all of these determinants. One of the most moving of the moments that evokes this irreducible mystery is Mortimer's outcry as he collapses unable to kill Herbert in the castle:

> Murder! asleep! blind! old! alone! betray'd!
> Drugg'd and in darkness! Here to strike the blow,
> Visible only to the eye of God!

> (2.3.203–5)

At this awful moment it is not at all clear who Herbert "is." Perhaps there are faint echoes of the sick, weak, dying widower father Wordsworth attended at age thirteen. But Mortimer's horror seems to stem from the contrast between the utter helplessness of his victim and his own contrasting absolute power over him. It is the theme that has haunted Wordsworth's poetry from the first, only now, through the political phase, there has been a reversal in which Wordsworth is all-powerful and the object of his anger is the fragile being on the margins that he himself once was. It was when Wordsworth became aware of what was associated for him with the idea of the "independent intellect"—a self-divinization whose aim, far from benevolence, was destructive omnipotence—that he recoiled from radical individuality with a shock of horror. Its reverberations are seen in Mortimer's self-sentencing to the fate of the wandering Jew (5.3.264–75), whose voice would never be heard by human ear—the ultimate punishment for a poet.

But the energy of the recoil was not wholly negative. For implicit in the rebellion, and available when the rebellion was abjured, was that source of power—nature—that had been not so much rebelled against as wholly internalized into the self. It had only to be partially restored to its externality to provide a new position, one much safer, but one that would enable Wordsworth to retain a modified principle of individuality, and with it the position of moralist, prophet, and poetic innovator.

IV) A Tenuous Resolution

For Wordsworth to return to nature, however, was not an easy step. Since 1792 his relationship with it had been mediated by politics. He had been able to perceive nature as sublime and to appropriate its power by sublimating his own ambitions and rages in an identification with heroic fighters for freedom, dignity, and benevolence. But, having come to suspect his own motives through reflection on the hidden personal absolutism of his revolutionary principle of individuality, he had abandoned political radicalism, and the integrated structure of self, social world, and nature he had built on it was no longer tenable. He was left with two problems that had both personal and poetic bearing. The loss of political mediation provided a complete rupture of his connectedness with nature and with humanity; his relationship to each had been rendered problematic and had to be reconceived. Once he had politicized his identification with the world's outcasts he could no longer return them to the ambiguous status the female beggar had occupied in "An Evening Walk" as the twice-removed object of a mindscape within a landscape. On the other hand, once he had exposed the dangerous meaning of his politicization, the outcasts could no longer be the objects of politically reformist concern. But the aesthetic moves made possible by the political phase could not be undone. Having restored the sublime to nature and assimilated its force into himself, he could not return to the merely picturesque, whose inadequacy in any case had helped trigger his poetic and political crises.

Both of these dilemmas are poignantly expressed in "Lines left upon a Seat in a Yew-tree," which date from the spring of 1797 and reflect Wordsworth's state after finishing *The Borderers*. The abrupt, urgent beginning, "Nay, Traveller! rest"[78] is a plea to the busy reader who would find no immediate reason to linger at the barren yew-tree bower, or, by extension, to pause with the poem, which is the story of the man who made the bower. It is apparently without human interest, being far from any habitation, and does not pulse with natural life either. Yet the sound of the waves lapping the shore—the still small voice of the poet—may speak a meaning through the emptiness itself.

For the bower is the image of the man who fashioned it, and his fate is the message. The description of the man contains the familiar phrases of Wordsworth's self-portraits.

> He was one who owned
> No common soul. In youth by science nursed,
> And led by nature into a wild scene
> Of lofty hopes, he to the world went forth
> A favoured Being, knowing no desire
> Which genius did not hallow; 'gainst the taint
> Of dissolute tongues, and jealousy, and hate,
> And scorn,—against all enemies prepared,
> All but neglect. The world, for so it thought,
> Owed him no service; wherefore he at once

With indignation turned himself away,
And with the food of pride sustained his soul
In solitude.

(12–24)

Crucial features of this self-portrait had already appeared in *The Borderers* and in the prefatory essay describing the Rivers's type, and they
would recur, not always in the same combination, throughout Wordsworth's poetry. The composite picture is of a specially favored being, who
plunges in youth into turbulent and hopeful times with great ambitions
justified by his genius, but who is beset, contradictorily, by both envious
hatred and neglect. Angry at his treatment, he withdraws from social life
and sustains himself with the "food of pride"—a description that condenses both the period of Wordsworth's belief in radical individuality and
of his recoil from it into political immobility. That recoil left him bereft,
with a diminished sense of nature, of whose sublimity he felt unworthy,
and isolated from men, from whose fellowship he felt excluded by the
consciousness of his own self-concern.

>   these gloomy boughs
> Had charms for him; and here he loved to sit,
> His only visitants a straggling sheep,
> The stone-chat, or the glancing sand-piper:
> And on these barren rocks . . .
>
>   .   .   .   .
>
> Fixing his downcast eye, he many an hour
> A morbid pleasure nourished, tracing here
> An emblem of his own unfrutful life:
> And, lifting up his head, he then would gaze
> On the more distant scene,—how lovely 'tis
> Thou seest,—and he would gaze till it became
> Far lovelier, and his heart could not sustain
> The beauty, still more beauteous! Nor, that time,
> When nature had subdued him to herself,
> Would he forget those Beings to whose minds
> Warm from the labours of benevolence
> The world, and human life, appeared a scene
> Of kindred loveliness: then he would sigh,
> Inly disturbed, to think that others felt
> What he must never feel. . . .

(24–44)

But this self-pitying isolation is untenable. The "lost Man" whose fancy
fed on "visionary views" dies; his death is a lesson that a different solution

to his dilemma is necessary. The hortatory ending admonishes the reader against the sins that created that dilemma:

> know that pride,
> Howe'er disguised in its own majesty,
> Is littleness . . .
>
> . . . . . .
>
> The man whose eye
> Is ever on himself doth look on one,
> The least of Nature's works, one who might move
> The wise man to that scorn which wisdom holds
> Unlawful, ever.
>
> (50–59)

But more poignant and relevant to the immediate situation is what must be seen as Wordsworth's self-admonition not to linger in guilt and immobility once the sin has been committed:

> True dignity abides with him alone
> Who, in the silent hour of inward thought,
> *Can still suspect, and still revere himself,*
> In lowliness of heart.
>
> (61–64; italics added)

Presently, "the silent hour of inward thought" will yield metaphysical visions of oneness with Nature, but here the issue is starkly, brilliantly psychological and moral: the ability, in Wordsworth's wonderful phrase, to "still suspect, and still revere oneself," the ultimate paradox where self-reverence runs the danger of vainglory but self-blame destroys the self-regard necessary for experiencing the sublime.

Wordsworth's task was to find the way to realize this paradox. A fragment of poetry from that period titled "Argument for Suicide" suggests how much that achievement would cost him. Compressed and ambiguous to the point of unintelligibility, it is a tortured return to the theme of violence with which Wordsworth had been wrestling since his defense of regicide.

> Send this man to the mine, this to the battle,
> Famish an aged beggar at your gates,
> And let him die by inches—but for worlds
> Lift not your hand against him—Live, live on,
> As if this earth owned neither steel nor arsenic,
> A rope, a river, or a standing pool.
> Live, if you dread the pains of hell, or think
> Your corpse would quarrel with a stake—alas

Has misery then no friend?—if you would die
By license, call the dropsy and the stone
And let them end you—strange it is;
And most fantastic are the magic circles
Drawn round the thing called life—till we have learned
To prize it less, we ne'er shall learn to prize
The things worth living for.[79]

It is not clear whether the opening lines are a sarcastic attack on the rulers of society, who in effect commit murder indirectly by letting the poor die through customary social policy, or a desperately grotesque recommendation of the writer for putting them out of their misery. In either case the lines reflect the agonizing dilemma facing one who has abjured a revolutionary political solution to the problem of poverty. He must either rail impotently at the criminal hypocrisy of established society, or, more horribly, support it by himself wishing for the death of the poor as the only solution to their suffering. The ironic exhortation beginning "Live, live on"—the plea for suicide—is also ambiguous; is it to the suffering poor, who are too frightened of the afterlife to end their real misery here on earth, or is it to the writer, who needs to punish himself for the terrible policy to which he sees no alternative? With regard to the second possibility, Johnston nicely observes, "The desire to kill a suffering fellow being arises from a very deep appreciation of life—and an arrogant one. Under guise of wishing to put the sufferer out of his misery, it may mask a need to remove a threat to one's sanity, either from an excess of empathy or from a sense of guilt."[80] The concluding moral of "Argument for Suicide," that the taboos against suicide and murder are irrational because they fetishize mere survival at the expense of truly human life, contains the deepest irony of all in the context of Wordsworth's development. Having abandoned revolution because it licensed murder in the name of individuality, he has come to the position that one must accept the death of the poor—and one's own death—as the price of learning to prize "The things worth living for."

The ultimate exemplar of learning "to prize life less" is given in "The Ruined Cottage," written in the summer of 1797; the meaning of "the things worth living for" is clarified in the additions to it in early 1798 called "The Pedlar." In retrospect, though the step obviously could not have been predicted, it seems inevitable that Wordsworth should have effected the recovery from his revolutionary crisis through a new solution to the problem of the poor and abandoned woman. Since "An Evening Walk" she had been the figure through whom Wordsworth had, in a complex network of identifications, connected his feelings about himself with the social world. In her first incarnation, she was the figure of human vulnerability and the threat of annihilation. In her politicized form, she was a victim of sociohistorical conditions whose suffering could be ended forever by political change. As Margaret in "The Ruined Cottage," she is the embodiment of the human condition and a sacrifice offered up by the poet to a new vision of reconciliation with human destiny.

As if to close the circle, "The Ruined Cottage" opens with a passage adapted from the opening lines of "An Evening Walk." Wordsworth is signaling that the very landscape whose harmony had been disrupted by the appearance of the female vagrant will be the scene of restoration. But the process is the reverse of "An Evening Walk." The only harmony initially present in the landscape exists for "the dreaming man" wishfully imagined by the young traveler, whose own journey across the meadow is exhausting and beset with the discomforts of slippery ground, heat, and buzzing insects. Nature to him is inhospitable. He has not yet learned to approach it in ways that can make it a haven; the landscape will have to be his scene of instruction. His pain is only intensified at first by the sight of the ruined cottage and the terrible story of Margaret's decline and death told to him by the Pedlar. But it is through that story—or more precisely, that story-telling, in which the narrator's attitude is the key—that enlightenment and reconciliation will come.

Mary Jacobus has neatly summarized the new significance of this version of the female vagrant: "The suffering of a single, ordinary woman is invested with the tragic significance of mortality itself. The symbolic method by which the decay of the cottage is identified with Margaret's own decline serves as a general metaphor for human transience. Now, the death of the individual and all that dies with him is reconciled by invoking the permanence of nature."[81] In Margaret, Wordsworth has realized the theme of human fatedness to suffering that haunted his poetry even at its most political, undercutting even then the possibility of a reformist solution. Margaret and her family are undone by external forces, accidents of nature and war, but these are not seen as modifiable causes of destruction. On the other hand, Wordsworth is not simply implying that poor harvests and war are ineluctable conditions of human existence and hence permanent sources of suffering. If they are the necessary conditions of Margaret's disintegration, they are not sufficient. It is Margaret's response to her losses that is the core of her collapse. Critics like De Quincey are on to something when they accuse Margaret of "criminal indulgence" for giving in to her despair and causing the death of her child by refusing to go on living.[82] It is that very refusal, the consequence of her attachment to her absent husband, which is the essence of Margaret's "mortality," the symptom of the human condition.

This aspect of her situation suggests, however, that Margaret is not just "a single, ordinary woman." Whatever Everywoman might look like, Wordsworth has gone to pains to give Margaret distinctive and unusual features. Her extreme benevolence alone, represented in her holding up to thirsty travelers water drawn from her well—a biblical allusion to Rebecca—and in her capacity to love all who come by her cottage, marks her as special, if not unique. But this characteristic by itself would only make the story a stereotypical emblem of the age-old challenge to faith inherent in the words uttered by the Pedlar, "The good die first / And they whose hearts are dry as summer dust / Burn to the socket."[83] Much more striking, partly because it is the constantly reiterated theme of her downfall, is her all-consuming longing for her husband Robert, which supersedes not only concern for self-preservation but maternal feeling as well. She deteriorates because as time passes and he does not return, she ceases to do what she needs to do—garden, spin, maintain the cottage—to sustain herself and her children. Wordsworth has her acknowledge this to the Pedlar, even judge it in apparent moral terms: "'I am changed, / And to myself,' said she, 'have done much wrong, / And to this helpless infant'" (405–7). But beyond her words she shows no remorse or contrition, and her admission has no consequence for her actions. What is more, not only does the Pedlar never admonish her, he does not seem to see her behavior as culpable. More even than does Margaret herself, he accepts it as a fact of nature. What is remarkable is the collusion between the two of them that consecrates the inevitability of her longing and the inertia it produces.[84]

This collusion points back to Wordsworth's lament in "A Night on Salisbury Plain" that it is man's "miserable dower / Only to taste of joy" that he may "pine / A loss, which rolling suns shall ne'er restore." The Pedlar takes Margaret's behavior for granted because it represents his own point of view, which, as these lines show, is also that of the poet. Loss is inevitable and irrecoverable, and human life is marked forever by an infinite and unsatisfiable longing. On one level the Pedlar is identified with Margaret, as the traveler on Salisbury Plain is with the female vagrant—as Wordsworth always is with his female outcasts. In this case there is a particularly striking piece of confirmatory evidence in a fragment of 1797 obviously related to "The Ruined Cottage" but not included in the poem.[85] A baker's cart passes the home of an impoverished widow—a prefigurement of Margaret—without stopping:

> She said: "that waggon does not care for us"—
> The words were simple, but her look and voice
> Made up their meaning, and bespoke a mind

Which being long neglected, and denied
The common food of hope, was now become
Sick and extravagant,—by *strong access*
Of momentary pangs driven to that state
In which all past experience melts away,
And the rebellious heart to its own will
Fashions the laws of nature.

(*Poetical Works*, 1:316.55–65; italics added)

The "rebellious heart fashioning the laws of nature to its own will" connects Margaret with Rivers in *The Borderers* as well as Wordsworth.

But that is not to say that Margaret is a projection of the poet. Even in her early incarnation in Wordsworth's poetry, where her features depended heavily on borrowings from other writers, the female outcast was meant as the representation of a real other; this was inherent in the nature of the problems with which Wordsworth was wrestling. The power of "The Ruined Cottage," as most critics have agreed, lies precisely in its brilliant, restrained, above all authentic evocation of the emotions of another person.[86] Indeed, as Johnston has pointed out, the evocation is so effective that it runs the danger of sensationalism.[87] The Pedlar himself warns against the temptations of his story, the "wantonness" of drawing "momentary pleasure" from the misery of the dead (280–84), a contradiction that would make no sense but for the voluptuous, almost sadomasochistic fascination with the relentlessness of Margaret's suffering and the sexual imagery in which some of it is presented.

She is dead.
The worm is on her cheek, and this poor hut,
Stripped of its outward garb of household flowers,
Of rose and jasmine, offers to the wind
A cold bare wall whose earthy top is tricked
With weeds and rank spear-grass. She is dead,
And nettles rot and adders sun themselves
Where we have sat together while she nursed
Her infant at her bosom.

(157–65)

There is a mysterious intimacy in the Pedlar's connection with Margaret that communicates itself to the traveler; though he never knew her, he is drawn to her personally: "In my own despite / I thought of that poor woman as of one / Whom I had known and loved" (264–66). All of this suggests that the "poor woman" has been layered over with powerful associations to Annette Vallon. Margaret's almost hallucinatory certainty that Robert will return despite all evidence to the contrary is powerfully rem-

iniscent of the tone of childlike hope and anticipation in the letters Annette was writing from France in 1793; even if Wordsworth did not see all
of them, the tenor of her attachment, which after all he knew at first
hand, resembles that of Margaret's to Robert. And there is the curious
specificity of the "Five tedious years" that Margaret "lingered in unquiet
widowhood / A wife, and widow" (482–84) before she died. It was almost
exactly five years before the poem was written that Wordsworth had left
Annette, and her status was precisely what he ascribed to Margaret;
among her friends, Annette was in fact known as both "Madame Williams" and "Veuve [widow] Williams."[88]

Wordsworth was coming to terms with a great many things in the figure
of Margaret: his own unappeased longing for his mother, his sense of
precariousness and imminent annihilation, his guilt over Annette, his
empathy with those who reminded him of any or all of these. The re-
morseless rehearsal of Margaret's accelerating decline, spontaneously
begun by the Pedlar, broken off in grief and taken up again only at the
almost reluctant bidding of the narrator in a rhythm of compulsion and
repulsion, has about it something of the quality of an endurance test; it is
as if both are trying to see how much they can bear. Only if the test is
ultimate, only if the traveler's pain is extended to the limit of endurance
by an encounter with his worst fears can it be cathartic. In "An Evening
Walk" the poet pulls abruptly away from the image of the dying woman
and her children because he has no way of integrating it and coming to
terms with it. The behavior of the traveler in "The Ruined Cottage" is in
telling contrast. Although he does turn aside in weakness,[89] he nonetheless "reviewed that Woman's suff'rings" and "blessed her with an impotence of grief," then "traced with milder interest / That secret spirit of
humanity / Which mid the calm oblivious tendencies / Of nature, 'mid her
plants, her weeds, and flowers, / And silent overgrowings, still survived"
(498–506). It is only when the Pedlar sees the traveler able to face human
impotence and still find the spirit of humanity in the remains of human
artifacts overgrown by nature, that he knows that he will be able to understand his lesson:

> My Friend, enough to sorrow have you given,
> The purposes of wisdom ask no more;
> Be wise and chearful, and no longer read
> The forms of things with an unworthy eye.
> She sleeps in the calm earth, and peace is here.
> I well remember that those very plumes,
> Those weeds, and the high spear-grass on that wall,
> By mist and silent rain-drops silver'd o'er,
> As once I passed did to my heart convey

So still an image of tranquillity,
So calm and still, and looked so beautiful
Amid the uneasy thoughts which filled my mind,
That what we feel of sorrow and despair
From ruin and from change, and all the grief
The passing shews of being leave behind,
Appeared an idle dream that could not live
Where meditation was. I turned away
And walked along my road in happiness.

(508–25)

The consolation for transience and nothingness is the eternity of nature, for the ugliness of life it is the sense that even the useless weeds, whose encroachment on the cottage was a symptom of its decay, can be as tranquil and beautiful as anything in nature. Nature is one, and humans too are part of its eternity and tranquil beauty—"She sleeps in the calm earth and peace is here." An important transition has taken place within the poem and through the poem. The longing that has been unappeased and unappeasable directed at an absent love is fulfilled when its object is displaced to nature herself.

But this displacement raises an obvious question in the light of Wordsworth's previous poetry. What enabled him to accomplish now what he wanted but was unable to achieve as far back as "An Evening Walk," when nature—or his ability to imagine nature—proved unequal to the task? The answer is that two necessary conditions had been fulfilled, one explicitly mentioned in "An Evening Walk" itself, the other only inherent in the nature of the crisis in that poem but finally fulfilled through Wordsworth's revolutionary period. The first condition was that he was finally in residence with Dorothy. At Racedown, where "The Ruined Cottage" was written, he shared with her that "gilded" cottage that he had declared the "Sole bourn, sole wish, sole object" of his way, the home whose evocation in the earlier poem had been the precondition of imagining the peaceful evening scene with which it ended. Now it was the realized condition of the healing vision of nature that enabled him to accommodate Margaret's destruction. Wordsworth twice paid tribute to Dorothy's role in his recovery. A famous passage in *The Prelude* makes the temporal connection explicit and emphasizes Dorothy's maternal functioning both as occasional monitor who yet does not compromise his independence and as omnipresent security and reminder of his better self.

                    then it was
That the beloved woman in whose sight
Those days were passed—now speaking in a voice
Of sudden admonition, like a brook

That does but cross a lonely road; and now
Seen, heard and felt, and caught at every turn,
Companion never lost through many a league—
Maintained for me a saving intercourse
With my true self . . .

.   .   .   .

She, in the midst of all, preserved me still
A poet, made me seek beneath that name
My office upon earth, and nowhere else.
And lastly, Nature's self, by human love
Assisted, through the wary labyrinth
Conducted me again to open day.

(X.907–24)

The other tribute to Dorothy, biographically less direct but conceptually more important, was of course in "Tintern Abbey."

The second condition of Wordsworth's recovery was the transformation of the image of nature, which meant transformation also of the imagination that could conceive it, so that it could withstand and contain the horror of Margaret's fate. It is this transformation that is accomplished in the figure of the Pedlar, whose history and philosophy were added to "The Ruined Cottage" only in the winter and spring of 1798. The first version of spring 1797 did not have any of the consolatory material discussed above and ended with the Pedlar's uninterpreted "and here she died / Last human tenant of these ruined walls." There has been much debate over whether the addition of the overt philosophical editorializing strengthens or weakens the poem. Whatever the judgment of its merit, current critical consensus on its origin is that Wordsworth turned to explicit philosophizing only under the influence of Coleridge, who entered his life in a sustained way in the summer of 1797, and that the purpose of the philosophical additions was to invest the Pedlar with metaphysical authority that would make him a plausible interpreter of Margaret's suffering.[90] The debate, but even more the emphasis on Coleridge, seems somewhat overdrawn, or more precisely, wrongly construed. The explicit consolation of the passage at the end of MS. D, a version of the poem dating from 1799, is implicit all along in "The Ruined Cottage"—it was after all the very purpose of the poem—and The Borderers is evidence enough that Wordsworth was not only thinking in philosophical terms before he met Coleridge but in terms of making philosophical statements. (It is interesting in this connection that a letter from one of Wordsworth's relatives to another describing the events surrounding the failure of the play reports that "the metaphysical obscurity of one character, was the great reason of its rejection" (Letters, 197). Unquestionably

Coleridge's more theoretical mind and wider reading were a powerful stimulus to a more self-conscious and self-confident philosophizing, but to attribute the very impulse to Coleridge is to misconstrue the whole course of Wordsworth's development.[91] Coleridge played a role in relationship to Wordsworth analogous to the role Schleiermacher played for Schlegel—functioning as a like-minded but strongly individual self who could enter into confirmatory dialogue and enable the other to crystallize latent thought. The more interesting question, however, is whether the Pedlar's philosophy does in fact make him a plausible interpreter of Margaret's experience. I want to argue that it does not, that in some sense Wordsworth was aware of that fact, and that this accounts for the excision of the Pedlar material from MS. D, for the future difficulties with the poem, and for much of his difficulty in completing *The Recluse*. The very imagination that could conceive a nature powerful enough to contain Margaret's fate undercut nature's objective power.

Jonathan Wordsworth has argued that "The Pedlar" is about the unity of man and nature, and that it was only later, with "Tintern Abbey" and especially *The Prelude*, that Wordsworth's faith in the "one life" uniting them began to weaken.[92] But from the very beginning of Wordsworth's description of their relationship in "The Pedlar," the focus is on the *activity* of the Pedlar in relationship to nature. As a child

> deep feelings had impressed
> Great objects on his mind . . .
>
> . . . .
> With these impressions would he still compare
> All his ideal stores, his shapes and forms,
> And, being still unsatisfied with aught
> Of dimmer character, he thence attained
> An *active* power to fasten images
> Upon his brain, and on their picture lines
> Intensely brooded . . .
>
> (30–42)

The italics are Wordsworth's, and every verb in the passage is self-referential and active; the only slight hedging is in the first line, where his feelings, rather than he himself, are said to act as autonomous agents. As the section continues, the emphasis on the mind's activity in producing the image of sublime nature increases:

> in the after day
> Of boyhood, many an hour in caves forlorn
> And in the hollow depths of naked crags
> He sate, and even in their fixed lineaments,
> Or from the power of a peculiar eye,

Or by creative feeling overborne,
Or by predominance of thought oppressed,
Even in their fixed and steady lineaments
He traced an ebbing and a flowing mind
Expression ever varying.

(48–57)

Of the three alternatives Wordsworth offers to explain how the "fixed and steady lineaments" of caves and crags took on the ebbing and flowing character of the mind, only one is perceptual, and even its ostensibly passive nature is undercut by the epithet "peculiar." The other two refer to intellectual activity and the creative imagination. Although Wordsworth wishes to insist on the objective presence of the living characteristics of nature through the repeated use of a perceptual vocabulary, the rhetoric of intensity continually pushes beyond sight to confound it with other faculties:

But in the mountains did he FEEL his faith,
There did he see the writing. All things there
Breathed immortality, revolving life,
And greatness still revolving, infinite.
There littleness was not, the least of things
Seemed infinite, and there his spirit shaped
Her prospects—nor did he *believe*; he saw.

(122–28)

The insistence on passive vision—contradicted by the italicizing of its opposite, "belief"—is lame in any case after the capitalizing of "feeling." Furthermore, what Wordsworth says he saw in the mountains is *writing*, and though the intended reference is to the true text of scripture, the idea of "writing" removes the object from the naive field of perception to the arena of interpretation, that is, from immediate objective presence to mediated existence. The ultimately uncontainable force of the mind's activity bursts through undisguisedly near the end of the poem:

From deep analogies *by thought supplied*,
Or consciousness not to be subdued,
To every natural form, rock, fruit, and flower,
Even the loose stones that cover the highway,
He gave a moral life; he saw them feel
Or *linked them* to some feeling.
. . . .
He had a world about him—'twas his own,
He made it.

(330–40; italics added)

The Pedlar is not a passive receiver of the consolations of eternal and objective nature, he *supplies* nature with the qualities that can console him.

Certainly Wordsworth also proclaims in the poem his vision of the one life in all things (217–18). But the real counterpart of the active mind within the poem is not the unity of mind and nature in the one life; it is the independent power of nature. And what is especially striking and important about the power of nature is that it is most often asserted in such a way as not to complement the active mind but in fact to efface it. When nature is evoked, the activity of the mind recedes or is absent; the mind becomes a humble vessel, a pure receptacle.

> But he had felt the power
> Of Nature, and already was prepared
> By his intense conceptions to receive
> Deeply the lesson deep of love, which he
> Whom Nature, by whatever means, has taught
> To feel intensely, cannot but receive.
>
> (86–91)

> yet was his heart
> Lowly, for he was meek in gratitude
> Oft as he called to mind those exstacies,
> And whence they flowed; and from them he acquired
> Wisdom which works through patience—thence he learned
> In many a calmer hour of sober thought
> To look on Nature with an humble heart,
> Self-questioned where it did not understand,
> And with a superstitious eye of love.
>
> (131–39)

> From Nature and her overflowing soul
> He had received so much that all his thoughts
> Were steeped in feeling.
>
> (203–5)

The characteristic trope in "The Pedlar" is *not* the "one life" but the oscillation between declarations of the absolute power of mind on the one hand and the absolute power of nature on the other. And what renders this apparently contradictory oscillation intelligible is yet another movement between active and passive, contained in the first, in which the activity is of quite a different character. That second oscillation is present in the difficult and ambiguous lines describing the Pedlar's epiphany in the mountains, where it is unclear to whom the different attributes belong, to him or to nature, and who is doing what to whom:

Oh then what soul was his, when on the tops
Of the high mountains he beheld the sun
Rise up and bathe the world in light. He looked,
The ocean and the earth beneath him lay
In gladness and deep joy. The clouds were touched,
And in their silent faces he did read
Unutterable love. Sound needed none,
Nor any voice of joy: *his spirit drank*
The spectacle. Sensation, soul, and form,
All melted into him; they swallowed up
His animal being. In them did he live,
And by them did he live—they were his life.
In such an access of mind, in such high hour
Of visitation from the living God,
He did not feel the God, he felt his works.

(94–106; italics added)

Jonathan Wordsworth points out the confusions in the passage. Sensation, soul, and form would seem to belong to the Pedlar, but they melt into him from the outside. His spirit actively drinks in the spectacle, but his being is passively swallowed up. The whole process is described as both "an access of mind" and a "visitation from the living God."[93] This last contradiction is congruent with a contradiction between creative mind and creative Nature. But the first two confusions represent activity as an active passivity, a taking in of the outside that can also be experienced as a being absorbed by the outside. The metaphors of drinking in and being swallowed up point plainly to the origin and nature of this dual experience. It is the relationship of infant and mother, in which the boundaries between the two are effaced and the child experiences the mother's power and bounty as his or her own while at the same time feeling contained within her.

Elsewhere Wordsworth is even more explicit about the maternal nature of the Pedlar's bond with nature.

Nature was at his heart, and he perceived,
Though yet he knew not how, a wasting power
In all things which from her sweet influence
Might tend to wean him.

(158–61)[94]

It is in the image of the maternal relationship that the apparent contradiction between the role of mind and nature is resolved in "The Pedlar"—not that it ceases to be a contradiction, but it is made to correspond to a contradictory actual experience. What is involved is not necessarily a psychological "regression" to an earlier stage but the poetic use of a regressive metaphor to stage a reconciliation. And through this metaphor it is finally apparent how Wordsworth has resolved the crisis of individuality. The vast claims Rivers makes for the absolute autonomy of the self are retained, indeed they are extended: the mind creates a unified yet infinite world. Nothing is lost, nothing is out of place, everything is related to everything else as parts of one whole, and everything lasts forever. The ability to create such a world depends wholly on the uniqueness of the Pedlar's spontaneous experience. That the Pedlar is "untaught, / In the dead lore of schools undisciplined" is precisely the condition of the possibility of such creation. He is an original, whose world-making is the negation of all previous thought, all external influence. Yet that very individuality is dependent not only in its origins but for its continuing sustenance on the very unity that it creates. That is why his "*being*" can become both "sublime and comprehensive" (129–30) while *he* remains lowly and meek in gratitude (132). This distinction between his being and his self is not "merely" rhetorical; it is the necessary splitting of the self through which Wordsworth can "still suspect, and still revere himself." The sublimity and comprehensiveness of the self is real, but it is also separable from the self because it is the gift of the Other, or rather, it is the presence of the Other. It is, in fact, the selfother within the self,[95] that part of the self Wordsworth sees as created through the internalization of what is sublime and comprehensive in nature. This presence, in all its infinite greatness, is wholly love. In it, all the dangers of infinite individuality have been eradicated by the attribution of the self's original and absolute power to a wholly benign source, so that when the self internalizes and exercises that power, the self cannot but be benign also. The problem for Wordsworth is that despite the distinction he wishes to make, he is unable to separate the "being" of the self and the self in wholly isolated compartments. His own self-awareness, which is the process of the poem itself, shuttles between the two, carrying the only half-suppressed news that what has been internalized has itself been created, that for the adult—and the poet—at any rate, internalization can be neither passive nor innocent but is an act of endowing the self with power. The external is already endowed before it is internalized and this fact is inescapable because the wish to see nature infinite in itself is an effort at escape from the self's frightening wish for its own infinity.

In the light of this reading of "The Pedlar," it seems to me necessary to reconsider once again the dating of the "Prospectus" to *The Recluse*, whose spirit and statement of aims accord so well with the philosophy of "The Pedlar." Older scholarship long assumed that the "Prospectus" was written at about the same time, in the late winter or early spring of 1798, but more recently, it has been assigned to a later date somewhere between 1800 and 1806.[96] Two kinds of arguments have been offered against the earlier dating—manuscript and textual. Manuscript evidence, however, as Jonathan Wordsworth points out, is unhelpful and remains inconclusive.[97] The textual argument is essentially twofold; first, that the only evidence in favor of the earlier dating is the resemblance of the opening words of the "Prospectus"—"On Man, on Nature and on human Life"—to Wordsworth's statement of his plan for *The Recluse* in the letter of March 1798 to James Tobin; and second, that the theme and language of the "Prospectus" bear far less similarity to writings from the spring of 1798 than to those of 1800 such as "Michael" and the "Glad Preamble" that appears later as the opening of Book I of *The Prelude*. The first point of course holds only if the second is true, and the second is a matter of interpretation. The currently favored interpretation can be sustained, however, only if one ignores not only the central role that Wordsworth assigned the active mind in "The Pedlar" but the whole dialectic of that poem. The triumphalist assertion in the "Prospectus" that enables Wordsworth to defy Jehovah's strength and terror and surpass Milton's Christian epic with his humanistic one captures not only the spirit of that heady spring of 1798 when Wordsworth had discovered his new message, but the spirit of "The Pedlar" as well.

> The darkest pit
> Of the profoundest hell, night, chaos, death
> Nor aught of blinder vacancy scoop'd out
> By help of dreams, can breed such fear and awe
> As fall upon me when I look
> Into my soul, into the soul of man
> My haunt, and the main region of my song
>
> (257.23–29)

Furthermore, if as I have argued, the "one life" exists in "The Pedlar" only in the context of a relationship between mind and nature, that relationship closely matches the famous idea in the "Prospectus" that paradisal unity need not be looked for only in history because "minds / Once wedded to this outward frame of things / In love, finds these the growth of the common day" (38–40). The "Prospectus" reproduces in much bolder and more compressed form the paradox of "The Pedlar." The mind of man is a sublime force higher and greater than heaven itself, existing in worlds "To which the Heaven of heavens is but a veil" (18). Yet its power, which makes the poet unafraid of Jehovah himself, is conditional, dependent on "this outward frame of things" to which it must be wedded in love to produce the Eden. The dependency holds even if the egalitarian relationship of marriage suggests a more balanced and stable dependency than the shifting domination submission of the mother-child dyad. There is one other striking piece of evidence for the earlier date. At the close, Wordsworth refers to himself as "In part a Fellow citizen, in part / An outl[aw], and a borderer of his age" (69–70), a self-reference that makes most sense in close proximity to the writing of *The Borderers* and the emotions connected with it.

If, however, the reading of "The Pedlar" I have ventured shows it to be closer in spirit to the "Prospectus" than has been previously suggested, it also helps to explain why the project announced in the "Prospectus" faced internal difficulties that ultimately prevented its ever coming to fruition. The proclamation of the absolute power of mind generates the immediate need to retreat to a regressive metaphor of maternal dependency. Even in the "Prospectus," the status of the mind as the sublime is reduced right after its annunciation to that of equal partnership with nature in marital union. In "Tintern Abbey," however, written a few months after "The Pedlar," the regression to dependency on the feminine is deeper, as we have seen, paralleling that of "The Pedlar" itself. "Tintern Abbey," furthermore, makes clear the cost of regression in relationship to other people and to the possibilities of social theory. In the dyadic relationship with nature, other selves are effaced because the essential problem has become the adjustment and regulation of the absolute self through a contradictory relationship with absolute nature (or an absolute counterpart female human, Dorothy, who is not an other but an alter ego). To be more precise, it is not true that others are simply obliterated. Just as all human artifacts have been blended into nature, all humans have blended into the hermit, who is at home alone with nature. Contrary to Levinson's assertion,[98] the vagrants she sees Wordsworth ignoring *are* explicitly in the poem, and they carry with them the intertextual weight of all the vagrants in Wordsworth's previous poetry. Their treatment in "Tintern Abbey" is a version of the solution he constructed for the problem of the vagrant through Margaret in "The Ruined Cottage." Just as he identified his plight with theirs ever since "An Evening Walk," he gathers them back to himself in the figure of the lonely hermit in "Tintern Abbey." But the hermit is no less "objective" a social figure than the vagrant; Wordsworth does not simply "subjectify" previously social figures by replacing them with his own consciousness. Identification is still mediated through social figures. Nevertheless, by blending the vagrants into the hermit, he does transform the existence of those in whom he once found his own image, those whom he had once chosen to try to save by revolutionary action. The hermit may be as poor as the vagrant, living as "houseless" in his cave as they in the woods. But unlike them, he has transcended his material situation by understanding his material suffering as an emblem of a finitude that can be overcome if it is rightly understood as the avenue to infinity. The move is an end-run around the basic premise of all social theory, the hypothesis of the social causation of misery.

That is not to say that Wordsworth understood himself this way, or that he did not try to have something like a social theory. There did, after all, seem to be a counterpart social vision to the hermit's lone communion with nature in Wordsworth's "implicit conviction about the human imagination as best thriving in a subsistence, agrarian economy of owner occupiers"[99] bound together by natural sympathy, a conviction expressed in poems such as "The Old Cumberland Beggar" and "Michael." But these poems represent only one part of the grand project Wordsworth announced to Tobin in March 1798. They omit the dimension of "Man" understood in terms of the vast claims for the human mind he intended to make. And it was the impossibility of integrating these claims with a social theory that defeated Wordsworth's larger project.

The best evidence for this thesis is in both Wordsworth's impetus to write the *Two-Part Prelude* of 1799 and the outcome of the poem itself. The 1799 *Prelude* is the climax of the effort at resolution I have traced so far, the best evidence of its tenuousness and partial failure, and the explanation of why Wordsworth would never complete the poetic project he announced with such hope the previous year.

It has been argued that the early *Prelude* is a much more unified poem with a stronger sense of formal structure than the 1805 version;[100] what is certainly true is that the structure of the 1799 *Prelude* reveals much about the nature of Wordsworth's conflict that was obscured in its later revision and expansion. One of the most important, and damaging, changes was the removal of the "spots of time" passage from its original position at the climax of Wordsworth's early recollections of childhood, where it takes on a crucial meaning not readily seen from its later placement far removed from them. Separating those memories that ostensibly revivify imagination from the other early memories and from the "infant babe" passage that followed them almost immediately in the original *Prelude* destroyed the narrative that told the crucial story.

The notoriously enigmatic question with which the poem abruptly begins, "What is for this," has occasioned endless interpretation; whatever else is true, it is unquestionably a lament for Wordsworth's apparent inability to carry out the poetic program he had announced to Tobin and discussed with Coleridge. With characteristic directness, Jonathan Wordsworth has said that Wordsworth wrote the 1799 *Prelude* to find out why he could not write the poem he was supposed to and that he went back to childhood in order to try to find out what was wrong.[101] The opening complaint, "Was it for this / That one, the fairest of all rivers, loved / To blend his murmurs with my nurse's song" (1.1–3), makes clear that he went back to memories of childhood also because, as "The Pedlar" had already claimed, he felt he had been prepared by his special relationship with nature in childhood for his great poetic task. Yet the sequence of memories that follows almost immediately tells a story that contradicts the privileged harmony evoked in the poem's first images, a story of childhood crimes. "The Pedlar" had stated that the poet's mind was nurtured in terror as well as love; it now emerges that the terror was the result of acts the poet remembers committing as a child, acts that in emotionally direct, if cognitively obscure, ways have conditioned the nature of his mind's power and led to the blockage he now experiences.

The initially benign memories of oneness with sun, stream, and field in early childhood play cannot be sustained; they modulate rapidly into an image of the four year old standing "alone / A naked savage in the thunder shower" (1.25–26). In the episodes immediately following, the "savage" is remembered as an older boy snaring woodcocks and stealing them from others' traps, robbing eggs from ravens' nests, and stealing a shepherd's boat to row across the lake at night. All of these are acts of "stealth and troubled pleasure" (1.90–91), as the boat-stealing episode is explicitly called. They involve challenges both to nature and to others' rights to her, declarations of superiority through thefts that are experienced as acts of destruction or of violent appropriation, and that are often followed by fears of retaliation. The boy trapping birds is not simply a thief but a "fell destroyer"; and after despoiling his competitors as well, he hears "Low breathings coming after me" (1.47). In the egg-robbing episode he celebrates a double triumph, turning an ignoble act to glory and defying mortality itself. Climbing precariously high on an almost sheer ridge of rock above the ravens' nest, he feels, instead of the expectable terror, a superhuman sensation of being suspended on air, buoyed by the very wind that threatens him (1.65). And in stealing the boat, the boy disables the shepherd and displaces him in the enjoyment of a "troubled pleasure" whose description virtually proclaims power, aggression, and sensuality: "I . . . struck the oars, and struck again / . . . . / twenty times / I dipped my oars into the silent lake, / And as I rose upon the stroke my boat / Went heaving through the water" (1.87, 103–6). Little wonder that the cliff that suddenly looms above a nearby hill as he moves further into the lake appears as an avenging giant striding after him.

Even the apparently unconflicted pleasure of the skating scene that follows the accounts of these crimes is described in military and hunting metaphors, partly hidden, partly displayed, in its brilliant onomatopoeic rendering: "All shod with steel / We hissed along the polished ice in games / Confederate, imitative of the chase" (1.156–58). And when the young Wordsworth stops short on his skates to enjoy the dizziness, he experiences the surrounding cliffs wheeling by him as the earth turning on its axis, the boy himself the very axis of the turning world. The theme of conflict, competition, and troubled triumph continues even into the quieter indoor amusements that Wordsworth recounts immediately afterwards. Tic-tac-toe is played with "head opposed to head, / In strife too humble to be named in verse," and the cards used in games are a "thick-ribbed army" led on "to the combat" (1.211–15).

Activities such as these impressed upon everything in nature—and in social life—for the young Wordsworth "the characters / Of danger or desire" (1.195–96), a fine phrase that neatly summarizes the significance of all the experiences the poet remembers in these first explorations of his childhood. The impressions are more accurately rendered conjunctively than disjunctively—danger *and* desire—for the objects of desire, or the desiring itself, were fraught with danger. His remembered reaction to the danger was equally significant. Thinking about the boat-stealing episode afterwards, the boy did not recall his fear or sense of threat; the emotion was isolated, the sensory images were repressed into a "darkness—call it solitude, / Or blank desertion" and displaced by "huge and mighty forms that do not live / Like living men" moving "slowly through my mind" (1.127–28). Thus external punitive forces were converted into only vaguely ominous internal powers, embodiments of a relatively benign transcendence of empirical perception, a sublimity stripped of anger, if not of awesomeness. The precipitating event itself—the trespass—becomes nothing but an occasion for the experience of these forces and loses its character as forbidden desire and act.

Crimes of destruction, appropriation, and aggrandizement, fear of retaliation, defensive neutralization through suppression of feeling and conversion of external sensory image to vague internal construct: this is the overall pattern of the chain of memory associations opening the poem.[102] The same pattern continues into the climactic memories of the first book, the "spots of time." The bridge to those more portentous memories, with their ostensible ability to repair the imaginative power, is the mysterious "drowned man" episode, which abruptly and ominously raises the emotional stakes of the already dangerous memory game by introducing the theme of death. Wordsworth remembers a scene in which, unlike all the others recalled so far, he was ostensibly passive, an observer rather than an actor; the passivity is as if in offset to the gravity of the event. Yet it is easy to sense in the description of his behavior the uneasiness of complicity and guilt. Catching sight of a pile of clothing across Esthwaite Lake, he watched for half an hour, until it grew too dark to see, for someone to recover them. He must have thought something was wrong, though he did nothing about it, because he returned to the scene the next day. He does not even report his return directly, however, as if troubled by his fascination. Rather the next lines describe men dragging the lake the following day, and the sudden apparition of the dead man rising "bolt upright" with his ghastly face—an image reminiscent of the cliff that "upreared its head" and followed the boy who had stolen the shepherd's boat. This episode, however, has no reported antecedents. It is described with narrative objectivity, almost without hint of any subjective reaction, and it is quickly submerged into a bland general reference to "numerous accidents in flood or field" (1.280) that impressed his mind "With images to which in following years / far other feelings were attached" (1.284–85). This memory too is clearly fraught with suppressed danger.

The two spots of time that follow are even more opaque, and their opacity seems in proportion to the even greater degree of danger they hold. Wordsworth recalls going riding with a servant while visiting his grandparents at Penrith when he was five years old. Although he was "an urchin, one who scarce / Could hold a bridle," he had, he says, "ambitious hopes." The hopes are not specified but the language suggests that the little boy wanted to be a grownup man: the phrase "I mounted" emphasizes his independence, just as the description of himself and the servant as "a pair of horsemen" asserts his equality with the adult. After only a short while, the boy as separated from "honest James" by "some mischance." The epithet, which seems to absolve the servant of blame, and the shift in the characterization of James from "encourager and guide" to "comrade" two lines later, at the point of separation, carry the strong implication that the two were separated not by accident but by the boy's willful act. The power and meaning of that act emerge in the images that follow. Frightened—though significantly it is James who is described as lost—the boy dismounts, and leading his horse down into a valley comes across the site where a man was executed for murdering his wife. Just what Wordsworth knew about the event as a boy is uncertain, for all that was visible then was a long green ridge of turf, "Whose shape was like a grave"; gibbet and bones are mentioned only as being no longer there. Furthermore, the description of the murder conflates two crimes, one of which, the one mentioned in the poem, Wordsworth could not have known about as a boy of this age because it had occurred not near Penrith but Hawkshead, where he did not go until four years later. Clearly the "memory" of 1798 is part retrospective creation. What is significant about it, however, is the association of murder with the boy's desire for independence and with the act of losing the adult authority whose guiding presence was embodiment and reminder of his lack of independence.

The "spot of time," however, does not come to focus on any of the components of this part of the event, that is, on the place of crime and punishment. Indeed, Wordsworth tells us abruptly, "I left the spot" and reascended the slope, as if it were too dangerous to linger at that depth of memory and desire. Instead, the boy's perception, and the poet's memory, focus on the "naked pool," the beacon on the "lonely eminence," and the girl with the pitcher on her head forcing her way against the wind. These "symbols" are hard to read, as commentators have noted; in one sense they are not meant to be read at all. They *may* suggest the frightened yet splendid isolation of the boy who having got rid of his adult guardian, plays at being the lone man, and the equivocal identities and inner struggles that his conflicted aims generate. But above all they are screen images, displacements to the periphery of frightening events that concentrate attention *away* from the content that is the center of emotional power while retaining all of its force. Even more than the "huge and mighty forms" that moved through his mind after the boat-stealing episode, the displaced images of pool, beacon, and girl neutralize events and feelings while functioning in their reinscription as evidence of internal transcendence, the "visionary dreariness" that invests the otherwise admittedly "ordinary sight." In this case memory is fixated on external visual images, that are better suited because of their externality and concreteness to hold more powerful and frightening impulses at bay.

The same dynamic operates in the second of the two spots, Wordsworth's memory of waiting for horses to take him and his brothers home from school for Christmas vacation when he was thirteen years old. Ten days after his return, his father died; the boy experienced this event as a "chastisement" from God who thus "corrected . . . desires" he had felt while waiting on the crag. The desires are not specified; as with the "drowned man" and Penrith episodes, ellipsis frustrates narrative and psychological connectedness. Weiskel has argued that punishment, let alone such dire punishment, for the presumably innocent desire of wanting to go home makes sense only if the desire was not innocent at all but an unconscious wish for his father's death.[103] To the details he adduces in support of this assumption, I would add Wordsworth's emphasis on his position high on the crag as he anxiously scanned for the horses. He describes it as "an eminence" overlooking all possible approaches and then underlines the superiority of his vantage point with repetition: "Thither I repaired / Up to the highest summit" (1.340–41). His sense of guilt seems to be connected with the assumption of preeminent position. Although his brothers were with him, the language of the passage indicates he climbed up by himself and waited above them alone. He refers to himself later upon his return home as "A dweller in my father's house" (351), as if to separate himself from his father's domain. And the sensory images to which this spot of time is fixed include the same emphasis on singleness, lonely isolation, and restless elements as in the first spot: a "single sheep," the "one blasted tree," "the bleak music" of an old stone wall, and "the wind and sleety rain" that accompanied his vigil for the horses (1.360–62). The similarity of the two spots in their elements and structure suggests an even greater closeness. Age five is the heart of the child's oedipal rebellion, as the onset of puberty is its repetition. Both episodes deal with a child's claim to autonomy and authority that is made at the cost of a desire to get rid of his father or the father's agent[104] and is punished by the imaginings of retaliatory death. And in both, the complex of wishes, fantasies, and fears is displaced onto obsessively fixed sensory images peripheral to the main event that, by keeping attention focused on the outside, prevent awareness of their inner meaning.

The spots of time are the climactic events in the chain of remembered crimes that Wordsworth's effort to understand his writing block has provoked. Superficially, the structure of the spots seems to bear out Weiskel's claim about how the spots of time restore the blocked imagination to its creative functioning. "The reviving of the imaginative power which the spots of time effect," he writes, "depends upon the continued repression of the signified"—that is, the external objects or events, like the grave-shaped ridge of turf, or the death of his father, which are not part of the visionary experience.[105] The very working of the imagination *is* its implication that the intensely-charged images (wind-blown girl, blasted tree) have a mysterious or transcendent meaning, and imagination produces this impression by refusing to supply the symbolic connection of these images with the other external objects. In this way, imagination "saves" itself as a creative or meaning-producing force by refusing the causal connections that would make purely external objects the causes of its meanings. But while Weiskel correctly, it seems to me, describes the process by which Wordsworth's mind suppresses its own knowledge in the spots of time, his overly abstract explanation finally concerns itself with the formal conditions of the symbolic function in Wordsworth, with the question of whether symbolism originates in the mind or in the external world; he thus pushes aside the *content* of the meaning of the spots of time, which he himself identifies as death, or death-wish, thus subtly colluding with Wordsworth's defensive maneuver. That is why Weiskel goes wrong, in a crucial way, in believing that the spots actually *do* revive the imagination. This is what Wordsworth claims they do, but the fact is that in the original poetic context of 1798 they do not succeed in overcoming the blockage of imagination that has stymied his writing of *The Recluse*. Wordsworth backhandedly acknowledges this to the addressee of the poem, Coleridge. "[M]y hope has been," he writes at the end of part one of the first *Prelude*,

> that I might fetch
> Reproaches from my former years, whose power
> May spur me on, in manhood now mature,
> To honourable toil. *Yet should it be*

That this is but an impotent desire—
That I by such inquiry am not taught
To understand myself . . .

. . . .
                        need I dread from thee
Harsh judgements if I am so loth to quit
Those recollected hours that have the charm
Of visionary things, and lovely forms
And sweet sensations, that throw back our life
And make our infancy a visible scene
On which the sun is shining?

                              (1.453–64; italics added)

Wordsworth acknowledges here both that he is not able to proceed with the writing of his philosophical poem on the power of imagination and that he has not understood himself sufficiently to learn why. He indicates instead, in his appeal to Coleridge's forbearance, that he is going to linger in childhood and to focus on happy memories, which in view of what has come before must be seen as a defense against what recollection has in fact revealed. If and when the poem continues, the "visionary dreariness" of murderous power will give way to an infancy "On which the sun is shining." Wordsworth's internal struggle is evident in some lines just after the original manuscript of part one that were not incorporated in the final version of 1799, lines that were written at the time of an abortive attempt to start the second part. "Here we pause / Doubtful; or lingering with a truant heart, / Slow and of stationary character, / Rarely adventurous, studious more of peace / And soothing quiet which we here have found" (*1799 Prelude*, 13n.). He seems to have feared that any resumption of the poem might take him where he did not wish again to tread— back to memories of "criminal" initiatives in childhood, with their ominous implications for the meaning of individuality in adulthood.

That such a danger existed is evident in the initial memory recounted in part two, which Wordsworth resumed only after many months delay. It is a memory of boat races on Lake Windermere, the boys beating along the lake "With rival oars" (2.56). But now, something different happens; the issues of competition and triumph are explicitly raised only to be denied. All the races end on islands whose descriptions ("musical with birds / That sang for ever") mark their mythic character as sheltered paradises free from strife.

                    In such a race,
        So ended, disappointment could be none,
        Uneasiness, or pain, or jealousy;

> We rested in the shade, all pleased alike,
> Conquered or conqueror. Thus our selfishness
> Was mellowed down, and thus the pride of strength
> And the vainglory of superior skill
> Were interfused with objects which subdued
> And tempered them, and gradually produced
> A quiet independence of the heart.
>
>   (2.63–72)

The struggle in this episode between the urge to competitive superiority and the need to subdue it in the interests of unity, harmony, and "quiet independence" (with its linguistic echoes of "Tintern Abbey") initiates an oscillation between memories of adventuresome boldness and retreat to protection and succor. An account of an aggressively overambitious schoolboy expedition on horseback to a destination "too distant far / For any cautious man" (2.106–7) shifts abruptly to the description of a boat ride in the shelter of a tunnel of overhanging tree branches, which ends with the boys being fed by the inhabitants of a neighboring mansion-house as they sit in the "covert" beneath the trees. This memory of womb-like nurturance in turn triggers another memory of feelings of warm attachment to the scene, expressed in lines taken almost directly from his boyhood poem "The Vale of Esthwaite," from the passage in which he laments having to leave the only home he knows, the substitute for his dead mother, to go up to Cambridge:

>   And there I said,
> That beauteous sight before me, there I said
> (*Then first beginning in my thoughts to mark*
> *That sense of dim similitude which links*
> *Our moral feelings with external forms*)
> That in whatever region I should close
> My mortal life I would remember you,
> Fair scenes—that dying I would think on you,
> My soul would send a longing look to you.
>
>   (2.161–69; italics added)

Here Wordsworth says explicitly that his first awareness of the symbolic *meaning* of external objects (as opposed to the empty signifying or symbolic *functioning* of the spots of time) took place in a state of maternal connectedness with nature. That meaning, as he says addressing Coleridge some lines later, is the "unity of all" (2.256) that is prior to the man-made distinctions of reason; but what must be noticed is that the sense of unity has been produced in the poem by a regression in memory to a preindividuated state of being, one developmentally prior to the independent, destructively aggressive initiatives of separateness that mark its first part. The regressive sequence of memories has prepared us for the famous "infant babe" passage.

Much can and has been said both about the insights of this amazing passage into the mother-infant relationship and about its significance for an understanding of the biographical origins of Wordsworth's longing for unity with nature.[106] A number of features of the passage, however, bear directly on the present discussion of the function of regression in Wordsworth. The first is the detailed description of what the symbiotic connection between mother and infant achieves for the child. The mother's passion for the child acts on him as an "awakening breeze" (a metaphor with a long future of displacements in Wordsworth), and in conjunction with her possession of the world, which he sees through her eyes and which bears for him the meaning she gives it, her love empowers the child. Her passion for him and her power over the world enable him to unify it, "to combine / In one appearance all the elements / And parts of the same object, else detached / And loth to coalesce" (2.276–80); she thus functions as his transcendental ego in the Kantian sense, producing the unity of apperception without which the experience of an organized world is impossible. Further, however, her passion and power enable him to "irradiate and exalt" the world into a sublimity that transcends mere sense perception and establishes its beauty and permanence. In the 1850 *Prelude*, Wordsworth added a few lines that make this process more explicit. "Is there a flower, to which he points with hand / Too weak to gather it, already love / drawn from love's purest earthly fount for him / Hath beautified that flower" (II.245–48). Finally, the passion of his mother's gaze allows him to feel connected with being, so that he is "No outcast . . . bewildered and depressed" (2.289–91). It is in the context of the mother-child relationship that Wordsworth's "indifference" to the priority of mind or nature seems much less astonishing than it does from the perspective of a "mature" sense of logic and reality. In the boundaryless triangular relationship that links infant, mother, and mother's world, there is no distinction between his mind and hers, between what he produces as "an agent of the one great mind" and what he receives through the perception already produced for him by that same mind.

Secondly, and most important, the location of the whole passage in the development of the poem provides a crucial insight into the psychological structure of the sublime imagination in Wordsworth, the imagination that, as we have seen, is the source of individuality's absolute power. My point here can be made most clearly by contrasting it with the positions of Weiskel and Hartman. Using psychoanalytic concepts to explicate the "deep structure" of the sublime experience, Weiskel summarizes the self's encounter with an object that inspires terror and awe: "the excessive

object excites a wish to be inundated, which yields an anxiety of incorpo-
ration; this anxiety is met by a reaction formation against the wish which
precipitates a recapitulation of the Oedipus complex; this in turn yields a
feeling of guilt (superego anxiety) and is resolved through identification
(introjection)." In Weiskel's interpretation of this sequence of reactions,
the "oedipal" response to the object that inspires sublime emotions—the
competitive desire for its power—is secondary, a defense against a more
primitive "pre-oedipal" relationship, the fear of being engulfed by it:
"The wish to be inundated is reversed into a wish to possess." Furthermore, since in Weiskel's estimation that aspect of the Oedipus complex that involves the aggressive wish against the father is not crucial to
the defensive maneuver against the fear of being overwhelmed by the
sublime object, aggression is only "structurally motivated and fails to
impress us as authentic."[107] The self's aim, in other words, is only to possess the sublime object, not to destroy it; any aggressiveness toward it is
incidental.

In any case, however, Weiskel does not believe that Wordsworth's particular version of the sublime ever reached the point of an oedipal defense
and identification with the sublime object. Wordsworth's "egotistical
sublime" remained at the level of a dependent relationship with the external object, in which both the subject and the object poles, ego and
nature, are retained intact. Wordsworth's defense against engulfment
"worked" by obfuscating the issue of priority—was the power in him or in
the object, or both?[109]

Although Hartman eschews Freudian vocabulary on this issue, his
view of Wordsworth's sublime is rather similar. He points out that the
common factor in many of Wordsworth's childhood memories is a violation of nature, which he sees as the result not of the boy's aggression
against it but of his separation from it. It is not clear why Hartman thinks
of separation as violation, but the result is that he misses the theme of
murder in the spots of time. "[W]here it [the violation of nature] is secret,
as in the two spots of time (for no clear desecration has occurred), we
must assume that the boy's very *awareness* of his individuality—a prophetic or anticipatory awareness nourished by self-isolating circumstances—reacts on him as already a violation."[109] But the "self-isolating
circumstances" in the spots of time are themselves acts of rebellion and
violence, though not against nature; and if they are anticipatory for the
child, they are retroactive for the poet, who remembers them in the light
of a present assertiveness of the power of his mind.

It is difficult to know just how to take Weiskel's psychoanalytic categories, since he rejects a biographical/psychological approach as reduction-
ist and accidental to the ultimate structure of the sublime. His categories
seem to be metaphors for that structure, though why he should think

them useful metaphors if the sublime is the more fundamental category is a question. In Wordsworth's poetry, however, psychological and familial configurations seem to be real experiences in and through which the sublime is experienced. And the psychodynamic story they tell is exactly the opposite of the one Weiskel narrates. The present analysis of the structure of the *1799 Prelude* shows clearly that for Wordsworth the regressive "pre-oedipal" memories of the "dual unity" of mother and child were defenses against memories of frightening "oedipal" rivalries rather than the other way around. More exactly, they are defenses against rivalries for power that included also important pre-oedipal conflicts with nature (mother) herself and the sibling (schoolmate) competitors for her, all of which came to a head and were organized in Wordsworth's memory under the domination of the oedipal conflict as evidenced in the spots of time. While the memories of conflict and usurpation of power were able to drive the poem forward up to a certain point, they could *not* renew the blocked poetic project of *The Recluse*. In fact, as the end of part one shows, they led to a new impasse within *The Prelude* itself, an impasse that was only undone by the regression of the second part of the poem, which resolves the relation of mind and nature into a more radical version of the ending of "Tintern Abbey." It is not the oedipal structure of the spots of time but the pre-oedipal structure of the "infant babe" passage that Wordsworth calls "the first / Poetic spirit of our human life" (2:305–6); in the autobiographical reminiscences of his mother that follow he attributes to this "first poetic spirit" his own poetic origins, his connection with nature after she died, and his ability to drink from her "the visionary power" (2:360). It is in the context of those memories and that relationship that he can then boldly declare the power of his own mind without fear, in a passage that might otherwise seem like an incongruous irruption of the very thing he is suppressing:

> An auxiliar light
> Came from my mind, which on the setting sun
> Bestowed new splendour; the melodious birds,
> The gentle breezes, fountains that ran on
> Murmuring so sweetly in themselves, obeyed
> A like dominion, and the midnight storm
> Grew darker in the presence of my eye.
> Hence my obeisance, my devotion hence,
> And *hence* my transport.
>
> (2:417–26)

The mind's light is auxiliar, not the sole or even primary creative force, as it is auxiliar in the original connection with the mother, where it does not *seem* contradictory that his "dominion" should also be his "obeisance" and his "devotion"; it is the infant's "transport" to "know" a situation that is at once absolute power and absolute security. It is within the framework of this experience that towards the end of the poem Wordsworth recaptures the position of "Tintern Abbey" and "The Pedlar": "I felt the sentiment of being spread / O'er all that moves, and all that seemeth still / . . . / in all things / I saw one life and it was joy" (2:450–51, 459–60). Safely ensconced in the dyad of mother and child, and only then, the mind can exert a benign dominion. When the mind rears itself up to undertake on its own the great self-imposed task of *The Recluse*, to encompass the whole of reality, it runs into its own fearsome claims to infinity and has to fight itself again.

But in at least two crucial ways, psychoanalytic categories, accurate as they may be in rendering the psychological atmosphere of Wordsworth's metaphors, are misleading, or at least radically incomplete. One way has already been alluded to: the relationship between the psychological and the ontological. The vision of the one life *is* a vision of timeless infinite unity, whether as propensity of mind or as feature of the world, and this desire goes beyond the usual biological or intrafamilial meaning of psychoanalytic categories of motivation. But this fact does not mean that psychoanalytic categories ought to be reduced to metaphors of ontological categories, any more than the reverse. It does mean that ontological or religious dimensions of human experience are phenomenologically lived in, through, and with the biological and psychological dimensions. It is fathers and mothers and lovers that are divinized and rebelled against and fused with in order to establish the divinity of the self.[110]

Secondly, the poem does not end with the metaphysical vision of the one life. In the lines that follow it, the visionary experience is explicitly offered as a response to a historical situation, to "these times of fear, / This melancholy waste of hopes o'erthrown" (2:479–80), when former political idealists turn in their disappointment with the French Revolution against all "visionary minds" that might hope for the unity of mankind. The "sentiment of being" spread over everything and the "one life" in all things seems in this context to be meant as a compensatory vision for the revolutionary hopes of political and social unity. Against the disillusioned, the indifferent, and the apathetic, against those who indulge their *Schadenfreude* at the discomfiture of revolutionary idealists or retreat into selfishness in the name of social order, Wordsworth asserts that "in this time of dereliction and dismay, I yet / Despair not of our nature, but retain / A more than Roman confidence, a faith / That fails not" (2:486–90). The end of the poem appears to make explicit what was only implicit in the link between *The Borderers* and "The Pedlar" or in the structure of "Tintern Abbey," the framing political context of Wordsworth's venture into the poetics of imagination in 1798. Nevertheless, the intimation that the social solidarity of the "one life" is the main compensation *The Prelude* holds out for the failed social and political hopes of the Revolution is misleading. As we know, the abruptly introduced reference to "hopes o'erthrown" was a response to a letter from Coleridge dating from September 1799 in which he begged Wordsworth to write a poem addressed to those who "have thrown all hopes of amelioration of mankind, and are sinking into an almost epicurean selfishness."[111] But for Wordsworth, the real compensation his poem offered was a replacement for the hopes of the absolute authority of individuality, abandoned of course in part because of its incompatability with the ideal of social solidarity. The consoling vision of the one life is part of a dialectic in one of whose moments all of nature obeys the "dominion" of the poet's mind. What a classical psychoanalytic reading ignores is that the regression in the *1799 Prelude* arises from a historically new sense of selfhood that has given oedipal impulses ultimate significance for the displacement of authority. All of the childhood memories in *The Prelude* are recollections reinterpreted in the light of the recent present. Their causal force for Wordsworth's poetic project and problem runs in the opposite direction from that normally assumed in psychoanalysis, from the present to the past; the memories have been poetically and ideologically potentiated by the radically new concept of selfhood Wordsworth generated out of the practice and the theory of modern revolutionary freedom. In turn those memories have forced him back further to yet another childhood "memory," or conceit, of the mother-infant dyad, potentiated by the present need to sustain the concept of a wholly autonomous self in a context of complete safety. As with Schlegel, it is the structuring of the contradiction between autonomy and dependency in the form of an infant-mother relationship that allows the writer to compartmentalize the contradiction uncontaminated by the corrosiveness of mature self-consciousness.[112]

What this means for the possibility of a genuinely *social* theory can be seen in the peculiarities of a poem that has been taken to be a locus classicus of Wordsworth's immediate postrevolutionary social ideas. "Michael," according to David Simpson, is "Wordsworth's most detailed exposition of the virtues of the rural statesman's life, and of the tragedy of its disappearance,"[113] but seen in this way, he concedes, the poem creates some difficulties. Contemporary indications suggest that it was common in eighteenth-century discussions of rural decline to focus on the relations between social classes as its cause. Wordsworth not only avoids any such implications in the poem but makes Luke's moral disintegration result from his willing co-optation by urban corruption. It seems necessary to Simpson therefore to hypothesize that Wordsworth was consciously or unconsciously uncomfortable with the "real background" to the events he narrates and chose to avoid it.[114] In fact, however, the problem disappears when the a priori assumption about the primarily social meaning of Wordsworth's poem is dropped. "Michael" is not "about" the decline of rural life as a socioeconomic fact at all, though it may well have this event as its historical background. As Wordsworth expressly says in the poem, he was drawn to tales of shepherds *not* because he loved such men "For their own sakes, but for the fields and hills / Where was their occupation and abode."[115] The subject of the poem is nature, more precisely, the right human understanding of and relationship to nature. Furthermore, it is about right relationship to nature as a precondition for poetry, that is, for the poetry that can save the unconditional authority of the self through its complete subordination to nature. Once again Wordsworth is explicit: he is writing the poem

> For the delight of a few natural hearts,
> And with yet fonder feeling, for the sake
> Of youthful Poets, who among these Hills
> Will be my second self when I am gone.[116]

Wordsworth looks to the immortality of his own individuality—not simple egotism but as we have seen, a necessary dimension of his general concept of individuality itself—through those poets who in repeating his understanding of nature will be incarnations of himself. It is central to this understanding that it is within the power of the individual to create the right connection with nature. That is why Wordsworth makes Luke responsible for his own corruption, rather than focusing on the external temptations that are its occasion. It is not that Wordsworth did not aspire to write social poetry; the project of *The Recluse* is ample evidence that he did. His doctrine of the self, however, only allowed for a social vision in which others were alter egos, struggling with his problem.

Wordsworth was not at this point interested in questions of social hierarchy or the distribution of political power, as he had been between 1792 and 1795. Unquestionably, "Michael" rests on the contrast between the good life of rootedness in landed property handed down from father to son and the evil ways of urban commerce. But it is the attitude to nature and to time that was primarily at stake for Wordsworth in this opposition between country and city, not the issue of social relationships. It is only in the rural life that nature is revered as sacred, not exploited, and it is only in a patrimonial society that the sense of nature's eternity can be preserved. The city and commerce are the very essence of ephemerality and of the utilitarian attitude that denies the objectivity and permanence of matter. What was essential for Wordsworth was to find absolute meaning in everything as it was, not to change it, for the human power to change detracted from the power of nature. Above all, he needed to find meaning in what had been the very emblem of exclusion from being, the poor, the vagrant, the social outcast. The point of "The Old Cumberland Beggar," written in 1798 during the composition of "The Ruined Cottage," is not so much the specific social role that the beggar supposedly plays as a stimulant to habits of charity but that "'Tis Nature's law / . . . that none / the meanest of created things, / . . . should exist / Divorced from good."[117] Although Chandler is certainly right that some of the poem's ideas are Burkean, its admonition to politicians not to consider the beggar a burden to be got rid of is not primarily intended as part of a Burkean argument that political change most often does more harm than good. Burke's notion of "prescription," the presumption in favor of the status quo, has ineradicably utilitarian—as well of course as ideological—implications. Wordsworth's position was metaphysical. Even the apparently useless and excluded is part of Being. Certainly the social implications of that metaphysical position shaded easily into a Burkean political philosophy. It was only as the doctrine of the self's subordination to nature gave way to a more orthodox religious belief, however, that the self would be resubordinated to a traditional divinity in a more conventional and straightforward way, and only then could Wordsworth come to a more genuinely social and political theory, a theory that as Chander has shown was strongly Burkean in cast, complete with Burkean views of social hierarchy and political deference. Only in the unassimilated residue of *The Prelude*, on which Wordsworth continued to work all his life, did the radical self continue to lead the underground existence to which he relegated it, continually fearful of its implications, as the post-1805 revisions of *The Prelude* show, but still able to sustain the tenuous synthesis that allowed it a precarious existence.

FOUR

FRANÇOIS-RENÉ DE CHATEAUBRIAND

I) *Le Vague des Passions*

THERE is a certain deceptiveness about the terms in which, at the beginning of the *Genius of Christianity*, Chateaubriand claimed to be offering his apologia for religion. It is the deceptiveness of introductory compression rather than of concealment, though it has had a persistent effect on the general image of his work. No longer, he argued, could one rely on unquestioning acceptance of religious first principles in order to ground other tenets of faith. The destructive work of Enlightenment critics had made older forms of theological apologetics untenable. In his time it was necessary "not to prove that *the Christian religion is excellent because it comes from God, but that it comes from God because it is excellent.*"[1] Chateaubriand's criterion of excellence was explicitly secular: responsiveness to universal human needs, but most particularly the claims of the imagination—the desire for beauty—and the "interests of the heart" (48), rather than the demands of reason. In apparent fulfillment of this self-imposed task, Chateaubriand's early works, the *Genius* and the short stories *Atala* and *René* that were intended as sections of it, represent and argue the aesthetic and emotional merits of religion, in a language whose sentimentality and melodrama have sometimes seemed to the twentieth-century sensibility to verge perilously on the comic.[2]

Yet none of the contributions to the religious revival for which Chateaubriand became famous—his claim that of all religions Christianity is the most poetic and the most favorable to the arts, the rhetorical evidence for this claim proferred in his famous descriptions of sea and forest (*Genius*, 170–74) supposedly made possible only by his faith in nature's divine creation, his celebration of the Gothic cathedral as the epitome of religiously-inspired human creativity (*Genius*, 384–87)—adequately or even accurately represents what for Chateaubriand was the true affective and aesthetic core of Christianity's superiority. That core is especially difficult to disengage in the vast sprawl of the *Genius*, whose lengthy and apparently disconnected catalogue of virtues seems designed to overwhelm through sheer quantity and the incantatory weight of rhetoric rather than to persuade by coherence of plan or organization. Chateaubriand does not even appear to be consistent in his repeatedly avowed aim of dispensing with rational argument. Arguing for the existence of God, for example (in Part I, Book Five), he claimed to rely not on abstract ideas but only on arguments "derived from poetical and sentimental considerations, or, in other words, from the wonders of nature and the moral feelings" (438). But in good Enlightenment fashion, he entered into scientific discussions about the age of the earth, contesting proposed dates for its origin that would make it older than the age assigned by biblical reckoning. A good part of Book Five offers a perfectly reasonable, if somewhat colorful, argument for divine creation from design, as well as an ingenious phenomenology of natural time-consciousness, reminiscent of St. Augustine, which proposes the coexistence of "absolute duration" and "progressive duration"—eternity and time—in the different ways the spectacle of nature can appear to human consciousness. Compelling as he undoubtedly meant this demonstration to be, however, its significance within the overall structure of the book is unclear. It is only one moment in a very long sequence of demonstrations appealing to a wide array of human functions and feelings—moral judgment, cognition, passion, familial attachment, habit, hope—each one of which, Chateaubriand argued, reached the highest form of expression in its Christian form, especially by contrast with the corresponding version to be found in classical culture. Whatever power each demonstration may have individually seems diminished rather than augmented by all the others, a crescendo whose force and finality is undermined by the others that precede and follow it.

Yet closer consideration of the *Genius* shows at least one theme recurring constantly in the resumé of achievements produced by Christian religion, a theme of interlinked elements not all of which appear at each repetition. The supreme virtues that Christianity infuses in everything it touches are the "evangelical sadness" of its awareness of mortality and the vanity of earthly ambition, and the sense that real existence does not begin until death (438). These are truths of the heart, not the head, and their importance explains the aesthetic focus of the *Genius*. Adam's original sin, whose modern manifestation can be seen in the pretensions of natural science, was that he "wanted to know everything at once. . . . [M]an had it in his power to destroy the harmony of his being in two ways, either by wanting to *love* too much or to *know* too much." Pride of knowledge, however, was much worse than pride of love: "the latter would have deserved pity rather than punishment" (117). Had Adam been guilty merely of desiring to *feel* too much rather than to *know* too much, he might have been able to expiate his sin. The difference between the two sins is that knowing is intrinsically incapable of reaching the ultimate human goal, whereas the danger in feeling is its potential for misdirection. Science is inherently uncertain and unstable; while scientific knowledge is cumulative over time, science can never produce total or ultimate knowledge. In words that anticipate certain relativist arguments in contemporary philosophy of science (and refer back to the seventeenth-century quarrel between the Ancients and the Moderns) Chateaubriand asserted, "Systems will eternally succeed systems, and truth will ever remain unknown" (389). "The sciences are a labyrinth in which you find yourself more than ever bewildered at the very moment when you imagine that you are just at the end of it" (400). Ultimate knowledge is to be found only in and through *desire* (a notion parallel to the idea of love that Schlegel derived from Fichte and Hemsterhuis), and the true realm of desire is literature. "The vice of the day consists in separating abstract studies rather too much from literary studies. The one belongs to the understanding, the other to the heart; we should therefore beware of sacrificing the part which *loves* to the part which *reasons*" (404).

But what does "the part which loves" really desire? What, in other words, is the true subject of literature? Chateaubriand's celebrated answer was *nothing*, or rather, nothingness. The form of desire with which he was centrally preoccupied—appropriately it makes its appearance near the middle of the *Genius*—was what he called *le vague des passions*, and its chief characteristic is that it is desire "without object and end" (296). Chateaubriand's phrase is so difficult to translate that most English critics are content to leave it in the original. In the 1805 preface to *René*, in a phrase extracted from the *Genius*, Chateaubriand referred to "that indeterminate state of the passions [*cet état indéterminé des passions*],"[3] and the 1856 translation of the *Genius*, perhaps relying on that phrase, titles the relevant chapter "the unsettled state of the passions." But this is of course quite misleading; "unsettled" and "indeterminate" are not synonymous, and Chateaubriand intended precisely what his words say, though not only what they say—a passion that is not for any determinate object.

Commenting on Chateaubriand's most famous fictional representative of the *vague des passions*, Eric Gans suggests one possible reason for its separation of desire from object: "From René who desires nothing to the modern consumer who desires everything, the distance is not indeed very great."[4] Without accepting Gans's consumerist model of "everything" and its implicitly Marxist market economy explanation of the *vague des passions*, we can see in his consumer a debased contemporary version of Chateaubriand's passionate human being restlessly seeking happiness without knowing what would bring it because he or she wants everything: "No sooner has [the soul] attained the object for which it yearned, than a new wish is formed; and the whole universe cannot satisfy it. Infinity is the only field adapted to its nature" (*Genius*, 184). Desire is without object because desire exceeds all finite objects; it is desire for the infinite. But this is an incomplete characterization of the actual manifestation of the *vague des passions*. As Gans himself points out, contradicting both his own and Chateaubriand's characterization of the *vague des passions* as a "desire without any object," René does in fact desire a particular object, which appears in two forms, one an object of the imagination, the notional "woman of his heart's desire," the other its living incarnation, his sister Amélie. Desire meant, for Chateaubriand as for Schlegel, that infinity was embodied in a woman, though Chateaubriand suggested more explicitly that this incarnation was provisional and mistaken.

In his acute and sensitive study of Chateaubriand, Jean-Pierre Richard gives a more complete picture of the mismatch of desire and object in an analysis that accommodates not only the fictional representations and theoretical discussions of the *vague des passions* in Chateaubriand's works but the contradictory oscillations in many of Chateaubriand's personal causes and enthusiasms as well, from love of women to politics to literature. On the one hand, Richard notes, since the object of desire is limited, it is exhausted or consumed by its possession, leaving the self unsatisfied: "[W]hat Chateaubriand discovers in *ennui* is quite simply his transcendence."[5] Each object proves disappointing because it does not meet the expectations of desire. But in another, parallel though opposite, kind of experience, the object is *not* possessed; it constantly flees the pursuer, leaving the self with an accompanying sense of exclusion and exile. Again there is the feeling of emptiness, but in this kind of experience, the object transcends the self; something is there but it is always receding, forever out of reach, as one's shadow is driven away by the very pursuit of it.

Richard discerns the difference between these two experiences of transcendence, both of which create an unbridgeable separation between the self and the object of its desire, but not their opposition. For him, they are different versions of the same reality, what he calls "a certain inconsistency of the outside—I lack the real, the object is refused me" (10). In both of these cases, the self desires to possess a real object. Where it is attained, it proves disappointing, and the quest goes on; the central experience in both cases is lack and perpetual yearning. But homogenizing the two experiences this way misses the contradictory experience of the self that they imply. Where the object disappoints, the self is everything and the object nothing; where the object remains unattainable, it is the object that is everything and the self nothing. It is this contradiction that justifies Chateaubriand's claim in *La Défence du génie du christianisme* that in the *vague des passions* he is describing an altogether new passion and attacking a vice never before addressed.[6] The insufficiency of earthly objects of desire is after all one of the oldest of religious and especially Christian topoi. What was new, however—even if it was not exclusive to Chateaubriand but shared with his Romantic contemporaries in Germany and England—was the depiction of an oscillation between a sense of being infinite on the one hand and on the other an abject sense of nothingness in the face of the infinite that reduced the self to pure craving.

Not that Chateaubriand explicitly understood this new aspect of desire in the way I have just described. Like Richard, he focused on desire as absence and perpetual yearning. He was obsessed by the self-destructive potential of the passivity of desire, the pernicious tendencies represented in Rousseau's *promeneur solitaire* and Goethe's Werther, René's acknowledged literary precursors, tendencies to solitude, longing, despair, and suicide. Chateaubriand even suggested in the *Genius* that the *vague des passions* was a specifically feminine condition that infected men through contagion; its "exaggerations . . . hopes and fears without object . . . instability in ideas and sentiments . . . perpetual inconstancy, which is but a continual disgust, [are] dispositions which we acquire in the familiar society of the fair sex. . . . Women . . . render the marks of the masculine character less distinct; and our passions, softened by the mixture of theirs, assume, at one and the same time, something uncertain and delicate" (297). In view of this phenomenology of desire, in which the revulsion and fear that incited Chateaubriand to project the *vague des passions* onto women is almost palpable, it is striking and puzzling that the most explicit expression of the powerful and active pole of the *vague des passions* in Chateaubriand's early work is given to a woman. Although René is supposedly its avatar, it is the feminine figure of Atala, in the first of the two stories that were to be included in the *Genius* to dramatize the *vague des passions*, who brings out more explicitly, if only for a moment, the claims to infinite power largely latent in it.

The moment, significantly, occurs in Atala's deathbed confession, when she can only describe a fantasy of power rather than hope to live it. The young Christianized Indian woman has rescued the pagan Chactas from death at the hands of her own tribe and fled with him into the forest, where the two have fallen in love. Their love, however, cannot be consummated; Atala's mother had consecrated her sickly infant to virginity at birth in an effort to save her life, and Atala had taken a vow of chastity herself as her mother lay dying. Tempted beyond endurance by her love for Chactas, Atala takes poison to prevent herself from yielding to her sexual desire. "It was yesterday—during the storm. I was about to break my vow. I was about to hurl my mother into the flames of damnation" (*Atala/René*, 62). Breaking the vow—defying God and killing her mother by consigning her to eternal spiritual death—would have violated the most powerful taboos on human behavior and so shattered the apparently most fundamental limitations on human freedom. But the vow of chastity turns out to be only a defense against an even more radical claim for freedom than absence of restraint, a claim inherent for Atala in her desire itself. "Sometimes," she confesses, explaining why so drastic a response to desire as suicide was necessary, "as I fixed my eyes upon you, my desires would go to the wildest and most forbidden extremes. *I wanted to be the only living creature on earth with you*, or else, feeling some divinity restraining me in my dreadful ecstasies, *I longed for the annihilation of the divinity*, if only, clasped in your arms, I could plunge through endless depths along with the ruins of God and the universe" (61; italics added). In this fantasy, sexual ecstasy takes on ontological significance; the lover wishes to command or incorporate the totality of being, destroying all rival claimants, if necessary, traversing infinity "on the ruins of God and the universe." The fantasy is the ultimate breaking of human limits, the ultimate rebellion against and usurpation of absolute power, reminiscent of the most extreme positions of Wordsworth's Rivers and Wordsworth himself, but in a much more consciously violent and destructive apocalyptic vision. Atala, of course, imagines herself in Chactas's arms, not alone; but Chactas, as she has learned, is her brother, the adopted son of her natural father, and the desired incestuous union would be a union with another who is also self. This fact explains the contradictions of Atala's otherwise strange phrase, "the only living creature on earth with you"; though two, they are parts of one whole.

Father Aubry, the priest who had earlier sheltered the young couple from a storm, and who now seeks both to chastise Atala for her passion and console her because her imminent death makes its fulfillment impossible, only confirms in his preachments the absolute character of the claims made by Atala's desire. What she is seeking in her union with Chactas is not given to humanity, he argues. "[I]f man were ever constant in his affections, if his feelings remained eternally fresh and he could strengthen them endlessly, then solitude and love would surely make him God's equal, for those are the Great Being's two eternal pleasures" (66). Constant yet ever renewing, complete at every instant yet infinitely growing, totally self-sufficient yet completely connected—were an individual able to reconcile these contrarieties he or she would indeed be not God's equal but God. What Atala represents and Father Aubry describes is a desire that is objectless because it embraces all objects, wishes to be all objects.

A similar moment of recognition recurs in *René*, though so intermingled with its opposite, the sense of emptiness and absence, that it is more difficult to distinguish. It is the moment when René climbs to the summit of Mt. Aetna and sits by the crater of the volcano. "A young man full of passion, sitting at the mouth of a volcano and weeping over mortal men whose dwellings he could barely distinguish far off below him . . . such a picture reveals my character and my whole being. Just so, throughout my life, I have had before my eyes an immense creation which I could barely discern, while a chasm yawned at my side" (*Atala/René*, 92). If there is something comically self-dramatizing to the contemporary eye in this image, it is also more complex and more ambiguous than it might first seem. The moment is simultaneously one of fullness and of emptiness for René, the infinity of creation before him and the yawning abyss beside him. To compound the contradiction, each symbol doubles back on itself. The "immense creation" that he perceives is his—is in fact him—because he encompasses it visually and imaginatively; yet he can barely see its details, and those he does discern, human dwellings, refer him to the smallness and mortality of men. Similarly, the volcano is an empty chasm, but also the fullness of his soul ready to explode from the force of a content and a pressure too great for its vessel to contain—"I was furiously driven by an excess of life. . . . I felt torrents of burning lava surging through my heart" (96). Yet in contrast with Atala, the emphasis in René's depiction is on lack. With his capacity to encompass infinity, René feels that he is unjustly accused of being dissatisfied with limitations, of considering everything finite unworthy—why should such a one settle for less—yet at the same time he feels the need for "something to fill the vast emptiness of my existence . . . for the ideal creature of some future passion" (96).

That ideal creature turns out to be his sister Amélie. The quasi-incestuous nature of desire in *Atala* (Atala is not biologically related to Chactas) is fully realized in *René*. But *René* also makes clear something else that was only implicit in *Atala*, that the sisters are also maternal figures for their brothers. Amélie, who after the death of their mother and the emotional and physical abandonment by their father became the substitute parent of René's youth, is still in later years "almost a mother. . . . Like a child, I had only to be consoled, and I quickly surrendered to Amélie's influence" (100). Similarly, in Atala's presence, Chactas finds himself "powerless to rise to man's mature reason, for I had suddenly sunk into a kind of childishness" (29). As he wanders with Atala in the forest, Chactas is reminded of the biblical story of Hagar in the wilderness of Beersheba—who, though it is not stated, was wandering with her son Ishmael. Furthermore, Atala and Amélie are endowed with not only maternal but with explicitly divine attributes, described in the terms Chateaubriand used elsewhere in the *Genius* to describe the Christian religion; they are unities of opposites, creatures of inexhaustible mystery. "The constant contradictions between Atala's love and her religion, her unrestrained tenderness and the purity of her ways, the pride of her character and her deep sensitivity, the loftiness of her soul in essential things and her delicacy in the little ones—everything made her an incomprehensible being. Atala's influence over a man could never be weak; she was as irresistible as she was passionate, and she had to be worshipped or hated" (41). As for Amélie, she "had received some divine attribute from nature. . . . It seemed as though her heart, her thought, and her voice were all sighing in harmony. From her womanly side came her shyness and love, while her purity and melody were angelic" (100). These attributes of sisters, maternal and divine, hold out to Chactas and René the promise that they can participate in the infinite existence the women represent. An "Eve drawn from myself,"[7] as René refers to the object of his quest for love, Amélie is literally René's selfother, flesh of his flesh, and hence his alter ego, able by virtue of a preexisting though yet-to-be-consummated union to supply with her infinite nature the infinite lack in himself. In *Atala* and *René* it is clear that the scene of the *vague des passions* is the scene of incestuous sexual passion. And satisfying the *vague des passions* through incestuous consummation depends on a contradiction. It is through subordination to the sister-mother that the self becomes infinite, dominating the self on which it is dependent. Eric Gans is only partly right when he claims that René is the quintessential Romantic figure in the narcissism of his refusal of desire, which keeps him at the center of stage and subordinates Amélie to him because she does desire him. It is true that René does not recognize his sexual desire for his sister, while it is her desire for him that drives her to the convent, and it is certainly true that René is self-centered. But René obviously desires Amélie as much as she does him; moreover, his whole being is dependent on her yielding to him by loving him rather than God. It is precisely that René's "self-centeredness" cannot be fulfilled without her that is the crux of the contradiction in Chateaubriand's incestuous construction of Romantic selfhood.

But of course the point of both stories is that incestuous passion cannot satisfy the *vague des passions*, that to look to human love is to look for love in the wrong place. The point is made implicitly by the fact that not only Chactas and René, but Atala and Amélie, are in love, and in the context woman's desire undermines the male construction of her as infinite and self-contained. Women too are driven by the *vague des passions*, they are as incomplete as the men and not the bearers of infinite perfection. If anything their desire is more intense; in any case they are aware of its forbidden nature, while the men are not. It is the women who undergo the Passion, renouncing earthly desire through the self-sacrifice of suicide or withdrawal from life in order to gain its object through religion, because they seem to learn the real reason for the impossibility of their desire: the impossibility of incestuous love.

Incestuous love is impossible, however, not because it is wrong; rather, it is wrong because it is impossible. Behind the categorical prohibition against incest, behind the visceral revulsion that enforces it, is the ontological truth that no human object, not even the one whose attributes make it the most tempting or plausible, can satisfy the *vague des passions*. Even where mutual desire coexists with mutual affection, Father Aubry says, as with sister and brother, humans cannot avoid jealousy or imperfect congruence of heart. Men are inconstant, the beloved is finite and doomed to death. Religion, however, does not tell these truths to negate desire but to fulfill it. Father Aubry promises Atala the consummation in heaven she could never have had on earth even if she had not been tragically misled by a perversion of religion to try to extirpate her desire by vowing lifelong chastity. "The sepulture which you have chosen for your nuptial bed will never be dishonored, and the embraces of your heavenly spouse will never end" (67). And Amélie, in a letter to René, describes the recompense she has received for her "immense sacrifices" of retirement to the convent. "It is here that religion gently beguiles a tender soul. For the most violent passion it substitutes a kind of burning chastity in which lover and virgin are one. It purifies every sigh, it makes the ephemeral flame inviolate, and it blends its divine calm and innocence with the remains of confusion and worldly joy in a heart seeking rest and a life seeking solitude" (111). "Chastity" is the state of desire without fulfillment; "burning chastity" is realized desire that does not lose its quality of infinite anticipation, because the love of God *means* fulfillment in absence. No Romantic image of the union of opposites was more sexually concrete, or more boldly contradictory than the image of Amélie in the convent, virgin and lover, enjoying simultaneously calm and ecstatic confusion, innocence and sensual fulfillment.

Yet if the overt message of the stories, a message literally preached in both by priests, is that only religion can satify the *vague des passions*, there is a another covert message that subverts it, in the process reversing the power relationships between men and women. Atala, who is already Christian, professes herself consoled by Father Aubry and extracts a promise from Chactas that he will convert. Yet when he tells the story many years later as an old man, he has not done so; and it is only in an epilogue by another narrator that it is reported that Chactas had converted just before his death. René, overtly more skeptical about Amélie's religious solution than Chactas is about Atala's, openly questions the finality of her haven in the convent. In a passage that builds a metaphor on his departure from France and the storm he encounters at sea, he contrasts his sister's composure in the convent with his own stormy reality, only to reverse their states of mind in the end: "Storm on the waves, and calm in your retreat; men shattered on the reefs before an unshakeable haven; infinity on the other side of a cell wall; the tossing lights of ships,

and the motionless beacon of the convent; the uncertain lot of the sea-
man, and the vestal's vision in a single day of all the days of her life; and
yet, O Amélie, a soul such as yours, stormy as the ocean; a catastrophe
more dreadful than the mariner's—this whole picture is still deeply en-
graved in my memory" (111). René's last words completely undo the contrast between his stormy restlessness and the religious peace she has ostensibly found in the convent, and with them the whole thrust of both
stories that Christianity alone can gratify the *vague des passions*.

Amélie dies in the convent caring for her sisters during an epidemic.
René is left with his grief and a stern rebuke from a priest, Father Souël,
who has listened to his story, for wallowing in self-pity rather than following his sister's example of Christian service to the human community.
The fact of his survival, like that of Chactas's failure to convert, seems
again to cast doubt on the promise of her religious salvation, though he
survives in barren misery. There is, however, one final turn that suggests
another alternative to the religiosity of Atala and Amélie and the longing
and despair of Chactas and René. At the end of René's first-person account, the narrator (who is also the narrator of *The Natchez*, the novel of
which *Atala* and *René* were also to be parts, though it did not appear until
more that twenty years later) announces René's death along with that of
Chactas and Father Souël. Only the author is left, writing their story.
Only the words that describe the religious experience remain as a tangi-
ble sign of immortality, like the rock mentioned in the last sentence of the
story, where René would go to sit in the setting sun.

In the end, then, despite the overt preaching of the work, the author—
and the act of writing—triumph, not religion. In this sense, what is implicitly proclaimed is the transcendence of the observing and narrating
self even over the message of religion. This unexpected subversion casts
new light on the question that Chateaubriand raised about his apologetic
enterprise at the beginning of the *Genius*. Commenting on his effort to
justify religion by its ability to satisfy universal human needs, he asked,
"May there not be some danger in considering religion in a merely human
point of view?" Although the question was meant rhetorically, the previous analysis suggests an unexpected answer. It is the "human point of
view" that undermines religion.

But Chateaubriand's triumph as the writing self that apparently rose
even above religion was itself equivocal and contradictory. If, by chroni-
cling the failure of religion, he turned it into yet another merely determinate object that inspired ennui in the self, he implicitly pronounced himself parasitical on religion by making it the indispensable subject of his
writing. He was caught in a contradictory relationship of dependence and
independence to religion, just as the male characters, who apparently

triumph over the women on whom they depend by rejecting or demystifying their religiosity and surviving them, live their lives mourning lost loves and telling their stories.

The contradictions within Chateaubriand's explicit view of religion and his implicit view of writing are mirror images of one another. Chateaubriand's polemic in the *Genius* was aimed as much against a religion of self-denial, asceticism, and submission as it was against atheism. The most striking feature of this epochal apologia for Catholicism is its subversion of traditional religion by a radical redefinition that promises salvation will mean the divinization of the human. But this divinization takes place only through surrender of human ambition. In reaction against this submission, in turn, the writing subject triumphs over religion, turning it into just another plot element in his story. But the writer is not the arbitrary master of the tale; he takes for his subject the necessity of religious submission as the only satisfactory channel for human desires. How are we to understand these contradictions?

There is another and surprising dimension of the *vague des passions* in the *Genius* that has been little remarked, perhaps because it seems quite inconsistent with the apparently solipsistic and narcissistic nature of the passion. In *René*, Father Souël opposes to the eternal dissatisfaction of the self with everything, which isolates it from the world in futile longing, the demand to rejoin the human community in a life of useful service. Christain duty is the antidote to the *vague des passions*: "Whoever has been endowed with talent," he says severely to René, "must devote it to serving his fellow men, for if he does not make use of it, he is first punished by an inner misery, and sooner or later, Heaven visits on him a fearful retribution" (113). But in the chapter in the *Genius* that introduces René, Chateaubriand first contrasted the *vague des passions* not with an ideal of Christian service but with the classical ideal of civic involvement and political participation. "The ancients," he wrote, "knew but little of this secret inquietude, this irritation of the stifled passions fermenting all together; political affairs, the sports of the Gymnasium and of the Campus Martius, the business of the forum and of the popular assemblies engaged all their time, and left no room for this tedium of the heart"(*Genius*, 297). In the familiar procedure of the *Genius*, he went on to contrast unfavorably the Greek and Roman focus on the pleasures of this world with Christianity's awareness of their transience and its consequent preoccupation with the world to come. But as he pointed out, in unwitting contradiction of his praise of Christian otherwordliness, this preoccupation led historically to desire, meditation, and the monastery, which is but another form of the isolation Father Souël condemns.

The invocation of the classical political and social ideal as a contrast to the *vague des passions* is not incidental. Despite his insistent assertion of the superiority of the Christian over the classical conception of the world, it is clear that the antitype of the *vague des passions* for Chateaubriand was not originally a purely individualized Christian service but the idea of classical civic virtue, the ideal of public life and public man that, as he said, "left no room for the tedium of the heart." The ideal of classical republicanism, however, was kept firmly in the past. What is notably missing from his description of it is any mention of the more recent revolutionary politics that had consumed the attention and energies of contemporaries and had clothed itself precisely in the language of virtue and ancient republicanism. There is only the barest hint of recent events in the *Genius*, but it is a telling one. In the chapter on "Politics and Government" towards the end of the work, Chateaubriand noted the contribution of Christianity to politics. "[T]he spirit of the gospel is eminently favorable to liberty. The Christian religion adopts as a tenet the doctrine of moral equality—the only kind of equality that it is possible to preach without convulsing the world" (*Genius*, 662). The notion of "convulsing the world" in quest of liberty and equality connects with Atala's fantasy of challenging the authority of the divinity and destroying the universe in the triumph of earthly desire. While classical politics were for Chateaubriand the antithesis of the *vague des passions*, it appears that the politics of the French Revolution were the very expression of it.

What emerges from Chateaubriand's appeal to republican politics as the exemplar of healthy activity in the world, on the one hand, and his rejection of the recent convulsive revolutionary politics on the other, is not simply the idea that the French Revolution was the equivalent of, or a manifestation of, the *vague des passions* in the world of action. It is rather the more striking realization that Chateaubriand understood the *vague des passions* first as an activist, political passion whose very archetype was the Revolution. As we will see, this passion in fact makes its first appearance in Chateaubriand's writings in an analysis of the reasons for the failure of the French Revolution. The equation suggests that the fear of and disgust for the *vague des passions* was born of the fear of and disgust for the Revolution. But this suggests in turn that the religious sublimation of the *vague des passions* is also a sublimation of the Revolution. Politics seems to underlie the contradictions of Chateaubriand's position. In this sense, we can agree with Gans that "René was intended as an all but dehistoricized model of an attitude to life that Chateaubriand's reader could not help but understand as resulting from the recent crises in political and cultural history."[8] But Gans does not make clear what specific aspects of the contemporary crises he has in mind or how they explain

René's "attitude to life," and his hints about René as exemplar of the consumerist ethic of postrevolutionary commercial society are not very helpful.[9] Furthermore, what must also be explained is why desire functions in Chateaubriand's work as an intermediary between politics and religion. For religion is offered in the fiction not directly as a replacement for or displacement of politics, but of love. What must be understood then, is not only how historical-political crisis shaped Chateaubriand's very idea of the *vague des passions* and his contradictory response to it, but how the issue of desire entered into and shaped his understanding of historical and political crisis.

II) Chateaubriand the Revolutionary

i) France

There is almost no contemporary information on either the nature or the warmth of Chateaubriand's revolutionary sentiments in 1789, much less on his reasons for supporting the French Revolution. Almost all the evidence is *post factum*, and Chateaubriand's direct testimony stems from long after the Revolution. Even the fictional critiques of pre-revolutionary society have to be reconstructed from later reworkings of earlier, unpublished documents. *The Natchez*, for example, which contains some of Chateaubriand's earliest written work, dating perhaps from even before his trip to America in 1791, was revised and published only in 1827, well after his political opinions had changed. It might be expected that, refracted through the fully developed political-religious positions of his later life, such testimony as there is would be all of a piece. Yet there is a curious discrepancy, for example, between what Chateaubriand says in the *Mémoires d'outre-tombe* and what he says in *Travels in America*.

The persona (or personae) Chateaubriand created in the *Mémoires* had other purposes than the concealment of early political views,[10] but the artful construction of the section that deals with the French Revolution does accomplish that. There is just the barest hint of his ideas and beliefs at the time, and the clearest expression of his sentiments is the moment at which, he claimed, they began to change. Change from what? is a question that the chapter never satisfactorily answers. The first image of Chateaubriand as political man in the chapter is of the Olympian political analyst observing the structure and dynamics of the Revolution *sub specie aeternitatis*. His observations, informed by the irony such a vantage point affords, are shrewd enough and to the contemporary reader surprisingly "modern." He noted, for example, how each social group or institution, in its selfish desire for power, unwittingly opened the way for the social enemies it had previously defeated or exploited, and despite his emphasis on the importance of ideas as motors of the Revolution, insisted that "Louis XVI and the parlements . . . were, without knowing it, the instruments of a social revolution."[11] It was only after establishing this stance that Chateaubriand introduced himself as political actor, and the self-image he offered was one of initial detachment even in the midst of passion and action. Describing the violent clash between the nobles and the Third Estate over taxation in the meetings of the Brittany Estates in 1789, which he attended, he wrote, "I perceived in the middle of these meetings a tendency of my character that I have rediscovered since both in politics and in war: the more my colleagues or my comrades got heated up, the cooler I became; I looked with indifference on fire whether started by oratory or artillery; I never bowed to the word or to the cannon ball" (*Mémoires*, 1:210). But when Chateaubriand was finally driven by circumstances to take part in physical battle, it was on the side of the aristocracy.

The events in Brittany, and Chateaubriand's involvement in them, foreshadowed the outbreak of the events in Paris and Chateaubriand's participation there. He arrived only after the momentous events in which the Third Estate created the National Assembly, toward the end of June, and one of his first acts was to accompany a visiting Breton poet on a sight-seeing trip to Versailles. "There are people," he wrote ambiguously—of his companion or of himself?—"who visit gardens and fountains while empires are being overthrown; scribblers in particular have the ability to abstract themselves in their mania during the greatest events; their phrase or their stanza takes the place of everything else for them" (1:214). Having affirmed his primary identity as writer, he then described catching Marie-Antoinette's attention during the visit and her smiling at him, an incident that, whether real or fictional—its veracity has been challenged—certainly underlines his royalist sympathies. It is only after this that we get Chateaubriand's first direct commentary on a revolutionary event, the taking of the Bastille. His description of the actual seizure is a sardonic deflation of the "heroic conquest" by a drunken mob of a fortress defended by a few invalids and a timid governor, but that is followed by an assessment of its significance that not only makes great claims for the event but for the originality and superiority of the analysis. "What should have been seen in the taking of the Bastille (and what was not seen at the time) was not the violent act of the emancipation of a people, but the emancipation which was the result of this act. What was admired, the accidental, should have been condemned, and no one proceeded to seek in the future the realized destinies of a people, the change of *moeurs*, of ideas, of political powers, a renewal of mankind, for which the taking of the Bastille opened the era, like a bloody jubilee" (1:217). These carefully crafted words remain ambiguous; they hint at a positive attitude but emphasize the magnitude rather than the merit of the transformation and reveal very little of Chateaubriand's personal feelings about them. The only show of passion that Chateaubriand reported was hostile to the Revolution. It is his often-cited reaction to another mob some days later parading with the heads of the minister Foulon and his son-in-law the intendant of Paris impaled on their pikes. "Brigands, I cried out, full of an indignation I couldn't contain, is that what you mean by liberty? If I had had a gun, I would have fired on these miserable creatures as on wolves. [They tried] to join my head to those of their victims. . . . These heads, and others which I encountered soon afterwards, changed my political inclinations" (1:220). It was obviously important for Chateaubriand to establish his credentials as above all an objective observer, theoretician, and writer and then as emotional royalist before he uttered the first words that gave any hint of revolutionary sympathies. Even then, the language is oblique and qualified. It indicates some support for the work of the Constituent Assembly and the constitutional monarchy it created. "The constituent assembly, despite the reproaches that can be levelled against it, remains nonetheless the most illustrious popular assembly that ever appeared among the nations, as much for the greatness [grandeur] of its transactions as for the immensity of their results. . . . [T]he Republic and the Empire were good for nothing" (1:224). Only a few pages later, however, Chateaubriand explicitly rejected any imputation of partisanship. "I had neither adopted nor rejected the new opinions," he claimed, "as little disposed to attack them as to serve them, I neither wanted to emigrate nor to continue my military career; I resigned. . . . From my youth, my political impartiality pleased no one. What is more, I attached no importance to the questions that were raised then, except as they concerned general ideals of human liberty and dignity; personal politics bored me; my real life was in higher regions" (1:239).

So persuasive is Chateaubriand's rhetoric, so plausible and apparently consistent the interlocking personae of the *Mémoires*, backed by an immensity of finely observed and rendered detail, that this picture of his revolutionary involvement has been accepted by many readers and critics. The most recent, and by far the best, of his biographers, George Painter, is often skeptical about the face value of many of the "facts" offered in the autobiography, but is largely in accord with Chateaubriand's account in this instance. He attributes Chateaubriand's ideas to his association with the group of late Enlightenment, mostly second-rate writers who made up the literary establishment of 1780s Paris and sees his adoption of their views more as an act of eighteenth-century sociability than of belief. "He too found it agreeable," Painter writes, "to believe ethically, in universal brotherhood, the perfectibility of man, the noble savage; metaphysically, in the remote existence of a benevolent God . . .

politically, in an urgent but painless reform which would begin with the liberalization of court, aristocracy and Church, and end with the stable, limited monarchy, and a contented nation."[12] This vague and watered-down set of beliefs—the Rousseauist state of nature, Deism, and mild constitutional reform—is more specific than anything Chateaubriand himself gave at the appropriate point in his autobiography, but even they, according to Painter, were not real. "In fact," he insists, "François-René's new views . . . were second-hand, factitious, and foreign to his deeper nature."[13]

Chateaubriand, however, said otherwise. He said it both directly, though without elaboration, and indirectly, at greater length and in many different ways. Chateaubriand's rebellion was deep, and both the hopes and needs that brought him to revolution and the complex disappointments and fears that the experience of it caused—an experience that encompassed his trip to America—played a decisive part in his self-creation. Even the first brief mention of his relationship to the Revolution at the end of the book in the *Mémoires* preceding the narrative of his part in it has a different tone. Writing of his close relationship with his sister-in-law's grandfather, the eminent *parlementaire* and former minister Lamoignon de Malesherbes, a severe critic of the monarchy, Chateaubriand pointed to their "common views" on politics (though without detailing them) and acknowledged that "The Revolution would have carried me away had it not started in crime" (1:188). Elsewhere he was even more blunt. "When I left France at the beginning of 1791," he wrote in his book on the American trip, published only in 1826, "the revolution was proceeding rapidly: the principles on which it was founded were mine, but I detested the violence which had already dishonored it. It was joyfully that I set out to seek an independence more in conformity with my tastes, more in sympathy with my character."[14] One need no more question the sincerity of Chateaubriand's detestation of violence than the authenticity of his avowal of revolutionary principles. In the *Travels in America*, Chateaubriand offered an explanation of his trip to the United States quite consistent with the idea that the cause of political independence was of personal importance to him and different from what he said about this trip in the *Mémoires*. The latter account needs not so much to be rejected as to be put in the context of the self-image he was constructing at that point in the work. He was, he wrote in the *Mémoires*, consumed with the idea of a trip to the United States, but needed a useful purpose to legitimate it and so came up with the idea of discovering the long-sought Northwest Passage to India. The wording of the section plainly states that the plan of exploration came *after* the intent to make the trip—though the idea of exploration had occurred in his conversations with Malesherbes—but it was no mere rationalization, if so ambitious a purpose could be appropriately referred to as "mere." Once again the context is revealing. The report of his resolution to go to America is immediately followed by Chateaubriand's comparison of himself with Bonaparte, a comparison that seems quite anachronistically out of place and is for that reason all the more illuminating. "I was thus the same as Bonaparte, a mere sublieutenant completely unknown; we were both starting from obscurity at the same time, I to seek my fame in solitude, he to seek his glory among men" (*Mémoires*, 1:240). Although this obviously could not have been even the most unconscious of associations in 1791, the comparison with Bonaparte, which played so big a role in Chateaubriand's later life, reveals a supremely important dimension of his needs that had much to do with both the purpose of the American trip and its results. Chateaubriand's ambition, even then, was enormous; as overseas traveler he was both repeating and trying to exceed the accomplishments of his father.

"[Its] principles . . . were mine," said Chateaubriand of the Revolution. But what principles? *Travels in America* reveals two agenda in Chateaubriand's quest for independence, one explicitly political and ideological, the other personal, but both for Chateaubriand almost seamlessly connected. Other writings add a good deal of explicit material to the ideological program; the personal agenda can only be amplified by the psychological connections Chateaubriand might not have been expected to be able to make himself, though he is surprisingly helpful even about these.

Chateaubriand's self-avowed political ideal was a form of classical republicanism modified to suit the conditions of modernity. It was a model derived from many sources, both classical and eighteenth century, and its eclecticism will need to be further parsed, because his political ideas attempted to fuse ultimately immiscible elements in a mixture that proved unstable and explosive. Long after Chateaubriand had abandoned it, however, he could still remain sympathetic to his younger self despite his irony:

> A man landing as I did in the United States, full of enthusiasm for the ancients, a Cato seeking everywhere for the rigidity of the early Roman manners, is necessarily shocked to find everywhere the elegance of dress, the luxury of carriages, the frivolity of conversations, the disproportion of fortunes, the immorality of banks and gaming houses, the noise of dance-halls and theaters. . . . [N]othing proclaimed that I had passed from a monarchy to a republic.
>
> [A]t that time . . . I admired republics greatly. But I did not believe them possible at the present age because I knew liberty only in the manner of the ancients, as a daughter of manners in a new-born society. (*Travels*, 15)

"C'est du Rousseau," as he had said of other aspects of his early views (in the 1826 notes to the *Essai sur les révolutions*), but also of Montesquieu, the abbés Mably and Raynal, and other eighteenth-century participants in the debate over the virtues of modernity who had proclaimed the superior virtue of ancient republics over modern commercial monarchies, if not necessarily their viability in modern times.[15] Despite his concession to change, Chateaubriand was, or seemed to be, decidedly of the "old party" from a moral point of view, the party of ancient republicanism and stern civic virtue, and against the commerce and luxury that corrupted the state and destroyed liberty and the common good. A republic might no longer be possible, as the proponents of modernity claimed, but Chateaubriand did not accept their positive argument that commerce, and both the collective search for opulence and the refined politeness that it brought with it, could be a satisfactory substitute for civic virtue as political cement. As late as 1821, when he wrote the books of the *Mémoires* covering his trip to America, he evaluated the prospects for the continued survival of the American political experiment with the skepticism born of a classical republican perspective:

> If hostilities came unexpectedly upon an unwarlike people, would it be able to offer resistance? Would its fortunes and habits [*moeurs*] consent to sacrifices? How could it give up the bland usages, the comfort, the indolent well being of life? . . .
>
> The commercial spirit is beginning to invade them; self-interest is becoming their national vice. Already the speculations of the banks of the different states clash with one another, and bankruptcies threaten the common wealth [*la fortune commune*]. So long as liberty produces gold, an industrial republic does wonders; but when the gold is acquired or exhausted, it loses its love of independence, which is not based upon a moral sentiment, but arises from the thrust for gain and the passion for trade. (*Mémoires*, 1:352–53)

So far as can be discerned, the values and perspectives reflected in this passage were an essential part of Chateaubriand's criticism of France in 1789. The most detailed specification of his charges against the monarchy is to be found in *The Natchez*, published in 1826 but partially based on an older manuscript that contains much earlier views.[16] Chateaubriand used the by-then hoary device of the innocent abroad, the noble savage (or quizzical foreigner) of Marmontel, La Bruyère and Montesquieu, to deliver his indictment of prerevolutionary French society. The Huron chief Chactas (who would figure in his younger years as the hero of *Atala*), brought to France as a prisoner, is given the opportunity to observe its civilization. His hopes of finding a "nation of free warriors" (*Natchez*, 1:244) are sharply disappointed. He discovers instead a nation that builds its palaces on the backs of slaves and apparently exhibits their flesh in "huts of trade"—a pointed misunderstanding of butcher shops that equates commerce with trafficking in human flesh or even cannibalism

(251); a nation that does not tolerate differences in beliefs, ferrets out dissident opinions through torture, and then strangles to death anyone who holds them "because he had the weakness to confess under torture a crime of which there is not other proof than the avowal wrung from him by pain" (253). Condemnation of the regime is not limited to the outsider but reinforced by internal critics. At the salon of a famous courtesan, a figure representing La Bruyère asks Chactas what he thinks of a society with "prelates differing as widely in talents as principles . . . ladies of pleasure intriguing with monks close to the throne, courtiers disputing the possession of their mutual prey . . . magistrates at variance, admirable ordinances but not enforced, the law proclaimed supreme but always suspended by royal command, property declared inviolable but confiscated at the good pleasure of the master, all the citizens at liberty to go wherever they want, and to say what they think, at the risk of being apprehended if it so pleases the king, and sent to the gallows" (263–64). "La Bruyère" concludes on an ambivalent note, praising the enduring glory of a regime that has, despite its faults, erected impressive edifices, established manufactures, founded colonies, created a navy, and subdued half of Europe, but Chactas will have none of this exculpation. Continuing on his way, he is sickened by the execution of a Huguenot minister who could not stand exile and sneaked back home, by the inhospitableness of the rich and the brutalization of the poor, whose poverty is not simply the result of misfortune but of social arrangements. "I consider," he concludes,

> the men of your country more unhappy than those of mine. They pride themselves on their arts . . . but if life be limited to a few days, what matters it whether we have made the voyage in a small bark canoe, or in a large vessel. . . . No, the canoe is to be preferred, for it glides on the river along the shore, where it can find a thousand places of shelter; but the European vessel sails on a stormy lake, where ports are rare and rocks frequent, and where it is impossible to cast anchor, because of the depth of the abyss.
>
> The arts, then, contribute nothing to the happiness of life, and yet that is the only point in which you appear to excel us. . . . I begin to perceive that this odious medley of ranks and fortunes, of extraordinary wealth and excessive privation, of unpunished guilt and suffering innocence, forms what is called society in Europe. This is not the case with us; enter the huts of the Iroquois, and you will find neither great nor small, neither rich nor poor, everywhere peace of mind and human liberty. (*Natchez*, 1:271)

Analyzing the origin of these sentiments, which are as much antimonarchist as Rousseauist, Pierre Barbéris points out that they derive in part from Chateaubriand's father as representative Breton aristocrat. René-Auguste, Count of Combourg, was an avid reader of the abbé Raynal, critic of the monarchy, and a fierce partisan of La Chalotais, leader of the Rennes parlement in its struggle for Breton privileges against the efforts of the military commandant d'Aiguillon to enforce a new royal tax on Brittany in the 1760s. The attitude of the provincial nobility defending its traditional privileges combined easily with that of the philosophe criticizing the irrational and despotic tendencies of modern absolutist monarchy, and it is not surprising to find a portrait of the noble savage condemning corruption in Versailles from the pen of a man whose father was so bitterly opposed to the court.[17]

The coherence of Chateaubriand's views with those of his father, however, is far from perfect. As Barbéris himself points out, Chateaubriand's father was not simply a provincial aristocrat of fierce local loyalties; he had been a merchant and a dealer in the slave trade. In fact, such a description understates the paradox of his position. René-Auguste was a proud but impoverished aristocrat of very ancient lineage who with single-minded determination had restored some of the patrimony and prestige of his family through very modern means—investing in ships, privateering, trading in slaves, and fishing for cod. He had purchased his castle and title with the proceeds of these ventures;[18] in the very year that François-René was born, his father had outfitted a new slave ship.[19] In attacking the monarchy, Chateaubriand may well have been identifying with his father's politics, but in attacking modern commercial society and the slavery on which it rested, he was attacking his father as well. In the *Histoire des deux Indes*,[20] René Auguste's bible, the abbé Raynal, friend of both Voltaire and Rousseau, took a somewhat equivocal stance in the luxury debate, but one with moral and political elements strongly congenial to Chateaubriand's father. "The taste for luxury and for commodities," Raynal wrote, "has produced the love of work, which today constitutes the main power of states. . . . A poor people can no longer become formidable to a rich nation. Force is today on the side of wealth because it is no longer the fruit of conquest but the product of assiduous labors and a life wholly occupied. Undoubtedly, it is nice to depict the Romans, with the art of war alone, subjugating all the other arts, all the idle or commercial nations . . . smashing . . . the vessels of Corinth, happier under their gods of clay than the others with gold statues of their emperors of mud. But it is much more pleasant to see the whole of Europe . . . open . . . all the sources of population and pleasure to pour them through a thousand channels over the face of the earth. In that way, perhaps, the divinity contemplates his handiwork with pleasure and does not regret having created man."[21] In passages that must have been particular favorites of Chateaubriand père, Raynal even singled out cod fishing for praise as a specially worthy commercial enterprise, both because it satisfied a (somewhat vulgarized) physiocratic criterion of reproductive wealth, in contrast with the sterile wealth of gold or manufacture, and because it did not harm, exploit, or infringe on the rights of others.[22] Somewhat ambivalently, Raynal did agree with the critics of commerce that its spirit was that of self-interest, and that therefore it always produced division in the polity.[23] The conclusion of the work repeated the standard republican charge that when commerce introduces great riches into a state, they become the object of public ambition, undermine the spirit of public service, and lead to the corruption of its public officials. But Raynal found a way of resolving the contradiction by blaming these evils not on wealth itself but on bad government, specifically government that is so constituted that those in authority can place themselves above the law and use their power to plunder.[24] The whole mercantilist regime, in which royal authority granted individuals monopolies over various items of commerce, was one of the methods used by modern rulers to exaggerate differences in wealth and social division. In this way Raynal joined his condemnation of absolute monarchy with his praise of commerce to attribute its deleterious effects not to its inherent vices but to its political perversions. His analysis of the exploitation of the natural, innocent, and virtuous New World by a tyrannical Europe was a displacement of the conflict he saw at home between the despotic court and the society it brutalized with its tax laws and administrative intrusions.[25]

Chateaubriand's republicanism was aimed quite explicitly at his father's kind of compromise. But it was not simply a version of the *thèse nobiliaire* of nostalgic aristocrats longing for an ancient constitution founded on a landed aristocracy free of royal despotism. It was the egalitarian republicanism of Rousseau, which, mixed with the notion of universal individual rights, was turned against the tyranny not only of kings but of all external authorities, aristocrats and fathers not least. One of Rousseau's most important accomplishments in the social and political theory of the eighteenth century was to develop a notion of individualism on a basis wholly different from the theory of commercial society, which equated individualism with self-interest, a notion, however, that was not constricted within the confines of the classical republican concept of independence. In classical theory, the highest goal was the civic virtue deriving from direct participation in public life on behalf of the common good; material independence was a prerequisite of participation, for the dependent man could not serve the common good if his own survival depended on serving a master. Such an instrumental notion of independence does play a role in Rousseau's political theory, for the possibility of sustaining the general will in *The Social Contract* depends on a rough equality of wealth and independence among the polity's citizens. Rousseau in fact democratized the idea of independence that in most versions of republican thought in the seventeenth and eighteenth centuries was an elitist concept restricting the idea of participation to those whose landed wealth made them independent. It was not, however, from *The Social Contract* but from *Emile* and the *Discourse on Inequality* that Chateaubriand took his inspiration. The definition of autonomy in the second *Discourse* goes far beyond material independence; it is an end in itself, not a means to civic virtue. It is also quite different in spirit from the individualist current in French thought that Nannerl Keohane traces back to the Jansenist psychology of the passions, with its focus on the connection between passion and self-interest.[26] Contrasting the savage's *amour propre* with the inauthenticity of modern life,[27] Rousseau wrote, "the savage lives in himself; the man accustomed to the ways of society is always outside himself and knows how to live only in the opinion of others. And it is, as it were, from their judgement alone that he draws the sentiment of his own existence. . . . [A]lways asking others what we are and never daring to question ourselves on this matter, in the midst of so much philosophy, humanity, politeness, and sublime maxims, we have merely a deceitful and frivolous exterior: honor without virtue, reason without wisdom, and pleasure without happiness."[28] Chateaubriand's early ideal of an egalitarian and authentic individuality, which derived in part from these Rousseauist ideas, struck directly at his father's hierarchical pride of caste as well as at his commercial mentality.

No reading between the lines is necessary to determine the extent of René-Auguste's influence on his son's life. There is an open avowal of it, as well as of its profoundly ambivalent nature, a few pages into the *Mémoires*. The very first words of the *Mémoires*, written in 1809, record Chateaubriand's recent purchase of a country house, an act analogous to the purchase that reestablished his father in his ancient honors; and though Chateaubriand initially tried to establish his independent identity as writer by linking the estate with Voltaire, whom he mistakenly believed to have been born in the neighboring town, he immediately asserted the primacy of the paternal significance of the purchase: "This spot pleases me; it has taken the place of my paternal acres." The displacement of his father continues in the competitive contrast of the next words that underline not only the son's difference from, but his moral superiority to, his father, in sentiments echoing Raynal's moral criticism of colonial enterprises: "I have bought it with the price of my dreams and my vigil; I owe the little wilderness of Aulnay to the vast wilderness of Atala; and I have not, in order to acquire this refuge, imitated the American planter and despoiled the Indian of the Two Floridas" (*Mémoires*, 1:4). What appears to be the wholly gratuitous mention of Napoleon in the next paragraph in fact continues the competitive theme. Having completed a number of works, Chateaubriand wonders what to do next; on the day that is both his saint's day and the anniversary of his entrance into Jerusalem—a day of blessing, and, one might think, of dauntingly grandiose identifications—he is tempted to begin his autobiography. First, however, the human authority who represents both competition and an actual threat to his security must be named and defied. "The man who today is endowing France with the empire of the world so that he may trample her under foot, the man whose genius I admire and whose despotism I abhor [a few pages later he will call his father both a despot and a man of genius], that man surrounds me with his tyranny as it were with a new solitude; but though he may crush the present, the past defies him, and I remain free in all that precedes his glory" (*Mémoires*, 1:15). So the evocation of the past through writing memoirs is in part a declaration of independence, a declaration that implies, in connection with his father, as the narrative will shortly show, that though his father crushed Chateaubriand's boyhood, the future defied his power, and Chateaubriand remained free in all that *followed* his father's glory.

"Let us commence, then," Chateaubriand begins the autobiography proper,[29] "and speak first of my family. This is essential, because the character of my father depended in a great measure upon his position, and, in its turn, exercised a great influence upon the nature of my ideas, by determining the manner of my education." This paragraph was later replaced by one that opens more abruptly, omitting the significant connection between "beginning" and "father"; this version is more revealing and blunt, however, about his father's emotional impact upon him. "My father's birth and the trials of his position caused his character to become one of the gloomiest ever known. Now this character influenced my ideas because it terrified me in childhood, saddened me in youth, and determined the manner of my education." That the consuming passion of René-Auguste's life was the restoration of his aristocratic status through castle and title had fateful implications for the meaning of François-René's life. His very reason for existing at all was as backup heir, not merely an appendage to his father's ambition but an appendage to an appendage, of no importance in himself except as a male and even then only if his brother were to die. François-René was the last of ten children, the first four of whom had died as infants. Of the remaining six, the oldest was a boy, the heir to the title and estate, the next four were girls, who "[p]robably . . . owed their existence to my father's desire to assure the perpetuation of his name through the arrival of a second boy" (*Mémoires*, 1:28). "I resisted," he added, referring perhaps not only to his difficult birth but to the destiny that declared his utter insignificance to his father. But if insignificance bred rebellion, defiance was not open, for the father's fundamental lack of interest in his second son did not mean benign neglect. "[T]aciturn, despotic, and threatening at home, the feeling which the sight of him inspired was one of fear" (1:26).

Chateaubriand's beginnings with his mother were no more auspicious. He was put out to wet nurse in a nearby town immediately after his birth—his first exile, he called it—and did not return home until age three. There he remembers his mother ignoring him, leaving him to the care of servants while she centered all her affection upon her eldest son. The only family member who lavished attention and affection on him was his sister Lucile, two years older than he, the youngest of the sisters, and neglected like himself. François-René returned the attachment ferociously, protecting her against the scoldings of her elderly tutors, once by scratching their faces. His father dismissed him as another in the long line of ne'er-do-well Chateaubriand younger sons, his mother "crowned her remonstrances with a panegyric on my brother, whom she called a Cato, a hero." His only family tie thus led to further exclusion, and he was inclined, he wrote, to adapt to their negative expectations and do all the ill they seemed to expect (1:34).

Chateaubriand anticipated the modern psychological question about his childhood by raising, only to reject the possibility that his upbringing made him hate his parents. Not at all, he said, though the sentiments he enunciated toward them—value, honor, gratitude—do not include love. In any case, his point in raising the issue was both broader and more polemical. No system of education is better than any other, he wrote, an obvious slam in 1809 at the Rousseau he once revered; children do not love their parents any better when they address them familiarly and have no fear of them, and the educational outcome of any parental treatment is finally unpredictable. Yet the description of his feelings and actions belies these assertions. He noted his melancholy, described his attachment to an outgoing, daring, and rebellious childhood friend, misunderstood like himself, and the sense they both shared of someday proving their worth. He wrote of becoming, without actively trying—"it happened"—the center of a gang at school, and of his touchy sense of honor, "the idol of my life," which led him not only to defy a punishment of beating for stealing some bird's eggs because of the shame it would cause, but to kick the prefect who was to administer it. His sensitivity to humiliation, his ambition for greatness and leadership, his defiance of authority seem in direct proportion to his apparent exclusion by a father for whom rank and status were everything and a mother who doted on the older brother who was destined to them.

How Chateaubriand was to realize his ambitions, however, was a difficult and uncertain question. There were limited possibilities available to the cadet of an aristocratic house—the church, the court, and the military—and his father, not surprisingly in view of his own history, decided on a career in the navy for his son. Despite a belief that he might have made a good naval officer, however, Chateaubriand used the accidental failure of his commission to arrive as anticipated after he had undergone two years of naval training as an excuse to take his destiny into his own hands. "[M]y spirit of independence . . . disinclined me to service of any kind: I was born with an incapacity for obedience. Voyages tempted me, but I felt that I should enjoy them only in solitude, left free to follow my own will" (1:98). At the age of sixteen, without securing permission or even informing anyone, he abandoned his naval career and went home. Not coincidentally, it was while this decision was germinating, as he stood on the shore at Brest, the tip of Brittany, and contemplated the "boundless ocean and unknown worlds" beyond, that he had his first vague thoughts about society, its blessings and its evils. Contemplating the constrictions and aspirations of his own life had led him to look beyond himself and to generalize the problem of freedom to society at large: the connection between the personal and the political made its first hazy appearance.

Any further development, however, had to await the crystallization of a more specific sense of identity that might give direction to Chateaubriand's inchoate yearnings for freedom and greatness. He had no idea what he wanted to do. He announced that he wanted to enter the priesthood and went for a time to the college at Dinan, but this was only a moratorium: "The truth is that I was only seeking to gain time, for I did not know what I wished" (1:105). He would often go home on weekends and finally settled in at home, apparently at an impasse.

Yet it was in his "two years of madness at home" that Chateaubriand found himself. "It was in the woods of Combourg that I became what I am."[30] He decided that he was, or would be, a writer, and the catalyst of this self-discovery was his sister Lucile. The family's routine during the period of François-René's adolescent residence at home was somewhat bizarre. René-Auguste cast an even deeper pall over the already gloomy setting of the castle by his distance and isolation. He dispersed his family and servants to rooms in separate corners of the castle, with his son in its most remote part. Meals were taken in silence, and even afterwards the children were too terror-stricken to talk. Only after their father retired did life return. "The spell was broken; my mother, my sister and myself, who had been changed into statues by my father's presence, recovered the functions of life. The first effect of our disenchantment took the form of an overflow of words: silence was made to pay us dear for having so long oppressed us" (1:111). Language, voluble, pressing, almost desperate in its liberating urgency, was not only a vehicle of expression; it was a life-giving rebellion that freed Chateaubriand from the hypnotic tyranny of his father's presence and gave him access to his mother and sister. It was on one of his long walks through the woods that were their chief pastime that Lucile, responding to his "rapturous" discourses on solitude, told him to write it all down. "These words revealed the muse to me. I began to lisp verses, as though it were my natural language" (1:120).

His main subject was his famous "sylphide," the fantasy image he built up of the ideal woman, by now a commonplace of male adolescence, though pursued by few, as Painter notes, with such lifelong intensity and persistence. Painter also points out the autobiographical referents of the fantasy, its embodiment of Chateaubriand's "lost birthright, the love of the mother who abandoned him in infancy," and the idealized though hardly desexualized sister who was to be at the core of the incest motifs of his later work. At a deeper level, however, Painter insists, Chateaubriand's sylphide was more than a mere autobiographical reincarnation. She was the symbol of an "archetypal and anonymous deprivation . . . a symbol of the truth . . . that in love there is always something false or factitious, a response that is never quite identical with the longing that demands it."[31] This splitting of the psychological from the existential, however, threatens to rob Chateaubriand's experience of its specificity. It was, for example, a crucial part of Chateaubriand's experience of his sylphide that she was a young queen belonging to a king, and that in his fantasy of possession he was successfully competing by taking her away from her royal husband, so that "the royal jealousy encompasses us" (1:127). But Painter's point about the fictive nature of the sylphide is crucial. She was not only a creature of the imagination but an object of linguistic address, identical with writing itself. Through her, Chateaubriand had found not only an object of longing but a métier that promised permanent value, and with it, the self he had been looking for. But through her, writing was also connected with competitive self-assertion.

It was not, therefore, a self Chateaubriand could be easy about in relationship to his father. For one thing, its very roots lay in defiance of him. At the peak of his intensifying fantasy, Chateaubriand saw his sylphide as a source not only of loving acceptance and erotic fulfillment but as a way of surpassing his father's values of glory and honor. To possess her would somehow be to transcend virtue and genius themselves. In the ultimate act of paternal usurpation, he imagined fusing with her and becoming pure spirit as well as man, infinite and self-contained, "at once passion given and received, love and the object of love" (1:132). The shattering vision and the equally shattering illusoriness of its fulfillment drove him to a double-edged despair, an oscillation between feelings of valueless mediocrity, nothingness, for not being able to realize his fantasy, and specialness unappreciated for the power that enabled him to visualize it. He left his tower room furtively, "like a murderer," and came back from a wild walk in the woods unable to face his father. Forced finally to do so at dinner, he sat in utter humiliation before the man he so passionately wanted both to please and surpass. The tension was too great. He tried, though half-heartedly, to shoot himself.

The immediate crisis passed. The gun didn't go off, a severe illness prevented another attempt, and the doctor ordered him to leave home as part of his recovery. But the military commission his brother procured for him, and his departure with his father's brusque blessing and old sword, did not change the underlying feeling. When a short time later his father died, Chateaubriand mourned him in an odd way. He reminisced about another harsh father, a notorious historical figure, the Maréchal de Montluc, whose mass execution of Huguenots in the sixteenth century had earned him the nickname of the Royalist Butcher. But what interested Chateaubriand in the Maréchal was how he had mourned the death of the son he had lost. Thus he converted his father's death into his own and relished the fantasy of how sorry his father would be for treating him as he had. He was sure, he remembered thinking, that his father would have had similar regrets had he died first. Writing about the event years later, he also raised a question he could not have posed at the time of his father's death, a question that had its origins at the time his muse opened up the prospects of a literary vocation. "Would [my father] . . . have set store by the fame that has sprung from my life? A literary reputation would have wounded his nobility; he would have seen nothing but degeneration in his son's gifts; even the Berlin Embassy, conquered by the pen, not the sword, would have barely satisfied him" (1:158). If his literary vocation represented his spiritual superiority to his father, it was at the same time by his father's standards utterly worthless. The vehicle he had chosen to realize his father's values of honor and glory and outdo him in them was condemned in advance by those very values.

The first major event Chateaubriand recorded in the *Mémoires* after reporting the death of his father is symbolic—his presentation at Versailles and his hunt with the king himself. The point of his narrative is his utter lack of interest in the honor, which was arranged by his brother as part of his own ambitions at court. In fact, the story reveals Chateaubriand's ongoing struggle with his ambition and the memory of his father. The hunters were instructed not to come between the king and his quarry. Sure enough, however, Chateaubriand's willful horse, which had already embarrassed him by charging into one of the women in the hunting party, brought him to the kill before the king was able to reach it. Instead of flying into the expected rage, Louis XVI uttered a casual pleasantry, and Chateaubriand was reprieved; indeed the story spread about that he had chatted with the king. Chateaubriand related the incident with open self-mockery, yet it is hard to miss his sense of pleasure at having beaten the king to the kill, a pleasure for which the king did not even make him pay.

It was not in this arena, however, that Chateaubriand wanted to fulfill his ambition. The episode of the chase ends with a little dialogue in which he tells his imaginary questioner that he did nothing to exploit his adventure with the king but that he did put effort and intrigue into publishing a poem a few years later. He would not, in other words, be a courtier or fawn on power, though he implied that he had the opportunity to do both. He would, instead be a citizen of the republic of letters. This opportunity came a year later when he was able to settle in Paris and join, if only as a tolerated observer, the literary circles of the capital.

Chateaubriand's entrée was not the result of his own merit. His brother had made a very advantageous match, marrying a young woman who was the daughter of the president of the *Parlement* of Paris and the granddaughter of the illustrious former president of the *Cour des Aides* and director of the royal censorship, Lamoignon de Malesherbes, who also served Louis XVI for a brief time as one of his chief ministers. Chateaubriand's sister Julie, whose charm effortlessly attracted the attention of men, decided to take advantage of her older brother's good fortune by moving to Paris to improve her social situation and persuaded Lucile and François-René to join her. It was through Julie that Chateaubriand met Delisle de Sales, the prolific, if second-rate, philosophe who had the prestige of having been imprisoned for his *Philosophy of Nature* in 1770, and through Delisle many of the last prerevolutionary generation of philosophes and writers—Flins des Oliviers, La Harpe, Parny, Ginguiné, Le Brun, Chamfort, and Fontanes.

Chateaubriand's brief descriptions of his literary associates, written from the later vantage point of his own literary preeminence, give little idea of their contemporary impact on him. He acknowledged that he once admired them, though he gave no direct indication of what he found admirable, since he consistently deflated them with ironic comments and mocking detail. Yet the group supplied him at the time both with an ideology and with literary models. Through them he was introduced to the Rousseauist notions that were widespread among writers in the last decade before the Revolution, concepts that combined the ideal of virtue in ancient republics with that of the natural benevolence and sociability of primitive peoples in a critique of the corruption of modern commercial monarchies. These ideas provided him with a set of terms, tropes, and models appropriate to his antiauthoritarian longings, yet not wholly inconsistent with his father's anticentralizing ideals. It is likely that the original plan for *The Natchez*, which was to be a saga of the noble savages of the New World fighting against the tyrannical oppression of the Old, was first sketched out under the influence of these ideas in the two years before the outbreak of the French Revolution.

Chateaubriand was supported and confirmed in these new ideas and projects by the sympathetic attention of Malesherbes. The elder statesman, who had been a patron and protector of the philosophes, who had used his position as director of the royal censorship to soften its effects, and who had acted as intermediary between Rousseau and his French editor at the time of the publication of *Emile*, took the intense, searching, and uncertain young man to his heart. He became a surrogate father not only for the one François-René had just lost but also for the father he had never had. Malesherbes was as different in personality from René-Auguste as possible, cheerful and playful where the latter had been dour, open and passionate where he had been withdrawn and reserved. Above all, Malesherbes talked volubly, and to François-René. He talked about his interests in botany, geography, and exploration, he talked about the philosophes, and he talked about contemporary politics. "M. de Malesherbes' free ways," Chateaubriand wrote, "removed all my constraint" (1:188). As a result he was able to talk freely too about all the things that had been important to him but which he had had to keep to himself in solitude.

Malesherbes not only listened, he agreed, at least to some extent, giving Chateaubriand the sense of being taken seriously, indeed of being treated as an equal by a very important member of an older generation. "We also held views in common on politics; the generous sentiments which were at the root of our earlier troubles appealed to the independence of my character; my natural antipathy to the court gave strength to this inclination. I was on the side of M. de Malesherbes and of Madame de Rosanbo [his sister-in-law's mother] as against M. de Rosanbo and my brother, who was nicknamed the fanatic Chateaubriand. The Revolution would have carried me away, had it not started in crime" (1:188). It is unlikely, however, that the views of the untried young man learning about politics at second hand from books and litterateurs and those of the sophisticated and experienced elder statesman who had participated in some of the most important political struggles in the eighteenth century were quite as similar as Chateaubriand claimed. As a distinguished *parlementaire* and former *Premier Président* of one of the most important courts in France, Malesherbes had forcefully argued the "constitutionalist" position of the parlementary opposition to the absolute monarchy at critical junctures in the struggle with the royal administration during the second half of the eighteenth century. In this view, the courts, representing the nation, were the only institution that could defend liberty and ensure consistent justice in France against the tendencies of administrative arbitrariness.[32] As George Kelly points out, there were few if any republican residues in Malesherbes; liberty was for him not the active participation of responsible citizens but the negative defense of particular rights guaranteed by the sovereign courts.[33] His affinity with Rousseau was based on an appreciation of the dignity of independent labor and thought and hence of the indignities of intellectuals' dependency on men of wealth and position, but his egalitarianism was very limited; while he argued against the inequality of noble exemption from the *taille*, he believed that respect was owed the nobility on the basis of a right of birth.[34] And although he criticized excessive luxury, by which he meant living beyond one's means, he believed so strongly in the virtues of commerce that he recommended that nobles should practice trade and that they should not suffer the dangers of derogation for doing so. Nonetheless, despite the real differences in their political views, François-René for the first time felt himself to be in the right as against both his brother and his father's generational representative—his brother's father-in-law, M. de Rosanbo. What he felt was being sanctioned by Malesherbes was less the particulars of his radicalism than his dignity and independence, his very rebellion against his father. With such heady support, it is not surprising that he felt that the Revolution might have swept him up in the enthusiasm of creating a world that would be totally different from the world he knew. In 1788, Malesherbes went beyond his previous position and advised against convoking the Estates-General in the forms of 1614 with the words "What the Nation demands is a new Constitution which has never before existed in France"[35]—words that would have sounded a deep echo in François-René.

We have already seen that it is almost impossible to know just what Chateaubriand's precise political ideas were with regard to the day-to-day events and issues of the early revolution and exactly why he decided to leave it for the United States. There is more to the vagueness on these matters than absence of contemporary documentation or the change of heart that preceded Chateaubriand's writing about them. Although Chateaubriand was to become deeply immersed in concrete politics in later years both as polemicist and politician and to know the realities of its intrigues, power struggles, and sudden shifts of fortune, in some sense he did not see the Revolution as a real political event. That is not to say that he did not locate himself on the spectrum of the constitutional opinions of the day. Ideal preferences and practical possibilities were kept in separate compartments. In 1789 Chateaubriand supported a constitutional monarchy; he believed, with Malesherbes, that the monarch was in theory, and ought to be in practice, the king of a free people able to express their legislative will through a representative assembly. He favored the abolition of aristocratic privilege, including primogeniture, a position notable for an enlightened aristocrat only in that in Chateaubriand's case it struck directly at his father's identity and destroyed his brother's status as his successor. At times, however, his egalitarian sentiments took him beyond the moderate position later associated with the Feuillants—precisely again where the issue touched on his personal motives for revolution. In the one extant letter in which Chateaubriand commented on current events, he directed some bitter remarks at the decree of the National Assembly of March 8, 1790, concerning the French overseas colonies, which left slavery untouched. "It has decreed that the colonies could adopt whatever constitution pleased them. Also there was no talk either of blacks or of anything else, and the colonists are quite happy to be able to do whatever they want to get rich; it's a nice country to live in now. You who are in Switzerland enjoy peace and nature while we others, inhabitants of France, are still plunged into chaos."[36] In general, he found himself fighting with his brother and M. de Rosanbo on the right and with his friends Ginguené, La Harpe, and Chamfort, who were becoming increasingly more radical, on the left. But his politics constantly betrayed his strong personal motives. He was drawn to Mirabeau, the renegade aristocrat who "like me, had been treated with severity by his father, who had like my own, preserved an inflexible tradition and absolute paternal authority" (1:227).

But despite an invitation, Chateaubriand did not get involved in Mirabeau's political intrigues. The reference to his correspondent's enjoyment of peace and nature in Switzerland in the letter cited above suggest that the realities of politics were for Chateaubriand pale copies of a more exalted program, the creation of an ideal mythic society derived from his reading and his desires. Under these circumstances it was easy for him to be disappointed by even small deviations of reality from the ideal. Chateaubriand became disillusioned with revolutionary actuality well before it became apparent that the constitutional monarchy would not work, before the massacres that later horrified other supporters. It was one thing for antirevolutionary aristocrats to leave the country after July 1789; it was quite another for Chateaubriand, who at first repudiated emigration, to do so even before the new constitution was installed.

This is not to say that his horror at the violence he did witness was not genuine but that it has to be understood within the psychological and mythic economy of his revolutionism. It is possible to read in this early recoil at violence a reaction to impulses that would appear later in his fiction as a concealed fascination with violence. Barbéris has pointed out a number of passages in *The Natchez* (early notes and drafts for which, it will be remembered, date from this period) that conjoin eroticism with violence, death, and murder, passages that indulge a horrified enjoyment of the sexual suffering of women;[37] they will prove to be of great significance for understanding Chateaubriand's political trajectory. But the outburst of Atala's frustrated desire when she declares herself ready to annihilate the divinity itself for blocking her passion is not the outcry of a feminine victim. She speaks for desire, for the author himself. Chateaubriand's adherence to the Revolution was too closely linked to his hatred for his father for him to be able to tolerate any violence in its name. His contradictory wish for a pacific utopia of free warriors reflected his conflicted desires and drove him to seek, as he put it, "an independence more in conformity with my tastes, more in sympathy with my character" than the messy reality of revolutionary France.

ii) The Meaning of American Freedom

Chateaubriand hoped to find his desired independence in the New World—though not necessarily in the new United States. Despite its apparent success as a republican experiment, Chateaubriand was primed by his mythic predilections to be disappointed by the American reality. The case was somewhat more complex than that of revolutionary France. In the United States the revolution was already achieved; he need not fear violence there. Theory prepared him to accept that modern commercial republics were imperfect by classical standards. The scale of modern states and the established, central role of commerce in them made compromise unavoidable for one who would salvage anything of republican ideals in the modern world. And in fact for polemical purposes later in his life, Chateaubriand could make much of the classical virtue of Americans. Both in the *Mémoires* and in the *Travels in America*, he used George Washington's simplicity and self-effacing patriotism as a foil to skewer Napoleon for the egotism of his purely personal quest for glory and renown. But though Chateaubriand claimed that before he arrived in the United States, Washington was "according to my ideas at the time . . . necessarily Cincinnatus" (*Mémoires*, 1:16), the dictator who saved the Roman republic in battle and then returned to his plough, it did not take very long for him to become disillusioned. Even Washington had his disappointing side. Chateaubriand caught his first glimpse of him in an elegant carriage that "upset my idea of the Roman republic of the year 246." And though Washington redeemed himself by showing in their later encounter "the simplicity of the old Roman,"[38] the United States did not. In a long note in the *Essai sur les révolutions*, Chateaubriand scathingly described the disillusioning information he was given about the Quakers, whom his reading of Raynal had prepared him to see as models of virtue. In America he was told instead that if he wanted to be cheated, all he had to do was enter a shop of one of the brothers and if he were curious to learn just how far the spirit of self-interest and mercantile immorality could go, he could be shown the spectacle of two Quakers engaged in a commercial transaction and trying to deceive one another.[39] The commercial American republic displayed little of the republican virtue Chateaubriand had expected to find.

Chateaubriand's real hopes, however, lay with the Indians of the New World, not with the European settlers and their descendants. "I was," he wrote, "impatient to continue my journey. I had not come to see the Americans, but something quite different from the men I knew, something more in harmony with the habitual order of my ideas" (*Mémoires*, 1:286). In the years just before the Revolution, he had planned to write "the epic of the man of nature," linking the mores of the Indians to a specific event, the massacre of French settlers by the Natchez of Louisiana in 1727. Following Raynal's (in fact mistaken) account, he interpreted the Indian revolt of 1727 as an uprising of all the Indian tribes of North America, after two centuries of oppression, to liberate the New World from the Europeans.[40] The appeal of the uprising in the light of Chateaubriand's personal issues was obvious. Even before revolution in France, he was imagining a rebellion of the natural, pure, and noble against oppression and tyranny. To write its history would be to find a subject that expressed the rebelliousness inherent for Chateaubriand in the act of writing, in language itself. The meaning of the French Revolution for him was already prefigured in the mythic historic framework of the revolt of the noble savage. When the Revolution failed to be what it was supposed to be, he did not find it difficult to abandon this historically flawed exemplar of the ideal in order to seek a living embodiment of it, however deformed it might be by the continuing domination of European society. But the project of writing after the outbreak of the Revolution was not the same as the project before. What had been an act of personal and cultural rebellion had been politically transformed into an act that envisioned the actual overthrow of a regime. It is certainly true, as Painter has seen in the murk of uncertainty and conflicting evidence regarding Chateaubriand's motives for his trip to America, that his main purpose was to write a book.[41] But he did not go, as Chateaubriand intimated in the preface to *Atala*, simply to get firsthand knowledge and experience of the people and places he wanted to write about. His voyage was a stage on his revolutionary journey. Having been disillusioned by the Revolution itself, he returned to an earlier writing project transformed into a substitute revolutionary act.

A first indication of what he was looking for came when he left Albany, New York, and crossed the Mohawk River into the as-yet uncleared forest.

When, during my travels among Indian nations of Canada, I left the European settlements behind and found myself, for the first time, alone in the midst of an ocean of forests, having, so to speak, the whole of nature prostrate at my feet, a strange revolution took place within me. Seized by a kind of delusion, I followed no path; I went from tree to tree, right and left indifferently, saying to myself "there, no more roads to follow, no more cities, no more confining houses, no more presidents, republics, kings, above all no more laws, and no more men. Men? yes, some noble Savages who were not ashamed of me nor I of them—who like me, wander freely wherever their ideas lead them, eating when they like, sleeping where and when it pleases them." And to test whether I was finally reestablished in my original rights, I indulged them in a thousand acts of will which enraged . . . [my] guide . . . who in his heart believed me mad. (*Essai*, 305–6)

Unfortunately the acts of will that shocked the European guide are left to his readers' imagination, but the sense of the event is unmistakable. As literary a moment as it no doubt partly was, its dimensions defined by Rousseau, it was also an explosion of anarchic freedom and power. The accents indeed go beyond Rousseau's moralized spontaneity to an unconstrained exuberance of domination in which Chateaubriand was alone and nature lay prostrate at his feet. He had translated Rousseau into lived experience, in the process metaphorically expanding the sense of independence in the trackless but object-filled forest to the unmarked and undifferentiated boundlessness of the sea. The moment of expansion was simultaneously a moment of negation, it was indeed expansion through negation, as the litany of "no more" and the defiant acts of will indicate. In the first primitive intoxication of independence, there was nothing there but him; only in reflection did he acknowledge the presence of what he denied at the time—other men—but as alter egos who felt as he felt and did as he did.

This initial moment of "revolution," as he himself called it, was not sustained, but was almost immediately undercut by an encounter that, though perhaps not as unexpected as Chateaubriand claimed it was in the *Mémoires*, was turned into a moment of ironic reversal. He "bumped" into a shed in which Iroquois in native dress were being taught European dances by a powdered and bewigged French dancing-master, and though he had apparently been told about this man earlier, he exclaimed, "Was it not an overwhelming thing for a disciple of Rousseau, this introduction to savage life through a ball which General Rochambeau's late scullion was giving to the Iroquois? I had a great longing to laugh, but I felt cruelly humiliated" (*Mémoires*, 1:291). The expansiveness was deflated, and reality undercut mythic ideal in a particularly painful way; the Indians who were put in a position where they appeared ridiculous were humiliating to Chateaubriand because they were him, and he was in effect the object of his own ironic laughter.

It is impossible to know with certainty whether Chateaubriand's disillusion was actually contemporary with the experience or whether, if it was, it was as keen as he described. The latter seems unlikely because the cycle of enthusiasm and disappointment is artfully repeated a number of times in the texts describing the voyage. Through the accounts of successive episodes there is a rising intensity of excitement, a progressive development in the sense of selfhood and its claims. The spiral structure of the whole experience seems to be an artifact of the writing, but it builds to a climax that the evidence suggests occurred during the trip itself. A few weeks later, as Chateaubriand lingered in a village near Niagara Falls, waiting permission to enter the region, he wrote to Malesherbes describing the way Iroquois children are brought up. The letter, later reprinted in slightly altered form in the *Travels*, is one of the few documents dating from the time of the trip itself and comes as close as anything can to reporting Chateaubriand's feelings at the time. The status of his observations of the Iroquois is uncertain; they were clearly combined, as were so many of his travel descriptions, with reports from the writings of European travelers before him. Whether they are true or not, however, whether they were personally observed or not, what is significant about his descriptions is that he chose to communicate them to Malesherbes. The Rousseauist ideals he partly shared with his mentor and Malesherbes's personal sympathy made him the appropriate recipient of a description of modes of child-rearing that point for point are the opposite of everything Chateaubriand suffered as a child and adolescent. What is striking conceptually and literarily about the letter is that the picture it gives of the character and freedom of the Iroquois child is at a more advanced social and developmental level than that of Chateaubriand's first outburst of freedom on reaching the virgin forest. That solipsistic moment of purely negative liberation is succeeded by a more socially concrete picture of intrafamilial relations. It is as if Chateaubriand were reliving a corrective maturational development in the course of his trip. The letter is worth quoting in detail.

> You reviewed the proofs of *Emile*. Why should you not glance at a page on the topic of education? Consider me a little Jean-Jacques. . . .
>
> The [Iroquois] child is never forcibly weaned; after feeding on other foods, he drains his mother's breast, like a cup drained at the end of a banquet. When the entire nation is dying of hunger, the child still finds in the maternal breast a source of life. . . .
>
> A savage about thirty years old called his son and suggested that he moderate his jumping; the child answered, "That is reasonable." And without doing what the father told him, jumped more vigorously.
>
> The grandfather of the child called him in turn, and said to him, "Do that"; and the little boy obeyed. Thus the child disobeyed his father, who asked him, and obeyed his grandfather, who ordered him. [In the version of the letter in the *Travels*, Chateaubriand added here, "The father is almost nothing for the child" (32).]

The child is never punished; he recognizes only the authority of age and of his mother. When she grows old, he feeds her.

As for the father, as long as he is young, the child discounts him completely, but as he progresses in life, his son honors him not as a father but as an old man, that is, a man of good advice and experience.

This manner of raising children should make them prey to ill humor and caprice; however, the children of the savages show neither caprice nor ill humor because they want only what they can obtain. If it does happen that a child cries for something that his mother does not have he is told to get that thing where he saw it; now, since he is not the stronger one and since he feels his weakness, he forgets the object he desires. If the savage child obeys no one, no one obeys him.

The Indian [children] do not quarrel, do not fight. They are neither noisy, annoying, nor surly; they have in their appearance some mysterious seriousness, like happiness, some nobility, like independence.

When the adolescent begins to feel the taste for fishing, hunting, war or politics, he studies and imitates the arts he sees being practiced. . . . What is an amusement for the son is the basis of the father's authority; the latter's right of force and intelligence is recognized. . . .

The girls enjoy the same liberty as the boys. [42]

Unlike Chateaubriand's mother, the Indian mother is always there, nurturing her children, even at seven or eight, until they decide to end their own dependency. Yet they are not allowed to expect total gratification of their wishes. They get what is in her power to give, which they thus learn is limited. Such frustration is not arbitrary and it both sustains their love for their mother and their own reasonableness and independence. They learn that they will one day be strong enough to satisfy their own needs and desires.

If the mother's authority is rationally based on her ability to nurture, the father—again quite unlike Chateaubriand's—initially has no authority, for he has at first nothing to give the young children. Paternal authority at this point would be irrational and arbitrary. It is only as the children mature to the point of wanting and being able to master the arts of their culture that the father takes on the authority of his powers and abilities. The obviously crucial point for Chateaubriand was that authority in child-rearing was never arbitrary, that the Indian child knew neither command nor obedience. As a result, with a taste neither for submission nor for domination, children could develop into beings who were so free that they were not even the slaves of their own desires, for they willed only what they could obtain.

This image is one of a seamless connection with nature. Children or adolescents are at one with themselves and the world, feeling neither deprived nor entitled.[43] They do not quarrel with siblings or peers because they have no reason to feel envious or jealous. The implication is that the need for competition and conquest is a response to powerlessness, and since the powerlessness that the child experiences is the shared experience of the universal infant condition and not the result of arbitrary distinctions, it is not individually humiliating.

And yet if the integrated self is the product of an ideal set of social relationships, the Iroquois family structure does not produce a social being. Even in this idyllic picture, the social behavior of the Indian child is limited to taking nourishment from the mother and imitating the father's skills; the only other interaction that is mentioned is the child's future caring for the mother in her time of need, the result of natural gratitude. Otherwise, the focus is on the lone individual and the development of his or her unfettered freedom and fulfillment. For Chateaubriand the initial revolutionary experience of the American wilderness was the vision of broken chains and unconstrained self-expression. Another passage contemporary with the trip, the "Diary Without Dates," likely written some weeks after the letter to Malesherbes as Chateaubriand journeyed down the Ohio towards the Mississippi, represents the climactic point of his vision of freedom, the *jouissance* of the liberty opened to him by the images of an ideal upbringing and the vistas of a virgin nature unspoiled by prior possession.

> The sky is pure over my head, the water limpid under my boat, which is flying before a light breeze. On my left are some hills rising like cliffs and flanked with rocks from which hang the morning glory with white and blue blossoms, festoons of begonias, long grasses, rock plants of all colors; to my right reign vast prairies. As the boat advances new scenes and new views open up: at times solitary and laughing valleys, at times bare hills; here the somber porticoes of a cypress forest, there the sun playing in a light maple forest as if shining through a piece of lace.
>
> Primitive liberty, I find you at last! I pass as that bird who flies before me, who travels haphazardly, who has only an embarrassment of riches among the shadows. Here I am as the Almighty created me, the sovereign of nature [another version of the "Diary" in the *Mémoires* includes the phrase "heir presumptive of the heavens" (*Mémoires*, 1:323)], borne triumphantly by the waters, while the inhabitants of the rivers accompany my course. The peoples of the air sing me their hymns, the animals of the earth salute me, and the forests bend their upmost branches over my passage. Is it on the forehead of the man of society or on mine that is engraved the immortal seal of our origin? Run and shut yourselves up in your cities; go and subject yourselves to your petty laws; earn your livelihood by the sweat of your brow, or

devour the pauper's bread; slaughter one another over a word, over a master; doubt the existence of God, or adore him in superstitious forms. I shall go wandering in my solitudes. Not a single beat of my heart will be constrained, not a single one of my thoughts will be enchained; I shall be free as nature, I shall recognize as sovereign only Him who lit the flame of the suns and who with one movement of this hand set in motion all the worlds. (*Travels*, 42–43)

The first paragraph of nature description is central to the experience. It depicts a landscape at once differentiated into pairs of opposites yet unified in a whole, complete yet ever open to novelty that is at once integrated into the closed structure, timeless and absolute yet organized from a shifting center, the constantly moving eye (and "I") of the traveler. All the spatial vectors—above/below, left/right, before/behind—are subsumed in the picture, which enfolds air, water, and earth, the dun barrenness of rock and the colorful abundance of vegetation, light and shadow, solemnity and play in a celebration of totality.

"I leave as they are these expressions of youth," Chateaubriand added in wry self-indulgence in a footnote when he published the diary extract years later (*Travels*, 213). Adolescent effusion they certainly were, at least from a later perspective; the sentiments and cadences of the sentence beginning "the peoples of the air sing me their hymns" are reminiscent in their naive candor of the words in which Joseph related his dream of being worshipped by his brothers and his father—the sun, moon, and stars. But they were more than expressions of youth. They were the breakthrough of a revolutionary sensibility in which the self appropriated the variety and creative force of nature through the constructive powers of language. The acknowledgment of God, while neither ritual nor pro forma, was not a pledge of submission or fealty. It was both an insistence on the reality of the divinity and an assumption by the self of divine power on earth and in heaven. In the beginning God set in motion all the worlds; it was for man to take over his absolute sovereignty in the present, recreating creation by the power of his mind and imagination. Chateaubriand's progress down the river was the triumphal procession of a monarch surveying his domains, his by virtue of his ability to mix his will with their unformed chaos through the power of describing, figuring, relating.

Later in the journal, the comparison between the traveler in the wilderness and the monarch is even more explicit. On an island in the river, Chateaubriand had a meal of seasoned fresh trout, "a dish worthy of a king's table. Thus was I much more than a king. If chance had placed me on the throne and a revolution had cast me from it, instead of eking out my misery in Europe as did Charles and James, I would have said to the covetous: 'You want my position, well try the job; you will see it is not so desirable. Slay one another over my old mantle; in the forests of America I shall enjoy the liberty you have given back to me" (*Travels*, 65). But this liberty was not simply freedom from the burden of a ruler's cares. It was rather a power greater than what a king could possibly exercise. Chateaubriand described his experience of it after the meal:

> After supper I sat down by myself on the shore. . . . I fell into that kind of reverie known to all travellers. No distinct remembrance of myself remained; I felt myself living as a part of the great whole and vegetating with the trees and flowers. [That is perhaps the most pleasant condition for man, for even when he is happy, there is in his pleasures a certain foundation of bitterness, an indefinable something that could be called the sadness of happiness. The traveller's reverie is a sort of plenitude of the heart and emptiness of the mind which allows one to enjoy his existence in repose; it is by thought that we trouble the felicity which God gives us.] (*Travels*, 65; the portion in square brackets is omitted from the version in the *Mémoires*.)

"Oh, man is a God when he dreams, a beggar when he thinks," Hölderlin would have Hyperion say a few years after the events this passage reports. The intimations of irony in the passage, however, are retrospective; the reflections on the corrosive effects of self-consciousness are not to be found in the version of the event described in the *Mémoires*. The climax of disillusion on this trip in the wilderness was yet to come, and when it did, it was not the result of philosophical reflection. It was in fact a crisis of the near-fulfillment of the last in the series of wilderness idylls that created a political rupture for Chateaubriand. The idyll represented the next stage of development in the sequence that began with his absolute negative liberation in the pristine wilderness and continued with his identification with the ideal Iroquois upbringing that produced the self-contained yet infinite natural being. It brought the youth to the stage of sexual desire and sociability. But this idyll, unlike the others, collapsed in disaster.

III) The Reversal

The political rupture that the collapse led to was Chateaubriand's decision to return to France to fight with the émigré army against the Revolution. On his return journey to Philadelphia in October 1791, he came across a newspaper report of Louis XVI's abortive flight to Varennes some four months before. Originally he had contemplated staying in Philadelphia over the winter and renewing his journey westward in the spring. Instead, on reading the report, he heard himself say, "Go back to France."

No adequate explanation has been given for this decision. Chateaubriand claimed that he acted out of a sense of duty to himself; he certainly did not feel needed in the sense that his contribution to the Bourbon cause would make a material difference. But duty to what? He had left for the United States precisely because he felt caught between a revolution with which he sympathized but whose course he could no longer defend or support and a counterrevolution to which, though it included his brother and brother's father-in-law—perhaps because it included them—he was fundamentally opposed. Arguably, he was acting in a way consistent with his own political views. The revolutionary constitution he could have supported was a constitutional monarchy created without violence, and when the king turned against the Constituent Assembly's work, his action invalidated the new constitution for Chateaubriand because it revealed that it was being forced on the monarch against his will.

Yet this reasoning—which Chateaubriand himself did not report as his own—seems somewhat out of focus. The course of events would seem calculated rather to keep him in America than to bring him home to France. He had seen the king under coercion before; he was present when Louis was forcibly brought from Versailles to Paris in October of 1789. He had no illusions that the Revolution had anything but the king's most reluctant acquiescence. Just a short time before reading of Louis's flight to Varennes, he had in the "Diary Without Date" proclaimed the superiority of loneliness in the American wilderness to any throne, and all the more to any attempt to reclaim a lost one. Chateaubriand himself suggested that something other, something more, than consequential reasoning according to his principles of duty and honor was the cause of his decision. "A sudden conversion," he wrote, "took place within my mind" (*Mémoires*, 1:346). The about-face was not only a reasoned reversal of plans; the word "conversion" is not too strong. It was a reversal of loyalties. In an abrupt act Chateaubriand was pledging himself to the very monarch against whom he had rebelled, the monarch who had fled the kind of constitutional regime Chateaubriand favored.

The best evidence for the real reasons for Chateaubriand's "conversion" lies in the narrative immediately preceding it. It is the story of the "two Floridians," his encounter with two young Indian women that is told at unusual length, with much detail, and with the linguistic markers of its emotional—and ideological—importance. At the end of the story Chateaubriand himself asserted the significance of the episode for his literary work; the two young women became the models for two of his most important fictional female protagonists. But the episode had political as well as literary significance.

Just prior to his meeting the two young women, Chateaubriand had been lamenting what were turning out to be the rather petty pleasures of paradise. Wonderful as the American landscape and its flora and fauna were, observing and classifying them seemed an increasingly trivial pursuit. "In the midst of these walks and studies, I was often struck by their futility. What! Did the Revolution, which already weighed down upon me and drove me into the woods, inspire me with no graver thoughts than these? What! Was the time of my country's confusion that which I chose to occupy myself with descriptions of plants, and butterflies, and flowers?" (*Mémoires*, 1:329–30). Even if these are fictionalized memories from the time of composition, a narrative preparation for the account of the decision to return to France, the sentiments described in the *Mémoires* are consistent with his contemporary sense, expressed in the older documents, of the disparity between the grandiosity of the liberation that the American wilderness provided him and the petty acts in which his liberty was exercised there.

The symbolic significance of the incident with the two young women, however, was another matter. On an island in the Ohio, his party met a group of Indians that included two women of mixed Cherokee and Castilian ancestry, whose beauty and mystery Chateaubriand found utterly seductive. When the men set out the next day from their mainland camp to hunt, he stayed behind with the women, playing and flirting. They did not understand one another's language; everything was gesture and action, with all their attendant ambiguities. The young women were twins, yet opposites, "sylvan goddesses," one proud, the other sad. He fetched them water, firewood, and moss for their beds. He placed ornaments on their heads; they submitted, somewhat frightened, or so he perceived them. "[W]itches themselves," Chateaubriand construed their reactions, "they thought I was working a charm on them" (*Mémoires*, 1:333).

Chateaubriand's desire for their company was only whetted. He arranged a fishing party that evening with the two women back on the island where they had first met. This was the occasion of the meal fit for a king and the pantheistic reverie cited earlier from the *Travels*. Set in the context of this event, the reverie takes on new meaning. After the meal he feel asleep, and upon awakening, he found the two women, one on each side of him, with their heads resting on his shoulders. The "sad" one began to sing, and he felt an enormous vulnerability and attachment: "No one who is unsure of who he is should ever expose himself like that; no one can know the kind of passion that insinuates itself with melody into a man's heart" (*Mémoires*, 1:336). His very being was put in the keeping of the singing woman. But the moment was suddenly and rudely shattered. A man who Chateaubriand later learned was in love with one of the women called out in a "rude and jealous voice" in response to the song. The magic night was over; it was time to leave not only the island but the young women. They returned to the shore and were taken away by their men, as if "snatched by the god of the nether world."

A trivial, fleeting dalliance—yet Chateaubriand described his subsequent state as "widowerhood." He was shocked to be told that his two "brides" were prostitutes, but, though his vanity was wounded, he still felt bereft. His sense of loss was compounded by the humiliating fact that his rival—his "favored" rival, he called him—was ugly and unprepossessing, a "mosquito," an "insect." Chateaubriand was inconsolable. He tried to summon up his sylphide to comfort him, but imaginary fulfillment was inadequate to his sense of real loss; he gave her the cold shoulder for the first time. From that moment, he wrote, "Solitude appeared empty to me. . . . I lost no time quitting the desert." In fact, textually it is immediately after this misadventure—though the actual lapse of time must have been days or weeks—that he describes coming across the headline of the king's flight and making the decision to return to France. On the very day he found the newspaper in the house in which he had taken shelter, he had been reminiscing bitterly about his lost happiness. "How happy should I have been there with the 'sad' one, had she been faithful to me, seated dreaming at her feet, my head laid upon her knees" (*Mémoires* 1:340). The "conversion" to the royalist cause and the decision to leave America were intimately connected with the shattered idyll of the "two Floridians."

The event has all the appearance of a doubly incestuous fantasy. Chateaubriand took over the two women—who functioned as mother and sister—while their men went off to do their grownup work. He served his witch-goddesses and adored them, and they in turn were bewitched by him. Not content with the completeness of his possession while the men were away, he isolated himself with the women on the island that even consciously had mythic dimensions—according to an Indian legend he related, there was an island in the middle of a lake where the most beautiful women in the world lived, an island containing a fountain of youth. Alone with his two Floridians, Chateaubriand was nurtured and fed; he dissolved into a reverie of oneness with nature, a symbiotic fusion, and awoke into the "reality" of possession and being possessed. But at the moment of greatest openness, when his separateness felt most threatened, and his need for identity through merger both most naked and closest to fulfillment, his exclusive relationship was destroyed by the demands of the real "husband." Although there is no evidence in Chateaubriand's account that the Indian woman actually loved or preferred the other man—except of course that she went off with him—he was in the fantasy the "favored" rival. Chateaubriand's would-be wife unaccountably abandoned him for someone he believed to be obviously inferior but who had unimpeachable claims of priority to her.

The degree of Chateaubriand's felt loss was proportional to the scope of his wish. It was not merely a wish for a sexual mother. The solitude that appeared as an infinite fullness as the woman sang to him now appeared as an emptiness. In the *Mémoires* Chateaubriand used the event as a paradigm of abortive experiences, lost opportunities, and ennui.

> Thus does everything prove abortive in my life, thus there is nothing left to me except images of what has passed so quickly. . . . The fault lies in my organization; I am never able to take advantage of any piece of good fortune; I can never take an interest in anything whatever that interests others. Putting religion aside, I have no beliefs. Shepherd or king, what should I have done with my sceptre or my crook: I should have wearied equally of glory or genius, work or leisure, prosperity or misfortune. Everything tires me; laboriously I drag my ennui through my days, and wherever I go, yawn away my life. (*Mémoires*, 1:337)

Both the context and the structure of the passage reveal the ennui not as an original metaphysical state but as a defense against loss. The "fault" was not his failure to take advantage of the situation with the two Floridians; in the circumstances, he had no realistic opportunity to do so. Putting the blame on his own lack of initiative and his fundamental ennui was a reaction against deprivation and helplessness and the impossibility of fulfilling his wishes.

But the event was also more than the mere incidence of a general pattern. In one way, it was a repetition of the original circumstances of his childhood, an effort to restore the maternal loss that had given rise to the need for repetition in the first place. But the repetition took place in ideological circumstances that gave it new meaning and additional causal force. It was because of this new meaning that the old vision of the sylphide could not console him. In its politicized context in the American wilderness, the idyll of the two Floridians and its shattering conclusion revealed in the most intimate and direct way the conflictual and dangerous aspects of revolutionary liberation and the dream of expansiveness. There were indeed kings—and fathers—in the wilderness after all. Sovereignty over nature, whose fullness Chateaubriand had realized in the episode with the Floridians meant for him the love of a "natural" woman, was not established in a social vacuum but only in conflict with and at the expense of others. The violence that had driven Chateaubriand out of France had burst through in his own impulses of rage against those who had taken away his goddesses. To win the real-life sylphide and enjoy eternal life with her on the blessed isle would have meant taking her away from someone else—just as it had in the original fantasy, when he had imagined taking the queen away from the king. With a rival in the real world, however, gratification demanded confrontation and combat. Chateaubriand surrendered because the only alternative—at least in fantasy—would have been pursuit and violence, perhaps murder. As it was, he assaulted his rival verbally, reducing him at least with his language to a loathsome insect.

It was these inner circumstances that lay behind Chateaubriand's "conversion," his readiness to fight for the helpless Louis XVI. It was, as he himself said, an internal rather than an external necessity. He was no longer a bystander of revolutionary evil, he was implicated in it by his personal extrapolation of the revolutionary ethic and the first real test of its concrete meaning. He dealt with that implication by reacting against it, defending the king whose destruction his claim to selfhood threatened.

It was not only immediate events that testified to the pivotal significance of the episode. Chateaubriand preserved it forever by transforming the two women into literature, the proud one into the unattainable Atala, the sad one into Céluta, unhappy wife of René in *The Natchez*. And although the published version of the novel did not appear until many years later and after many rewritings, the main plot of the story of René, Céluta, and the Indian revolt, which probably did not change very much from the lost American drafts, tells a good deal about the forces that went into Chateaubriand's conversion into a reluctant, if resolute, royalist soldier.

The Natchez seems to enfold two stories, the individual story of René, a melancholy exile from France with a mysteriously tragic past who is adopted into the tribe by its sachem, Chactas, and the political story of the rising of the Natchez against the French in the colony of Louisiana in 1727. The relationship between the two stories is unclear and, to the extent that it is ascertainable, somewhat odd. René, sympathetic to the desires of the Indians to liberate themselves from the oppressive exploitation of French civilization, sides with his adoptive people against his native people. Arrested at one point by the French authorities for complicity in a conspiracy against them, of which he in fact knows nothing, he not only acknowledges his more general guilt in opposing French colonization, he proclaims it defiantly even while protesting his innocence of the particular charge: "A vile rabble, composed of men who are the refuse of European corruption, has deprived an independent nation of its lands. . . . I will not enter into justifications which I disdain, not knowing, moreover, of what I am accused: the suspicion of men is of itself a presumption of innocence . . . [but] if there be a conspirator among the Natchez, I am he, for I have always opposed your oppressions. As a Frenchman I may appear guilty; as a man I am innocent."[44] Yet the epicenter of René's story is his ennui, his inability to care deeply about anything or commit himself to person, cause, or purpose. He inspires sympathy, friendship, love, jealousy, and hatred, but he feels little of any emotion himself and is not an initiator of action of any kind, much less a leader of the Indian rebellion. Whatever fighting he does with the Natchez is against their Indian enemies, not against the French. He does not even know about the planned uprising, and this points to the second part of the puzzle, for the uprising of which he professes ignorance but whose purpose he claims to favor is tainted. It has been engineered by the malevolent Ondouré as a means for promoting his own power among the Natchez. A usurper who has climbed his way to leadership through seduction of the female chief, Ondouré has conspired to get rid of René and of his rivals for leadership within the tribe by lying about them to the French and has conspired with other Indian tribes to slaughter helpless French colonists on the pretext of French mistreatment of the Natchez sachems. His purpose is not liberation and a renewal of the Indians' pristine way of life before the coming of the white man. "Disgust with the state of nature, and a desire to possess the enjoyments of social life aggravated the uneasiness of Ondouré: he devoured with his eyes all that he saw in the habitations of the Whites" (*Natchez*, 1:128).

A tainted revolution and a passive revolutionary: the political themes of Chateaubriand's own flight from France. But the contrast in fact resolves itself into something more personal; a conflict between a tainted but active revolutionary and a noble but passive and impotent one. For a large part of Ondouré's motive is a consuming personal jealousy of René. He is erotically obsessed with Céluta, the beautiful, sad young woman who loves René passionately, the woman whom René marries, though reluctantly. Ondouré wishes to destroy René in order to possess Céluta; at the climax of the novel he murders him and rapes Céluta in her husband's blood. René, on the other hand, does not desire his own wife any more than he desires anything else. He marries her out of obligation to her brother Outougamiz, who has saved his life, and to her puzzled sorrow remains emotionally, and often physically, aloof from her.

Yet for all René's passivity, he sees himself, and is ultimately seen by the narrator, as the motor of all events.

> The wilderness had not satisfied René any more than the world; and in the insatiability of his vague desires he had already drained solitude, as he had exhausted society. Motionless amid so many moving persons; the center of a thousand passions which he did not share; the object of all thoughts for widely different reasons; the brother of Amélie became the invisible cause of every effect; to love and to suffer was the double fatality which he imposed on all who came near him. Thrown into the world like some great calamity, his baleful influence extended to surrounding objects: thus there are beautiful trees, under which it is death to sit or to breathe. (*Natchez*, 1:276)

René sees himself as the cause of the war between the Illinois and the Natchez, because in a beaver hunt with his adopted tribe he has killed some female beaver, not knowing the injunction that makes the act a legitimate casus belli between tribes. But his reflections are in fact incited by his awareness of Céluta's passion for him and his own indifference. It is this passion that has incited Ondouré to the actions that will lead to disaster for the Natchez, the French, and his own family—though René is not aware of any of this. He somehow knows nonetheless that to love him is a misfortune. The reference to him throughout the novel as "the brother of Amélie" points to the prior event on which this self-knowledge is based, the mysterious relationship to his sister in France that has already brought her some undescribed misfortune. There are thus two central events for which René feels responsible—and is so held by the narrator. "The life and death of René were pursued by illegitimate flames which gave heaven to Amélie and hell to Ondouré. René suffered the double chastisement of these two criminal passions. No one can produce disorder in others without having some principle of disorder in himself; and he who even involuntarily is the cause of misfortune or of crime, is never innocent in the sight of God" (*Natchez*, 3:321–22).

On the surface, the canon of moral responsibility that the narrator invokes here to explain and judge René's sense of guilt is an impossible one. He makes René responsible not only for the fates of Amélie and Ondouré, which he acknowledges René did not intend, but for their very passions. And the narrator's insistence on René's responsibility, while in part echoing René himself, is also aimed against him, for René is constantly protesting his innocence even as he confesses his guilt. René's guilty ambivalence and the narrator's draconian standard of judgement become intelligible only when it is understood that René is responsible for Ondouré's passion not merely because Céluta loves him instead of Ondouré, but because he *is* Ondouré, more exactly, Ondouré is René's other self, his hidden, but not quite unacknowledged self.

René's fatal passivity in America is a response to his belief that he had been fatally active in France. In a dramatic letter to Céluta near the end of the novel, he reveals some of the secret—the part he understands himself—of his mysterious melancholy and his inability to love her. In his youth, he was loved—"too much"—by his sister Amélie. The "too much" implies an exclusive, as well as a forbidden, sexual passion; it made all love "horrible" to him because "a model of womankind was before me, whom nothing human could approach," and so "closed forever, without drying up, the sources of my existence" (*Natchez*, 3:143). But her passion was his doing, the response to his passion for her. "From this heart issue flames which want nourishment, which would devour the creation, without being satisfied." This consuming passion has ultimately been the cause of Amélie's death; he hears, he tells Céluta, the voice of God calling him, "'René! René! what hast thou done with thy sister?' Am I then a Cain?" (*Natchez*, 3:146).

What he has done to Amélie is what he has all along feared doing to Céluta; he has constantly warned Céluta away from him because his flames would consume her as well. René's identification of Céluta with Amélie retroactively explains his previous behavior, and nonbehavior, towards Céluta. It is not that he does not have sexual desires for her and wishes for a normal life with her. "René," the narrator tells us, "had wished for a desert, a wife, and liberty; he possessed them all, and yet something poisoned this possession" (*Natchez*, 2:126). The "poison" is the psychic congruence of Céluta and Amélie. Céluta is an orphan (like René and Amélie) and her primary identity in the novel is as a sister—she is generally referred to as "the sister of Outougamiz." Toward René, however, her instincts and behavior are both erotic and maternal. In a critical scene, after Outougamiz has rescued an ill and famished René from captivity, Céluta laments that she has nothing with which to feed and revive him. "Oh that he had been my husband, and I had born him a pledge of love, he might then have drunk with the child at the fountain of life." To which the narrator adds, "Divine wish of the lover and the mother!" (*Natchez*, 2:107–8). As Barbéris says of René's relationship to Céluta, "René, desiring the breasts of Céluta as those of a woman, desires them in fact like those of the mother he didn't have and like those of the sister who could only be for him something other than a sister. Images which are distinct in a world where there is no lack here are blurred together: the maternal breast for the son, the woman's breast for the lover, non-sexualization of the sister for the brother and so the complete absence of possibility of desire by the brother for the sister's breasts."[45] The failure of René's desire is the reaction to an incestuous wish.

But René's incapacity to feel is not only the result of his fantasy (re)enactment of incestuous desire with Céluta. In this repetition of desire, René reveals something shockingly new about it. What lies behind René's guilt over Amélie's fate and his fears for Céluta if she too loves him is not simply awareness of the unhappy but unintended calamity that befalls the objects of his passion. As we have seen, there is a logical gap between René's desires and his sense of guilt; why should he be held responsible for Amélie's ill-fated desire for him and her subsequent death? The answer that emerges in the letter to Céluta is that his passion is something more than, other than, love. It is a consuming, and finally murderous, passion; he has *wished* Céluta's death, and through her identification with Amélie, he is confessing that he wished his sister's death as well.

> Finally, Céluta, if I should die, you may perhaps search after my life is extinct, for a union with a soul more perfect than mine. But think not even then to receive with impunity the caresses of any other man; think not that his feeble embraces can efface from your heart those of René. I have clasped

you to my bosom amid the desert, amid the howlings of the storm; *and when I had carried you safely over a torrent, I have wished to stab you to the heart in order to fix happiness there, and to punish myself for having given you that blessing.* . . .

Yes Céluta, if you love me, you will remain a widow; who could surround you with that flame which I always bear about me, even when I love not! Those solitudes which I rendered torrid would seem frozen to you by the side of another spouse. What would you seek among the woods and in the shade? There is no longer for you illusion, intoxication of the fancy, enthusiasm! In giving you all, or rather in having given you nothing, I have despoiled you of everything: an incurable wound was rankling in the depths of my heart. Don't think, Céluta, that a woman to whom I make avowals so cruel, for whom I have formed wishes so odious—*don't think that such a woman can ever forget the man who loved her with so extraordinary a love and so singular a hatred.* (*Natchez*, 3:150–51; italics added)

Here René reveals himself in his thoughts and fantasies to be what Ondouré is in his acts. Like Ondouré, René hates what he professes to love. Like Ondouré's, his love is partly a jealousy of potential rivals; he wants to kill Céluta in order that no one else can have her. But beyond that, his love for her is a displaced yet also defeated narcissism, self-inflation coupled with rageful self-negation. No possible rival, he tells her grandiloquently, could equal him. His passion is infinite; it contains everything, so that to be its object is to be fulfilled beyond the possibility of want and to have it withdrawn is to be empty beyond the possibility of satisfaction. Thus he even envies Céluta for the fulfillment his love would give her. He has withheld himself to prevent it ("in having given you nothing, I have despoiled you of everything"), and in the fantasy of taking her and giving her happiness, he has to kill her for having given her that blessing.

Of course, he speaks of killing Céluta as a self-punishment. This is not merely grotesque rationalization; he has openly admitted to hating her. But he hates himself as well, because he implicitly recognizes that if he needs her, his passion cannot be self-sufficient and infinite, as he describes. It goes out of itself to another and thus recognizes itself as emptiness, as lack. Yet this lack, which he experiences, is not seen by the object of his desire, the woman who loves him. She will feel fulfilled by it, even if her fulfillment is, as he recognizes, "illusion, intoxication of the fancy, enthusiasm." Hence his split consciousness, a compartmentalization of awareness that is never broken down. She will be fulfilled by a desire that he knows is need or lack, and he can clothe himself in her illusion. In her death he loses his own infinity.

Ondouré does what René cannot even fantasize directly. He kills the rival and forcibly takes the woman; René can only fantasize killing the woman and dying himself, but not confronting rivals. Ondouré is the realization of René's repressed action. One element, however, seems still missing in the twinship of the two. Ondouré is a public, political figure, a leader at the head of a revolution; René is a solitary. Within the framework of complementarity between them that the present analysis suggests, it would perhaps not be necessary that René himself be a political figure, though in fact as we have seen, he is given strong revolutionary sympathies in the novel. But the text provides one powerful, if indirect, clue to the political meaning of René's sexual passions themselves. It is the moment in which Mila, a young woman who has been in love with René and has jealously tried to displace Céluta, has decided to give him up because he is too remote and turns toward the simpler and more giving Outougamiz. "Alas!" says the narrator, "those simple and gracious loves, which ought to have glided on beneath a serene sky, were formed at a period of storms. *Unhappy you who begin life at the breaking out of revolutions*: you lack love, friendship, peace, those blessings which constitute the felicity of other men; you will not have time to love or be loved. In the age when all is illusion, the frightful truth will pursue you; at the age when all is hope, you will cherish none" (*Natchez*, 2:156–57; italics added).

There is unconscious irony in this passage. It seems to refer to the innocent love of Mila and Outougamiz, spoiled from the outside by political upheaval, but it refers to "loves" in the plural, and even Mila's love is hardly innocent, tainted as it is by rivalry and aggression. It is the emotions themselves that have been perverted by the Revolution. More accurately, the emotions at play in love are revolutionary emotions. The Revolution has created the sense of self René brings to love, transforming the desire for negative liberty and the innocence of nature into a desire for infinite selfhood that is baffled by its own internal nature. It is baffled first by being desire that arises as revolt. Such desire posits a preexisting absolute authority that must be defeated and replaced. It is baffled secondly by its demand for a totality that, precisely insofar as it remains the object of desire, is forever beyond, out of reach. And it is baffled finally by the awareness of murderous impulses toward the transcendent object that is imagined to incorporate that totality. To the extent that the totality becomes embodied in another person, he or she becomes an object of envious hate as well as desire. Desire itself thus threatens its own object with destruction. Chateaubriand clearly saw more deeply into the dangerous ambivalence of idealization than did Schlegel.

Just how much of all this Chateaubriand worked out while still in America is difficult to ascertain with certainty. Between the first (though extensive) notes for *The Natchez* put down in America and the draft of the novel written in London around 1797 (then left behind and not recovered or revised for publication until 1826), six years were to pass, years that included his loveless marriage shortly after his return to France, his disastrous few months as a soldier in the émigré army, his exile in England, and especially his aborted romance there with his young pupil Charlotte Ives. In the *Mémoires* Chateaubriand spoke of Charlotte as his first real love. But in his description of the episode with her, there is apparent a clear connection between his reaction and the psychology of René in *The Natchez*. He could not marry Charlotte because he was already married, a fact that he had guiltily concealed during the months he tutored her without any plan except a desire not to snuff out the growing feeling on both sides. "It was then," he wrote in the *Mémoires*, having broken the news of his marriage to Charlotte's distraught mother and left their home, "that embittered as I was by misfortunes, already a pilgrim from beyond the seas, having begun my solitary travels, it was then that I became obsessed by the mad ideas depicted in the mystery of René which turned me into the most tormented being on the face of the earth" (*Mémoires*, 1:465). This was written in 1822, after a surprise meeting with Charlotte Ives, now Mrs. Sutton, while Chateaubriand was ambassador to England. His feelings toward her in that meeting were very complicated, no longer the candor and innocence, he says, of first desire. "[I]f I had pressed in my arms, as a wife and a mother, her who was destined for me as a virgin and a bride, it would have been with a sort of rage, to blight, to fill with sorrow, to crush out of existence those twenty-five years which had been given to another after having been offered to me" (*Mémoires*, 1:464). The jealous rage Chateaubriand attributed to Ondouré and René he reported experiencing himself, but at a much later date, closer to the revision and publication of *The Natchez*.

For reasons such as these, there have been many critical discussions about the biographical originals of Céluta, and much doubt has been cast on the notion that the Floridian was her prototype. But the text of *The Natchez* contains strong suggestions that whatever later experiences contributed to the evolution of the novel and its figures (aside from the Christianization that is a post-1797 development and must be examined in its own right later), Chateaubriand himself associated the climactic, horrifying revelation about the true nature of his desires with the emotions excited by the idyll with the two Floridians. Two critical junctures in the novel link *The Natchez* to the narration of the episode with the Floridians in the *Mémoires*. The first is the description of René's effort to find happiness in his marriage with Céluta. "He strove to realize his old chimeras: what woman was more beautiful than Céluta? He conducted her into the recesses of the forests, from solitude to solitude. But when he had pressed his young spouse to his bosom amidst precipices, when he had lost himself with her in the region of the clouds, he did not find the pleasures of which he dreamt" (*Natchez*, 2:126–27). The "old chimeras" are a reference to Chateaubriand's fantasy, the sylphide; they are strongly reminiscent of his attempt to console himself with her image after the encounter with the Floridians. They, like Céluta for the fictional René, were François-René's first living embodiments of his imaginary lover, his first romantic infatuation in life under the aegis of his wilderness liberation. The novel does reverse the situation described in the autobiography; in the novel, the real woman does not live up to the fantasy, whereas in the memoirs the fantasy does not measure up to the reality of the young women. The reversal, however, does not negate the significance of the parallel. In both works a comparison between fantasy and reality is being made. The novel refers the fantasy ideal back to René's sister Amélie, but since Céluta is her substitute, the psychological problem for René is that Céluta is too real, too much his sister; the failure of desire for her is actually a repression of desire. This repression is necessary because in the novel René actually marries Céluta, whereas in Chateaubriand's experience with the young Indian women, he only fantasized marriage, and the physical play with them was displaced far enough from sexuality to be admissible. The novel, then, is really the more complete development of the dangerous incestuous desire for the fantasy of the Floridians. As if to confirm this, Chateaubriand ended René's letter to Céluta with almost the same reflections on ennui that form the conclusion to the episode of the young Indian women in the *Mémoires.* "I am weary of life; ennui has always preyed upon me; what interests other men doesn't touch me. Shepherd or king, what should I have done with either crook or crown? . . . In Europe and America, both society and nature have fatigued me" (*Natchez,* 3:151–52). In the context of the novel, however, much more is disclosed about the "weariness of life" than in the *Mémoires* episode of the Floridians; it is a recoil not only from disappointed desires but, more significantly, from desire itself. And the recoil from desire is at the same time a retreat from the ideal of political liberation, for desire and liberation as Chateaubriand then conceived them were one. The sexual and the political were two sides of the same coin; both represented a new ethos of individuality under the aegis of revolution and both encompassed the aggrandizement of the self at the expense of others.

IV) Transition: Religion and Selfhood

Nothing could better demonstrate the interrelatedness of the erotic and the political for Chateaubriand than the relationship between *The Natchez* and the *Essai sur les révolutions.* Chateaubriand began the latter in 1794, shortly after his arrival in London as an émigré. The two works were intertwined textually and temporally. Chateaubriand drew on the thousands of folio pages of *The Natchez* already in existence for his nature descriptions in the *Essai*, and he returned to *The Natchez* immediately after the publication of the *Essai*. The external link is the emblem of the internal. The *Essai* is the public side of the lessons Chateaubriand had learned by observation during the French Revolution and in his own body and psyche in America; it constitutes the political moral of René's apprenticeship to the wilderness. And just as the political appears in the narrative of individuals not only as subtext but as text, the personal appears explicitly in the *Essai*, a work intended as a historical and theoretical contribution to contemporary thinking about the French Revolution. "[I]f the 'I' appears here often, it is because this work was first undertaken for myself and myself alone," Chateaubriand wrote when he republished the work in 1826; "the apparent disorder which reigns in these pages [reveals] the whole interior of a man" (*Essai*, 1:51–52).

"Who am I?" Chateaubriand began the *Essai* (1:55), meaning to present his credentials for the ensuing work of political theory, credentials that he claims consist of his nonpartisanship in a partisan age. It was a question he may well have asked, was implicitly asking, on other grounds. All his previous gods (except, perhaps, the god of writing) had failed him. Among other things, the essay is a farewell to politics, premature, as it turned out, of course, but sincere at the time. Between the monarchy he had rejected and the republicanism and natural life that had failed him, there was no way to turn. He evoked the state of nature throughout and especially at the end of the work, but it was now an act of nostalgia. Chateaubriand recognized that he was debarred from that Eden. If the impossibility of politics had led him to believe that no government is better than even government by the people, he knew that he himself, at least, was unfit for the primitive state.

Insofar as the elegiac description of a "Night with the Savages of America," the last chapter of the *Essai*, can be said to offer reasons for this exclusion, two emerge. The first is Chateaubriand's inescapable sense of identification with the European civilization that had despoiled the native population. He remembered lying awake in a camp not far from Niagara Falls, contemplating a young Indian asleep amidst the party of European travelers. He was moved to tears by the young man's innocent trust: "Europeans, what a lesson for us! These same Savages whom we have pursued with steel and flame; to whom our avarice has left not even a spadeful of earth to cover their corpses, in this whole universe, once their vast patrimony; these same Savages, receiving their enemy under their hospitable roofs, sharing with him their miserable meal, their innocent bed, and sleeping alongside him the deep sleep of the just! Those virtues are as far above our conventional virtues, as the soul of this man of nature is above that of the mass of society" (*Essai*, 2:310).

But why then could Chateaubriand not have joined the "savages," as in the same chapter he says other Europeans have done? A passage further on suggests that mere change of location can't change his fundamental nature. Contemplating the endless, untouched landscape, his soul for a moment traverses its varied contours and merges with its immensities only to be brought back to uncomfortable consciousness: "These delights [*jouissances*] are too poignant; such is our weakness that exquisite pleasures become griefs, as if nature is afraid that we will forget that we are men. Absorbed in my existence, or rather extended completely outside myself, having neither feeling nor distinct thought but an ineffable something which resembled that mental happiness which it is claimed we will enjoy in the other life, I was suddenly recalled to this one. I felt bad, and I saw that it was necessary to bring things to an end" (*Essai*, 2:313). It is consciousness of self, the self whose claims Chateaubriand had learned in America, the self that did not permit the self-effacement of dissolution in nature, that brings him out of revery. The experience described in this last chapter explains the shape and purpose of the whole *Essai*, which doubles back on Chateaubriand's experience. He had not had to account before now, even to himself, for the failure of the French Revolution, because he had not fully identified with it; the better Eden in America had still lain before him. Thrust from it by the sins of individuality, as both corrupt European and as importunate ego—he did not explore the relationship between the historical and the universal dimension of this feeling—Chateaubriand could only go back to deal with the civilization he knew and was a part of. Now he felt a need to account for the failure of France and the Revolution, which were his failures.

Of monarchy there is not even a serious question in the *Essai*; it is the form of polity that precedes and follows republics, both the tyranny that makes republics desirable and desired and the unhappy consequence of their inevitable degeneration. The decision to fight in the army of the princes for the restoration of Louis XVI had not made him a monarchist. "[M]y zeal [to join the émigrés] exceeded my faith," he wrote in the *Mémoires*. "I felt that the emigration was a stupidity and a madness. . . . My distaste for absolute monarchy left me with no illusions concerning the step I was taking" (*Mémoires*, 1:382). In fact, he took each step in the direction of joining the émigrés reluctantly and ambivalently, refusing to assume responsibility for it. Without money for the venture, he allowed his family to arrange a marriage with a young girl he had never met who was supposed to have a large inheritance. "My family," he wrote in a witty double irony even more ironic than he knew, "married me in order to procure me the means of going to get killed in support of a cause which I did not love" (*Mémoires*, 1:363). Forced to borrow money when he learned that his wife's estate was virtually valueless, he lost almost the whole sum in an impulsive gambling binge—his first—on the way home from the lender and left the rest in his wallet in the carriage. He consulted his mentor Malesherbes on the morality of turning to the enemies of one's country in order to save it and rejected the strong and reasoned support for emigration that he got. In the end, despite all his contrivances, he managed to leave France and join the aristocratic émigrés, for whose style of existence he had expressed nothing but contempt. He conducted himself bravely enough, if without special distinction, and was wounded severely enough to satisfy honor and almost lose his life. He had satisfied his inner need to defend the king without becoming his supporter.

In a footnote from 1826, Chateaubriand remarked of his attitudes toward politics in the original 1797 edition of the *Essai*, "The author shows himself here to be a royalist out of despair at not being able to be a republican, judging the republic impossible" (*Essai*, 2:52). Even this explicit acknowledgment of his grudging monarchism of 1797 understates his antipathy to the ancien régime at that time. Chateaubriand wrote in 1797 as a bitterly disappointed and disillusioned republican. "Just because the Jacobins committed crimes," he said, rather boldly for an émigré, "does not stop me from believing that a republic is the best of all governments when a people has *moeurs* and the worst of all when they are corrupt" (*Essai*, 2:222). The position echoes Montesquieu, with the difference at this point—Chateaubriand was, as we will see, not consistent—that he saw civic virtue as being possible at any time in the history of civilization, not just in its early phase. The problem with republicanism in the French Revolution was that the revolutionaries tried to create a republic precisely during a time of corruption. Significantly, Chateaubriand identified "corruption" not with commerce and luxury but with a concern for political liberty. The difference between ancient and modern republicanism was for him in the ideas of the intellectuals who furnished each form with its ideological foundation. The ancient philosophers were concerned above all with morals, their modern degenerate counterparts, the philosophes, with politics. The former said, "Be virtuous, then you will be free," while the latter said, "Be free, then you will be virtuous" (*Essai*, 1:183). It was this reversal of priorities that caused the Revolution to be so destructive. Without public virtue and the readiness to subordinate self-interest to the good of the whole, modern freedom was not benign anarchy but something much worse. "I acknowledge that I believe in theory in the principle of the sovereignty of the people, but I also add that if it is put into practice rigorously, it would be much better for the human race to revert to the savage state and flee completely naked into the woods" (*Essai*, 2:65). Before we can understand in more detail what this modern freedom was that Chateaubriand so feared, however, we must examine an apparently inconsistent strand in his argument.

From the beginning, Chateaubriand's history of republicanism argued that corruption was not exclusively a feature of modern republics but part of the life cycle of all republics, including those of antiquity. The Athenian republic, unlike that of modern France, was founded on virtue but that did not ultimately prevent its corruption. In a sense, corruption was the inevitable result of republican virtue itself. The essential principle of popular government, Chateaubriand asserted, is ambition. Freed from internal tyranny, Athens was led to try to enslave the rest of the world, and it was precisely the civic virtue, patriotism, self-sacrifice, military valor, and courage of the Greeks that made them successful in conquest. The imperialist successes of republics, however, contained the seeds of their own destruction. The wealth accumulated through plunder of conquered peoples led to demagoguery, factions, and division within the city; the way was prepared for the loss of Greek liberties to Philip of Macedonia and Alexander the Great.

By this point the argument seems no longer historical but a priori. Chateaubriand supported his political generalizations about the development of republics with generalizations about human nature. "The thirst for liberty and that for tyranny have been mixed together in the heart of man by the hand of nature: independence for oneself alone, slavery for all the others, is the motto of the human species" (*Essai*, 1:109). Thirty years later, Chateaubriand recognized the bleaker moral hidden within the conscious pessimism of the original enterprise. His plan, he said, had been to prove that a republic could not be established in contemporary France because its *moeurs* were not innocent enough. But, he recognized, he had made of that observation a universal instead of a historical principle. In advanced civilizations of the past, he had argued, men of enlightenment could not prevent periods of corruption, an assertion that made it seem impossible for even an ancient civilized people to sustain a republic. It seemed to follow—the Chateaubriand of 1826 professed himself horrified by the logical conclusion of 1797—that civilization as such condemned men to perpetual slavery (*Essai*, 1:317).

Chateaubriand believed that it was his study of ancient republics that had led him to this conclusion. In fact, however, the methodology of his *Essai* undercut any such possibility. The comparative focus and the constant use of analogies to the present both point to Chateaubriand's effort to abstract a model of republicanism from contemporary events and project it backwards. All the republics of the past turned out to be forerunners of the present because they were seen in the light of the present. As a comparative study, then, the *Essai* is of little value. On the other hand, it says a great deal about Chateaubriand's views of the causes of corruption in eighteenth-century France. He held the philosophes and the culture of the eighteenth century crucially responsible for the creation of conditions that guaranteed the Revolution's failure. But he too was a philosophe and part of the culture. To that extent, his portrait of the philosophes is a self-portrait.

The main fault of the philosophes was the historical abstractness of their thought, which failed to address itself to the realities of contemporary France. "A distinctive characteristic of our revolution is that one must include speculative thought and abstract doctrines as playing a huge role among its causes. It was partly a product of men of letters who, more inhabitants of Rome and Athens than their own country, tried to restore ancient *moeurs* to Europe" (*Essai*, 1:127). The attack on abstract ideas smacks of Burke, whose influence on an émigré in England is not surprising, but one is reminded of Chateaubriand's own quest for Cato in America. "As for me I too wanted to spend my days under a democracy such as I had too often dreamed of as the most sublime of governments in theory; I also lived as a citizen of Italy and Greece" (*Essai*, 2:47). But what made this anachronistic quest so harmful in its consequences was the state of the society in which it was attempted. And here Chateaubriand offered a series of political and social descriptions, some of which were the stock of eighteenth century critics, but the most original of which have questionable empirical value and make little sense as social history; their ultimate origins are autobiographical.

During the eighteenth century, according to Chateaubriand, a weak court was easily deceived by incapable or evil ministers, corrupted, whether their social origins were aristocratic or plebeian, by the combination of power and wealth. Intrigue and competition produced constant change in the governing personnel and chronic inconsistency of policy, except for the consistent policy of sucking the blood of the poor. In the meantime, moral disorder was spreading among the populace. The numbers of bachelors increased, and "These men, isolated and consequently egoists, tried to fill the emptiness of their lives by troubling the families of others." Selfishness was on the rise even among those who were married. Couples had fewer children: "A father and a mother did not want to sacrifice the comfort of life to the education of a large family, and this narcissistic self-love [amour de soi] was covered over with the pretences of philosophy. Why produce unhappy people? said some; why produce beggars, said others" (*Essai*, 2:44). "The man who no longer found his happiness in the union of a family . . . got used to being happy independently of others. Excluded from the bosom of nature by the *moeurs* of his century, he enclosed himself within a hard egotism which sullied virtue to its roots." The philosophy of the century deprived such men of religious hopes for a better life in the hereafter. "In this situation, finding himself alone in the middle of the universe, not having anything to consume except an empty and solitary heart . . . should one be surprised that the Frenchman was ready to embrace the first phantom which showed him a new world?" (*Essai*, 2:45). This analysis, Chateaubriand asserted, was not refuted by the counter-claims that France was populous and flourishing in the eighteenth century. Those who were content and virtuous lived in the countryside, and it was not the peasants who had made the Revolution. As for the well-to-do of the city, their smiles covered an inner anxiety, discontent, and malaise that were not the right conditions for a revolution. Yet it was precisely at this moment that a group of men arose to sound the return of Sparta and Athens (*Essai*, 2:46).

Aside from the rather impressionistic nature of the social analysis, there seems to be a gap in the logic of Chateaubriand's argument. Why should the goal of restoring civic virtue have foundered on selfishness when its primary purpose would seem to have been to counter selfishness with the cause of the general good? The answer, implicit in the categories of his analysis, is that in the context of modernity, the very goals of republicanism, whatever its official rhetoric, turned into something else. Modern society had so transformed men that they were incapable of virtue, or even the independence that is its counterpart and precondition.

> [I]t is in vain that we claim to be politically free. Independence, individual independence, that is the internal cry that pursues us. Let us listen to the voice of conscience. What does it tell us, according to nature? "Be free." According to society? "Rule." Whoever denies it lies. Civil [i.e., political] liberty is only a dream, a factitious sentiment which we do not really feel. . . . Until we return to the life of the savage, we depend always on other men. And what does it then matter whether we are devoured by a court, a directory, or an assembly of the people? . . . Every government is an evil . . . but let us not conclude from this that it is necessary to break it. Since it is our lot only to be slaves, let us bear our chains without complaint" (*Essai*, 2:49–50).

"This is a kind of black orgy of a wounded heart," Chateaubriand wrote of these words in 1826 (*Essai*, 2:51). By what, however, had it been wounded? It is possible to inscribe Chateaubriand's words, unique as they may be in their passion and eloquence, in the tradition of the republican and Rousseauist indictment of commercial society, so central, we have seen, in *The Natchez*. All the code words—corruption, avarice, luxury—are there, though with few specifics. Barbéris indeed insists that the essence of Chateaubriand's diagnosis of blockage and hopelessness in the *Essai* is historical and social, in sharp contrast, for example, with his later diagnosis of René's ennui, which is purely personal. He underlines three aspects of Chateaubriand's analysis of developments in France in the eighteenth century—the birth of the philosophe sect, the upheaval created by John Law's abortive effort to create a national bank, and the role of the press. "The spirit of infinite criticism, the destructive power of speculation and the placing of a commercial press in the service of particular interests are presented as the very signs of the modern world. . . . It is not the Revolution as single event, as a brutal, contingent historical act that destroyed the poetry of the ancestral village . . . the original community. It is civil [bourgeois] society. From 1725 on one could present the destruction of all these things as the result . . . of the action of the bourgeoisie and the bourgeoisified, their philosophy and their action."[46] In fact, however, Chateaubriand's most passionate language is not the language of social and economic analysis, nor is it even the language of morals, despite the consistent recurrence of the idea of *moeurs*. It is a psychological language to which, when he is generalizing, he attempts to give a social context, a language that becomes less theorized, more supple, more expressive, when he is speaking of himself. It is true that Chateaubriand was not alone at the time in criticizing bachelors who trouble the happiness of others; writers on the nobility such as Chérin wrote about this problem even before the Revolution. But this issue had powerful personal significance for Chateaubriand and at least a double reference in his life. It points first of all to the brief period of Chateaubriand's "libertinism" during his residence in Paris just before the Revolution, when, along with his political free-thinking, he adopted a pose of sexual liberation as well. There is a revealing letter to a friend at that time that not only affects the insouciance of a jaded roué but comes as close as Chateaubriand ever came to expressing directly sexual interest in his sister. His friend had a mistress but was courting Lucile: "With two or three beings such as you and a mistress (because that is a necessary evil) a country retreat some distance from Paris or even in Brittany, we could have a good time for a few days. . . . Handle her [Lucile] gently. If you seduce her, my dear Châtenet, remember that she is a virgin."[47] The passage in the *Essai* thus connects his incestuous thoughts with the origins of rebellion/revolution. But the reference to those who trouble the happiness of others is also to the duplication of this situation with the Floridians in America, when the political dimension of his impulses had not only become more explicit but magnified by the infinite content that the wilderness experience had given to his definition of freedom.

This is not to say that Chateaubriand's own sentiments and experiences were without cause or that the cause was purely psychological. Chateaubriand was working with the conceptual tools furnished by eighteenth-century theory to understand himself. But those tools were not adequate to the new reality Chateaubriand was struggling with, the reality, ultimately, of the meaning of his own revolutionary desires. They had revealed to him that, at least within the confines of civilization, the desire to be radically free turns into the desire to expand infinitely and dominate the whole of being. The purity of mere negative liberation was a chimera. The soul did not merely wish to be left alone in solitude. The ideal savage, Chateaubriand wrote, wanted freedom from dependence, wanted to be nothing but himself, not to have to dissimulate, hide his feelings, flatter, work for mercenary ends (*Essai*, 2:303). European man, however, had learned another side of freedom; independence meant detachment from limits—familial, political, divine—and the next step was for the self to fill the space of possibility left when all limitations were seen as illegitimate. In the moment of consciousness, that step felt like ecstasy, an explosion of the kind that drove Chateaubriand from tree to tree in the American forests shouting the absence of restraints, taking untold liberties of behavior, feeling godlike in his sense of possibility. Lived in relation to others, that same consciousness revealed the emptiness of the mere sense of infinite possibility that grudged what others have that one did not possess—most especially it grudged the woman who incarnated totality—revealed through the totality of the drive directed toward her—the very totality she embodied. It was all this, and more, that Chateaubriand had learned about his own political impulse, and hence about the true meaning of revolutionary freedom.

> So! unhappy, we torment ourselves to achieve a perfect government, and we are flawed; a good one, and we are wicked. We get agitated today over a meaningless system, and we won't even be here tomorrow. . . . *Is it some indeterminate instinct, an internal void that we do not know how to fill, that torments us? I have felt it too, this vague thirst for something. It has accompanied me in the mute solitudes of America and in the turbulent cities of Europe.* (*Essai*, 2:48; italics added)

The *vague des passions* makes its first appearance here in the *Essai*, and quite explicitly in connection with the French Revolution, with the desire for a new polity. But that desire, Chateaubriand claimed, had not known itself for what it really was in the Revolution. It was not primarily concerned with the creation of a virtuous political structure, but with creating personal perfection, with filling an infinite void in the self, with satisfying the indeterminate individual will. What Chateaubriand had learned was that it was both impossible and dangerous to try to satisfy this desire in politics. The "indeterminate instinct" led to tyranny and violence in politics as it did in love, not only because it brooked no competition, was not interested in a tolerant pluralism that worked toward a compromise of interests, but because the polity represented the totality one wished both to create and to be embraced by. Freedom, the very desire to create, if one was the sole creator, was a "totalitarian," in the sense of totalizing, impulse. It made no difference, it was perhaps all the worse, when what one was trying to create was the republic of virtue, the general good. Chateaubriand wrote of the Jacobins in 1797, "These spirits rarefied by the fire of republican enthusiasm, and so to speak, reduced by their purifying gaze to the quintessence of crime, displayed simultaneously an energy the likes of which had never existed before and crimes which could hardly be equalled by all the previous ones of history put together" (*Essai*, 1:119). It was the very sincerity of their absolute passion that made the Jacobins so destructive. But unlike both contemporary and later interpretations of Jacobinism as old religious fanaticism or new ideological totalitarianism, Chateaubriand understood its links not only with ancient pagan republicanism but with modern individual freedom.

The net result of this realization, however, was not only political bankruptcy but despair about the possibility of any future activity. Even writing was implicated. Chateaubriand's identity as a writer was inextricably interwoven with politics, not specifically in terms of doctrine but as a way of being, as liberation, as advocacy, as self-presentation and self-assertion. In the wake of the loss of politics, there was little if anything left: "Man, if it is your destiny to bear with you everywhere a heart undermined by an unknown desire, if that is your illness, you have one resource left. Let the sciences, those daughters of heaven, come to fill that fatal void which sooner or later will lead you to your doom. . . . [S]eek in Newton's footsteps, the hidden laws which magnificently conduct these globes of fire across the celestial blue, or, if the Divinity touches your soul, meditate in adoring him in that incomprehensible Being who fills these spaces without limits with his immensity" (*Essai*, 2:48–49). In the light of Chateaubriand's imminent religious conversion, these words might seem like an anticipation. He himself argued as much in the *Mémoires*. "The *Essai*," he wrote, "was not an impious book, but a book of doubt, of sorrow. Through the darkness of that book glides a ray of the Christian light that shone upon my cradle. It needed no great effort to return from the skepticism of the *Essai* to the certainty of the *Génie du Christianisme*" (*Mémoires*, 1:492). This is more than misleading. The religious note sounded in the previous passage was not new to Chateaubriand. He had always been a believer, in the emotional mode of Rousseau's Savoyard Vicar, a mode that did not preclude his sense of himself, at the height of his liberationist fervor, as the "heir presumptive of heaven." It was a very long step, however, from this kind of faith to the Catholic church, a step that the ferocious criticism of the clergy in the *Essai* seemed to make highly unlikely. The last part of the *Essai* is a Voltairean diatribe against the *infâme*. Some form of religion might be a useful illusion, Chateaubriand conceded, but Christianity was almost wholly deleterious to freedom. Its priests were "vampires who suck your money, your blood, even your very thought . . . the rearguard of tyranny [who] render slavery legitimate and holy in the eyes of the people" (*Essai*, 2:260, 263); as a faith, it had long been on the decline and would soon fall into (well-deserved) "absolute discredit" (*Essai*, 2:283).

But aside from the fact that the sentiment in the passage cited above is not a harbinger of religious conversion, it is clearly a counsel of despair. It represents rhetoric in the negative sense of that term; Chateaubriand was writing here for the sake of writing. The attitude of passive appreciation of the objective world, whether as scientist or worshipper, was antithetical to the self Chateaubriand had created through his revolutionary and American experiences. If the object of science and contemplation satisfied the quest for the infinite, the purely mimetic or reproductive aspect of the activities did not satisfy the need for creative freedom, control, fashioning. When Chateaubriand turned to Catholicism, it was not in the spirit of this passage.

Chateaubriand had reached a dead end with the *Essai*. It is impossible to imagine his being able to complete and publish *Atala* or *The Natchez* in the frame of mind it represented. He had not ceased to "believe" in the noble savage, but now only as an ideal outside history, or at any rate, outside "civilization" to which he as a European was doomed. It made no sense to proselytize on behalf of such an ideal when it was no longer even a possible yardstick by which to measure corruption. And simply to describe lost or impossible Edens as a passive observer of nature was inconsistent with his notion of freedom.

It is against this background that Chateaubriand's account of his "conversion" to Catholicism has to be understood. Few of his readers have wanted to credit his story fully. It is too simple, too abrupt, too pious, too "literary," too much in keeping with the kind of religious self he wanted to represent after his conversion. As Charles Porter has put it, "There is simply not enough evidence to enable us to understand how the cynical, not so young author of the chapter in the *Essai sur les révolutions* titled 'Quelle sera la réligion qui remplaçera le Christianisme' . . . came in four years or less to write the *Genius of Christianity*. The claims of crassest opportunism made by his detractors are not wholly credible; neither is the instant conversion implied by the 'j'ai pleut et j'ai cru' [of his account]."[48] Indeed, as Chateaubriand related his conversion in the *Mémoires*, there are omissions serious enough to warrant charges not only of fictionalization but of outright falsification. Yet if one attends closely to his words, and if they are understood in the full density of the context created by his history, the story seems not only just but almost necessary—necessary in the sense of a continuity of theme in the face of radically changed circumstances.

On July 1, 1798, Chateaubriand received a letter from his sister Julie announcing the death of his mother. The letter blamed him for the sadness his "errors had cost her [his mother] in her last years and implored him to give up writing" (*Mémoires*, 1:491). As Chateaubriand summarized the impact of the letter, an impact intensified by the fact that Julie had (he said) died by the time the letter reached him, "These two voices from the tomb, that death which acted as death's interpreter impressed me. I became a Christian. I did not yield, I admit, to great supernatural enlightenment: my conviction came from the heart; I wept and I believed" (*Mémoires*, 1:492).

This account seems to give the impression that Chateaubriand first learned of his mother's death from this letter. In fact, however, he had learned of it on May 31, shortly after it had occurred, from his uncle (*Mémoires*, 1:490; editor's footnote). Yet Chateaubriand was not deliberately misleading here. His first lines after citing the letter are "Ah, why did I not follow my sister's advice! Why did I continue to write?" The "news" that the letter had brought him was not of his mother's death but of his culpability—specifically the culpability of his writing. "The idea that I had poisoned the old age of the woman who bore me in the womb filled me with despair; I flung copies of the *Essai* into the fire with horror, as the instrument of my crime." Language had always been Chateaubriand's crime. It was the mode of his rebellion against his father; it was the instrument of the seduction of his sister. In the pages of the unpublished *Natchez*, he had raped and stabbed Céluta, and in his first important publication, he had uttered rebellious impieties that had wounded his mother. The hurt to her was the culmination of a series of hurts he had inflicted, mostly, but not only, in imagination, on her surrogates in the preceding years. It seems to have brought home the full implications of his idea of freedom. The paradox of his crime and despair was that it suggested the means of atonement and reparation. "I did not recover from my distress until the thought occurred to me of expiating my first work by means of a religious work: this was the origin of *Le Génie du christianisme*" (*Mémoires*, 1:491).

It was indeed a stroke of genius. The wound that had been created by writing would be healed through writing in the cause of religion. He would surrender to the higher power, as he had when he abandoned revolution for the king's cause in 1791. But, as we have seen at the beginning of this chapter, his surrender was also a conquest. Chateaubriand accepted religion only by reinterpreting it, making of it an expression in displaced form of the aspirations of his revolutionary desires. The same combination of surrender and self-assertion would mark his future politics and his idea of writing as well. It would be found in the peculiar blend of arrogant independence and submission to authority that would enable him to serve, then defy, Napoleon, and to oscillate after 1814 between a conservative monarchism that at times made him seem more royalist than the king and a liberal insistence on constitutional hedges and limits to royal power that could put him in direct opposition to his monarch.[49] These contradictions would also be the source of his master-work, the main writing project of the second half of his life, the self-celebration of his memoirs; while continually mourning the futility and ennui of human life in the face of the eternity of God, they expressed in their very title as well as in their detail the hope that from beyond the grave he would be remembered by posterity and would thus sustain the eternal value of his self.

The combination of surrender and assertion in politics is already found in the apparently apolitical Christian works that preceded Chateaubriand's active involvement in government and political theorizing. *Atala* is a work of Christian *political* apologetics that subverts its political message through both its love story and the structure of its narrative. The titles Chateaubriand chose for the first two subsections of the main body of the story, "The Hunters" and "The Tillers," situate the love tragedy within a socioeconomic and religiopolitical argument that recapitulates Chateaubriand's own ideological history. The story begins as an apparent defense of the superiority of the state of nature over that of civilization. The opening "Prologue" portrays with mythic exoticism the Edenic perfection, the "grace joined with splendor" (*Atala/René*, 17) that is untouched nature. Chactas meets Atala when he escapes from the "distasteful" life of the Spanish city of Saint Augustine, where he has been held prisoner, to the freedom of his native forests. But the superiority of Indian life in the wild is provisional, relative to the corruption of the European city. The virtues of Christianity are pitched against those of the state of nature not only in the contrast between the character of the Christianized Atala and her "savage" fellow tribesmen, but above all in the contrast between the Christian communist agrarian society founded and guided by Father Aubry ("The Tillers") and the native Indian society ("The Hunters") to which Chactas returns and falls victim. The naturalness of primitive society is also its defect. Unconstrained by the artificial inequalities of "civilized" private property and the authoritarian hierarchies they produce, primitive society is nonetheless subject to the vagaries of nature and the uncertain bounties of the hunt. Natural emotions allow the most exquisitely delicate sensibilities, reflected in the customs, rituals, and forms of expression surrounding birth, courtship, and death, but they also include extreme passions that sanction the barbarisms of war and take pleasure in torturing enemies. Into the "fierce customs" and "pitiful way of life" of the nomadic tribes, Father Aubry has introduced the tempering message of Christian love and just enough of the basic arts of life to create economic stability and security without ruining simplicity of manners. In the exclusively agrarian society he has helped fashion, land is divided, so that individuals take responsibility for their own production, but harvests are placed in community granaries and distributed equally by four elders. Father Aubry's own role is formally that of teacher and preacher, not lawgiver, but his charismatic presence makes him a revered authority with powers greater than those of even the most absolute of rulers. His authority stems from his faith in a transcendent God, a faith that has given him the wisdom to understand the human heart and the humility of knowing that his wisdom does not come from himself. The society combines radical republicanism with a voluntary theocratic monarchy, complete equality with the most extreme, if benevolent, paternalism. Father Aubry is the rediscovered good father who loves his children, and loves them equally, who attends to their needs, but in a noncoercive way that leaves them feeling completely free. It is a utopia that looks back to the idyll of a childhood that never was, a childhood that Chateaubriand had longed for; but it is also a revised vision of an ideal polity in the retrospect of a disastrously failed revolution whose ideals of equality Chateaubriand could never give up, even though he believed the revolutionaries' grandiosely egotistical aspirations had been the cause of their failure.

"How joyous my life had been could I have settled with Atala in a hut by those shores," Chactas exclaims on describing this social paradise (56). It is too late for the two of them, however. The train of events leading to tragedy had begun long before they arrived, when Atala's mother consecrated her daughter to virginity. But while Atala's vow of chastity gives Father Aubry the opportunity to rail at ill-informed and superstitious versions of religion, which does not in fact demand the sacrifice of sexual passion, her vow is something of a red herring, a decoy. *Atala* is not a melodrama whose tragedy depends on a potentially avoidable misunderstanding of the requirements of faith. The real barrier between Atala and Chactas, we have seen, is incest. *Atala* does not yet have the courage of *René*. The sibling relationship is much attenuated; the Spaniard Lopez who informally "adopted" Chactas in St. Augustine is Atala's natural father, and the relationship seems to be a loose plot element with no apparent consequence. But unlike the vow of chastity, the incestuous relationship is not fortuitous. In making Atala and Chactas brother and sister, Chateaubriand made incestuous love the natural erotic form of the *vague des passions*. It is when the pair discover that they are related—appropriately enough, in the wild, in the midst of a storm—that their sexual passion reaches its peak and pushes them toward consummation: "This fraternal affection which had come upon us, joining its love to our own love, proved too powerful for our hearts" (46). They are saved from themselves by the violence of the storm, which not only mirrors the force of their natural passion but their guilt, represented in the lightning bolt that splits the tree they are under and sends them fleeing; and they are saved from the storm by the appearance of Father Aubry, who is on the lookout for those in danger.

It is also Father Aubry who reveals the deep structure of incestuous desire. Incestuous love is not only developmentally and psychologically "natural" because of the simple proximity of brother and sister in the family. By adding to the natural sexual desire between male and female the purity of selfless love that binds a brother and sister, the particular bond that exists between two who are sexual opposites but in virtue of common parentage alter egos, incest creates the illusion of the possible fulfillment of the desire for infinity, the complete self-containment in fusion with the selfother that would make the self, as Father Aubry says, equal to God. (For the male, especially given the role Lucile played biographically for Chateaubriand, the image of the omnipotent nurturing mother in the sister could only make this fantasy more plausible.) Father Aubry calls Atala's immoderate desire "unnatural," though not culpable in the eyes of God, because it is an error of the mind rather than a vice of the heart (61). What Father Aubry is conceding is that the ultimate goal of incestuous desire *is* natural; it is only wrong because it is directed at the wrong object, since no mortal, not even one's ideal other half, can supply what the self needs to gratify it. The desire can only be realized in heaven, that is, in the sphere of the beyond, the unreal. In this sense, Christianity, which can appear permissive in relation to the mistaken asceticism of the vow of Atala's mother, does in fact aim at subduing the passions on earth, though with the promise of eternal fulfillment later.

But in arguing the insufficiency of earthly objects, Father Aubry is himself undermining the viability of the earthly Christian paradise he has created with his ideal society. That society can at best be a remedy for the selfish passions artificially created by the destructive social arrangements of modern commercial societies; it cannot contain the "natural" passions. The human heart is not satisfied with the moderate happiness of limited achievement and peaceful fraternity. That the tragedy of desire unfolds in the story *after* the brief glimpse of Father Aubry's utopian community is the expression in narrative structure of this fatal truth of the *vague des passions*. The infinite demands of desire undermine any possibility of earthly sociopolitical satisfaction or containment.

This might seem not just a paradoxical but a dubious conclusion in the light of Chateaubriand's deep involvment in the political theory and the actual politics of the Restoration, an involvement that reached its high point when he became foreign minister of France in 1822. Politics were important to him partly because they were a sphere of power and partly because they were necessary for the regulation of the political passions that had almost destroyed France in the process of bringing her liberty. Chateaubriand tried to fashion a form of politics that would preserve liberty while serving as a bulwark against the injection of the *vague des passions* into public life, which, as we have seen, he identified with the politics of Jacobinism. This is the meaning of the often-quoted political formula he offered in his most important political pamphlet, *The Monarchy According to the Charter* of 1816: "Religion, the basis of a new structure, the Charter, and the virtuous people [*les honnêtes gens*], *the political goals [choses] of the revolution and not the political men of the revolution*; that is my whole system" (italics added).[50] The most plausible interpretation of Chateaubriand's political twists and turns is that he was trying to convert the traditional ruling elites into protectors of the legacy of the Revolution, in the actual event an unrealistic hope but the only way he could see to combine liberty with moderation and order.[51] His monarchism, even his political elitism, were in largest part concessions to reality, not ideals in themselves: "A gentleman and a writer, I have been a Bourbonist out of a sense of honor, a royalist by reason, and a republican by taste."[52] Politics for Chateaubriand after the Revolution was primarily a realm of defense, not a realm of full self-realization. While it offered real power in the world, identity was not to be found there, both because absolute power was precisely the danger to be avoided and because it was not to be had in the world in any case.

Self-fulfillment is presumably reserved for the sphere of religion. But as we have seen, it is not only Christian *society* that proves inadequate in *Atala*. The promise of Christian faith for the fulfillment of desires in the afterlife is not persuasive enough to make Chactas convert. As if to underline his own inconsistency, Chactas himself expresses surprise that he is not yet a Christian and criticizes the "petty motives of politics and patriotism" that have kept him in the error of his fathers (*Atala/René*, 70). These excuses may seem like rationalizations when weighed against the supposedly transformative emotional and spiritual power of the events surrounding Atala's death that have shaken him out of his former being, but they point to a significant rebellion. What Chactas has been unable to give up for the sake of Christianity is power in the world, specifically his role as sachem of his own tribe and his standing among all the Indians as "patriarch of the wilderness." And though René, unlike Chactas, is both nominally a Christian and resolutely a solitary rather than a political figure, he too refuses to follow the Christian model and remains stubbornly mired in his longing for his sister. Taken together, the two figures reveal how Chateaubriand dealt fictionally with the contradiction inherent in the ideal of infinite expansion through total self-surrender: rhetorical submission masking defiant self-assertion.

It was finally not through religion but through the working-out of the drama of incest that Chateaubriand arrived at the unstable equilibrium between expansion and surrender that defines his version of the Romantic self. This is a troubled issue, with regard to Chateaubriand in particular and to textual interpretation in general, for to attribute such central importance to that theme seems to put the major focus of interpretation on Chateaubriand's relation to his sister Lucile and thereby to reduce literature to nothing but an expression of the (concealed) life. Barbéris, steering between what he sees as the interpretive dangers of biographical reductionism on the one hand and sterile explanation by "literary influence" on the other, suggests that it is as wrong to deny the presence of incest in the text because it might reflect on Chateaubriand's life as it is to insist that its presence merely reflects literary fashion;[53] what is decisive is what is in the text and how it functions there. But as he notes, there is no clear line between Chateaubriand's autobiographical texts and his fictional ones; each partakes of both genres. *René* is "self-referential but not auto-biographical"; the story, that is, tells the truth about Chateaubriand's psyche but does not necessarily accurately recount the outward facts of his life.

In both *Atala* and *René*, it is the women who have the guilty sexual desire (though only in *René* is it explicitly incestuous.) Nevertheless, as Barbéris insists, there is no question that René desires his sister; it is evident even in the style of the story itself: "Whenever the narrative is about to reveal the secret, it changes language. It never says desire or gratification but beauty, genius, even poetry itself, which will be named, and enacted so that it does not enact something else."[54] If René expresses the wish to love and then to die, it can only be because his object is the forbidden sister, not because Chateaubriand believes sexuality is inherently evil and must be punished. René's incestuous wish unquestionably reflects on Chateaubriand, but what is equally important about it is its refusal in the text. Amélie represents the old order, tradition, and the faith of infancy, from which René has been forever separated; the impossibility of incest symbolizes the impossibility of political and religious restorations.[55] By rejecting incest for René, Chateaubriand is undermining the message of faith that is supposedly the burden of his story. "*In appearance*, Chateaubriand the man rallied [to the church]; but his writing and the way he makes his hero live prove the contrary."[56]

Barbéris is unquestionably right when he asserts that *René* is a psychodrama that contests its own religious apologetics but I believe he is wrong when he claims that the novel is unable to produce its own solution.[57] Because he sees Amélie as essentially a symbol of the sociohistorical past, he mistakes the nature of the contradiction and its outcome. If Chateaubriand displaced his own incestuous wishes onto his female figures, he also granted them the idealized fulfillment of infinite, God-like love in the glories of their religious faith. The cost of this infinite existence, however, is self-surrender. We should recall the passage in the *Genius* in which Chateaubriand described the *vague des passions* as "feminine," a restless yearning for something greater than the self; for the male, its fulfillment would be an emasculation. The insurmountable dilemma derives from the paradoxical fact that it is surrender that empowers the self, makes it divine. Chateaubriand coped with this dilemma by splitting and dividing himself between his masculine and feminine figures. It is the feminine half that surrenders, is transfigured, and dies; it is the masculine half that remains behind, not only to nourish the *vague des passions* in unrepentant solitude, but to write. René, after all, is not the end of his own story. There is a third character other than himself and Amélie: the one who writes their story. This character rises above the alternatives of submission to the infinite, which would be loss of self, and refusal of such submission, which would be mere finite existence. It is the writer, finally, who arrogates to himself the divinity René aspires to through surrender to Amélie and Amélie aspires to through surrender to God.

But the power to write is not an absolute, ungrounded power of the self; it is parasitical on the contested religious surrender. What the writer writes is the story of the refusal of surrender. And when Chateaubriand came to write his autobiography, he conceived of it ultimately as a Gothic cathedral (*Mémoires*, 1:435). That crown of human architecture, which symbolized man's homage to the infinite, was made possible by religious faith. Within the formal shelter of that faith, Chateaubriand erected, over long years and part by part, a cathedral to another divinity, the infinite self, inevitably autobiography, a story of a unique and finite individuality that nonetheless in speaking on behalf of eternity, could speak eternally from beyond the grave.

CONCLUSION

IN a popular stereotype, the Romantic artist dies young, his premature death a symbol of incompleteness and unfulfillable yearning. Schlegel was nearly fifty-seven when he died, Wordsworth was eighty, and Chateaubriand just short of that age; at the point in their lives where this study breaks off, they had many years of literary and political activity ahead of them. But the foundations of what we can call early Romanticism, extending the German term to England and France, had already been established by around 1802, and most of its great documents had been written, or at least, as in the case of Wordsworth's *Prelude*, begun. And though these men would continue writing until the end of their lives, this early phase of their lives did not last long. Wordsworth's "great decade" of 1797–1807 is a notorious cliché, but a period also came to a close in Schlegel's life with his trip to Paris in 1802 and his Cologne lectures of 1804–06, and in Chateaubriand's as well with the assumption of his first diplomatic post in Rome in 1803 and his trip to the Holy Land and North Africa in 1806. Whether or not this closure also marks a decline in their work, as has been alleged in the case of Wordsworth—the idea of decline is plausible for Schlegel, at least in literary theory, but much less so for Chateaubriand, who was soon to begin his *Mémoires*—it certainly represented a change. In each case that change was in the direction of greater orthodoxy in religion and conservatism in politics, culminating, for example, in Schlegel's case with his conversion to Catholicism in 1808; the highly personalized syntheses of the earlier period gave way to, or were infused by, more traditional concepts and formulae.

In the light of the present analysis, the reification of these syntheses should come as no surprise. Their contradictoriness made them inherently unstable, and the quasi-awareness that the writers had invented their own absolutes, projecting the idea of totality on aesthetic form, nature, or the ideal woman, so that in turn these could confer absoluteness on the self, made them unreliable protections against the dangers of self-aggrandizement they had been invented to domesticate. The turn to conservatism and orthodoxy did not quite mean the end of Romantic individuality, in the work of the three men, but an effort to hedge it more securely in long-established structures of authority, which of course modified it radically. For Friedrich Schlegel, for example, the (idealized) medieval Hapsburg Empire became the political model for reconciling individuality and totality; as a federation of separate nationalities and ethnic groups united only by a common loyalty to one ruler, it represented diversity and pluralism in unity, in contrast to the homogenizing centralized nation-state.

The major figures of this study were literary figures, though the exception of Schleiermacher is telling. I have argued that even for the creative writers and critics, the Romantic idea was never a narrowly conceived literary or aesthetic ideal; it was a concept of ideal self-formation and transformation and, they hoped, an ideal for society as well. But it is not coincidental that Romanticism was largely a literary movement. The concept of the self that the Romantics invented had to remain fictive or notional, for at least two reasons. As a striving for infinity or totality, it was unrealizable in the world except as an abstraction or allegory; and as the Romantics had learned, an attempt to live the ideal of totality, whether in personal relations or in political activity, was destructive to the liberty, even the personhood, of others.

It is a central contention of this work that the figures discussed in it extended the idea of the autonomy of the individual self beyond anything previously imagined in European thought, except perhaps in the reified and negative Christian imagery of Satan. What makes this fact so striking is that the early Romantics worked independently of one another, yet in close homology. Of course, this was not coincidence. Their different national cultures, social situations, and religious faiths were coordinate constituents of a larger European world whose economic, social, political, and intellectual transformation over the preceding century or more had generated new ideas and expectations of freedom within the framework of old structures of authority. I have argued that the vicissitudes of the personal histories of these writers were extremely important in shaping their needs and ideas, but even those histories show striking similarities. Children of absent mothers and remote, authoritarian fathers, these men all experienced a sense of marginality and exclusion and a competitive desire for high personal achievement enhanced by a sense of specialness partly compensatory, partly generated by extraordinary personal endowment. Working with the materials of their cultures, interpreting their personal issues through those materials, they all each tried to find some way of integrating and asserting their selves. It could be argued that their personal dilemmas were also products of typical structures of European society, or at least of the pathologies of those structures. Silvio Vietta claims, as I have noted, that Schlegel's oscillation between grandiosity and depression was typical of the weakened self-structures of all of the early German Romantics and attributes it to the combination of a strict bourgeois patriarchal-hierarchical family structure on the one hand, and the glorification of the subjective self in Enlightenment philosophy on the other. The psychological syndrome is easy to see, but much more work would have to be done to substantiate the sociocultural hypothesis for Germany, let alone to show that it had analogues in the family structures of a middle-class servitor of the English high gentry and aristocracy or of a Breton noble of ancient lineage. On the individual level, the parallelism is suggestive, however. Wordsworth and Chateaubriand, as well as Schlegel, felt themselves blocked by family and social authorities from extending the cultural traditions and pursuing the career paths they hoped would produce solutions for their personal dilemmas.

Although Schlegel and Wordsworth were late in adhering to the French Revolution, it was a natural step for all of these writers. The Revolution came at a time when the barriers to their goals either loomed close or had actually become larger. By furnishing a social model and a set of public symbols for what had seemed purely personal issues, the Revolution enabled them to transpose the problem of autonomy into the world of political action and public authority. But even politicized, those issues never lost their personal dimension. The Romantics remained concerned with the problem of the nature and extent of individual freedom even within the framework of revolutionary political theory. And if they did not remain revolutionaries, it was not simply because the Revolution became too radical, too violent, for them. It was because they themselves became in a sense too violent, too radical through it. Novices in political theory and philosophy, they imbibed it eagerly, but they did not remain mere disciples to their intellectual masters. Out of Fichte, Godwin, and Rousseau primarily, but others as well, Schlegel, Wordsworth, and Chateaubriand fashioned a concept of the freedom of the unique self that made it not only the sole legitimate source of meaning and judgment but entailed its infinite expansion. The logic of the idea is clearest in Schlegel and Schleiermacher, the Germans being the most philosophically self-conscious of the Romantics, but the claims for individuality are equally evident in the assertions and figures of Wordorth's poetry and Chateaubriand's stories and prose.

The danger of these claims emerged for the Romantics not primarily as a theoretical implication but in personal feeling and action, above all in desire. Desire was the testing ground of the new concept of self; it was the most intimate arena of social relationships. Not directly involved in politics themselves (Chateaubriand did not join the émigré armies until after he tested the new ethic in Anerica), it was in personal relations that the Romantics came to see the costs of their idea of individuality and to understand its implications for politics as well. It meant destructive danger to others, to the objects of desire, but also to the competitors for those objects, figured as the defunct authorities who were to be displaced by the self. However much the Romantics tried to see the human quest for the infinite as a cooperative venture, a bond that united people rather than set them against one another, the self-aggrandizement of desire made its competitive, grandiose, and destructive dimension unavoidable. For the Romantics there was a seamless connection between erotics and politics, as *The Borderers* and *The Natchez*, and even *Lucinde*, make clear; Novalis's *Belief and Love* only makes that connection explicit in self-conscious, if unorthodox, political theorizing.

The result was that the Romantics recoiled from their most advanced claims for the absolute authority and infinity of the self. But in this recoil they tried to preserve the essence of what they had achieved and the way they found to do it was through a form of male-female relationship that then became the template for their conception of the self's relationship to the work of art, to nature, and to the divine. They retreated to a position repeatedly described in these pages that made the infinity of the self dependent on its fusion with a totality both other and greater than itself, yet at the same time a creation of the self, a projection of its own aspiration for infinity. What made this apparently blatant contradiction sustainable was precisely its "regressed" structure. Figured as a child-mother relationship, it adverted to a developmental stage in which there was no consciousness of the contradiction. The result was the compartmentalized coexistence of contradiction and the self-consciousness of Romantic irony that exposed it.

This tenuous synthesis had undoubted political implications. I have argued that on the whole, the concept of the infinite self was not really compatible with political theory because no theory whose aim was the coordination of the individual and society could accomodate it. This was clearest in the early Romanticism of Schlegel, who at its peak even eschewed politics completely, but it was true for Wordsworth and Chateaubriand also, who (apart from Chateabriand's brief Napoleonic temptation) became largely "defensive" conservatives, their political theory primarily negative, aimed against the claims of absolute egotism. If however, the polity could be figured so as itself to take on the characteristics of totality and individuality, the self, merging with it, could realize its own wholeness and uniqueness through that fusion. Something like this happened in some strands of German Romanticism, as we saw in the introduction to this book, and produced the organic statism or nationalism that some have regarded as the quintessential Romantic politics. In fact, in England and in France, a later generation of Romantics would revive the original radical impulse of Romanticism and show that conservative holism was only one pole of a Romantic dialectic. But whether as a direct claim for the self, or as a claim for the collective entity through which the self achieved its realization, the Romantics' concept of individuality as ultimate authority and as infinite foundation of meaning left a legacy of problems for psychological identity, gender relations, social ethics, and political theory that we are far from having mastered.

NOTES

INTRODUCTION

1. R. N. Bellah et al., *Habits of the Heart: Individualism and Commitment in American Life* (Berkeley, 1985), 333–34, 336.

2. K. J. Weintraub, *The Value of the Individual: Self and Circumstance in Autobiography* (Chicago, 1978), xvii.

3. Bellah, *Habits*, 32. This is evident from the titles that introduce the section.

4. Weintraub, *Value of the Individual*, xvii.

5. N. L. Rosenblum, *Another Liberalism: Romanticism and the Reconstruction of Liberal Thought* (Cambridge, Mass., 1987), 2.

6. G. Simmel, *The Sociology of Georg Simmel*, ed. K. H. Wolff (New York, 1950), 78, 80–81. For a brief overview of the German contribution to the idea of individuality, essentially a summary of the ideas of Simmel and Meinecke, see S. Lukes, *Individualism* (New York, 1973), 17–22.

7. F. Meinecke, *Die Idee der Staatsräson*, *Werke* (Munich, 1957–62), 1:425.

8. Simmel, *Sociology*, 82.

9. Among the significant analyses of this development are F. Stern, *The Failures of Illiberalism: Essays in the Political Culture of Modern Germany* (New York, 1972), especially the essay "The Political Consequences of the Unpolitical German," and F. K. Ringer, *The Decline of the German Mandarins: The German Academic Community, 1890–1933* (Cambridge, Mass., 1969).

10. W. von Humboldt, *The Limits of State Action*, ed. J. W. Burrough (Cambridge, 1969).

11. Lukes, *Individualism*, 18, 69.

12. F. Hölderlin, *Hyperion*, *Sämtliche Werke*, ed. F. Beissner (Stuttgart, 1969–73) 3:202.

13. T. Rajan, *Dark Interpreter: The Discourse of Romanticism* (Ithaca, 1980), 260.

14. I include under this rubric existentialist-inspired work such as that of Hartman on Wordsworth and Richard on Chateaubriand, as well as deconstructionist criticism. Although deconstruction and poststructuralism generally have tried to eliminate self and subjectivity, central to existentialism, by subordinating them to the supposedly superordinate structures of language or discourse, there is a close affinity between the existentialist and deconstructionist projects of undermining the claims of beliefs to objectivity, universality, and totality. In any case, deconstructionist criticism of Romanticism does not necessarily deny the Romantic preoccupation with self even where it believes it to be in error. Rajan distinguishes between "first generation deconstruction," inspired by de Man's early phenomenological work, which explored textual contradictions without giving up the idea of a consciousness enmeshed in its own representation, and a "second generation" of deconstruction that sees constructs like "self" as figures produced by language and therefore subordinates psychology to rhetoric. "The Erasure of Narrative in Post-Structuralist Representations of Wordsworth," in *Romantic Revolutions: Criticism and Theory*, ed. K. R. Johnston, G. Chaitin, K. Hanson,

and H. Marks (Bloomington, 1989), 350–51. I have argued elsewhere that de Man's arguments for the subordination of psychology to rhetoric are deeply flawed and contradictory. See my forthcoming "Text, Context, and Psychology in Intellectual History" in *Developments in Modern Historiography*, ed. H. Kozicki (New York, 1993).

15. Rajan, *Dark Interpreter*, 262.

16. M. H. Abrams, *Natural Supernaturalism: Tradition and Revolution in Romantic Literature* (New York, 1973), 182.

17. Ibid., 255.

18. Novalis, *Glaube und Liebe*, in *Schriften*, ed. R. Samuel (Stuttgart, 1965), 2:490. This summary is of course a highly compressed version of a complex dialectic Novalis derives from the ideas of Fichte. Much more will be said about these ideas in the chapter on Schlegel.

19. J. H. Miller, "On Edge," in *Romanticism and Contemporary Criticism*, ed. M. Eaves and M. Fischer (Ithaca, 1986), 109.

20. M. H. Abrams, "Construing and Deconstructing," in *Romanticism and Contemporary Criticism*, 147–54.

21. Even in more purely logocentric texts, it is not enough to rely on the inherent structure of language to explain contradictions. The notion that language is an automatic machine that disseminates meanings infinitely without any check by a controlling consciousness is based on misconceptions within the poststructuralist account of language about the origins of meaning. See my "Text, Context, and Psychology."

22. J. J. McGann, *The Romantic Ideology: A Critical Investigation* (Chicago, 1983), 26.

23. Ibid., 1.

24. For Germany, among others, R. Brinkman, "Deutsche Frühromantik und Französische Revolution," in *Deutsche Literatur und Französische Revolution* (Göttingen, 1974), 172–89; C. Behrens, *Friedrich Schlegels Geschichtsphilosophie (1794–1808)* (Tübingen, 1984); B. Bräutigam, *Leben wie im Roman. Untersuchungen zum ästhetischen Imperativ im Frühwerk Friedrich Schlegels (1794–1800)* (Paderborn, 1986).

25. McGann, *The Romantic Ideology*, 1.

26. Ibid., 91.

27. Ibid.

28. A. Liu, *Wordsworth: The Sense of History* (Stanford, 1989), 23.

29. As Liu puts it in one of the initial summary statements of his conclusion, "Both these propositions are true: first, that Wordsworth's largest and most sustained theme is the realization of history; and second, that his largest theme is the denial of history" (39).

30. P. Gilbert, "Boundaries and the Self in Romanticism," in *English and German Romanticism: Cross-Currents and Controversies*, ed. J. Pipkin (Heidelberg, 1985), 143–53.

31. W. Wordsworth, *Home at Grasmere: Part First, Book First of The Recluse*, ed. B. Darlington (Ithaca, New York), "Prospectus," MS.1, 261.63–71.

32. For this formulation I thank an anonymous reader for Princeton University Press.

CHAPTER ONE

1. F.D.E. Schleiermacher, *Über die Religion: Reden an die Gebildeten unter ihren Verächtern*, 2d ed. (Berlin, 1806), 6–7.

2. F.D.E. Schleiermacher, *Über die Religion* [1799 ed.], *Werke*, ed. O. Braun and J. Bauer (Leipzig, 1911), 4:214. Most citations are from this edition, though I have occasionally used F.D.E. Schleiermacher, *On Religion: Speeches to Its Cultured Despisers*, trans. J. Oman (New York), a translation of the third edition of 1821.

3. F.D.E. Schleiermacher, *Monologen*, *Werke*, 4:420; *Schleiermacher's Soliloquies*, ed. and trans. H. L. Friess (Chicago, 1957), 31. Translation slightly modified.

4. Schleiermacher had already challenged Kant in a series of youthful writings in which he attempted to counter Kant's doctrine of transcendental freedom with a version of determinism partly indebted to Spinoza. I will have more to say about this below.

5. Humboldt, *Limits*, 16–17.

6. M. Redeker, *Schleiermacher: Life and Thought*, trans. J. Wahlhauser (Philadelphia, 1973), 55.

7. This tradition has been much studied in Anglo-American thought under the impetus of J.G.A. Pocock's work, particularly *The Machiavellian Moment: Florentine Political Thought and the Atlantic Republican Tradition* (Princeton, 1975) and *Virtue, Commerce, and Society: Essays on Political Thought and History, Chiefly in the Eighteenth Century* (Cambridge, 1985), but little research has been done on it in Germany. See below, however, for Rudolf Vierhaus's discussion of republican ideas in Germany.

8. P. R. Sweet, *Wilhelm von Humboldt: A Biography*, 2 vols. (Columbus, 1978–80), 1:58–59.

9. Humboldt, *Limits*, editor's introduction, xi.

10. Rudolf Vierhaus argues that there existed a distinctive political consciousness within the cultivated classes in Germany before the French Revolution, based on both the classical republican and natural law traditions with their concepts of citizenship, patriotism, utility, and rights. Although this outlook was interwoven with ethical issues, and not concerned with concrete problems of political representation, it envisioned a reform of society in the direction of wider participation, social betterment, and the securing of equal rights before the law. Such reform was considered quite compatible with absolutist government and was indeed in the view of many *gebildete* well underway before the Revolution. R. Vierhaus, "Politische Bewusstsein in Deutschland vor 1789," in *Deutschland im 18. Jahrhundert: Politische Verfassung, Soziales Gefüge, Geistige Bewegungen* (Göttingen, 1987), 187–91. Humboldt's extension of this political consciousness to the previously apolitical concept of individuality, however, was new. Moreover, the attitude that Germany could accomplish reform without Revolution could only be a response to the Revolution itself. In this sense it is somewhat misleading to suggest that such an attitude preceded the Revolution because it obscures the radicalization of German political consciousness under the impact of the Revolution even if, as in Humboldt's case, the hope for reform

was still invested in enlightened authority. The implications of Humboldt's program of 1791–92 were so radical that they would have entailed the total transformation of the Prussian political system.

11. Sweet, *Humboldt* 1:3–4. As Sweet points out, Humboldt's ancestry was one of blurred class lines because of its rapid upward mobility over the generations.

12. Schleiermacher, *On Religion*, 27.

13. W. Dilthey, *Leben Schleiermachers*, 3d ed., ed. M. Redeker (Berlin, 1970).

14. K. Nowak, "Die Französische Revolution in Leben und Werk des jungen Schleiermacher," in *Internationaler Schleiermacher-Kongress Berlin 1984*, ed. K-V. Selge (Berlin, 1985), 103–25.

15. Ibid., 119.

16. Ibid., 118.

17. J. Droz, *L'Allemagne et la révolution française* (Paris, 1949).

18. F.D.E. Schleiermacher, *The Life of Schleiermacher. As Unfolded In His Autobiography and Letters*, trans. F. Rowan (London, 1860), 109. Cited as *Life*.

19. Cited in Nowak, "Die Französische Revolution," 116–17.

20. J. Dawson, *Friedrich Schleiermacher: The Evolution of a Nationalist* (Austin, 1966), 86–87. See also Sweet, *Humboldt*, 2:55–58.

21. F.D.E. Schleiermacher, *Kritische Gesamtausgabe*, ed. G. Meckenstock, pt. 1, vol. 2, *Schriften aus der Berliner Zeit, 1796–1799* (Berlin, 1984), *Gedanken*, 1:3, 1. Cited as *KG*.

22. Schleiermacher, "Notizen und Exzerpte zur Vertragslehre" (1796–97), in *KG* 1:2:53–69 and "Entwurf zur Abhandlung über die Vertragslehre," ibid., 73–74.

23. F.D.E. Schleiermacher, *Jugenschriften, 1787–1796*, KG, 1:1:217–357.

24. For example, in Dilthey's biography and in A. L. Blackwell, *Schleiermacher's Early Philosophy of Life: Determinism, Freedom, and Phantasy* (Chico, 1982).

25. Dilthey, *Leben*, 62.

26. F. W. Katzenbach, *Friedrich Daniel Ernst Schleiermacher in Selbstzeugnissen und Bilddokumenten* (Hamburg, 1967), 32.

27. Dilthey, *Leben*, 60.

28. Ibid., 71.

29. Redeker, *Schleiermacher*, 22.

30. Blackwell, *Schleiermacher's Early Philosophy*, 43.

31. Ibid., 45.

32. Ibid., 87.

33. For some useful remarks on the Berlin Jewish salon, see H. Arendt's book on one of its leaders, *Rahel Varnhagen, The Life of a Jewish Woman*, trans. R. and C. Winston (New York, 1974), 57–59.

34. F.D.E. Schleiermacher, *Aus Schleiermachers Leben. In Briefen*, 4 vols., ed. W. Dilthey (Berlin, 1863), 1:186–87. Cited as *Briefen*.

35. Sweet, *Humboldt*, 1:18–19, 35.

36. Ibid., 42–43.

37. Ibid., 95.

38. Ibid., 96–97.

39. F.D.E. Schleiermacher, *Vertraute Briefe Über Friedrich Schlegels 'Lucinde.'*

40. Sweet, *Humboldt*, 1:60. Sweet disagrees with conventional assessments of Humboldt's enthusiasm for the French Revolution and points out that what is striking about Humboldt's visit is how much he kept his distance from events while in Paris.

41. Ibid., 62.

42. R. Samuel, *Die poetische Staats- und Geschichtsauffassung Friedrich von Hardenbergs* (Frankfurt am Main, 1925), 66.

43. J. E. Toews, *Hegelianism: The Path Toward Dialectical Humanism, 1805–1841* (Cambridge, 1980), 63.

44. Novalis (Friedrich von Hardenberg), *Schriften*, ed. R. Samuel (Stuttgart, 1965), 2:500.

45. Ibid., 459.

46. M. Delon, "Du Vague des Passions à la Passion des Vagues," in *Le Préromantisme: Hypothèque ou Hypothèse*, ed. P. Viallaneix (Paris, 1975), 490.

47. J. R. Gillis, *Youth and History: Tradition and Change in European Age Relations, 1770–Present* (New York, 1974), 8–9.

48. See K. O'Flaherty, "Adolescence in the Work of Chateaubriand," in *Chateaubriand Today: Proceedings of the Commemoration of the Bicentenary of the Birth of Chateaubriand, 1968*, ed. R. Switzer (Madison, 1970), 273–82.

49. See for example, H. Segeberg, "Deutsche Literatur und Französische Revolution. Zum Verhältnis von Weimarer Klassik, Frühromantk und Spätaufklärung," in *Deutsche Literatur zur Zeit der Klassik*, ed. K. O. Conrady (Stuttgart, 1977) 243–66; W. Rasch, "Zum Verhältnis der Romantik zur Aufklärung," in *Romantik: Ein literaturwissenschaftliches Studienbuch*, ed. E. Ribbat (Königstein, 1979) 7–22; and Viallaneix, *Le Préromantisme*.

CHAPTER TWO

1. *Kritische Friedrich-Schlegel-Ausgabe*, ed. E. Behler with J-J. Anstett and H. Eichner (Munich, 1958–), 18:24, 64. The *Kritische Ausgabe* is cited throughout as KA with volume, page, and fragment number where relevant.

2. F. Schlegel, *Literary Notebooks, 1797–1801*, ed. H. Eichner (Toronto, 1957), 46, 307. Cited as *Notebooks*, with page and fragment number.

3. *Athenaeum* fragment 262, *Friedrich Schlegel's "Lucinde" and the Fragments*, trans. and ed. P. Virchow (Minneapolis, 1971), 200. All references to the *Lyceum* and *Athenaeum* fragments and to *Lucinde* are from this edition, cited as *Lyceum*, *Athenaeum*, and *Lucinde*, respectively; page and fragment number are given where relevant.

4. F. Schlegel, *Dialogue on Poetry and Literary Aphorisms*, trans. and intro. E. Behler and R. Struc (University Park and London, 1968), 54. Cited as *Dialogue*.

5. Schlegel, KA, 18, editor's introduction, xviii.

6. See J. Hörisch, *Die fröhliche Wissenschaft der Poesie* (Frankfurt, 1976),

15–20; I. Strohschneider-Kohrs, *Die romantische Ironie in Theorie und Gestaltung* (Tübingen, 1960), 8, 67–68, and F. N. Mennemeier, *Friedrich Schlegels Poesiebegriff* (Munich, 1971), 65.

7. P. de Man, "The Rhetoric of Temporality," *Blindness and Insight: Essays in the Rhetoric of Contemporary Criticism*, 2d ed. (Minneapolis, 1983), 220.

8. M. P. Bullock, *Romanticism and Marxism: The Philosophical Development of Literary Theory and Literary History in Walter Benjamin and Friedrich Schlegel* (New York, 1987), 129.

9. H. Eichner, *Friedrich Schlegel* (New York, 1970), 63.

10. Anne Mellors seems to take a similar position when she argues that "the authentic romantic ironist is as filled with enthusiasm as skepticism. He is as much a romantic as an ironist." *English Romantic Irony* (Cambridge, Mass., 1980), 5. Although this seems to go beyond Szondi and Behler in affirming the positive aspect of Romanticism, it still falls short of Schlegel's contradiction; what Mellors calls Schlegel's "celebration" of Romantic creativity is a celebration of the continuing process of creation and destruction, but not of any of the totalizing syntheses along the way.

11. Bullock raises this question in *Romanticism and Marxism*, 36–37. See also M. Brown, *The Shape of German Romanticism* (Ithaca, 1979).

12. Bernd Bräutigam sees Schlegel's insistence on the "homology" between art and life, his insistence that aesthetic theory and literary practice furnish models for practical action in the world, as the characteristic feature that distinguishes Schlegel's early Romanticism from Schiller's Kant-inspired humanism. Bräutigam, *Leben wie im Roman*, 18–19.

13. These conclusions differ sharply from those of Karl Heinz Bohrer and Jürgen Habermas, who see in Schlegel's ideas between 1797 and 1800 (particularly in the "Talk on Mythology") an abandonment of the political foundations of aesthetics for an absolutizing of literature, and differ particularly from those of Bräutigam, who argues than Schlegel was never really political, even in his supposedly republican phase. K. H. Bohrer, *Mythos und Moderne. Begriff und Bild einer Rekonstruktion* (Frankfurt, 1983) 53–60; J. Habermas, *Der philosophische Diskurs der Moderne. Zwölf Vorlesungen* (Frankfurt, 1985), 112; Bräutigam, *Leben wie im Roman*, 55–70. As my remarks suggest, however, the question of Schlegel's political versus his aesthetic intentions is not a matter of either/or and can only be clarified in a developmental analysis of his successive positions.

14. E. Behler, *Friedrich Schlegel In Selbstzeugnissen und Bilddokumenten* (Hamburg, 1966), 12.

15. For important analyses of this group, see R. Vierhaus, *Germany in the Age of Absolutism* (Göttingen, 1968; trans. Cambridge, 1988), 84–86, his "Umrisse einer Sozialgeschichte der Gebildeten in Deutschland" in *Deutschland im 18. Jahrhundert: Politische Verfassung, soziales Gefüge; geistige Bewegungen* (Göttingen, 1987), 167–82, and his essay also titled "Deutschland im 18. Jahrhundert" in *Lessing und die Zeit der Aufklärung* (Göttingen, 1968). See also the section on "Movers and Doers" in M. Walker, *German Home Towns: Community, State, and General Estate, 1648–1871* (Ithaca, 1971). The standard older work on the subject is H. Gerth, *Die sozialgeschichtliche Lage der bürgerlichen Intelligenz um die Wende des 18. Jahrhunderts* (Frankfurt am Main, 1935).

16. C. Enders, *Friedrich Schlegel, Die Quellen seines Wesens und Werdens* (Leipzig, 1913), 6.

17. J. S. Rutledge, *Johann Adolph Schlegel* (Bern and Frankfurt am Main, 1974), 39–40.

18. Ibid., 65ff.

19. Ibid., 218.

20. Ibid., 215–16.

21. Enders, *Schlegel*, 16.

22. H. W. Ziegler, "Friedrich Schlegels Jugendentwicklung," *Archiv für die Gesamte Psychologie* 60, (1927): 15.

23. Enders, *Schlegel*, 160–79.

24. Vierhaus, "Deutschland im 18. Jahrhundert," 19–20, and *Germany in the Age of Absolutism*, 84; J. Whaley, "The Protestant Enlightenment in Germany," in *The Enlightenment in National Context*, ed. R. Porter and M. Teich (Cambridge, 1981).

25. Vierhaus, "Deutschland im 18. Jahrhundert," 84.

26. V. Lange, *The Classical Age of German Literature, 1740–1815* (New York, 1982), 26.

27. K. Epstein, *The Genesis of German Conservatism* (Princeton, 1966), 547.

28. Enders, *Schlegel*, 182.

29. Ibid., 187.

30. For a discussion of Rehberg and the "Hanoverian School" of political thought, see Epstein, *Genesis*, 547–94.

31. Silvio Vietta takes this oscillation between grandiosity and depression to be typical of the weakened self-structures of all of the early German Romantics and attributes it to the combination of the strict bourgeois patriarchal-hierarchical family structure in Germany on the one hand and the glorification of the subjective self in German Enlightenment philosophy on the other. S. Vietta, "Frühromantik und Aufklärung" in *Die literarische Frühromantik*, ed. S. Vietta (Göttingen, 1983), 38–42. Although somewhat schematic, in part due to the condensation of the essay, both Vietta's psychological analysis, which specifically alludes to the psychoanalytic work of Heinz Kohut and Otto Kernberg on narcissism, as well as his sociological comments about the structure of the German family, are highly suggestive. Without further large-scale research, the familial causation must remain conjectural—research on the early modern family is not extensive or fine-grained enough to establish it—but the details of Schlegel's states of mind as reported in his letters directly support, and extend, Vietta's psychological conclusions and indirectly, through their internalized effects, suggest the impact of familial structure. The parallels with Schleiermacher are clear; they are equally, if not more, striking in the case of Novalis.

32. R. Murtfeld, *Caroline Schlegel-Schelling: Moderne Frau in revolutionärer Zeit* (Bonn, 1973), 23.

33. Behler, *Friedrich Schlegel* 27–28, and editor's introduction and notes, 23:xxvii, 407.

34. Murtfeld, *Caroline*, 31.

35. Behler, *Friedrich Schlegel*, 28.

36. See, for example, E. M. Butler, *The Tyranny of Greece Over Germany*

(Cambridge, 1935) and H. Hatfield, *Aesthetic Paganism in German Literature From Winckelmann to the Death of Goethe* (Cambridge, 1964).

37. On this issue see H. R. Jauss, "Schlegels und Schillers Replik auf die 'Querelle des Anciens et des Modernes'" in *Literaturgeschichte als Provokation* (Frankfurt am Main, 1970), 67–106.

38. J. J. Winckelmann, *Thoughts on the Imitation of the Painting and Sculpture of the Greeks*, in *German Aesthetic and Literary Criticism: Winckelmann, Lessing, Hamann, Herder, Schiller, Goethe*, ed. H. B. Nisbet (Cambridge, 1985), 33.

39. Ibid., 42.

40. "Römische Staatsnation und griechische Kulturnation: Zum Paradigmawechsel zwischen Gottsched und Winckelmann," in *Akten des VII. Internationales Germanistik-Kongresses* (Göttingen, 1985).

41. Pointing to the ecstatic sensuousness of Winckelmann's descriptive language, Hugh Honour calls Winckelmann's theory of art "expressive." *Neo-Classicism* (Middlesex, 1968), 61. Peter Gay has noted the paradox of Winckelmann's advocacy of objectivity in art and his discovery of his own preferences in his homoerotic passions, *The Enlightenment, An Interpretation*, vol. 2, *The Science of Freedom* (New York, 1977), 293. This paradox may well help explain the continuing tension in Winckelmann's synthesis; the effort to deal with the unruly subjective is of interest in Schlegel's classicism as well.

42. G. E. Lessing, *Laocoon*, in *German Aesthetic and Literary Criticism*, 61–62.

43. "Über das Studium der Griechischen Posie," Schlegel, KA, 1:253.

44. That Schlegel shared his sense of personal conflict with others such as Winckelmann and Schiller, so that the feeling of inner disharmony bespoke a broad cultural dilemma, in no way lessens the personal referentiality of the essay.

45. See Vierhaus, "'Patriotismus'—Begriff und Realität einer moralisch-politischen Haltung," in *Deutschland im 18. Jahrhundert*, 96–109, which shows that even participatory rather than authoritarian notions of patriotic service were consistent with hierarchical subordination, whether to *Reich* or modern absolutist state.

46. My position here differs essentially from that taken by such critics as Mennemeier and Bräutigam and is closer to that of Oesterle, though for different reasons than the ones she gives. Bräutigam, for example, while insisting on the explicitly political nature of Schlegel's attack on modern literature, even directly associating Schlegel's characterization of modern literature as "interested" or arbitrary with his critique of despotism (*Leben wie im Roman*, 46–47), argues that for Schlegel the French Revolution was only an incitement to its own sublimation in aesthetics. In his view Schlegel was opposed to the idea of actual revolution in Germany; the aesthetic revolution not only replaced but precluded political revolution. Its purpose was to displace into the literary imagination the problem of realizing the goals of political revolution in reality; the aesthetic revolution thus sidestepped the problem that was created once revolutionary political action was rejected (62–63, 65–70, and 171, n. 177). For Oesterle's contrary view, see I. Oesterle, "Der 'glückliche Anstoss' aesthetischer Revolution und die Anstössigkeit politischer Revolution. Ein Denk- und Belegversuch zum Zussamen-

hang von politischer Form-veränderung und kultureller Revolution im Studim-Aufsatz Friedrich Schlegels," in *Literaturwissenschaft und Sozialwissenschaften*, vol. 8, *Zur Modernität der Romantik*, ed. D. Bänsch (Stuttgart, 1977), 169, 176.

One serious problem in Bräutigam's approach is that he does not differentiate between Schlegel's classical and romantic phases and sees no crucial difference between Schlegel's politics before and after his move to Berlin. As I have noted earlier, Schlegel's political position is indeed much more ambiguous and conflicted after 1797 and it confuses the situation to import the later position into the earlier one.

47. "Über die Grenzen des Schönen," Schlegel, KA, 1:35.

48. See note 46. See also C. Behrens, *Friedrich Schlegels Geschichtsphilosophie, (1794–1808): Ein Beitrag zur politischen Romantik* (Tübingen, 1984), 66–67; R. Brinkman, "Deutsche Frühromantik," 178, 188–89; E. Behler, "Die Auffassung der Revolution in der deutschen Frühromantik," in *Essays on European Literature. In Honor of Lieselotte Dieckmann* (St. Louis, 1972), 191–215. For a contrasting view, see W. Weiland, *Der junge Friedrich Schlegel oder die Revolution in der Frühromantik* (Stuttgart, 1968).

49. Schlegel, KA, 7:11–25.

50. L. Krieger, *The German Idea of Freedom: History of a Political Tradition* (Boston, 1957), 117–22.

51. For an appreciation of the radically democratic character of the *Versuch*, see H. Meixner, "Politische Aspekte der Frühromantik," in S. Vietta, *Die literarische Frühromantik*, 185–86.

52. Behrens, quoting G. Birtsch (150, n. 213), points out that in recent Schlegel research it has been repeatedly suggested that even in Schlegel's decisive avowal of republicanism there can already be seen the elements of his future conservative critique of majoritarian democratic republicanism. This, however, is the vantage point of hindsight. At the time, Schlegel's position was, and was intended to be, a radical step beyond Kant.

53. Schlegel, KA, 2:78–99.

54. Behrens, *Geschichtsphilosophie*, 19.

55. Ibid., 20.

56. One way in which this is done is to confuse Schlegel's opposition to the extension of the French Revolution to Germany with rejection of the primacy of politics in cultural transformation. See F. N. Mennemeier, "Klassizität und Progressivität. Zu einigen Aspekten der Poetik des jungen Friedrich Schlegel," in *Deutsche Literatur zur Zeit der Klassik*, ed. K. O. Conrady (Stuttgart, 1977), 289. But Schlegel's repudiation of violence was not a repudiation of republicanism as the necessary condition and aim of cultural transformation.

57. J. G. Fichte, *Die Grundlagen der gesamten Wissenschaftslehre*, vol. 1, part 2 of *Gesamtausgabe, Werke, 1793–1795* (Stuttgart, 1965), 1:2:173–451. The English version used here is the translation by P. Heath and J. Lacks, *The Foundation of the Entire Theory of Knowledge* (New York, 1970). Cited as *Theory of Knowledge*.

58. G. Kelly, *Idealism, History and Politics: Sources of Hegelian Thought* (Cambridge, 1968), 209.

59. Fichte himself repudiates any such reading in the *Grundlage des Naturrechts* of 1796–97 and the *System der Sittenlehre* of 1798. Only the first would have been available to Schlegel at this point, but he makes no mention of it or its point of view.

60. Kelly, *Idealism*, 207.

61. M. Preitz, ed., *Friedrich Schlegel und Novalis. Biographie einer Romantiker-Freundschaft in ihren Briefen* (Darmstadt, 1957), 64.

62. J. Körner, *Krisenjahre der Frühromantik: Briefe aus dem Schlegelkreis*, 3 vols. (Brünn, 1936–1958) 1:8–9.

63. E. Behler, "Friedrich Schlegels erster Aufenthalt in Jena: Vom 6. August 1796 bis zum 3. Juli 1797," *Modern Language Notes* 102, no. 3 (1987), 557.

64. Preitz, *Biographie*, 88.

65. Ibid., 85.

66. Ibid., 92.

67. See I. Oesterle, "Der 'gluckliche Anstoss,'" 167.

68. Schlegel, KA, 2:xi–xii.

69. Ibid.

70. S. Friedrichsmeyer, *The Androgyne in Early German Romanticism: Friedrich Schlegel, Novalis, and the Metaphysics of Love* (Berlin, 1983), 116.

71. Schlegel, KA, 1:87.

72. "Über die Diotima," KA 1:70–115.

73. S. Moenkmeyer, *Francois Hemsterhuis* (Boston, 1975), 146.

74. Ibid., 49–51. See also P. Kluckhohn, *Die Auffassung der Liebe in der Literatur des 18. Jahrhunderts und in der deutschen Romantik* (Tubingen, 1966), 228–32.

75. This was a concern of course widely shared by his contemporaries. The importance of friendship in the German Enlightenment lay partly in the fact that it rooted morality in natural feeling, and partly in its furnishing a nonsexual basis for intimacy between the sexes. See Kluckhohn, *Auffassung*, 181–82.

76. Schlegel, KA, 2:57–77.

77. Virchow, *Lucinde*, editor's introduction, 26.

78. Schlegel, KA, 2:126–46.

79. Ernst Behler argues that the novel's structure is in part temporal, the first six sections describing the spiritual present of Julius's fulfillment through Lucinde, the long central section his past chaotic state before fulfillment, and the last six sections the future and Julius's entrance into the world that has been made possible by his union with Lucinde. E. Behler, "Friedrich Schlegel: *Lucinde* (1799)," in *Romane und Erzählungen der deutschen Romantik*, ed. P. M. Luetzeler (Stuttgart, 1981), 98–124. Behler, however, does not see the inconsistency between the middle and the last sections.

80. A. Schlagdenhaufen, *Fréderic Schlegel et son groupe: la doctrine de l'Athenaeum (1798–1800)* (Paris, 1934).

81. The first major steps in this journey can be followed in Schlegel's Cologne lectures on philosophy and universal history delivered in 1804–1806. They represent the complete repudiation of his earlier republicanism, which he now saw as the political rationalization of clashing interests in a modern individualistic commercial society. "Unity is essential to state power," he claimed, "otherwise wild

freedom and equality, whose evil consequences would hinder the goal of the state, would again enter [society]" (KA, 13:125). But this unity was not to obliterate the distinctive individuality of the estates, representing different social functions in the necessary division of labor in society, or the different national cultures and traditions of Europe. These individualities were like the different parts of a person, and their integration made the properly constructed state a "self-sufficient, self-subsistent individual" (KA, 13:164). Only the medieval Holy Roman Empire came close to this model: "The confusions of an ideal federation of nations are mostly avoided in the system of the Empire. . . . The Empire is specifically distinguished from a kingdom insofar as it is a kingdom of kingdoms" (KA, 13:165).

CHAPTER THREE

1. W. Wordsworth, *The Prelude (1805)*, in *The Prelude: 1799, 1805, 1850*, ed. J. Wordsworth, M. H. Abrams, and S. Gill (New York, 1979), I:212–13. All citations from the long version are from the *1805 Prelude* unless otherwise noted.

2. H. M. Scurr, *Henry Brooke* (Minnesota, 1922), 63–67.

3. E. de Selincourt, ed., *The Letters of William and Dorothy Wordsworth*, vol. 1, *The Early Years 1787–1805*, 2d ed. (Oxford, 1967), 210–12. Cited as *Letters*.

4. W. Wordsworth, *The Borderers*, ed. R. Osborn (Ithaca, 1982), 4.2.134–35. References are to the early version, 1797–99.

5. W. Wordsworth, *"The Pedlar," "Tintern Abbey," "The Two-Part Prelude,"* ed. J. Wordsworth (Cambridge, 1985), 29–31. All references to "The Pedlar" are from this edition.

6. T. Weiskel, *The Romantic Sublime: Studies in the Structure and Psychology of Transcendence* (Baltimore, 1976, 1986), 50–51.

7. I disagree here with Kenneth Johnston, who writes that imagination did not become independent of material limitation until *The Prelude* of 1805, though he does see anticipations of it even in 1797–98. K. R. Johnston, *Wordsworth and "The Recluse"* (New Haven, 1984), 15. I have learned much from his sensitive and nuanced explanation of Wordsworth's failure to complete *The Recluse*, though my interpretation of the tensions that hampered the poem is different.

8. H. Bloom, *The Visionary Company* (New York, 1961); G. H. Hartman, *Wordsworth's Poetry, 1787–1814* (New Haven, 1964).

9. Among proponents of the second viewpoint are J. K. Chandler, *Wordsworth's Second Nature: A Study of the Poetry and Politics* (Chicago, 1982); J. McGann, *The Romantic Ideology* (Chicago, 1983); D. Simpson, "Criticism, Politics and Style in Wordsworth's Poetry," *Critical Inquiry* 11 (Spring 1984): 52–81 and *Wordsworth's Historical Imagination: The Poetry of Displacement* (New York, 1987); A. Liu, "Wordsworth: The History in 'Imagination,'" *English Literary History* 51 (Fall 1984): 505–48 and *Wordsworth: The Sense of History* (Stanford, 1989); M. Levinson, *Wordsworth's Great Period Poems: Four Essays* (Cambridge, 1986).

10. M. H. Abrams, *Natural Supernaturalism: Tradition and Revolution in Romantic Literature* (New York, 1973); e.g., "Wordsworth . . . salvaged his earlier millennial hope by a turn both from political revolution and from utopian plan-

ning to a process which, in the phrase from the Prospectus, is available to 'the individual Mind that keeps her own / Inviolate retirement.' The recourse is from mass action to individual quietism, and from outer revolution to a revolutionary mode of imaginative perception which accomplishes nothing less than the creation of a new world" (338).

11. G. H. Hartman, "Wordsworth Revisited," in *The Unremarkable Wordsworth* (Minneapolis, 1987), 5.

12. This is the central theme of Hartman's work as it is of the closely allied early position of Paul de Man (in the first edition of *Blindness and Insight* and in *The Rhetoric of Romanticism*) and of Tillotama Rajan's *Dark Interpreter*, which, however, does not discuss Wordsworth explicitly.

13. Levinson, *Four Essays*, 7–8; Chandler, *Wordsworth's Second Nature*, 74–75. For a definition of "historicism" as contrasted with the older historical approach of Woodring, Erdman, and others, see Levinson, *Four Essays*, 135, n. 1.

14. Levinson, *Four Essays*, 5.

15. Hartman, *Wordsworth's Poetry*, 184.

16. Ibid., 254.

17. H. Bloom, "The Scene of Instruction: Tintern Abbey," in *William Wordsworth: Modern Critical Views*, ed. H. Bloom (New York, 1985), 130. Bloom accepts the earlier and now generally discredited date of winter-spring 1798 for the composition of the "Prospectus." At the end of the chapter, in the context of my own argument, I will attempt a reassessment of the "revisionist" position.

18. "Lines Composed a Few Miles Above Tintern Abbey, On Revisiting the Banks of the Wye During a Tour, July 13, 1798," in *Selected Poems and Prefaces by William Wordsworth*, ed. J. Stillinger (Boston, 1965), 108.5–8.

19. Levinson, *Four Essays*, 37.

20. I will argue later that the simultaneous suppression of the vagrants surrounding the Abbey, whose absence Levinson makes a good deal of, also has a far different significance from what she attributes to it.

21. Surveying the melancholy themes of Wordsworth's earliest poetry, Paul Sheats writes that "before he was a poet of nature he was emphatically a poet of the human heart." P. D. Sheats, *The Making of Wordsworth's Poetry, 1785–1798* (Cambridge, 1973), 6.

22. J. Purkis, *A Preface to Wordsworth* (London, 1986), 58.

23. G. E. Mingay, *English Landed Society in the Eighteenth Century* (London, 1963), 112.

24. B. Bonsall, *Sir James Lowther and Cumberland and Westmoreland Elections, 1754–1775* (Manchester, 1960), vi.

25. I owe this information to my colleague Richard Davis.

26. B. R. Schneider, *Wordsworth's Cambridge Education* (Cambridge, 1957), 11, 21.

27. M. H. Abrams, "*The Prelude* as a Portrait of the Artist," *Bicentenary Wordsworth Studies*, ed. J. Wordsworth (Ithaca, 1970), 183. Cited as *Bicentenary*.

28. N. Roe, *Wordsworth and Coleridge, The Radical Years* (Oxford, 1988), 65.

29. H. T. Dickinson, *British Radicalism and the French Revolution, 1789–1815* (Oxford, 1985), 6–20; J. C. D. Clark, *English Society, 1688–1832* (Cam-

bridge, 1985), 315–48; I. Kramnick, "Religion and Radicalism: English Political Theory in the Age of Revolution," *Political Theory* 4 (1977): 503–34, and "Republican Revisionism Revisited," *American Historical Review* 87, no. 3 (1982): 629–64. Nor, given his social origins, does Wordsworth fit the country gentry model of reform of the Yorkshire Association.

30. Sheats, *Making*, 33.

31. W. Wordsworth, *The Poetical Works of William Wordsworth*, vol. I, ed. E. de Selincourt (Oxford, 1952), 281.506. Cited as *Poetical Works*.

32. R. J. Onorato, *The Character of the Poet: Wordsworth in "The Prelude"* (Princeton, 1971).

33. Hartman says that the subject of the poem is the "mind of Wordsworth understood as the mind of a poet" (78), separate, that is, from his biography and psychology.

34. De Quincey, quoted in F. W. Bateson, *Wordsworth: A Re-Interpretation* (London, 1954), 44.

35. M. Moorman, *William Wordsworth: A Biography*, vol. 1, *The Early Years, 1770–1803* (Oxford, 1957), 19.

36. Bateson, *Wordsworth*, 47.

37. W. Wordsworth, *An Evening Walk*, ed. J. Averill (Ithaca, 1984), 301.

38. Sheats notes that the stylistic change from the subjectivity of the Hawkshead poetry to the prevalence of objective natural imagery in "An Evening Walk" was intensified "consciously or unconsciously" by the unsettled state of Wordsworth's feelings and that such imagery offered not only relationship to nature but forgetfulness of self (*Making*, 56, 58). At this point in the poem, however, self is reasserted as imagined image replaces perceptual image, a shift Sheats apparently misses.

39. They need not be, of course, but only they can be; they are "privileged" experiences for the breakthrough of the experience of finitude. This is what Kierkegaard understood in his psychology of anxiety.

40. My interpretation here conflicts with two other approaches that also contradict one another. Jonathan Wordsworth claims that at this time Wordsworth's interest in suffering seems to have been entirely literary and that the dying woman and her children were an excuse for a sentimental episode in the manner of Thomson and Darwin, in *The Music of Humanity: A Critical Study of Wordsworth's "Ruined Cottage"* (London, 1969), 50. Mary Jacobus concurs with her suggestion that the female beggar is in the poem to satisfy contemporary sensibility rather than the demands of the poem itself, *Tradition and Experiment in Wordsworth's "Lyrical Ballads"* (Oxford, 1976), 135. This seems an insufficient understanding in view both of the structure of the poem and the central role of such figures throughout Wordsworth's poetry. As Kenneth Johnston points out, the use of literary conventions does not preclude their significance as the expression of personal needs (*The Recluse*, 28). Jacobus herself cites other Wordsworth poems as examples of how inherited material provides Wordsworth with vehicles for personal preoccupations (e.g., 16, 151).

On the other hand, in a more recent historicist approach, Marilyn Butler insists that humanitarian feeling for the social "underdog" is a strong vein in British literature after 1760; in the poetry and novels of Sterne, Mackenzie, and Goldsmith, "Representative men and women are studied in some of the common crises of life; they are counters for human sympathy." Marilyn Butler, *Romantics, Rebels and Reactionaries: English Literature and its Background, 1760–1830* (Oxford, 1982), 22. She links this literary development with the political radicalization that took place in England after 1760 with the Wilksite agitation, the ferment over the American Revolution, and the movement of the Yorkshire gentry for parliamentary reform, and argues that rather than illuminating inner concerns of the author, the literary representation of the socially downtrodden reflects "collective anxieties." This generalization does not fit the tone or the structure of Wordsworth's poem, and in any case, as in the matter of literary convention, inner concern and collective anxiety need not be mutually exclusive. Much the same can be said about John Williams's more explicitly political interpretation that tightly links the eighteenth-century pastoral tradition of "An Evening Walk" to the Commonwealthman political tradition of dissident Whig and country gentry republicanism. J. Williams, *Wordsworth: Romantic Poetry and Revolution Politics* (Manchester, 1989). As Williams himself acknowledges, "An Evening Walk" shows very little of the political awareness of other poems supposedly in the same tradition (19).

41. "The Pedlar," 19, n. 1.

42. Schneider, *Cambridge Years*, 7–8.

43. M. L. Reed, *Wordsworth: The Chronology* of the Early *Years, 1770–1799* (Cambridge, Mass., 1967), 130.

44. Roe, *Radical Years*, 56–65.

45. Ibid., 22.

46. John Williams sees an "ideological confusion" in the eclecticism of Wordsworth's choices of political authorities, though he also suggests that his political ideas were weighted towards the republican or Commonwealth tradition and hence failed to integrate Paine's ideas. Williams, *Romantic Poetry and Revolution Politics*, 58. This misses both the coherence and the originality of Wordsworth's ideas. On British radical thought during the French Revolution, see J. Brewer, "English Radicalism in the Age of George III," in *Three British Revolutions*, ed. J.G.A. Pocock (Princeton, 1980), 323–67; C. Cone, *The English Jacobins* (New York, 1968); G. Claeys, *Thomas Paine: Social and Political Thought* (Boston, 1989); H. T. Dickinson, *British Radicalism and the French Revolution 1789–1815* (London, 1985); A. Goodwin, *The Friends of Liberty. The English Democratic Movement in the Age of the French Revolution* (Cambridge Mass., 1979); S. Maccoby, *English Radicalism 1786–1832* (London, 1955).

47. *The Prose Works of William Wordsworth*, ed. W.J.B. Owen and J. W. Smyser, vol. I (Oxford, 1974), 33. Cited as *Prose Works*.

48. On this issue see Claeys, *Thomas Paine*, 78–82.

49. W. Wordsworth, *Descriptive Sketches*, ed. E. Birdsall (Ithaca, 1984), 115–16.

50. E. Birdsall, "Nature and Society in 'Descriptive Sketches,'" *Modern Philology* 48, no. 1 (1986): 39–52.

51. "Descriptive Sketches," 72.

52. *The Salisbury Plain Poems of William Wordsworth*, ed. S. Gill (Ithaca, 1975), 1793, 404–5.

53. Jacobus, *Tradition and Experiment*, 150.

54. Moorman, *Wordsworth*, 212–13.

55. W. Godwin, *An Enquiry Concerning Political Justice*, 2 vols. (Dublin, 1793). See also Roe, *Radical Years*, 80.

56. I find Jonathan Wordsworth's idea that the passage most probably refers to the idea of animated matter put forward by scientists such as Darwin, Priestley, and Hutton far too restrictive (*Music of Humanity*, 184–88). The line "and sees not any line where being ends" in the Windy Brow revisions parallels "He felt the sentiment of being spread / O'er all that moves and all that seemeth still" in "The Pedlar." Contextually, Jonathan Wordsworth ignores the continuity from "Descriptive Sketches," where the idea of nature has been transformed for the poet into the unifying "secret power" of line 131. Wordsworth is proceeding from the erroneous assumption that the poetry of this period was concerned with man rather than with nature (188); as we have seen, the two cannot be separated.

57. Roe, *Radical Years*, 197, 223.

58. Ibid., 134.

59. Chandler, *Wordsworth's Second Nature*, 224.

60. Ibid., 229.

61. Personal communication from G. Claeys. In the original 1805 edition, "Philosophy" is capitalized.

62. *Poetical Works*, 1:292.205–213.

63. Johnston, *The Recluse*, 30.

64. R. Osborn, "Meaningful Obscurity: The Antecedents and Character of Rivers," in *Bicentenary*, 345.

65. See the editor's introduction to *The Borderers*, 28–31.

66. D. V. Erdman, "Wordsworth as Heartsworth; or, Was Regicide the Prophetic Ground of those 'Moral Questions'?" in *The Evidence of the Imagination: Studies of Interactions between Life and Art in English Romantic Literature*, ed. D. H. Reiman, M. C. Jaye, and B. T. Bennett (New York, 1978), 17.

67. Osborn, "Meaningful Obscurity," 228.

68. This is the general thesis of Chandler, *Wordsworth's Second Nature*.

69. M. Philp, *Godwin's Political Justice* (Ithaca, 1986), 141. By the second edition of 1795, Godwin had reversed himself and admitted the importance and legitimacy of passion.

70. J. Jones, *The Egotistical Sublime* (London, 1954).

71. Wordsworth, *The Borderers*, 34.

72. Hartman, *Wordsworth's Poetry*, 128.

73. F. Hölderlin, *Hyperion*, trans. W. R. Trask (New York, 1965), 129.

74. Erdman, "Wordsworth as Heartsworth," 26.

75. M. H. Friedman, *The Making of a Tory Humanist: William Wordsworth and the Idea of Community* (New York, 1979) 125.

76. Erdman, "Wordsworth as Heartsworth," 17.

77. Ibid., 19.

78. *Poetical Works*, 1:92.1.

79. *Poetical Works*, 1:316.1–15.

80. Johnston, *The Recluse*, 32

81. Jacobus, *Tradition and Experiment*, 177.

82. Quoted in J. Wordsworth, *Music of Humanity*, 85, 134n.

83. W. Wordsworth, *"The Ruined Cottage" and "The Pedlar,"* ed. J. Butler (Ithaca, 1979), MS. B, 1.150–52.

84. De Quincey also blames the Pedlar for not taking the practical and available step of finding the local station of the detachment in which Robert had enlisted and using the information to locate him: "To have overlooked a point of policy so broadly apparent as this vitiates and nullifies the very basis of the story." See J. Wordsworth, *Music of Humanity*, 85. De Quincey has put his finger on the issue, though it is the opposite of what he says: the Pedlar's "overlooking" is the basis of the story.

85. J. Wordsworth, *Music of Humanity*, 5–7

86. Ibid., 153.

87. Johnston, *The Recluse*, 43–47.

88. Moorman, *Wordsworth*, 1:554.

89. Butler, *Ruined Cottage*, MS. D., 495.

90. Johnston, *The Recluse*, 20. Jonathan Wordsworth is the first modern critic to argue thoroughly the case for Coleridge's influence, and his approach is essentially followed by Jacobus and Johnston.

91. Much less the content. As Jonathan Wordsworth writes, "Wordsworth did not at the end of 1797 arbitrarily take over the beliefs of another man, he accepted a way of thinking that was essentially sympathetic" (*Music of Humanity*, 245).

92. Ibid., 212.

93. Ibid., 224.

94. Cf. Jonathan Wordsworth's footnote to this passage in his edition of *"The Pedlar," "Tintern Abbey," "The Two-Part Prelude"*: "a child is 'weaned' from its mother when she ceases to breast-feed it. Wordsworth's use of the metaphor here suggests a tendency, seen elsewhere, to think of Nature as replacing his own mother, who died when he was seven" (25).

95. I use the term in deliberate imitation of the notion of "selfobject" coined by the psychoanalytic theorist Heinz Kohut. Kohut retained the word "object" out of homage to Freud, for whom it was the characteristic term for a person as the object of a drive. It is particularly inapt not only for my purposes but for Kohut's, for it is precisely the characteristic of this dimension of the "bipolar" self that it is expanded by its identification not with an object but with another self. In my usage the term also has an ontological dimension not present in Kohut's usage. See H. Kohut, *The Analysis of the Self: A Systematic Approach to the Psychoanalytic Treatment of Narcissistic Personality Disorders* (New York, 1971).

96. See J. Wordsworth, *Music of Humanity*, 213, and especially, "On Man, on Nature and on Human Life," *Review of English Studies*, n.s., 21, no. 121 (1980): 17–29. Also J. Finch, "On the Dating of Home at Grasmere: A New Approach," in *Bicentenary*, 14–29, and the discussions by Beth Darlington, editor of the Cornell edition of *Home at Grasmere*, 19–22, and by Kenneth Johnston, *The Recluse*, 95–99 and 372, n. 26.

97. The argument that Dorothy Wordsworth copied the poems her brother wrote in 1798 into a number of notebooks that, however, contain no trace of the "Prospectus" (Darlington, citing Finch, 20) suffers the weakness of all negative arguments.

98. Levinson, *Four Essays*, 37.

99. Simpson, *Wordsworth's Historical Imagination*, 47.

100. J. R. MacGillivray, "The Three Forms of the Prelude," quoted in *The Prelude*, editor's notes on the texts, 512.

101. J. Wordsworth, "The Two-Part *Prelude* of 1799," *The Prelude*, 572.

102. Jonathan Wordsworth makes a persuasive argument for Wordsworth's deliberate use of vague and obscure language as the necessary means to approach infinity, linking it with Burke's argument that "A clear idea is . . . another name for a little idea." J. Wordsworth, *The Borders of Vision* (Oxford, 1982), 21. Vagueness and obscurity, however, can also have defensive functions, as they clearly seem to have in this episode.

103. Weiskel, *Romantic Sublime*, 182–83.

104. "Honest James," the family servant, was certainly in some sense the symbolic representative of Wordsworth's father, though this way of putting it is a somewhat simplistic version of symbolic functioning. Friedman, *The Making of a Tory Humanist*, 18.

105. Weiskel, *Romantic Sublime*, 185.

106. The passage is a highly compressed adumbration of some themes in the psychoanalytic view of the symbiotic stage of child development developed by Margaret Mahler in *The Psychological Birth of the Human Infant: Symbiosis and Individuation*, M. S. Mahler, F. Pine, and A. Bergman (New York, 1975). For its biographical-poetic significance see R. J. Onorato, *The Character of the Poet*, 61–65.

107. Weiskel, *Romantic Sublime*, 105. I am not sure what Weiskel means by "structurally motivated."

108. Ibid., 50.

109. Hartman, *Wordsworth's Poetry*, 214–15.

110. In his critique of Freud, Sartre argues that the Oedipus complex should be understood as a "theological complex" rather than as a sexual complex based on biological desire and biological fear. Idealization of parents (as the word "idealization" itself seems to suggest) and the sense of the legitimacy of their authority cannot be derived from purely biological categories; it derives from a need for transcendence that turns parents into sacred objects. But there is no need to make the choice between biological and transcendental needs; the child's relation to the parents fuses both. The desire for the mother can be both a sexual desire and a desire for the absolute object that confers on the child his or her sense of absolute identity. The competition with the father can be a desire to replace the rival for the mother or to take over as the incarnation of absolute authority. See G. N. Izenberg, *The Existentialist Critique of Freud: The Crisis of Autonomy* (Princeton, 1976), 244.

111. Quoted in J. Wordsworth, ed., *The Prelude*, 26, n. 9.

112. I readily concede Andrej Warminski's argument that the contradiction remains inscribed in the "infant babe" passage because it takes a linguistic "act" for the baby to constitute the (absolute) mother, who in turn has the power to constitute the baby's sense of self. A. Warminski, "Facing Language: Wordsworth's First Poetic Spirits," in Johnston et al., *Romantic Revolutions*, 34–35. My point is that it is precisely this "infantile" trope that makes evasion of self-knowledge plausible.

113. Simpson, *Wordsworth's Historical Imagination*, 141.

114. Ibid., 143.

115. W. Wordsworth, "Michael," in Stillinger, *Selected Poems*, 146.25–26.

116. Ibid., l46.36–40.

117. W. Wordsworth, "The Old Cumberland Beggar," in Stillinger, *Selected Poems*, 15.73–77. I agree fully with Chandler's interpretation, as against Harold Bloom's, that Wordsworth is "preaching" the value of beggary, though not with his further contention that the poem is intended as (Burkean) political and social theory. See Chandler, *Wordsworth's Second Nature*, 84–89.

CHAPTER FOUR

1. F-R. de Chateaubriand, *Le Génie du christianisme*, 2 vols. (Paris, 1851); English translation, *The Genius of Christianity; or the Spirit and Beauty of the Christian Religion*, trans. C. I. White (1856; reprinted New York, 1976), 48. Cited as *Genius*.

2. F-R. de Chateaubriand, *Atala/René*, trans. I. Putter (Berkeley, 1952), editor's introduction, 9.

3. F-R. de Chateaubriand, *Oeuvres romanesques et voyages*, vol. 1 (Paris, 1969), 112.

4. E. Gans, "Self-Centralization in René," *Studies in Romanticism* 27, no. 3 (1983): 424.

5. J.-P. Richard, *Paysage de Chateaubriand* (Paris, 1967), 9.

6. Chateaubriand, *Oeuvres romanesques*, 116.

7. "Une Eve tireé de moi-même," ibid., 130. The English translation loses the sense of René's narcisssistic identification of the desired lover with himself.

8. Gans, "Self-Centralization," 422.

9. Gans may have in mind the much more elaborate interpretation of P. Barbéris in his *A la recherche d'une écriture: Chateaubriand* (Paris, 1974), which puts great explanatory weight on the commercial transformation of French society in the eighteenth century. I will address Barbéris's book in detail at a later point.

10. See for example, A. Vial, *La Dialectique de Chateaubriand: "Transformation" et "changement" dans Les Mémoires d'outre- tombe* (Paris, 1978).

11. F-R de Chateaubriand, *Mémoires d'outre-tombe*, 4 vols., ed. M. Levaillant (Paris, 1948) 1:193. Cited as *Mémoires*. In the light of contemporary revisionist denials of the social nature of the Revolution, it is interesting to see a contemporary and participant affirm that dimension of it. For the contemporary point of view, see W. Doyle, *Origins of the French Revolution* (Oxford, 1980); F. Furet and M. Ozouf, eds., *A Critical Dictionary of the French Revolution*, trans. A. Goldhammer (Cambridge, Mass., 1989); and S. Schama, *Citizens* (Cambridge, Mass., 1989).

12. G. D. Painter, *Chateaubriand: A Biography*, vol. 1 *(1768–1793): The Longed-for Tempests* (New York, 1978), 98.

13. Ibid.

14. F-R. de Chateaubriand, *Travels in America*, trans. R. Switzer (Lexington, Ky., 1969), 7.

15. One form that the argument took was the "luxury debate" in the eighteenth

century, among whose most famous disputants were Voltaire in *Le Mondain* and Rousseau in the two discourses. The issue could also be argued in more specifically political and constitutional terms. See among others, K. M. Baker, "A Script for a French Revolution: The Political Consciousness of the Abbé Mably," in *Eighteenth Century Studies*, no. 14 (1981): 235–63; H. Ellis, "Montesquieu's Modern Politics: The Spirit of the Laws and the Problem of Modern Monarchy in Old Regime France," in *History of Political Thought* 10, no. 4 (1989): 665–700.

16. For a detailed description of the genesis of the manuscript, see the introduction to *Oeuvres romanesques* 1:149–55. For a discussion and defense of the legitimacy of using *The Natchez* as a source for Chateaubriand's views in 1789, see P. Barbéris, *A la recherche*, 43, 78–80. Barbéris builds an elaborate case for a distinction between Chateaubriand's critique of the France of Louis XIV and his critique of the postregency eighteenth-century monarchy. Barbéris sees the "rupture" of 1715–25 as decisive for the completion of the transformation of France into a modern commercial monarchy and therefore as the end of any hope on Chateaubriand's part for the reform of France itself. Chateaubriand's interpretation of that rupture is what made it possible for him, according to Barbéris, to set René's history in the earlier period and to make the new society of the eighteenth century that caused and destroyed the Indian uprising symbolic of the social structure that caused the failure of the French Revolution. I find this part of Barbéris's argument problematic because it seems to deny an independent causal role to the Revolution, but my difference with him is irrelevant as regards the acuity of his summary of Chateabriand's critique of the Old Regime.

17. Barbéris, *A la recherche*, 50.

18. Painter, *Chateaubriand*, 10–12.

19. Ibid., 32.

20. The full title of the work is *l'Histoire philosophique et politique des établissements et du commerce des Européens dans les deux Indes*, published in three edtions in 1770, 1774, and 1781.

21. H. Wolpe, *Raynal et sa machine de guerre: L'Histoire des deux Indes et ses perfectionnements* (Stanford, 1957), 59–60.

22. Ibid., 67–68.

23. Ibid., 62.

24. Abbé Raynal, *A Philosophical and Political History of the Settlements and Trade of the Europeans in the East and West Indies*, 5 vols., trans. J. Justamond (London, 1776) 5:601–2.

25. R. Koselleck, *Critique and Crisis: Enlightenment and the Pathogenesis of Modern Society* (Cambridge, Mass., 1988), 176–80.

26. N. O. Keohane, *Philosophy and the State in France: The Renaissance to the Enlightenment* (Princeton, 1980), 21.

27. On the idea of authenticity, see M. Berman, *The Politics of Authenticity: Radical Individualism and the Emergence of Modern Society* (New York, 1970).

28. J-J. Rousseau, *On the Social Contract, Discourse on the Origin of Inequality, Discourse on Political Economy*, trans. D. A. Cress (Indianapolis, 1983), 161. On Chateaubriand and Rousseau, see C. Dedeyan, *Chateaubriand et Rousseau* (Paris, 1973).

29. *Mémoires*, 1:15, in the 1826 version; the passage was omitted later.

30. Painter, *Chateaubriand*, 59.

31. Ibid., 69.

32. G. A. Kelly, "The Political Thought of Lamoignon de Malesherbes," *Political Theory* 7, no. 4 (1979): 485–508; K. M. Baker, "French Political Thought at the Accession of Louis XVI," *Journal of Modern History* 50, no. 2 (1978): 291–95. See also Baker, "Representation," in *The French Revolution and the Creation of Modern Political Culture*, vol. 1, *The Political Culture of the Old Regime* (Oxford, 1987), 472–78.

33. G. A. Kelly, *Victims, Authority and Terror: The Parallel Deaths of d'Orléans, Custine, Bailly and Malesherbes* (Chapel Hill, 1982), 247.

34. Ibid., 248.

35. Ibid.

36. F-R. de Chateaubriand, *Correspondance générale*, vol. 1, *1789–1807* (Paris, 1977) 1:49.

37. Barbéris, *A la recherche*, 61–64.

38. Painter has argued persuasively that the encounter, long thought by readers to be one of Chateaubriand's fabrications, most likely did in fact take place, though at the end rather than at the beginning of his trip.

39. F-R. de Chateaubriand, *Essai historique, politique et moral, sur les révolutions, anciennes et modernes, considérées dans leur rapports avec la révolution françoise de nos jours, Oeuvres complètes*, vols. 1–2 (Paris, 1837), 1:211–12, n. 3. Cited as *Essai*.

40. Chateaubriand, Preface to *Atala, Oeuvres romanesques*, 16.

41. Painter, *Chateaubriand*, 138.

42. Chateaubriand, *Correspondance*, 61–62.

43. Chateaubriand's conception of ideal child-rearing makes an interesting contrast with that of Hölderlin, also derived from Rousseau, who similarly inflected it with needs stemming from his own background. For Hölderlin, the historical model was the ideal development of ancient Athens. "Leave the human being undisturbed from the cradle! Do not force him . . . out of the small house of his childhood! Do not too little, lest he make shift without you, and hence distingushes you from himself; do not do too much, lest he feel your power or his own and hence distingushes you from himself; in short, let him not learn until late that there are men, that there is something else outside himself, for only thus will he become man. But man is a god as soon as he is a man. And once he is a god, he is beautiful" (*Hyperion*, 91). This narcissistic solution to the twin dangers of inadequate nurturing and overprotective interference reflects Hölderlin's inner and outer conflict with his widowed mother's oscillation between emotional absence and smothering intrusiveness.

44. F-R. de Chateaubriand, *Les Natchez*, in *Oeuvres Romanesques*; English translation, *The Natchez: An Indian Tale*, 3 vols., trans. H. Colburn (1827; reprinted New York, 1978), 2:209–10.

45. Barbéris, *A la recherche*, 106.

46. Ibid., 159.

47. Chateaubriand, *Correspondance*, 3.

48. C. A. Porter, *Chateaubriand: Composition, Imagination, and Poetry* (Saratoga, 1978), 80.

49. On the contradictions in Chateaubriand's politics and the difficulty of classifying them, see J-A. Bedé, "Chateaubriand as a Constitutionalist and Political Strategist" and P. J. Siegel, "Chateaubriand, révolutionnaire politique," in *Chateaubriand Today*, ed. R. Switzer (Madison, 1970), 29–44, 177–84.

50. Quoted in Siegel, "Chateaubriand," 182.

51. Bedé, "Chateaubriand as a Constitutionalist," 42.

52. Quoted in Siegel, "Chateaubriand," 178.

53. There is a large literature representing both views; see Barbéris, *A la recherche*, 260–280.

54. Ibid., 270.

55. Ibid., 300. Barbéris is summarizing here the argument of E. Picon in his article "Chateaubriand" in the *Histoire de la litérature*, vol. 3 of *Encyclopédie de la Pléiade*.

56. Barbéris, *A la recherche*, 290.

57. Ibid., 302.

BIBLIOGRAPHY

ROMANTICISM: GENERAL

Abrams, M. H. *Natural Supernaturalism: Tradition and Revolution in Romantic Literature*. New York, 1973.

Behler, E. *Unendliche Perfektabilität: Europäische Romantik und Französische Revolution*. Paderborn, 1989.

De Man, P. *Blindness and Insight: Essays in the Rhetoric of Contemporary Criticism*. 2d ed. Minneapolis, 1983.

———. *The Rhetoric of Romanticism*. New York, 1984.

Furst, L. R. *The Contours of European Romanticism*. Lincoln, 1979.

Gilbertson, P. "Boundaries and Self in Romanticism." In *English and German Romanticism: Cross-Currents and Controversies*, edited by J. Pipkin. Heidelberg, 1985.

McGann, J. J. *The Romantic Ideology: A Critical Investigation*. Chicago, 1983.

Menhennet, A. *The Romantic Movement*. London, 1981.

Pipkin, J., ed. *English and German Romanticism: Cross-Currents and Controversies*. Heidelberg, 1985.

Rosenblum, N. L. *Another Liberalism: Romanticism and the Reconstruction of Liberal Thought*. Cambridge, Mass., 1987.

SCHLEIERMACHER

Primary Sources

Schleiermacher, F.D.E. *Aus Schleiermachers Leben. In Briefen*. Edited by W. Dilthey. 4 vols. Berlin, 1863.

———. *Jugendschriften 1787–1796*. Part 1, vol. 1 of *Kritische Gesamtausgabe*. Edited by G. Meckenstock. Berlin, 1984.

———. *The Life of Schleiermacher. As Unfolded In His Autobiography and Letters*. Translated by F. Rowan. London, 1860.

———. *Monologen, Werke*. Edited by O. Braun and J. Bauer, vol. 4. Leipzig, 1911.

———. *On Religion: Speeches to Its Cultured Despisers*. Translated by J. Oman. London, 1893.

———. *Schriften aus der Berliner Zeit, 1796–1799*. Part 1, vol. 2 of *Kritische Gesamtausgabe*. Edited by G. Meckenstock. Berlin, 1984.

———. *Soliloquies*. Translated by H. L. Friess. Chicago, 1957.

———. *Über die Religion: Reden an die Gebildeten unter ihren Verächtern*. 2d ed. Vol. 4 of *Werke*. Berlin, 1806.

Secondary Sources

Blackwell, A. L. *Schleiermacher's Early Philosophy of Life: Determinism, Freedom and Phantasy*. Chico, 1982.

Dawson, J. *Friedrich Schleiermacher: The Evolution of a Nationalist*. Austin, 1966.

Dilthey, W. *Leben Schleiermachers*. 3d ed. Vol. I. Edited by M. Redeker. Berlin, 1970.

Forstman, J. *A Romantic Triangle: Schleiermacher and Early German Romanticism*. Missoula, 1977.

Katzenbach, F. W. *Friedrich Daniel Ernst Schleiermacher in Selbstzeugnissen und Bilddokumenten*. Hamburg, 1967.

Nowak, K. "Die Französische Revolution in Leben und Werk des Jungen Schleiermacher." In *Internationaler Schleiermacher-Kongress Berlin 1984*, edited by K. V. Selge, 103–25.

Redeker, M. *Schleiermacher: Life and Thought*. Translated by J. Walhouser. Philadelphia, 1973.

Selge, K-V., ed. *Internationaler Schleiermacher-Kongress Berlin 1984*. Berlin, 1985.

SCHLEGEL

Primary Sources

Schlegel, F. *Dialogue on Poetry and Literary Aphorisms*. Translated by E. Behler and R. Struc. University Park and London, 1968.

———. *Kritische Friedrich-Schlegel-Ausgabe*. Edited by E. Behler, with J-J. Anstett and H. Eichner. 36 vols. Munich, 1958–.

———. *Literary Notebooks, 1797–1801*. Edited by H. Eichner. Toronto, 1957.

———. *"Lucinde" and the Fragments*. Translated by P. Virchow. Minneapolis, 1971.

Körner, J. *Krisenjahre der Frühromantik: Briefe aus dem Schlegelkreis*. Vol. 1. Brünn, 1936.

Preitz, M., ed. *Friedrich Schlegel und Novalis. Biographie einer Romantiker-Freundschaft in ihren Briefen*. Darmstadt, 1957.

Secondary Sources

Behler, E. "Die Wirkung Goethes und Schillers auf die Brüder Schlegel." In *Unser Commercium: Goethes und Schillers Literaturpolitik*, edited by W. Barner, E. Lammert, and N. Dellers, 559–83. Stuttgart, 1984.

———. *Friedrich Schlegel in Selbstzeugnissen und Bilddokumenten*. Hamburg, 1966.

———. "Friedrich Schlegel: *Lucinde* (1799)." In *Romane und Erzählungen der deutschen Romantik*, edited by P. M. Luetzeler, 98–124. Stuttgart, 1981.

———. "Friedrich Schlegels erster Aufenthalt in Jena: Vom 6. August 1796 bis zum 3. Juli 1797" *Modern Language Notes* 102, no. 3 (1987): 544–69.

Behrens, K. *Friedrich Schlegels Geschichtsphilosophie, 1794–1808*. Tübingen, 1984.

Bräutigam, B. *Leben wie im Roman: Untersuchungen zum ästhetischen Frühwerk Friedrich Schlegels (1794–1800)*. Paderborn, 1986.

Bullock, M. P. *Romanticism and Marxism: The Philosophical Development of*

Literary Theory and Literary History in Walter Benjamin and Friedrich Schlegel. New York, 1987.

Eichner, H. *Friedrich Schlegel.* New York, 1970.

———. "Friedrich Schlegel's Theory of Romantic Poetry." PMLA 71, no. 5: 1018–41.

Enders, C. *Friedrich Schlegel, Die Quellen seines Wesens und Werdens.* Leipzig, 1913.

Friedrichsmeyer, S. *The Androgyne in Early German Romanticism: Friedrich Schlegel, Novalis, and the Metaphysics of Love.* Frankfurt, 1983.

Handwerk, G. J. *Irony and Ethics in Narrative: From Schlegel to Lacan.* New Haven, 1985.

Heiner, H-J. *Das Ganzheitsdenken Friedrich Schlegels: Wissenssoziologische Deutung einer Denkform.* Stuttgart, 1971.

Holz-Steinmeyer, C. *Friedrich Schlegels "Lucinde" als "Neue Mythologie."* Frankfurt, 1985.

Hörisch, J. *Die fröhliche Wissenschaft der Poesie.* Frankfurt, 1976.

Mennemeier, F. N. *Friedrich Schlegels Posiebegriff.* Munich, 1971.

———. "Klassizität und Progressivität. Zu einigen Aspekten der Poetik des jungen Friedrich Schlegel." In *Deutsche Literatur zur Zeit der Klassik*, edited by K. O. Conrady. Stuttgart, 1977.

Murtfeld, R. *Caroline Schlegel-Schelling: Moderne Frau in Revolutionärer Zeit.* Bonn, 1973.

Oesterle, I. "Der 'glückliche Anstoss' aesthetischer Revolution und die Anstössigkeit politischer Revolution. Ein Denk- und Belegversuch zum Zusammenhang von politischer Formveränderung und kultureller Revolution im Studium-Aufsatz Friedrich Schlegels." In *Literaturwissenschaft und Sozialwissenschaft*, edited by D. Bänsch. Stuttgart, 1977.

Peter, K. *Friedrich Schlegel.* Stuttgart, 1978.

———. *Stadien der Aufklärung: Moral und Politik bei Lessing, Novalis und Friedrich Schlegel.* Wiesbaden, 1980.

Polheim, K. K. "Friedrich Schlegel's *Lucinde*." In *Friedrich Schlegel und die Romantik, Zeitschrift für Deutsche Philologie.* No. 88 (1969), Sonderheft.

Rutledge, J. S. *Johann Adolph Schlegel.* Bern and Frankfurt, 1974.

Schlagdenhaufen, A. *Fréderic Schlegel et son groupe: La doctrine de l'Athenaeum, (1798–1800).* Paris, 1934.

Volpers, R. *Friedrich Schlegel als politischer Denker und deutscher Patriot.* Berlin und Leipzig, 1917.

Weiland, W. *Der Junge Friedrich Schlegel, oder die Revolution in der Frühromantik.* Stuttgart, 1968.

Ziegler, H. W. "Friedrich Schlegels Jugendentwicklung." *Archiv für die Gesamte Psychologie* 60 (1927): 1–128.

German Romanticism and Intellectual History

Arendt, H. *Rahel Varnhagen, The Life of a Jewish Woman.* Translated by R. and C. Winston. New York, 1974.

Bänsch, D. *Literaturwissenschaft und Sozialwissenschaft.* Vol. 8, *Zur Modernität der Romantik.* Stuttgart, 1977.

Behler, E. "Die Auffassung der Revolution in der deutschen Frühromantik." In *Essays on European Literature. In Honor of Lieselotte Dieckmann*, 191–215. St. Louis, 1972.

Brinkman, R. "Deutsche Frühromantik und Französische Revolution." In *Deutsche Literatur und Französische Revolution*, 172–89. Göttingen, 1974.

Brown, M. *The Shape of German Romanticism*. Ithaca, 1979.

Bruford, W. H. *Germany in the Eighteenth Century: The Social Background of the Literary Revival*. Cambridge, 1935, 1971.

Brunschwig, H. *Enlightenment and Romanticism in Eighteenth Century Prussia*. 1947. Translated by F. Jellinek. Chicago, 1974.

Butler, E. M. *The Tyranny of Greece Over Germany*. Cambridge, 1935.

Conrady, K. O., ed. *Deutsche Literatur zur Zeit der Klassik*. Stuttgart, 1977.

Dickey, L. *Hegel: Religion, Economics, and the Politics of Spirit, 1770–1807*. Cambridge, 1987.

Epsteins, K. *The Genesis of German Conservatism*, Princeton, 1966.

Fichte, J. G. *Die Grundlagen der gesamten Wissenschaftslehre. Werke, 1793–1795*. Vol. 1, part 2 of *Gesamtausgabe*. Stuttgart, 1965.

———. *The Foundation of the Entire Theory of Knowledge*. Translated by P. Heath and J. Lacks. New York, 1970.

Habermas, J. *Der philosophische Diskurs der Moderne. Zwölf Vorlesungen*. Frankfurt, 1985.

Hatfield, H. *Aesthetic Paganism in German Literature from Winckelmann to the Death of Goethe*. Cambridge, 1964.

Hölderlin, F. *Hyperion*. Vol. 3 of *Sämtliche Werke*. Edited by F. Beissner. Stuttgart, 1969–1973.

———. *Hyperion*. Translated by W. R. Trask. New York, 1965.

Hughes, G. T. *German Romantic Literature*. London, 1979.

Humboldt, W. von. *The Limits of State Action*. Edited by J. W. Burrow. Cambridge, 1969.

Kahn, L. W. *Social Ideals in German Literature, 1770–1830*. 1938. Reprint. New York, 1969.

Kelly, G. *Idealism, History and Politics: Sources of Hegelian Thought*. Cambridge, 1968.

Kistler, M. O. *Drama of the Storm and Stress*. New York, 1969.

Kluckhohn, P. *Die Auffassung der Liebe in der Literatur des 18. Jahrhunderts und in der deutschen Romantik*. Tübingen, 1966.

Krieger, L. *The German Idea of Freedom: History of a Political Tradition*. Boston, 1957.

Lamport, F. J. *Lessing and the Drama*. Oxford, 1981.

Lange, V. *The Classical Age of German Literature, 1740–1815*. New York, 1982.

Lessing, G. E. *Laocoon*. In *German Aesthetic and Literary Criticism*, edited by H. B. Nisbet. Cambridge, 1985.

Luetzeler, P. M., ed. *Romane und Erzählungen der deutschen Romantik*. Stuttgart, 1981.

Meixner, H. "Politische Aspekte der Frühromantik." In S. Vietta, *Die literarische Frühromantik*. Göttingen, 1983.

Nisbet, H. B., ed. *German Aesthetic and Literary Criticism: Winckelmann, Lessing, Hamann, Herder, Schiller, Goethe.* Cambridge, 1985.

Novalis (Friedrich von Hardenberg). *Glaube und Liebe.* Vol. 2 of *Schriften.* Edited by R. Samuel. Stuttgart, 1965.

Rasch, W. "Zum Verhältnis der Romantik zur Aufklärung." In *Romantik: Ein literaturwissenschaftliches Studienbuch,* edited by E. Ribbat, 7–22. Königstein, 1979.

Ribbat, E., ed. *Romantik: Ein literturwissenschaftliches Studienbuch.* Königstein, 1979.

Samuel, R. *Die poetishce Staats- und Geschichtsauffassung Friedrich von Hardenbergs.* Frankfurt am Main, 1925.

Seegeberg, H. "Deutsche Literatur und Französische Revolution. Zum Verhältnis von Weimarer Klassik, Frühromantik und Spätaufklärung." In *Deutsche Literatur zur Zeit der Klassik,* edited by K. O. Conrady. Stuttgart, 1977.

Strohschneider-Kors, I. *Die Romantische Ironie in Theorie und Gestaltung.* Tübingen, 1960.

Sweet, P. R. *Wilhelm von Humboldt: A Biography.* Two vols. Columbus, 1978.

Toews, J. E. *Hegelianism: The Path Toward Dialectical Humanism, 1805–1841.* Cambridge, 1980.

Vietta, S. ed. *Die literarische Frühromantik.* Göttingen, 1983.

———. "Frühromantik und Aufklärung." In *Die literarische Frühromantik,* edited by S. Vietta.

Whaley, J. "The Protestant Enlightenment in Germany." In *The Enlightenment in National Context,* edited by R. Porter and M. Teich, 106–17. Cambridge, 1981.

Winckelmann, J. J. *Thoughts on the Imitation of the Painting and Sculpture of the Greeks.* In *German Aesthetic and Literary Criticism,* edited by H. B. Nisbet. Cambridge, 1985.

Ziolkowski, T. *German Romanticism and Its Institutions.* Princeton, 1990.

German Political and Social History

Droz, J. *L'Allemagne et la révolution française.* Paris, 1949.

Fulbrook, M. *Piety and Politics: Religion and the Rise of Absolutism in England, Württemberg and Prussia.* Cambridge, 1983.

Gagliardo, J. G. *Reich and Nation: The Holy Roman Empire as Idea and Reality, 1763–1806.* Bloomington, 1980.

Gerth, H. *Die sozialgeschichtliche Lage der bürgerlichen Intelligenz um die Wende des 18. Jahrhunderts.* Frankfurt am Main, 1935.

Vierhaus, R. *Germany in the Age of Absolutism.* 1968. Translated by J. B. Knudsen. Cambridge, 1988.

———. *Deutschland im 18. Jahrhundert: Politische Verfassung, Soziales Gefüge, Geistige Bewegungen.* Göttingen, 1987.

———. "Deutschland im 18. Jahrhundert: Politische Verfassung, Soziales Gefüge, Geistige Bewegungen." In *Lessing und die Zeit der Aufklärung.* Göttingen, 1968.

Walker, M. *German Home Towns: Community, State, and General Estate, 1648–1871*. Ithaca, 1971.

WORDSWORTH

Primary Sources

Wordsworth, W. *The Borderers*. Edited by R. Osborn. Ithaca, 1982.

————. *Descriptive Sketches*. Edited by E. Birdsall. Ithaca, 1984.

————. *An Evening Walk*. Edited by J. Averill. Ithaca, 1984.

————. *Home at Grasmere: Part First, Book First of The Recluse*. Edited by B. Darlington. Ithaca, 1977.

————. *The Letters of William and Dorothy Wordsworth*. Vol. 1, *The Early Years, 1787–1805*. 2d ed. Edited by E. de Selincourt. Oxford, 1967.

————. *"The Pedlar," "Tintern Abbey," "The Two-Part Prelude."* Edited by J. Wordsworth. Cambridge, 1985.

————. *The Poetical Works of William Wordsworth*. Vol. 1. Edited by E. de Selincourt. Oxford, 1952.

————. *The Prelude: 1799, 1805, 1850*. Edited by J. Wordsworth, M. H. Abrams, and S. Gill. New York, 1979.

————. *The Prose Works of William Wordsworth*. Vol. 1. Edited by W.J.B. Owen and J. W. Smyser. Oxford, 1974.

————. *"The Ruined Cottage" and "The Pedlar."* Edited by J. Butler. Ithaca, 1979.

————. *The Salisbury Plain Poems of William Wordsworth*. Edited by S. Gill. Ithaca, 1975.

————. *Selected Poems and Prefaces by William Wordsworth*. Edited by J. Stillinger. Boston, 1965.

Secondary Sources

Abrams, M. H. "'The Prelude' as a Portrait of the Artist." *Bicentenary Wordsworth Studies*. Ithaca, 1970.

Bateson, F. W. *Wordsworth: A Re-Interpretation*. London, 1954.

Birdsall, E. "Nature and Society in 'Descriptive Sketches.'" *Modern Philology* 48, no. 1 (1986): 39–52.

Bloom, H. "The Scene of Instruction: Tintern Abbey." In *William Wordsworth: Modern Critical Views*, edited by H. Bloom, 113–37. New York, 1985.

Chandler, J. K. *Wordsworth's Second Nature: A Study of the Poetry and Politics*. Chicago, 1982.

Ellis, D. *Wordsworth, Freud and the Spots of Time*. Cambridge, 1985.

Erdman, D. V. "Wordsworth as Heartsworth; or, Was Regicide the Prophetic Ground of those 'Moral Questions'?" In *The Evidence of the Imagination: Studies of Interactions Between Life and Art in English Romantic Literature*, edited by D. H. Reiman, M. C. Jaye, and B. T. Bennett. New York, 1978.

Finch, J. "On the Dating of 'Home at Grasmere': A New Approach." In *Bicentenary Wordsworth Studies*, 14–29. Ithaca, 1970.

Friedman, M. H. *The Making of a Tory Humanist: William Wordsworth and the Idea of Community*. New York, 1979.

Hartman, G. H. *Wordsworth's Poetry, 1787–1814.* New Haven, 1964.

———. *The Unremarkable Wordsworth.* Minneapolis, 1987.

Jacobus, M. *Tradition and Experiment in Wordsworth's "Lyrical Ballads."* Oxford, 1976.

Johnston, K. R. *Wordsworth and "The Recluse."* New Haven, 1984.

Jones, J. *The Egotistical Sublime.* London, 1954.

Levinson, M. *Wordsworth's Great Period Poems: Four Essays.* Cambridge, 1986.

Liu, A. "Wordsworth: The History in 'Imagination.'" *English Literary History* 51 (Fall 1984): 505–48.

———. *Wordsworth: The Sense of History.* Stanford, 1989.

Meyer, G. W. *Wordsworth's Formative Years.* Ann Arbor, 1943.

Moorman, M. *William Wordsworth: A Biography.* Vol. 1, *The Early Years, 1770–1803.* Oxford, 1957.

Onorato, R. J. *The Character of the Poet: Wordsworth in "The Prelude."* Princeton, 1971.

Osborn, R. "Meaningful Obscurity: The Antecedents and Character of Rivers." In *Bicentenary Wordsworth Studies.* Ithaca, 1970.

Purkis, J. *A Preface to Wordsworth.* London, 1986.

Rajan, T. "The Erasure of Narrative in Post-Structuralist Representations of Wordsworth." In *Romantic Revolutions*, edited by K. R. Johnston et al. Bloomington, 1990.

Read, H. *Wordsworth.* London, 1958.

Reed, M. L. *Wordsworth: The Chronology of the Early Years, 1770–1799.* Cambridge, Mass., 1967.

Roe, N. *Wordsworth and Coleridge, The Radical Years.* Oxford, 1988.

Schapiro, B. A. *The Romantic Mother: Narcissistic Patterns in Romantic Poetry.* Baltimore, 1983.

Schneider, B. R. *Wordsworth's Cambridge Education.* Cambridge, 1957.

Simpson, D. "Criticism, Politics, and Style in Wordsworth's Poetry." *Critical Inquiry* 11 (Spring 1984): 52–81.

———. *Wordsworth's Historical Imagination: The Poetry of Displacment.* New York, 1987.

Sheats, P. D. *The Making of Wordsworth's Poetry, 1785–1798.* Cambridge, 1973.

Warminski, A. "Facing Language: Wordsworth's First Poetic Spirits." In *Romantic Revolutions*, edited by K. R. Johnston et al. Bloomington, 1990.

Williams, J. *Wordsworth: Romantic Poetry and Revolution Politics.* Manchester, 1989.

Wordsworth, J. *The Borders of Vision.* Oxford, 1982.

———. "On Man, on Nature, and on Human Life." *Review of English Studies*, n.s. 21, No. 121 (1980): 17–29.

———. "The Two-Part Prelude of 1799." In *The Prelude: 1799, 1805, 1850.* New York, 1979.

———. *The Music of Humanity: A Critical Study of Wordsworth's "Ruined Cottage."* Edited by J. Wordsworth et al. London, 1969.

———. *Bicentenary Wordsworth Studies.* Ithaca, 1970.

English Romanticism and Intellectual History

Abrams, M. H. "Construing and Deconstructing." In *Romanticism and Contemporary Criticism*, edited by M. Eaves and M. Fischer. Ithaca, 1986.

Bloom, H. *The Visionary Company*. New York, 1961.

Butler, M. *Romantics, Rebels, and Reactionaries: English Literature and Its Background, 1760–1830*. Oxford, 1982.

Claeys, G. *Thomas Paine: Social and Political Thought*. Boston, 1989.

Deane, S. *The French Revolution and Enlightenment in England, 1789–1832*. Cambridge, Mass., 1988.

Eaves, M., and M. Fischer. *Romanticism and Contemporary Criticism*. Ithaca, 1986.

Godwin, W. *An Enquiry Concerning Political Justice*. Two vols. Dublin, 1793.

Johnston, K. R., G. Chaitin, K. Hanson, and H. Marks, eds. *Romantic Revolutions: Criticism and Theory*. Bloomington, 1990.

Kramnick, I. "Religion and Radicalism: English Political Theory in the Age of Revolution." *Political Theory* 4 (1977): 503–34.

———. "Republican Revisionism Revisited." *American Historical Review* 87, no. 3 (1982): 629–64.

Mellors, A. *English Romantic Irony*. Cambridge, Mass., 1980.

Miller, J. H. "On Edge." In *Romanticism and Contemporary Criticism*, edited by M. Eaves and M. Fischer. Ithaca, 1986.

Philp, M. *Godwin's Political Justice*. Ithaca, 1986.

Rajan, T. *Dark Interpreter: the Discourse of Romanticism*. Ithaca, 1980.

Weiskel, T. *The Romantic Sublime: Studies in the Structure and Psychology of Transcendence*. Baltimore, 1976, 1986.

English Political and Social History

Bonsall, B. *Sir James Lowther and Cumberland and Westmoreland Elections, 1754–1775*. Manchester, 1960.

Bonwick, C. *English Radicals and the American Revolution*. North Carolina, 1977.

Brewer, J. "English Radicalism in the Age of George III." In *Three British Revolutions*, edited by J.G.A. Pocock, 323–67. Princeton, 1980.

Clark, J.C.D. *English Society, 1688–1832*. Cambridge, 1985.

Cone, C. *The English Jacobins*. New York, 1968.

Dickinson, H. T. *British Radicalism and the French Revolution, 1789–1815*. Oxford, 1985.

Goodwin, A. *The Friends of Liberty. The English Democratic Movement in the Age of the French Revolution*. Cambridge, Mass., 1979.

Maccoby, S. *English Radicalism 1786–1832*. London, 1955.

Mingay, G. E. *English Landed Society in the Eighteenth Century*. London, 1963.

CHATEAUBRIAND

Primary Sources

Chateaubriand, F-R. de. *Atala/René*. Translated by I. Putter. Berkeley, 1952.

———. *Correspondance générale*. Vol. 1, *1789–1807*. Paris, 1977.

———. *Essai historique, politique et moral, sur les révolutions, anciennes et modernes, considérées dans leur rapports avec la révolution françoise de nos jours*. Vols. 1–2 of *Oeuvres complètes*. Paris, 1837.

———. *Le Génie du christianisme*. Two vols. Paris, 1851.

———. *The Genius of Christianity; or the Spirit and Beauty of the Christian Religion*. Translated by C. I. White. 1856. Reprint. New York, 1976.

———. *Mémoires d'outre-tombe*. Edited by M. Levaillant. Vol. 1. Paris, 1948.

———. *The Natchez: An Indian Tale*. Translated by H. Colburn. Three vols. 1827. Reprint. New York, 1978.

———. *Oeuvres romanesques et voyages*. Vol. 1. Paris, 1969.

———. *Travels in America*. Translated by R. Switzer. Lexington, 1969.

Secondary Sources

Barbéris, P. *A la recherche d'une écriture: Chateaubriand*. Paris, 1974.

Bedé, J-A. "Chateaubriand as a Constitutionalist and Political Strategist." In *Chateaubriand Today*, edited by R. Switzer, 29–44. Madison, 1970.

Dedeyan, C. *Chateaubriand et Rousseau*. Paris, 1973.

Gans, E. "Self-Centralization in René." *Studies in Romanticism* 27, no. 3 (1983): 421–35.

Lelièvre, M. *Chateaubriand Polémiste*. Paris, 1983.

O'Flaherty, K. "Adolescence in the Work of Chateaubriand." In *Chateaubriand Today*, edited by R. Switzer. Madison, 1970.

Painter, G. D. *Chateaubriand: A Biography*. Vol. 1 *(1768–1793): The Longed-For Tempests*. New York, 1978.

Porter, C. A. *Chateaubriand: Composition, Imagination, and Poetry*. Saratoga, 1978.

Richard, J-P. *Paysage de Chateaubriand*. Paris, 1967.

Siegel, P. J. "Chateaubriand, révolutionnaire politique." In *Chateaubriand Today*, edited by R. Switzer, 177–84. Madison, 1970.

Switzer, R. *Chateaubriand*. New York, 1971.

———, ed. *Chateaubriand Today: Proceedings of the Commemoration of the Bicentenary of the Birth of Chateaubriand, 1968*. Madison, 1970.

Tabart. C-A. *De "René" aux "Mémoires d'outre-tombe": Chateaubriand*. Paris, 1984.

Vial, A. *La Dialectique de Chateaubriand: "Transformation" et "changement" dans 'Les Mémoires d'Outre-Tombe.'* Paris, 1978.

French Romanticism and Intellectual History

Baker, K. M. "French Political Thought at the Accession of Louis XVI." *Journal of Modern History* 50, no. 2 (1978): 291–95.

———. "Representation." In *The French Revolution and the Creation of Modern Political Culture*. Vol. 1, *The Political Culture of the Old Regime*. Oxford, 1987.

———. "A Script for a French Revolution: The Political Consciousness of the Abbé Mably." *Eighteenth Century Studies*, no. 14 (1981): 235–63.

Barny, R. *Prélude idéologique à la révolution française*. Paris, 1985.

Berman, M. *The Politics of Authenticity: Radical Individualism and the Emergence of Modern Society*. New York, 1971.

Bryson, N. *Tradition and Desire: From David to Delacroix*. Cambridge, 1984.

Delon, M. "Du vague des passions à la passion des vagues." In *Le Préromantisme: Hypothèque ou hypothèse*, edited by P. Viallaneix. Paris, 1975.

Ellis, H. "Montesquieu's Modern Politics: The Spirit of the Laws and the Problem of the Modern Monarchy in Old Regime France." *History of Political Thought* 10, no. 4 (1989): 665–700.

Kelly, G. A. "The Political Thought of Lamoignon de Malesherbes." *Political Theory* 7, no. 4 (1979): 485–508.

——. *Victims, Authority, and Terror: The Parallel Deaths of d'Orléans, Custine, Bailly, and Malesherbes*. Chapel Hill, 1982.

Keohane, N. O. *Philosophy and the State in France: The Renaissance to the Enlightenment*. Princeton, 1980.

Koselleck, R. *Critique and Crisis: Enlightenment and the Pathogenesis of Modern Society*. Cambridge, Mass., 1988.

Porter, L. M. *The Literary Dream in French Romanticism*. Detroit, 1979.

Raynal, Abbé. *A Philosophical and Political History of the Settlements and Trade of the Europeans in the East and West Indies*. Translated by J. Justamond. 5 vols. London, 1776.

Rex. W. E. *The Attraction of the Contrary: Essays on the Literature of the French Enlightenment*. Berkeley, 1987.

Rousseau, J-J. *On the Social Contract, Discourse on the Origin of Inequality, Discourse on Political Economy*. Translated by D. A. Cress. Indianapolis, 1983.

Viallaneix, P., ed. *Le Préromantisme: Hypothèque ou hypothèse*. Paris, 1975.

Wolpe, H. *Raynal et sa machine de guerre: L'Histoire des deux indes et ses perfectionnements*. Stanford, 1957.

French Political and Social History

Behrens, C.B.A. *The Ancien Régime*. London, 1967.

Chaussinand-Nogaret, G. *The French Nobility in the Eighteenth Century: From Feudalism to Enlightenment*. Cambridge, 1985.

Cobban, A. *A History of Modern France*. Vol. 1, *Old Regime and Revolution, 1715–1799*. Harmondsworth, 1971.

Doyle, W. *Origins of the French Revolution*. Oxford, 1980.

Furet, F., and M. Ozouf, eds. *A Critical Dictionary of the French Revolution*. Translated by A. Goldhammer. Cambridge, Mass. 1989.

MISCELLANEOUS

Bellah, R. N. et al. *Habits of the Heart: Individualism and Commitment in American Life*. Berkeley, 1985.

Gay, P. *The Enlightenment, An Interpretation*. Vol. 2, *The Science of Freedom*. New York, 1977.

Gillis, J. R. *Youth and History: Tradition and Change in European Age Relations, 1770–Present*. New York, 1974.

Honour, H. *Neo-Classicism*. Middlesex, 1968.

Kohut, H. *The Analysis of the Self: A Systematic Approach to the Psychoanalytic Treatment of Narcississtic Personality Disorders*. New York, 1971.

Lukes, S. *Individualism*. New York, 1973.

Meinecke, F. *Die Idee der Staatsräson, Werke*. Vol. 1. Munich, 1957–62.

Moenkemeyer, S. *Francois Hemsterhuis*. Boston, 1975.

Pocock, J.G.A. *The Machiavellian Moment: Florentine Political Thought and the Atlantic Republican Tradition*. Princeton, 1975.

———. *Virtue, Commerce, and Society: Essays on Political Thought and History, Chiefly in the Eighteenth Century*. Cambridge, 1985.

Porter, R., and M. Teich, eds. *The Enlightenment in National Context*. Cambridge, 1981.

Ringer, F. K. *The Decline of the German Mandarins: The German Academic Community, 1890–1930*. Cambridge, Mass., 1969.

Simmel, G. *The Sociology of Georg Simmel*. Edited by K. H. Wolff. New York, 1950.

Stern, F. *The Failures of Illiberalism: Essays in the Political Culture of Modern Germany*. New York, 1972.

Weintraub, K. J. *The Value of the Individual: Self and Circumstance in Autobiography*. Chicago, 1978.

INDEX